Freedom's Ballot

Freedom's Ballot

African American Political Struggles in Chicago from Abolition to the Great Migration

MARGARET GARB

The University of Chicago Press
Chicago and London

Margaret Garb is associate professor of history at Washington University in St. Louis.

The University of Chicago Press, Chicago 60637
The University of Chicago Press, Ltd., London
© 2014 by The University of Chicago
All rights reserved. Published 2014.
Printed in the United States of America

23 22 21 20 19 18 17 16 15 14   1 2 3 4 5

ISBN-13: 978-0-226-13590-8 (cloth)
ISBN-13: 978-0-226-13606-6 (e-book)
DOI: 10.7208/chicago/9780226136066.001.0001

Library of Congress Cataloging-in-Publication Data

Garb, Margaret, author.
   Freedom's ballot : African American political struggles in Chicago from abolition to the Great Migration / Margaret Garb.
      pages ; cm
   Includes bibliographical references and index.
   ISBN 978-0-226-13590-8 (cloth : alk. paper)—ISBN 978-0-226-13606-6 (e-book)   1. African Americans—Illinois—Chicago—Politics and government—19th century.   2. African Americans—Illinois—Chicago—Politics and government—20th century.   3. African Americans—Civil rights—Illinois—Chicago—History—19th century.   4. African Americans—Civil rights—Illinois—Chicago—History—20th century.   5. Chicago (Ill.)—Race relations—Political aspects.   I. Title.
   F548.9.N4G37 2014
   323.1196′073077311—dc23

                                                            2013039202

♾ This paper meets the requirements of ANSI/NISO Z39.48-1992 (Permanence of Paper).

For Mark and Eva

The ruling of men is the effort to direct the individual actions of many persons toward some end. This end theoretically should be the greatest good of all, but no human group has ever reached this ideal because of ignorance and selfishness.

W. E. B. DUBOIS, "Of the Ruling of Men," *Darkwater*

I believe in Liberty for all men: the space to stretch their arms and their souls, the right to breathe and the right to vote, the freedom to choose their friends, enjoy the sunshine, and ride on the railroads, uncursed by color; thinking, dreaming, working, as they will in a kingdom of beauty and love.

W. E. B. DUBOIS, "Credo," *Darkwater*

Vote for the advantage of ourselves and our race.

SLOGAN OF THE ALPHA SUFFRAGE CLUB, established by Ida B. Wells-Barnett and Belle Squire

CONTENTS

African Americans living in Chicago in 1910, by Dennis McClendon.

From Party to Race

In the final decades of the nineteenth century and the early years of the twentieth, northern black activists, angry at Republicans and distrusting Democrats, used their race to claim political leadership and cement the support of an always-divided constituency of black voters. They were a tiny but surprisingly influential force. While their southern counterparts built communities bounded by disfranchisement and racial terror, African Americans in northern cities sent representatives to state legislatures and county boards, won positions in municipal agencies, and gained influence in urban politics. Their agendas, hotly debated in the press and from the pulpit, were guided by the dynamic social conditions of the industrializing North. They were neither the bland voices of racial uplift nor pliant puppets of Republican machines. They were outspoken, exacting, and pragmatic politicians who aimed to use electoral politics as a tool in the struggle for racial equality. Their history highlights the revolutionary potential and the tragic limits of American democracy.

This book is about three generations of African American activists—the ministers, professionals, labor leaders, clubwomen, and striving entrepreneurs—who engaged in political struggles and constituted themselves as political actors in a society that dismissed and denied their claims. This book explores the making of a political culture and tracks the ways a small and marginalized group claimed rights, gained influence within a political system, and put racial struggles at the center of urban politics. It is a study of how African Americans moved from slavery to citizenship, from debating their place within the nation to demanding representation in government, and ultimately, as journalist T. Thomas Fortune urged, from party to race.

Until the Second World War, the majority of black Americans lived in the American South. It is not surprising that most studies of black politics in the decades after the Civil War have been southern histories. These studies—some of the most important work in American history—focus on a region that was largely rural and that within a generation after emancipation disfranchised black voters.[1] The traditional narrative of black politics in the half century after Reconstruction emphasized a steady loss of civil rights and social power. This long-standing account assumed African Americans stood outside the massive economic and social forces transforming late nineteenth-century America. All too frequently, it played on a kind of nostalgia for rural folkways, which, William Jones contends, "understood black southerners as essentially incompatible with modernity."[2] Labor histories, by contrast, highlight the ways black workers were part of and, in some cases, on the vanguard of the gradual rise of industry in the post-Reconstruction South. Yet all agree that disfranchisement and mob violence severely limited the political activities of black southerners, especially by the end of the nineteenth century.[3]

The political struggles of African Americans in northern cities tell a very different story.[4] African Americans made up just 2.5 percent of northern urban dwellers in 1900, yet 70.5 percent of northern African Americans lived in cities.[5] Northern black activists, though constrained by law, racist customs, and mob violence, operated in a political culture that was dramatically different from that of the rural South. Theirs was an industrial society that relied on wage labor and was rapidly filling with European immigrants. The diversity of economic opportunities and nationalities—the rapid changes of an urbanizing society—chipped away at older institutions and opened new spaces for political activism for black Americans.

Students of black politics have long argued that black voters stuck with the party of Lincoln until the 1936 presidential election, when African Americans, grateful for the few benefits bestowed by the New Deal, shifted to the Democratic Party.[6] What gets lost in accounts of national trends is the ways northern black activists openly and aggressively debated, particularly in the 1880s and 1890s, whether to ally with local Democrats, to turn away from the voting booth in favor of the courts, or to establish black political parties. Black activists were regularly angered by the policies of the national Republican Party and frustrated by local Democrats and Republicans who did not make good on patronage promises. Their solution was to expand and redirect the party system. In Chicago, these were not necessarily black nationalists, though some supported emigration out of the United States. They were instead "race men," determined that black men become visible, vocal, and effective forces in local politics.

"Negroes in Chicago are bolder and more courageous as political pioneers than in any other city," commented Howard University sociologist Kelly Miller in 1935. Chicago, he added, is "a model for study for all of the large cities in the North with a considerable Negro contingency."[7] Chicago, after all, elected its first black alderman in 1915, twenty-six years before New York did, and the city was the first to elect a black congressman after the collapse of Reconstruction. Chicago was home to the nation's leading antilynching crusader, Ida B. Wells-Barnett; to some of the most vocal women's club activists; to several of the most prominent black ministers; to one of the earliest African American hospitals; and to influential African American newspapers—the *Conservator*, the *Broad Ax*, and most powerful of all, the *Chicago Defender*. Chicago's political activists, just a tiny portion of the nation's black population, had a disproportionate impact on local and national African American politics.[8]

This book is a history of Chicago as much as it is a study of long-neglected corners of American politics and African American history. I take seriously the old adage that all politics is local; to understand the workings of American democracy, we need to pay close attention to the hard-fought battles on clearly defined terrain. *Local* refers to more than sly handshakes and backroom deals. By "local," I mean an actual place—and the ways that urban space simultaneously structured and was structured by political struggles. Political battles in Chicago differed from those in the American South precisely because Chicago's activists were working in a rapidly industrializing northern city. Chicago politics was determined by changing social geography, a fragmented urban government, and a dynamic, rapidly swelling urban populace, as well as national events and global flows of capital and labor migrations. The city of industry and immigration, of racial and labor violence, of a World's Fair and a race riot, offered new opportunities and simultaneously constrained activists. The local determined—though not completely—the bounds of legitimate political action and rhetoric, and the possibilities for social change.[9]

And yet Chicago's activists were more than local figures. Their debates and campaigns played out in the national and at times international arenas. They forged alliances with activists along the East Coast and across the South, attended national conventions, read newspapers published in southern towns and northern cities, and petitioned Congress and the president. Even before the Civil War northern activists saw themselves as representing a national movement to abolish slavery and demand their own civil rights. Most significantly, the local political terrain was made and steadily transformed by European immigrants and American migrants seeking jobs and fueling the city's mass-production industries. Between 1850 and 1900, Chicago's population grew from 29,963 to 1,698,575; the city's population doubled again by 1920. In 1900, immigrants and their children made up 80 percent of Chicago's population.[10] Newcomers from Ireland, Italy, Poland, Scandinavia, and Lithuania, along with Yankee entrepreneurs and black laborers from the American South typically brought new values, customs, and tastes, and as their numbers grew, they made powerful demands on local government. The city's black population remained relatively small, less than 2 percent of Chicago's population until 1910. African American activists had to work within and among, in competition with and sometimes alongside a dynamic, splintered, multicultural political community. For black activists, the global complemented the local.

Life in the immigrant city sharpened social differences and heightened newcomers' sense of shared experience and values with fellow countrymen. The local hierarchies that had given order to rural regions and small towns shattered under the impersonal forces of urbanization, industrialization, standardization, and mass migration. New arrivals were faced with building new communities, drawing on the ideals and values they carried from abroad, and responding to the new pressures of the city. They established churches and civic organizations and networks of mutual support bound together by common language, beliefs, and shared struggles for survival.

Collective identities were constituted in neighborhoods and workplaces, giving spatial form to cultural bonds. Chicago was—and still is—a city of neighborhoods, and though most city blocks in the nineteenth through the twentieth century contained a mix of nationalities, residents tended to classify each neighborhood with an immigrant group. Job sites also tended to be segmented by nationality, as jobs designated high-skilled tended to go to German, Swedish, and English workers, with Italians, Poles, Lithuanians, and Bohemians—Jews and Catholics—and African Americans often grouped by nationality in less skilled, lower-paying work. Segmentation in the labor force replicated and reinforced segregation of racial and immigrant groups in the housing market. "The elaboration of space-bound identities," David Harvey notes, "became more rather than less important in a world of diminishing spatial barriers to exchange, movement and communication."[11]

Race entered Chicago's spatial order slowly but after the turn of the twentieth century with violent speed as real estate entrepreneurs backed by vicious white mobs began drawing the "color line" through the South Side. The racial segregation of the city's neighborhoods did not eliminate class differences, and black Chicagoans continued to separate respectable churchgoing families from others. But heavily policed neighborhood boundaries, which led European immigrants gradually to see themselves as part of a white working class, generated new institutions of self-support and new solidarities among black Chicagoans, particularly when it came to political organizing.[12] Churches and social organizations addressed the material struggles of black workers while also framing political agendas and generating new leaders whose interests traversed regional boundaries but whose authority sprung from an increasingly constricted economic and social foundation. South State Street, the city's African American commercial core, produced a new generation of urban black entrepreneurs, who supported black activists and financed the careers of several of the city's early twentieth-century black politicians. Black politicians and activists charted a new racial solidarity and gradually carved a separate African American political culture.[13] It was a politics guided by a small black elite that sought to elide class differences. Racial segregation paradoxically helped forge economic and cultural bonds (and mystify class differences, at least in the voting booth), which became a crucial base for urban black politics.

The interconnection of racial identities and urban space was widely visible in American towns and cities in the late nineteenth and twentieth centuries. The codification and institutionalization of racial segregation gave urban space—public and private, domestic and commercial—a racial character, determining literally the boundaries of work and neighborhood for millions of people. By the early twentieth century, segregation laws and local customs affected Native Americans, Asian Americans, Jewish Americans, and African Americans. Black Americans challenged racial segregation in real estate, commercial entities, and public spaces. Black Americans' efforts to ride in white-only rail cars, to be served in restaurants or seated in theaters were the subject of court cases and the basis for new rights claims. Racial segregation made the very ground on which black Americans lived the subject of political struggle.[14]

Yet segregation concealed as much as it affirmed. Black domestic workers regularly crossed the urban racial divide, daily traveling to and from their employers' white neighborhoods. White Americans expressed and asserted their racial identity both by enforcing segregation and by claiming the prerogative of crossing the "color line." White men owned shops in black neighborhoods and spent their money in the cabarets, dance halls, brothels, and gambling houses along South State Street. The color line functioned as an ideological barrier that mystified actual relationships of work, leisure, and housing. It obscured the ways people moved through the city and made inequalities in pay and in the distribution of municipal services to urban neighborhoods seem natural and ordinary. The color line was held up as a visible threat aimed at maintaining a racial hierarchy while vigorously concealing the regular interactions between black workers and white employers, black entrepreneurs and their white customers, white officials and black constituents, and ultimately the interdependence of white and black politicians.[15]

The emergence of racially segregated African American neighborhoods in northern cities in many ways transformed the structures and substance of urban politics. Chicago was not always a segregated city, and the process of racial segregation with its unequal distribution of investment capital and government resources in urban space powerfully defined urban politics in the twentieth century. South State Street, the commercial heart of the Black Belt, became a wellspring for economic autonomy and political authority for black Chicagoans. Denied access to bank loans and commercial credit, many black entrepreneurs got their start and made their fortunes in the vice trades, whether in gambling, semilegal saloons, or brothels. Those entrepreneurs, even as they crossed into licit businesses, gave legitimacy to an expanding political system of payoffs for protection and votes in exchange for city hall jobs, the methods of the emerging and increasingly powerful political machines. At the same time, widely sanctioned illicit business generated a new force in local politics, the politically engaged social reformers. The unequal distribution of investment capital made vice a viable, sometimes the only, strategy for launching businesses in the segregated South Side. Black activists and politicians, building careers on the investments of South Side entrepreneurs, made vice a crucial force in urban politics.[16]

The growth of the city—its rapidly expanding population, rising skyscrapers, and modern technologies of production and consumption—seemed to many observers a natural and inevitable result of scientific progress and the achievements of the reunified American nation in the late nineteenth century. Inequality too was widely portrayed as part of the natural order, an expression of the Darwinian competition that put the fittest, richest, most powerful men on top. Just as so many organic metaphors were applied to the densely packed city—Chicago was repeatedly described as a "breathing, belching organism"—so too were the racial (and racist) taxonomies of nineteenth-century race scientists presented as expressions of a natural order. The unequal distribution of power in social space—in the city—was easily naturalized and its operations veiled. Spaces, as Henri

Lefebvre famously observed, obscure the conditions of their own production. It was ultimately political organizing, the aggressive challenges to celebrations of national progress (like the World's Columbian Exposition in Chicago in 1893), and direct protests against racial discrimination that began to strip away the apparently inevitable development of racial inequality and racially segregated urban space. Political struggle in the modern city meant taking seriously both the city's history—challenging the monuments to its growth and the narratives of its Phoenix-like rise—and the history of racial violence and inequality across the nation.[17]

The question of the nation, its civic boundaries, and where they fit within it was a source of much debate and division among black activists in the decades surrounding the Civil War. The war violently opened the possibility of making a new national citizenry. War and Reconstruction shifted the ground of citizenship from the states to the nation, an expansion of federal power manifest in the new amendments to the Constitution, which abolished slavery, gave black men the vote, and defined citizens as those born in or naturalized in the United States. For black Americans, federal authority was personal; it transformed fundamental conditions of their daily lives. To some activists, government, once vilified for maintaining slavery, seemed a viable tool for affirming and expanding individual rights.

But if the postwar constitutional amendments set the contours of citizenship, local officials determined the practice. African Americans, north and south, faced a growing stack of local ordinances designed to limit their newly won rights. When law would not suffice, local groups, often parts of national organizations—the Ku Klux Klan and others—sought to bludgeon and brutalize black Americans into relinquishing rights. Federal officials, especially after the mid-1870s, offered little protection and often endorsed the violence. Despite the centralization of state power, it was in the many municipalities, county offices, courthouses, and jails across the nation where meaningful struggles over and for black civil rights occurred.

New arrivals to Chicago and other American cities in the years after the Civil War transformed political rhetoric and political processes on the local level. Breaking the hold of the Yankee elite on urban politics, immigrants and American-born laborers claimed rights as citizens. Most powerfully, they demanded representation in local governance and in the process transformed the meaning of political representation. Their claims were not rooted in the liberal ideal of individual rights or in leaders representing the universal interests of an abstract citizenry but in their collective interests as national groups living in new urban communities.

Spatial expressions of collective identity translated easily into politics in a city organized according to a ward system of governance, where ward and neighborhood boundaries often overlapped and aldermen used their influence in city hall to direct resources to their wards. Representation tied to a particular place was increasingly conceived in terms of the collective interests of various national groups. Representation increasingly had to do with representatives who "looked like" or shared cultural backgrounds with their constituents, political scientist Hannah Pitkin notes. This shift in popular theories of representation occurred initially in cities filling with immigrants and migrants. Gradually, it became commonplace in national politics as race and region—black or white, north or south—became a powerful call to political commitment, often superseding class interests expressed by organized labor.[18]

The move from collective interests to collective representation was not immediate or inevitable for black Chicagoans. African Americans had based their demands for rights on their membership in the nation. "We are American citizens," was the common refrain of black activists from the 1850s through the 1870s. But by the final decades of the century, black leaders, disappointed with the federal retreat from protecting their rights, strengthened political alliances that crossed regional and state lines while at the same time seeking greater access to local governance. Racial segregation in residences produced a new political constituency: black voters crowded into segregated wards, though black Chicagoans were not a majority in any ward until 1920. Just as significantly, segregation renewed a sense of common purpose as reformers, church leaders, and civic organizations moved to address the needs of a growing and often impoverished urban black population. Racial segregation, an emblem of the unequal distribution of urban resources, meant both spatial separation and political solidarity.[19]

"Union is strength and division is weakness," proclaimed John Jones, Chicago's first black elected official. Jones in 1872 had already experienced what activists would contend with through the following century: black leaders were rarely in agreement over agendas or strategy.[20] The widely chronicled early twentieth-century dispute between scholar and journalist W. E. B. DuBois and educator and writer Booker T. Washington was just one of the cracks and fissures that defined African American politics. There were, as political scientists and historians have recently recognized, significant conflicts and social differences among black activists. There was no united or cohesive "black community." Activists could see that education, earnings, gender, claims to "respectability," political alliances, and personal commitments, along with an array of seemingly trivial qualities, divided black Chicagoans.[21] Agendas set by the elite at times conflicted with the interests and aims of others. Unity, so often needed in political struggles, was not easy to achieve. How activists worked to forge unity and find common ground, especially during crucial moments in their long struggle for representation on the city council, is central to the history of black politics in Chicago.

Chicagoans in the tumultuous years around the turn of the twentieth century redefined politics for their communities, broadening the reach of urban politics to include working and housing conditions, public health and children's nurseries, as well as other social issues that had long remained outside the scope of formal politics. They used the political processes to regulate dance halls and to protest the local release of new films. Chicagoans saw politics in the trash-strewn alleys and overcrowded tenements on the West Side, in the adulterated meats shipped out of the stockyards, and in the willingness of the city's police, usually Irish immigrants, to slow and even halt investigations into fire bombings of homes and shops owned by African Americans. They heard political exhortations from the pulpit on Sundays and in cramped saloons where immigrants debated wages and working conditions in the city's booming industries.

Chicago was simultaneously a laboratory and a model for students of urban politics, just as it was for scholars of early twentieth-century American cities. The urban sociologists at the University of Chicago in the 1920s were more famous than the political scientists. Ernest Burgess and Robert Park, along with their students, produced some of the most influential and enduring studies of urban social change. The political scientists Charles E. Merriam and his student Harold Foote Gosnell also had a broad reach both within and outside the academy. Both men wrote books and articles analyzing the Chicago political scene with the aim of explaining it to other scholars but also of unveiling the workings of local governance to nonacademic readers. Both scholars took local politics seriously, believing that it was the local that, to a large extent, shaped the daily lives of the city's citizens. In emphasizing the local, Merriam and Gosnell translated the language of the street—boodlers, goo-goos, and bosses—into scholarly tomes. Each, responding to the dramatic economic and social changes in the city, recognized that the mechanisms of governance very often lay beyond formal structures. Government, they argued, derived its authority from the appearance of representation as much as if not more than from its actions. Chicago and to a lesser extent New York were the models for what Merriam, Gosnell, and many other scholars saw as the dominant form of urban politics in the first half of the twentieth century. Their views remain persuasive.[22]

In this study politics and political practice are broadly conceived. Politics is understood as relational and historically and geographically specific and involves collective and self-conscious struggles over social power.[23] My primary interest lies in understanding how activists maneuvered to gain influence in government and how they used the tools of protest available in the modern city to become integral participants in the electoral system.

Though this book is about politics at the grassroots level, it traces a handful of activists who devoted themselves to promoting what they called "the race." Black leaders often were in the paradoxical position of being both "elite" and working class, Elizabeth Jones Lapsansky writes of nineteenth-century Philadelphia.[24] A significant number of late nineteenth-century Chicago's activists were lawyers and successful businessmen; many were laborers, waiters, or Pullman porters; none, unlike some white politicians, had enough wealth to free them from regular work. Some black activists were born into slavery, others into tenuous freedom. The activists described in this study had distinguished themselves through education or economic achievements (or both). Even as they fought over strategies and agendas, over leadership of civic institutions and political parties, all claimed to speak for the black metropolis. Clearly, no individual represented the views of all of the city's African Americans, but in their struggle to articulate a vision for "the race," the activists effectively constituted an energetic urban—sometimes cohesive—African American constituency.

Chicagoans like to claim that the city's first non-Indian settler was a black man. Jean Baptiste Point du Sable, a fur trapper born in San Domingue, arrived in Chicago by way of New Orleans and the Mississippi River sometime before 1779. Du Sable built a cabin, mill, and trading post where the Chicago River meets Lake Michigan, establishing the first permanent settlement at the lake's southwestern corner. Most discussions of the city's black leaders jump from Du Sable across 150 years to Congressman William L. Dawson, long portrayed as a servant to Richard J. Daley's Democratic machine.[25] The story then moves to the 1980s and Harold Washington, the city's first black mayor, who for one bright political moment broke the hold of the machine and then died in office, and on to Barack Obama, the nation's first black president, who acquired a political education on the city's politically treacherous South Side. There are powerful studies of African American life in Chicago in the decades leading to World War II, a chaotic era of community building in the face of increasingly virulent mob violence. "The Making of a Negro Ghetto" Allan Spear angrily labeled this period (not surprisingly, as he was writing in the late 1960s).[26] No doubt, the "ghetto"—an impoverished though not entirely disfranchised community—was made in the early twentieth century. Yet from a slightly different angle and a longer view this era also marks the growth of a black political class, increasing strength of black activists, and the mobilization of African American voters.

This book spans nearly seventy years of Chicago's African American history. It begins in the 1850s when a small group of African American activists, mainly businessmen allied with white abolitionists, fought for civil rights in Illinois. Attending a series of "colored" conventions across the North, black Chicagoans helped build a national network of activists and in 1865 won the elimination the state's black codes. Black leaders, especially after the Civil War, were staunch Republicans and largely integrationist. Celebrating its achievements, this generation believed African Americans would be incorporated fairly and quickly into the reconstructed nation.

The alliance with white politicians shattered in the late 1880s as African American activists became disillusioned with the Republican Party, resentful of the paternalism of local white officials, and determined to launch autonomous black organizations. After a chapter on the "colored" convention movement and its impact on postwar Chicago politics, the chapters that follow trace local efforts to shape a political culture among black residents. Each chapter examines a site—sometimes material, sometimes metaphorical, sometimes both—where political consciousness emerged and strategies were debated. My study looks at literary societies, the black press (the *Conservator*, the *Whip*, and the *Defender*, and the *Broad Ax*), black labor organizations (especially the great waiters' strike in the early 1890s), turn-of-the-century reform associations, ministers and church organizations, and the rise of South State Street as the center of black commercial life. These chapters trace the growth of black-owned businesses, the emergence of new forms of popular culture (particularly film and dance-hall music), and rising conflicts between those who profited from vice and those who promoted virtue, between progressive reformers and pragmatic politicians.

This book concludes with the growing domination of the Republican machine, dramatic increases in mob attacks on African American homes, a growing black population living in run-down and overcrowded housing, and a bloody race riot. If the conclusion is depressing, it is not because black activists lowered their aspirations, became mere clients to white patrons, or were terrorized into submitting to the machine. Black activists worked with the Republican machine precisely because it was the only avenue to political influence. Labor unions largely rejected black workers; white progressives, though joining with some elite black activists, largely neglected African American communities. The machine was hardly a guardian of black civil rights, but machine politicians welcomed black activists who could bring a growing black constituency to the machine ticket. In return, African American politicians got a few jobs in city hall, jobs and work contracts for their supporters, a few municipal services, and financial donations to sympathetic black churches and civic organizations. It was not a fair deal, certainly. It did not eliminate racial discrimination in housing and labor markets and did not protect black homeowners from mob violence. But to many (though not all) black politicians, the machine proved a useful path to personal and "race advancement."

From the perspective of the twenty-first century and the tenure of America's first black president, African American activists in the early twentieth century might seem quaint, cautious, unimaginative, or short-sighted. They could not predict the impact of the Great Migration, much less of World War II, on African American politics. They could not foresee the great freedom struggle of the mid-twentieth century or the historic victory of Barack Obama. What they did know was their own history. They built their struggle—set strategies and agendas—on their understanding of the past. Some of Chicago's activists were simply pragmatic politicians, willing to sacrifice fundamental change for incremental advances. Others, like Ida Wells-Barnett, were stubborn visionaries. Some were both. All used the victories and defeats of the past to imagine, argue for, and create strategies that pushed African Americans into politics.

Chicago's activists understood the power of history itself, that narratives are malleable and images influential. They used newspapers, public protests, and eventually film to battle over how African Americans were represented in public life and defend their visions of American history. They understood that history had a politics; how the past was narrated revealed much about social power in the present. John Jones, the city's first black elected official, was explicit in his efforts to place himself within a larger panorama of American history. For those who followed Jones, participating in the political process—from checking a ballot to campaigning for office—was a means of writing history. Political activism meant, as Jones proclaimed, that black Americans could, to some degree, begin to make their own history.

It is possible to imagine a smooth path from Oscar DePriest, elected Chicago's first black alderman in 1915, to President Barack Obama. But such simple visions flatten history and lose sight of the profound and hard-fought transformations in American politics in the twentieth century. Such straight lines through time overlook the hard work of organizing voters faced with a long string of defeats, the unexpected courage of activists confronting horrible violence, and all the twists, turns, temporal contingencies, and specific conditions that led to unexpected and transformative events. Oscar DePriest, just like Barack Obama nearly a century later, owed his victory to the tireless local activists who worked the precincts, organized their neighbors, protested, petitioned, and demanded representation in government. Politics, like history itself, requires paying close attention to those local activists.

ONE

History, Memory, and One Man's Vote

"Where shall we lay our chains?" demanded the former abolitionist John Jones of a crowd of "colored men" gathered in a workingmen's association hall at Van Buren and Clark Streets in Chicago in January 1872. "Where? Where?" he cried. The audience of former slaves, Civil War veterans, and a few lifelong Chicagoans roared their approval when Jones offered his answer: "Upon the altar of the Republican Party. Thank God for the Republican Party." In a speech that rambled through the major events in America's past, Jones underscored black people's contributions to the nation's history. The "respect of the civilized world," he contended, goes to those who have a history. "Freedom and Progress" in the future would go to those who supported the Republican Party.[1]

Jones was asking his fellow citizens to do what he had been doing for nearly thirty years. "Let me exhort you to attend the political meetings of your neighborhood, towns and wards," he pleaded. It was through such meetings, where black Americans were schooled in politics, that the newly enfranchised were taught to "vote intelligently."[2] This was how Jones understood his own command of American politics and his own transformation over two decades of abolitionist and civil rights campaigns into a national leader. Less than a decade after emancipation and just two years after black men gained the right to vote, Jones urged Chicago's tiny black population to claim a place in municipal politics, to support the Republican Party, and to use their votes to assert their rights in urban society. Politics, he contended, was the means by which black Americans could write their own history.

The unquestioned leader of Chicago's black community, Jones was a powerful figure. He was barrel-chested, with muttonchop sideburns that curled into the middle of his cheeks. He had a full head of hair well into

Photo of portrait of John Jones, oil painting by Aaron E. Darling, ca. 1865.
Courtesy of Chicago History Museum (file iCHI-62629).

his fifties.[3] Jones was born on a plantation in Greene County, North Carolina, in 1816 to a free "mulatto" woman and a German-born man. He arrived in Chicago nearly two decades before emancipation and by the time of his speech had built a fortune in real estate and established a reputation as an outspoken advocate for an immediate end to the slave system and for the civil rights of black Americans. His home on Ray Street (later Wells Street) had before emancipation welcomed the antislavery fighter John Brown and sheltered runaway slaves seeking freedom further north across the border. His wealth and status as a spokesman for his race had in 1871 propelled him to victory in citywide elections for the Cook County Board of Commissioners, making Jones the first black man elected to a public office in Chicago.[4]

Jones, in his rousing appeal, asked the crucial question facing late nineteenth-century African Americans: where would black Americans "lay [their] chains." In other words, how would black Americans move from slavery to citizenship? The Republican Party was a good part of Jones's answer. On a deeper level, Jones was raising questions about black Americans' place within the postemancipation nation. Here was the core of African American political debates, argued over among activists, intellectuals, journalists, farmers, businessmen, and labor leaders, but never finally resolved.

As Jones well knew, where black Americans chose to lay their chains was determined, in large part, by where they lived. Black activists living in northern cities, though just a tiny portion of the nation's black population, saw themselves as guiding the national movement for freedom and political rights. Enslaved African Americans had challenged their owners' authority and undermined the slave system in acts large and small. But slaveholders and their representatives in government considered enslaved people "politically inert."[5] Black northerners, by contrast, were visible and vocal political activists. In their published writing, public lectures, and daily lives, free black people represented both the potential achievements of freedom and the lies at the heart of the slave system, which denied black Americans' ability to govern themselves.

Free black people were more than symbols on the political landscape. Many were activists, though denied the rights of citizenship—even recognition of their status as citizens. They organized public gatherings, articulated collective interests, built institutions, and used their resources to advocate for black Americans.[6] Men like Jones (and John Malvin in Cleveland, Robert Purvis in Philadelphia, or the more radical David Ruggles in New York) in the middle decades of the nineteenth century called into being an African American polity and constituted themselves legitimate political actors.[7]

In Chicago, during the decades surrounding the Civil War, Jones worked with black and white activists, establishing political ties with abolitionists across the North and building an interracial, largely elite coalition to fight for civil rights for black people in Illinois. Working with printer Henry Wagoner, white newsman and abolitionist Zebina Eastman, former slave Ford Douglas, and others, Jones elaborated theories of social change and racial equality tailored to the specific experiences of black men and women living in a northern city. This tiny group fought for the abolition of slavery and, with as much determination, demanded civil rights for northern black Americans. Their speeches were passionate calls to black Chicagoans to enter local political contests, first as petitioners and organizers and eventually as voters and candidates. Their work proved essential to mobilizing the city's black population in the years before the Civil War and to spurring a political consciousness among the churchgoers, laborers, aspiring entrepreneurs, and refugees from slavery. Their campaigns for suffrage and civil rights contributed to the formation of a small, vibrant, and highly contested Afro-American political culture in late nineteenth-century Chicago.

Jones's success in politics and business was the result of some shrewd alliances with the city's midcentury Republican business elite and, significantly of the rapidly changing character of mid-nineteenth-century Chicago. The city, when Jones, his wife, Mary, and their baby daughter, Lavinia, arrived in 1845, was fast recovering from the economic depression of the late 1830s and widely seen as a frontier town where a hardworking young man could make his fortune. Just a decade earlier, the Illinois Potawatomi had, after nearly fifteen years of war and a handful of treaty payments, been pushed to lands farther west; the French fur-trading families who had built the swampy village's first tavern and hotel had moved on. Chicago was barely a city with just twenty thousand people—compared to three hundred thousand in New York and ninety-three thousand in Philadelphia—and fewer than two hundred residents of African descent. It was a jumble of houses, shops, and warehouses stretching just four miles along the lakefront and west across the Chicago River to Western Avenue. "Its bustling streets," William Cullen Bryant wrote in a series of letters published in the *New York Post*, "its villas embowered with trees; and its suburbs, consisting of the cottages of German and Irish laborers . . . [are] widening every day." What had been a "raw" and "slovenly" settlement had by 1846, when Bryant's steamer landed at the city's busy harbor, become a "thriving commercial center."[8]

In 1845, Chicago's leaders were engaged in raising funds to restart work on the Illinois and Michigan Canal, among the earliest of the major infrastructure projects that tied the city's economy to eastern capital and established Chicago as a commercial center connecting markets to the east with farmers, planters, ranchers, and miners in the West and South. The ninety-six-mile waterway opened April 19, 1848. Two weeks later a canal boat carrying sugar from New Orleans arrived in Chicago, ostentatiously linking the slave regime to Chicago's fortunes. The sugar would be transferred to a steamboat and shipped across the Great Lakes to Buffalo, where it was held up two weeks while the Erie Canal was cleared of winter ice, and was then shipped to New York City.[9] The canal "brought stone, brick, food and fuel in vast quantities to build up her [Chicago's] trade, and carried away an inconceivable mass of lumber and merchandise."[10]

Over the following decades, railroads, telegraph lines, the arrival of German and Irish workers from eastern port cities, and investment capital funneled west by eastern banks and industrialists transformed the sleepy commercial post into a major industrial center. "It is the type of that class of American towns which have made themselves conspicuous, and almost ridiculous, by their rapid growth," commented a visitor in the 1850s.[11] The railroad along with entrepreneurs like reaper manufacturer Cyrus McCormick and meat-packer Philip Armor propelled Chicago's expansion. Trains deposited Wisconsin pine at the lumberyards just west of the Chicago River, spurring construction of frame cottages that lined the city's muddy streets. "In 1860, Chicago was a thriving young city . . . with many large factories; many papers, daily and weekly," wrote Joseph Kirkland in his 1892 history of the city. It was, "in short, a place of great pretensions and still greater hopes."[12]

The Civil War triggered rapid industrialization. Ready-made clothing firms were established during the war to manufacture uniforms for Union soldiers and sailors, producing $12 million in goods annually by 1863. It was the opening of the Union Stockyards on Christmas Day 1865 that in many ways signaled the emergence of the industrial city. The stockyards, built in the town of Lake just south of the city (later annexed to Chicago), introduced the mass-production techniques that were widely used in the following years, though the slaughtering and meatpacking plants used a "disassembly" line to transform livestock into packages of beef and pork. Chicago did not become a center for slaughtering and packing until the 1880s, when refrigerated railcars were introduced. But the packing plants, like McCormick's reaper factory, the planing mills, brass and iron foundries, breweries, and workshops making wagons, gloves, pumps, saddles, and other goods, employed the growing number of skilled and unskilled laborers arriving in the city.

The growth of factory production affected black Chicagoans in important but indirect ways. Industrialization generated new hierarchies in urban labor forces, designating some work as skilled, other work as "menial" and "servile." Skilled workers earned higher wages, enjoyed higher social status, and became leaders in labor and political organizations. Black workers were rarely included among the skilled labor force. More often, they were Chicago's cheapest labor and, designated unskilled, were trapped at the bottom of the urban wage scale. Merchants and artisans used these low-wage black workers—just as they used low wages paid to unskilled European immigrants—to accumulate profits, which could be invested in new technologies and new businesses, and to build their fortunes.[13]

Not until the early twentieth century would significant numbers of African Americans find jobs in industry. Before the Civil War, black men in Chicago owned some commercial property; one was a successful grocer, another a barber, and Jones started out in the city with a tiny tailoring shop. Most black men, however, were stuck in low-wage service jobs, refused work in the higher-paying construction trades or industry. The 1870 census listed nearly 80 percent of African Americans as restaurant and hotel workers, domestic servants, or dockworkers. Dock laborers earned $1.00 to $2.00 per day, while white workers in the building trades could earn as much as $3.50 or $4.00, and the iron and steel mills paid $1.50 to $6.00 depending on the job's skill level. The Great Fire of October 1871 apparently spurred the mayor to approve the formation of Fire Company 21, an all-black force, and in the mid-1870s, city officials hired a small number of black men as police officers. But even as Chicago's industries recovered from the economic depression of the early 1870s, black men found few jobs in manufacturing. More than 60 percent of the black workforce continued to work in domestic and personal services through the 1890s, earning significantly less than even the lowest-paid unskilled white laborers.[14]

African American women, facing equally dismal prospects, worked as servants in white homes or as laundresses and seamstresses for white clientele. Immigrant girls and women often worked as seamstresses in sweatshops, earning as little as a dollar per week or up to five or six dollars per week for skilled seamstresses. All, black and white, worked ten- to fourteen-hour days. The city's commercial laundries were among the major employers of black laboring women. "The colored people have done and are doing remarkably well considering the disadvantages and discouragements under which they live," commented the condescending white writer Joseph Kirkland in *Scribner's Magazine* in 1892,[15] failing to acknowledge that low-wage, low-skill jobs kept most black families mired in poverty.

Chicago's population expanded rapidly in the years surrounding the Civil War, fed largely by immigrants from northern and western Europe, along with a steady flow of Yankee strivers and a small but growing number of African American refugees from the slave South. In 1860, foreign-born residents made up 50 percent of Chicago's population; ten years later the foreign born were slightly less than half, yet the foreign born and their American-born children would make up close to 80 percent of Chicago's population from the 1870s through World War I. The 1850 census found just 323 people of African descent in Chicago; that number would jump to nearly 6,000 in 1880, still less than 2 percent of the city's population. The wide array of nationalities living in the city, along with the sharpening of collective interests among each national group, created some economic and political opportunities for even a tiny minority like African Americans.[16]

Chicago, even with its economic ties to the slave South, was widely known as an abolitionist stronghold. Antislavery politics, promoted from the pulpit and exhorted by civic leaders, expanded in the 1840s and 1850s. Many exhibited their abolitionist views by participating in a network of safe havens called the Underground Railroad. In any particular week, there were probably a dozen refugees, typically overlooked by census takers, staying in the homes and churches of the city's abolitionist leaders. Decades later, some of the early settlers remembered black families stopping in the city for a few days or a few months as they "fled from the Kentucky farm or plantation . . . anxious to move farther northward, away from any pursuers."[17] Southern Illinois remained generally proslavery; in Chicago, black men and women found sympathetic white friends. The city's white political leaders, mostly of New England birth, were generally well disposed to the abolitionist cause. The Chicago Common Council openly condemned the Fugitive Slave Act of 1850, calling it a "cruel and unjust law" and directing the city's police department to ignore requests to round up fugitive slaves.[18]

Chicago politics in the years before the Civil War was governed by a few white men who had made fortunes in Illinois real estate and local commerce. They were, in Donald L. Miller's words, "a frontier aristocracy," an urban elite of self-made men with interlocking business interests and, eventually, family ties. The city's charter, approved by the state legislature on March 4, 1837, established a common council composed of a mayor and aldermen, and divided the city into wards from which the aldermen were elected.[19] Cook County was organized January 15, 1831, with Chicago as county seat. The city's first mayoral election was "sharp and spirited," like nearly all those that followed, pitting John H. Kinzie, the Whig candidate, against William B. Ogden, a Democrat. "Both were members of the old St. James Episcopal Church, both men of wealth for that time and there was nothing in the character of either of the men to give either one an advantage over the other," commented the newspaper owner and later two-term mayor John Wentworth. Ogden won with 469 votes to Kinzie's 237.[20]

Only two of the city's nineteen mayors before the Civil War—a bartender and a blacksmith—were of the laboring classes. As Miller notes, all but three came from New York or New England; all were native-born Americans with strong views of the "city's first proletariat—the 'poor and vicious foreigners,' as Ogden called the Irish who lived in the squalid 'shanties' and 'rookeries' of Canalport."[21] Chicago's elite—the old-stock Yankee businessmen who owned most of the city's real estate and filled most municipal offices—seemed more likely to disparage Irish immigrants than African Americans. Most were antislavery, though hardly believers in racial equality or integration.

In the city's early years, property ownership and racial identity were marks of success and keys to political participation. The Illinois state constitution, approved in 1818, set a property qualification for the vote, which in effect prevented most black men and poor white men from voting. (Women were specifically denied suffrage.) A year later, the legislature specified race as a qualification for the franchise, barring black men from voting. Chicago, under its 1837 charter, affirmed the property requirement, setting "a nominal tax" of three dollars to be paid within one year before the election. "This restriction was not excessive, but sufficient to identify the suffrage with the interests of municipal expenditure," commented Samuel Edwin Sparling in his meticulous study of municipal governance published in 1898. Without commenting on the racial restriction of the franchise, Sparling suggested that the tax was designed to limit the political influence of propertyless immigrants. The tax "must be considered sensible and wise in the midst of a population of diverse elements, when a transient vote was proportionately large." Yet the "property test" was abolished in 1841, just as immigrants from Ireland, Bavaria, Saxony, and Prussia began to flow into the city. The Common Council periodically adjusted the residency requirement but never lengthened it to more than six months for adult male immigrants from Europe. Black men acquired voting rights only after the Civil War, with the passage of the Fifteenth Amendment to the US Constitution in 1870.[22] In the city at least, European immigrants were seen as a politically distinct group, though not nearly as constrained legally as black Americans.

State law further placed African Americans under a separate legal category, denying them the rights and responsibilities enjoyed by white residents of any nationality. Beginning in the territorial period and continuing through the Civil War, Illinois law, like ordinances in Ohio and Indiana, placed rigid and in some cases draconian restrictions on the actions of black residents. Indeed, the state constitution permitted slavery. It allowed long-term indentured servitude, authorized the enslavement of workers in salt manufacturing in southern Illinois, and did not free enslaved people brought into the territory before statehood. Until 1845, state law permitted immigrating slave owners to sign "labor contracts" with their black servants.[23]

The state legislature adopted a comprehensive Black Code in 1819, just a year after Illinois achieved statehood. The law barred black men from serving on juries, testifying against white men, or serving in the state militia and limited the franchise to white men. The law further barred marriage between the races. In later revisions, the state black laws required free African American men and women entering Illinois to carry their freedom papers or to post $1,000 bond.[24]

Chicago's Common Council and mayor's office, though sheltering many who opposed the slave system, never challenged the state's race laws. They also rarely enforced them. As in Boston, Philadelphia, and New York, racial separation in commercial spaces, rather than an outright ban on black residents, was common and customary. Racial segregation in common carriers, cemeteries, theaters, and schools was widespread, though not mandated by law.[25]

Chicago's African American leaders succeeded in business and politics despite the black codes. They effectively merged financial with political interests, forming friendships and business ties across racial lines. The same year Jones settled in Chicago, Abraham T. and Joanna Hall arrived. When black congregants established the city's first African American church, Quinn Chapel, in 1847, Rev. Hall became its first minister, receiving significant financial support from white Chicagoans. By 1860, the city's African American churches were "at least partially dependent on the good will of the white community" for funding. In the late 1840s, Henry O. Wagoner arrived in Chicago with his wife of two years. Wagoner was born into slavery in Maryland; his mother was enslaved, and his father was a German physician. The Wagoners lived in Chicago for just a few years before moving in the late 1850s to Denver, where he was active in Republican politics and was known as the "Douglass of Colorado." In Chicago, Jones, Wagoner, and others found among white abolitionists a ready, if sometimes condescending, supply of white educators and, in a few cases, investment capital. Wagoner acquired printing skills while working for the region's antislavery weekly, the *Western Appeal*, owned by white abolitionist Zebina

Eastman. Jones and Hall developed deep business ties with other white abolitionists.[26]

The racial division of labor meant that black men who had the skills to move out of laboring occupations relied heavily on white clients, white capital, and often political connections to whites involved in abolitionist work. Jones was probably the most visible of the city's black entrepreneurs. After settling his family in a cottage on Ray Street, Jones opened a tailoring shop, which he quickly transformed into a thriving business. (He had learned his craft through an indenture with a tailor in Memphis, where he met his wife, the daughter of a free blacksmith.) The Jones family attended the Tabernacle Baptist Church, also called Second Baptist, across from First Baptist Church at Washington and LaSalle Streets. Tabernacle Baptist, established by white antislavery men on August 13, 1843, was widely considered the first religious institution in the city to take a stand against slavery. At Tabernacle, political activists—leaders of the Illinois Liberty and Free Soil Parties—mingled with white Garrisonians like Allan Pinkerton and more militant black abolitionists. Jones would later work with Pinkerton and other white abolitionists to fight for civil rights for black people in Illinois.[27]

In the early 1850s, Jones formed a partnership with another prominent black abolitionist, John D. Bonner. The two men, using their connections to elite white Chicagoans, launched a business that supplied servants to families and bought and sold residential real estate and city lots. Jones, it seems, was recruiting African American women to work in white households, reinforcing his influence among well-to-do whites. The business prospered so quickly that Jones and Bonner opened an office at 88 Dearborn Street in the city's commercial center. Bonner died suddenly of typhoid on December 5, 1855, "a public as well as a private loss," one friend reported. Jones continued to invest in real estate and remained active in politics. Twenty-five years after arriving in the city, Jones had amassed a fortune of nearly $85,000. Much of his real estate was destroyed by the fire of 1871, but Jones recovered his business and when he died in 1879 left an estate worth between $50,000 and $60,000.[28]

Their servant employment service likely put Jones and Bonner in a difficult political position, especially as activists in the 1850s began to debate the merits of domestic service work for black women. There was widespread concern that women domestic workers risked sexual abuse from employers. Those who lived with their employers were separated from their families and from the protection of husbands or fathers. The situation, claimed activist and writer Martin Delaney, was similar to slavery. Delaney, who in the late 1840s traveled through the Midwest giving speeches and writing for Frederick Douglass's *North Star*, urged black men to seek education and skilled occupations and to keep their wives' labor within the home. (Delaney's wife largely supported the family through her work as a seamstress.) Other activists recognized that domestic work was a necessity for many black women. The issue was hotly debated at black political conventions and in the press in the early 1850s. Douglass commented that while service occupations were "right in themselves," the jobs were "degrading to us as a class." For Jones and Bonner, the business helped to cement ties to white elite families, apparently without hampering Jones's political support among black laborers.[29]

Well-to-do black Chicagoans like Jones and Rev. Hall effectively used white patronage to undercut their legal subordination to whites and to link themselves to the city's social elite. Their political work, as well as their business success, separated them from the city's black laborers. Ambitious African Americans regularly and publically expressed gratitude to their white patrons, entrenching a narrative of black dependence in popular literature (and in much later scholarship). In the most widely published vignette of his life, Jones claimed that two "friends of his race," Dr. Charles Volney Dyer and Lemuel Covell Paine Freer, taught him to read and write.[30] For Jones, the public recounting of the welcome support of white abolitionists was likely a genuine show of appreciation, but it also proved a successful method of placing himself among and equal to the city's white elite. The portrait of white guidance for ambitious African Americans, repeated in newspaper profiles of Jones and Wagoner, suggested a black reliance on whites in politics and business while at the same time introducing an image of a racially integrated Chicago elite. Neither was entirely accurate.

Black entrepreneurs relied on white patronage and when possible worked with white abolitionists. Yet the trope of African American dependence belied an increasingly aggressive black political culture. The city's black leaders, well schooled in legal rhetoric and the language of the Constitution, met regularly in the late 1840s and 1850s, arguing strategy and issuing demands for equal rights. Theirs was an integrationist vision resting on collective African American action. This approach was most obvious in the long struggle against the Illinois black codes.

Jones quickly became the city's most prominent black activist in 1847 when he published two letters in the *Chicago Tribune* demanding the full rights of citizenship for black Chicagoans. Jones contended that it was "anti-republican" and "unconstitutional to look upon us in any other light" than as full citizens. Working with a group of black leaders, including Rev. Hall, Wagoner, and William Johnson, Jones had helped draft a petition to the state legislature requesting a repeal of "all laws making a distinction between the negro and the white man." The group, working with a couple of black activists from southern Illinois, sent petitions to a state constitutional convention in Springfield in June 1847. Though the convention debated voting rights for European immigrants, it did not address African American rights. The Senate Judiciary Committee responded with a brief report rejecting the petition. The legislature claimed in 1847 that black men would never be considered full citizens of the state of Illinois. "The committee believe that no acts of legislation will or can ever raise the African in this country above the level in which the petitions find him," the report commented, and then explicitly rejected the petitioners' request for voting rights for black men.[31]

Despite such a sharp rebuke, the activists apparently remained optimistic; their experience with this political coalition gave them hope that black men, forming larger associations and using the petition as their only political tool, could achieve civil rights. They affirmed this faith when a small committee of black Chicagoans meeting at Tabernacle Baptist Church on August 7, 1848, selected Jones and Rev. Hall to speak for Chicago at the National Convention of Black Freemen in Cleveland that September.[32]

Jones and Hall, an aspiring businessman and a minister, were a fitting pair to represent Chicago at the convention. Both men had been born free—Hall in Pennsylvania and Jones in North Carolina. Both had arrived in the growing city in 1845, and both were outspoken abolitionists, opening their homes to runaway slaves. Hall had quickly established himself as a leader of the city's well-to-do black Christians; Quinn Chapel, located at Dearborn and Jackson Streets, was considered "one of the best appearing and best conducted congregations in the city." Both were men of broad ambitions, for themselves and for their fellow black Chicagoans.[33]

The series of "colored" conventions held in northern cities in the three decades before the Civil War provided a political education to a generation of free black men like Jones and Hall. The conventions brought together clergy, business, and professional men who claimed to represent the interests of northern black men and women. In attending the conventions and engaging in wide-ranging discussions of the economic and political needs of black Americans, those assembled constituted themselves as a new class

of regional and national political leaders. Convention proceedings, generally reprinted in the *North Star* or in the 1850s *Frederick Douglass' Paper*,
highlighted the elegant rhetoric of established leaders and helped draw attention to talented younger men.[34]

The conventions of the 1830s often merged pleas for temperance and
discussions about education for black children and moral reform of black
families with abolitionist rhetoric. In the 1840s, the conventions became
more overtly political, convulsed with disputes over the strategies of the
antislavery movement and the political goals of free black men. Attendees
debated and sometimes rejected William Lloyd Garrison's calls for "moral
suasion," instead promoting political activism or violence to destroy the
slave regime. Northern black leaders in the 1840s and 1850s, whether Gar-
risonian or not, demanded not only abolition but also civil rights and suffrage for black men. The conventions of the 1840s too marked an expansion of abolitionist activism into the Ohio River valley and westward to the
Mississippi River, spreading the aims of a politically engaged, increasingly
organized, and often contentious African American leadership into Illinois
just as Jones arrived in the state.[35]

The 1848 Cleveland convention lifted Jones into the national African
American leadership and fortified his friendship with the former slave
Frederick Douglass, already famous after publishing his best-selling autobiography three years earlier. Between fifty and seventy delegates, mostly
self-made men from west of the Appalachians and north of the Ohio River,
gathered in Cleveland for three days of speeches and political debate. They
were printers, carpenters, blacksmiths, clergymen, grocers, barbers, dentists, and farmers, men who could afford the cost of travel and who had
achieved some prominence in their congregations and communities. There
were also a few nationally known figures like Martin R. Delany, newspaper
editor Henry Bibb, and Cleveland real estate entrepreneur John Malvin.
Douglass was elected president, and Jones, was selected vice president of
the convention, a sign of his rising status in regional politics. All were "men
who were highly respectable in appearance and who manifested a high degree of talent," commented the Cleveland-based *True Democrat*.[36]

Douglass's speech on the convention's opening morning, widely reprinted in northern newspapers and disparaged in the proslavery press,
expressed the confidence and optimism of many black leaders in the late
1840s. It also issued a call to action to those living in northern states.
"Great changes for the better have taken place and are still taking place,"
he proclaimed. Emancipation had come to the colonies of England and
France; black men in America had in recent years achieved status as au-

thors, editors, doctors, and lawyers. But even though "mountains of prejudice have been removed," great work remained for the "most learned and
respectable" free black men. "Every one of us should be ashamed to consider himself free, while his brother is a slave." Black men should "act with
white Abolition societies wherever you can"—to end slavery and "rise in
the scale of human improvement." For Douglass, referring to the surge of
democratic revolutions in Europe that year, the 1848 convention came at
a propitious time in world history. "The world is in commotion," he wrote
in the *North Star*. "Subjects are shaking down kingdoms, and asserting their
rights as citizens."[37]

Meeting just two months before the presidential election and two
months after the first women's rights convention at Seneca Falls, New York,
the delegates gathered in Cleveland boldly and self-consciously took on
many of the major issues of the mid-nineteenth century. They saw themselves, as Douglass suggested, as part of a national, even international,
movement of oppressed people asserting their individual rights and freeing
themselves from entrenched and obsolete aristocracies. The Cleveland convention was the first of the national black conventions to recognize women
as participants, but only after substantial debate; delegates did not consider
women's education or employment. Douglass, who had argued for giving
women the right to vote at Seneca, was silent on the issue in Cleveland. Instead, the gathering debated the quality and content of education and vo-
cational training for African American men, with Jones and, even more vigorously, Delany arguing that young black men should pursue "honorable
occupations" that would lift them out of "menial labor." Douglass pushed
for moral improvement of men and women through thrift, education, and
hard work. "We beg and intreat you, to save your money," he added. "Not
for the senseless purpose of being better off than your neighbor, but that
you may be able to educate your children, and render your share to the
common stock of prosperity and happiness around you."[38]

Many others used the 1848 convention to assert that formal politics—
voting rights, party platforms, and elections—would determine the status
and future of African Americans, those still in bondage as well as free men
and women. Of primary concern to the delegates was the presidential campaign and the candidates' position on slavery. "Whereas American slavery
is politically and morally an evil of which this country stands guilty," the
convention proclaimed, "the two great political parties of the Union have
by their acts and nominations betrayed the sacred cause of human freedom." Delegates rejected both parties' nominees, the Whigs' Zachary Taylor and the Democrats' Lewis Cass. Sharp debate erupted around a pro-

posal that the delegates support the Free Soil Party, which had nominated
Martin Van Buren under the banner "Free Soil, Free Speech, Free Labor,
and Free Men." Jones, demonstrating his nascent skill at the political art
of compromise, helped resolve the dispute. He suggested a resolution that
stated that the Free Soil slogan was in the interest of the "downtrodden and
oppressed of this land" and that the movement "be recommended to our
people." The convention adopted the resolution. Western men like Jones
were pushing eastern abolitionists to become more explicitly political and
rhetorically aggressive.[39]

The presidential election of 1848 hardly fulfilled even the limited aims
of the black convention movement. Black men could not vote, but many
had hoped to bring moral pressure to bear on antislavery Whigs and Democrats. The Liberty Party, formed less than a decade earlier, had put antislavery on a national party platform. Many black leaders hoped the newly
formed Free Soil Party might push the agenda forward. Chicagoans, like
their antislavery neighbors in Ohio and northern Indiana, were particularly inspired by the Free Soilers' stance. Antislavery Whigs and Democrats
paraded through Chicago's streets in July, chanting Martin Van Buren's
name.[40]

Douglass, Henry Bibb, Henry Highland Garnett, and a few other black
abolitionists had attended the Buffalo National Free Soil Convention that
nominated Van Buren on an antislavery platform. But many in the crowd
of antislavery Democrats and Whigs along with more radical Liberty Party
men refused to address black civil rights in the national platform. It was
an imperfect but "noble step in the right direction," Douglass commented.
Still Van Buren was widely distrusted, even abhorred, by many abolitionists
unwilling to forgive his years of political maneuvering for Andrew Jackson
and the Democrats. The Whigs, though fractured, were not yet broken. Van
Buren won just 10 percent of the national popular vote and 15 percent of
the vote in the free states, but he carried Chicago. Taylor became president
of a nation barely united.[41]

The 1848 Cleveland convention marked the height of abolitionist optimism and probably the final moment when compromise was possible on
the major issues dividing African American men. Two years later, Congress
passed the Compromise of 1850, tenuously holding the Union together
but including the Fugitive Slave Act, which shattered the hopes of black
Americans. The new law, which required citizens of free states to assist
in the capture of runaway slaves, sparked outrage among black men and

women across the North. In northern cities and towns, black and white abolitionists gathered to protest the legislation and develop plans to protect refugees from slavery. At the same time, the law fractured the organized black leadership, dividing those who urged black Americans to establish a new homeland overseas from those who continued to assert that black people should fight for the full rights of American citizenship. Some black leaders, like the eloquent New York minister Henry Highland Garnet and the charismatic abolitionist lecturer H. Ford Douglas, argued for emigration while also seeking to establish autonomous black institutions in the United States. The compromise, stitched together by a sharply divided Congress, galvanized black northerners with a new sense of political purpose.[42]

In Chicago, anger over the Fugitive Slave Act prompted the first citywide political meeting of African Americans when three hundred people, more than half of the city's adult black population, gathered in Quinn Chapel. Some among them formed a Liberty Association to fight for civil rights. They issued a resolution opposing the Fugitive Slave Act. The Liberty Association quickly organized several teams of men who would patrol the city, prepared to attack slave hunters and asserting black Chicagoans' extralegal rights to guard the city's muddy streets and alleys. "We are determined to defend ourselves at all hazards," the association's resolution proclaimed, "even should it be to the shedding of human blood." Petitions and political organizing might be useful for some civil rights issues, but black Chicagoans, like those across the North, when "driven to the extreme" would use violence to protect their limited freedom.[43]

Liberty associations, appearing in northern cities and towns, further cemented ties forged at the "colored" conventions.[44] Small groups of free black men and women had helped to rescue fugitives from slave hunters in the 1830s and 1840s, but after 1850 defiance of the Fugitive Slave Act was widespread and brought together black and white abolitionists. In a series of daring and dramatic confrontations, vigilante groups from Massachusetts to the old Northwest rescued runaways from the custody of local sheriffs or courts, risking violence or prosecution from local officials. Among the most highly publicized was the Christiana Riot in mid-September 1851 in southern Pennsylvania. In the months that followed, when thirty-five black men were charged with treason in the shooting death of a Maryland slave owner who had been searching for four fugitives, black leaders across the North held meetings to raise money for legal counsel for the defendants. Donations came from as far west as San Francisco.[45] Jones was appointed chairman of a committee to receive donations from black Chicagoans and communicate with those supporting the defense in Philadelphia. Wagoner and William Johnson served on the committee. A year later, Jones led an effort to visit the homes of black and white abolitionists in Chicago to raise money to purchase and liberate a former Tennessee slave, Albert Pettit. Jones and his wife apparently took in Pettit's daughters. Rachel and Louisa Pettit lived with the Jones family at least until the early years of the Civil War, when the young women were in their late teens. The daring rescues of purported runaways along with the fund-raising drives for those charged with lawbreaking in the release of black prisoners brought well-publicized victories to the abolitionist cause and deepened ties among free black political organizers.[46]

"My friend, Illinois is aroused," wrote Jones in a letter published in *Frederick Douglass' Paper* on November 18, 1853. Jones drew attention to the political work of Illinois's activists and to his own role in leading the movement. Lecturers were traveling the state "addressing large and spirited meetings of colored men and women." Cities and villages were nominating candidates to state and national councils, and black Chicagoans had organized a debating society to consider issues related to black civil rights. The Literary and Debating Society, under the presidency of Henry O. Wagoner, held a mass meeting on December 2, 1852. Jones addressed the crowd, denouncing state legislators for denying black Americans the right to vote and to testify in court. Activists, Jones reported, were moving "passengers" along the underground railroad. "We will take care of them, and see that they are snugly shipped for Queen Victoria's land," meaning north to Canada. Black activists were organized, linked throughout the state and across the North, and publicizing their work.[47]

While the Fugitive Slave Act galvanized abolitionists, it also opened a sharp and heated dispute among black leaders over the place of black people in America. Until passage of the Compromise of 1850, many African Americans had criticized the American Colonization Society, which had been formed in 1817 and aimed to find a site suitable for the relocation of America's black residents. Black leaders had encouraged emigration for personal safety or advancement in the 1820s, but in the following decades many, like Douglass, felt it was their duty to remain and fight for an end to slavery. After 1850, many abolitionists took a new look at emigration. Delany, long disparaging of the colonization society, was equally pessimistic about the future of black Americans after the compromise. At a convention of emigrationists in Cleveland in late August 1854, Delany asserted that the issue pertained to "our destiny and that of our posterity." "Nothing less than a national indemnity," he proclaimed, "indelibly fixed by virtue of our own sovereign potency, will satisfy us as a redress of grievances for the unparalleled wrongs . . . [and] unmitigated oppression, which we have suffered at the hands of this American people." Emigrationists of the 1850s entertained several locations, including sites in Liberia, Haiti, and Canada. Mary Ann Shadd Carey, a newspaper editor and traveling lecturer, became a leading advocate for migration to Canada. "Many look with dreadful forebodings," she wrote, "to the probability of worse than inquisitorial inhumanity in the Southern States from the operation of the Fugitive Law." An estimated nine thousand free black men and women fearing capture by slave hunters fled to Canada. Carey argued that black people were making greater "social progress" in Canada than they ever could in the United States.[48] Few in the mid-1850s disagreed with that contention.

But the broader question of whether black Americans should seek to establish permanent, self-governing communities outside of the United States proved deeply divisive. For Jones, as for Douglass, Delany, and others, the answer hinged largely on a vision of American society, its history, and its future.[49] Delany argued that America, home to people of European descent, would never make a place for black people. "We must have a position independently of anything pertaining to white men or nations," he wrote. Henry Highland Garnet, whose support for emigration predated the Fugitive Slave Act, wrote in 1848 that black people should seek freedom wherever they could find it. "I would rather see a man free in Liberia than a slave in the United States," he wrote. A year later, he added suffrage to his demands, urging black Americans to move to any nation that promised them freedom and the franchise.[50] Opponents of emigration argued that African Americans should fight for abolition and the vote in America precisely because black people were American. "What do I know of Africa?" asked William H. Topp of Albany at the annual meeting of the Pennsylvania Anti-Slavery Society in 1852. "I am part Indian and part German."[51] Jones could make a similar claim.

Jones's opposition to emigration, despite his light complexion and interracial parentage, was based on notions of individual rights and of a collective national history. He asserted again and again that "we are American citizens." Individual ancestry, like skin color, hardly entered his public speeches. Instead, using Douglass's paper to attack the emigrationists in the mid-1850s, Jones argued that black people should fight the slave power and struggle for civil rights. "Within the meaning of the United States Constitution, we are American citizens," he wrote. "By the facts of history and the admissions of American statesmen . . . by the hardships and trials endured, by the courage and fidelity displayed by our ancestors in defending the liberties and in achieving the independence of our land, we are American citizens." His tone was less militant than that of Delany; his politics followed Douglass's almost precisely.[52]

Jones' antiemigration sentiments put him in opposition to H. Ford Douglas, whose support for emigration grew even more determined after passage of the Kansas-Nebraska Act and the Supreme Court's Dred Scott decision. Douglas, born in 1831 on a Virginia plantation, the son of a slave owner and an enslaved woman, had escaped north at age fifteen. He arrived in Chicago in 1855, several months after attending the National Emigration Convention in Cleveland, where he declared that he would not be a traitor if he joined a foreign army against the United States, since America "treats me as a stranger and an alien." Douglas, who spent a year (possibly two) in Canada in the late 1850s, often traveled in the South and lectured in northeastern cities, carrying information about the conditions of slaves and the status of abolitionists in other states to free men and women in Chicago.[53] Jones and Douglas remained friendly enough to work together to fight what had become the most prominent political issue for black Chicagoans: the state's black laws. The two men, working with several of the city's black leaders, issued a call for a state colored convention in 1856 to "exercise a Constitutional Right" and to "Petition the Government for a Redress of Grievances."[54]

What outraged Jones, Ford Douglas, and others was an 1853 law that, in effect, removed black Americans from northern society. The law, designed to severely restrict African Americans from entering Illinois, provided that any person who brought a "negro or mulatto," free or slave, into the state would be fined from $100 to $500 and imprisoned for up to a year. Any black person entering the state and remaining ten days would be fined fifty dollars; if the fine was not paid, the person would be sold to anyone who would pay the fine. "Our legislature thus assumes more power on the subject of slavery, than was claimed by Congress in the passage of the Fugitive Slave Law," the *Western Citizen* angrily asserted.[55] Legislators apparently felt that free black people could not live among free whites.

Chicago's antislavery activists were furious. The city's Baptist Association, which included black and white members, asserted its "astonishment and horror" over the legislation. The association issued a resolution declaring "our determination to treat all such legislation null and void." With regard to such legislation, its members would "obey God rather than man." The *Western Citizen*, calling it "the Illinois Slave Law," published a series of letters attacking the legislation. Chicagoans' fury did not change the law, but the law was rarely enforced, even as growing numbers of runaways in the 1850s and war refuges in the early 1860s arrived in the state. "To the credit of the people, as well as to the lasting disgrace of their lawmakers, it must be said that the 1853 statute has been a dead letter in all but two or three counties," the *Chicago Daily Tribune* reported. Jones admitted some sections of the black laws were not enforced, though "some of the disabilities laid upon negroes were a living active reality."[56]

The Illinois convention was planned to challenge those "disabilities." Like most of the state and national colored conventions of the decade, the convention turned explicitly to civil rights, suffrage, and the political status of free black men in America. About seventeen men from northern and central Illinois counties, gathered in the Colored Baptist Church in Alton from Thursday through Saturday, November 13 to 15, 1856. Slavery was hardly forgotten, but the language of moral reform that had permeated conventions of earlier decades was nearly absent in Alton. The primary achievement of the convention, aside from bringing together old friends and political allies, was the establishment of the State Repeal Association, whose aim was to "repeal the Black Laws of the State and for the final accession of our political rights." Jones was chosen president and Ford Douglas secretary of what would become the state's most aggressive African American political organization.[57]

The convention delegates, like those meeting in cities and towns across the North in the 1850s, aimed to radically redefine the American nation by demanding the full inclusion of black Americans in the national polity. The Liberty Association, with its proposed sponsorship of paid lecturers to travel the state denouncing Illinois's black laws, was the initial weapon in this larger campaign. Drawing on the nation's founding documents, the assembled men, in committee reports and speeches, asserted their status as American citizens. "We, the colored citizens of Illinois," began the Declaration of Sentiment and Plan of Action, "feel ourselves *deeply aggrieved* by reason of the cruel prejudice we are compelled to suffer in this our 'native land.'" The document declared "That all men are born free and equal, possessing certain inalienable rights, that can neither be conferred nor taken away." After detailing the promises of the preamble of the US Constitution, the declaration asserted, "We claim to be citizens of Illinois to all intents and purposes," adding "we believe with the fathers of '*Seventy Six*' that taxation and representation should go together." The declaration's writers had rhetorically situated the men gathered in Alton, and the rest of Illinois's free black people, within the narrative of American history alongside the men who founded the nation.[58]

Though all agreed on the Committee of Sentiment's assertions, there was heated debate over strategy. R. J. Robinson, a minister from Madison County, was concerned that the preamble to the Declaration of Sentiment was too aggressive. Urging the crowd to "be more mild in our language when asking for our rights," Robinson moved that the convention strike the words "Neither asking nor giving quarter, spurning all compromises." After much debate, which carried into Friday evening, the motion to strike that phrase failed in a narrow vote. Jones and Douglas were on the same side in this debate: both favored the more assertive language; both opposed compromising on their civil rights.[59]

The struggle for civil rights, for Jones, Douglas, and others, was an assertion both of citizenship and manhood, a term that appeared repeatedly in convention proceedings in Illinois and elsewhere. The black laws, the delegates asserted, "destroy whatever manhood there remains within us." African American women, all agreed, should garner status and respect as citizens, but the black laws were a particular burden to black men. Without the right to vote and lacking the right to testify against a white man, black men were denied the ability to protect their dependents: their wives and children. The convention delegates, like black leaders across the North, fashioned a vision of citizenship that explicitly linked economic independence and civil rights with "manhood." While African American leaders would after the outbreak of Civil War contend that military service proved black manhood and affirmed black men's citizenship rights, in the mid-1850s many viewed participation in the rituals of politics—claiming to represent the interests of their communities and engaging in public debate—as evidence of their status as "men." Attendance at the convention and the increasingly aggressive language issued in convention resolutions and petitions were, in Ford Douglas's words, the way "we will assert our manhood in the right way."[60]

The men gathered at Alton were participating in a national political drama played out in state legislatures, at political party meetings, and at conventions of black and white abolitionists across the North. They were closely watching the legal struggles of Dred and Harriet Scott as their case made its way from the Missouri courts to the US Supreme Court. "The doctrine that Slavery goes wherever the Constitution goes is now openly maintained by [Georgia senator Robert F.] Toombs and others in the South, and dough-faces innumerable in the North," Ford Douglas proclaimed. The court's decision, wrote Henry O. Wagoner in a letter read at the convention, was a "staggering blow, not only to the liberties of the *black* man, but to the *white* man as well." But Wagoner still believed in the abolitionist project.

"Even a small 'radical' minority, with *principles planted on the whole truth,*
with God upon their side, is a majority against the universe," he declared.
Joined in sentiment and organized in political purpose, Wagoner and others declared, abolitionists could transform the American nation.[61]

How they would remake the nation, which tools and tactics would serve
their political purposes, was disputed. By late1859 both Jones and Douglas had turned away from the newly formed Republican Party, "one of the
wildest delusions that ever entered into the conceptions of men professing
anti-Slavery," Douglas commented. (Both would return to the party after
emancipation.) The Republican Party, established in 1854 as the Whigs collapsed and antislavery men left the Democratic Party, was a pragmatic mix
of radical abolitionists, racist Free Soilers, and northern antislavery Whigs
and Democrats. Douglas and Jones initially supported the new party, but
both came to believe the Republicans had abandoned abolition in favor of
union. Jones was particularly disturbed by the Republicans' refusal to support civil rights laws for free black men. The Republican Party might have
been the only issue over which Frederick Douglass and Jones disagreed.
Douglass steadily supported the Republicans, while Jones and Ford Douglas wrote and spoke against the party throughout the 1860 presidential
election. (If black families dared to send their children to Illinois schools,
Ford Douglas wrote in 1860, "Abraham Lincoln would kick them out in
the name of Republicanism and anti-slavery.") Though the Alton convention resolutions called on the state legislature to give black men the vote,
which of the "barren and unfruitful" parties black men should support remained an open question.[62]

On the Alton convention's final evening, Saturday, November 15, white
abolitionists were invited to join the delegates meeting in Liberty Hall to
hear speeches from Jones, Douglas, and William Johnson. Only Douglas's
eloquent address was reprinted in full. In this well-attended and widely
publicized oration, Douglas framed the future of the nation in powerful
and prophetic terms. "The doctrine now advanced by anti-Slavery men, that
Freedom is national while Slavery is sectional," he said, "is in itself destruc-
tive and fatal to American liberty." The US Constitution, he argued, did not
create "a slave empire—a barbarian people." Rather, the founders had kept
"the word slave" out of the Constitution; slavery, he contended, "had its
birth amidst the darkest conceptions of atheism." For Douglas, abolition
was as much a political as a religious crusade. America, he suggested, had
fallen away from its founding principles and its Christian roots. "To advocate the sectional right of Slavery," he declared, "would be to break up the
throne of God and spit in the face of the Deity."[63]

With their attendance at the convention and the launching of a local campaign against the state's black laws, Jones, Ford Douglas, and others participated in a national debate about America's future. Jones and John Bonner had attended a meeting of the National Council launched by Douglass in Rochester in 1853.[64] Over the following years, even as fighting broke out in Kansas and the Supreme Court ruled that black people did not have the legal status of American citizens, Jones and other black Chicagoans gave speeches in small towns throughout Illinois. Jones's family home on Ray Street would in the 1850s serve as both a haven for slavery's refugees and a meeting place for some of the nation's leading crusaders against the slave regime. Jones's alliance with national figures like Douglass and Allan Pinkerton along with his local organizing against the state's black laws made him the most visible black politician in Chicago by the eve of the Civil War.

In the spring of 1861, when fighting began in South Carolina, there were about a thousand black men and women living in Chicago, less than 1 percent of the city's population. Fearing retribution from angry whites and renewed efforts to enforce the black laws, about three hundred black people headed to Canada and another forty-seven moved to Haiti. As the war expanded in the following year and a half, refugees from the western front—Alabama, Mississippi, Louisiana, Arkansas, Tennessee, Missouri, and Kentucky—flowed into the city, lifting the city's African American population to more than thirty-five hundred by 1870, when Chicago's population had reached more than three hundred thousand people. At least four new African American churches were established during the 1860s, and black immigrants, desperate for jobs and housing, began constructing a neighborhood of shacks and shanties along the western edge of the city's commercial center. For the first time in Chicago's brief history, there was a clearly designated African American neighborhood, though most of the city's black residents lived in other, largely white neighborhoods.

There were during the war years growing tensions between black laborers and European immigrants, particularly Irish workers, as unskilled laborers competed for jobs in the city's booming economy. But the Irish were also angry about conscription for the Union army. There were regular announcements that Chicago was falling behind its quota. The newspapers carried reports of several violent clashes between black laborers and Irish immigrants, one in which a black man was beaten to death. Violence erupted in other northern cities, most horribly in the draft riots in New

York City in 1863. Recent arrivals from the slave South also faced tensions with the "old settlers," the well-to-do black families like the Joneses who had allied socially and in many cases, politically, with the city's white elite. The war helped unify black leaders locally and nationally—all almost immediately understood it as a "second American revolution," a struggle for freedom for black Americans. But in a city on the cusp of rapid industrial growth, fueled by a wartime boom and weakened by postwar depression, the war and the resulting sudden growth in the city's African American population generated a more diverse and increasingly stratified black Chicago.[65]

The new arrivals, many smuggled into the state to avoid capture under the black laws, found freedom in Chicago, but many also faced tremendous burdens of reuniting family members separated during the flight from slavery. Finding jobs and housing in their new urban home was a struggle. "Arrived here [and] I [rented housing]," Nancy Clary, a former slave from Tuscumbia, Alabama, remembered thirty years later. "And did washing & finally got my children with me and after I had been here about 7 months, Elijah [her husband] & Louis [her twenty-year-old son] came here." In the following years, Elijah and Nancy Clary lost six of their twelve children to cholera, measles, tuberculosis, typhoid fever, and lung disease.[66] The war caused terrible hardship as young men joined the city's only black regiment, the Twenty-Ninth United States Colored Infantry. (William Johnson, a twenty-three-year-old waiter who lived less than a block from the Joneses, joined the new regiment in 1864.) Edward and Louise Flowers fled slavery in Tennessee and arrived in Chicago with their teenage son, Cato, in November 1862. Cato worked as a day laborer to support his parents—his father was nearly sixty and his mother in her late forties—until at age nineteen he enlisted in Company C of the Twenty-Ninth Regiment. Cato Flowers died of smallpox on August 12, 1864. His parents never recovered. They lived in poverty, dependent on charity from friends and the church, until dying in the 1870s.[67]

The war added urgency to African American political work. As Chicago became a center for organizing support for Union troops, the war effort expanded Jones's reputation as a local leader linked to the national cause. He lent the use of his business offices for recruiting soldiers for the Fifty-Fourth Massachusetts Regiment before Illinois's black regiment was formed. Frederick Douglass visited the Jones household in January and in February 1863 and, in a vignette that joined Jones's political work to the gentility of his household, the *Chicago Daily Tribune* reported that Jones's daughter Lavinia and several amateur musicians "serenaded" the visiting dignitary. Martin Delany arrived in Chicago a month later, also visiting Jones's home. Delany gave two public lectures about his recent travels in Africa, again urging black Chicagoans to seek freedom in more hospitable nations. On Delany's final visit to Chicago, Jones, still strongly opposed to emigration, presided over a meeting at Quinn Chapel where Delany was the honored guest.[68]

Emancipation brought much rejoicing but also renewed the struggle to expand the meanings of American citizenship to include black men and women. Quinn Chapel, a center for organizing abolitionists and civil rights activists before the war, hosted a daylong celebration when Abraham Lincoln issued the Emancipation Proclamation on January 1, 1863. The *Tribune*, the city's Republican antislavery daily, celebrated the "Jubilee." That evening the crowds at Quinn Chapel approved a resolution calling the president "a Christian patriot and honest man," celebrating the day that "four millions of African-Americans were redeemed from the thralldom of American slavery into the noonday of universal life" and mourning the loss of "so many soldiers of freedom . . . fallen in the struggle." The resolution concluded with a demand for more than "the genius of universal emancipation," asking for "the rights of man." Quoting from the Declaration of Independence, the assembled Christians pledged loyalty to the federal government in return for the full rights of citizenship.[69] The Chicagoans saw emancipation as the first step toward their full inclusion in nation's political life.

Just a year later, Jones wrote and published what would become his most widely acclaimed political statement, urging the state legislature to erase the racial barriers to citizenship rights. In a pamphlet titled *The Black Laws of Illinois and a Few Reasons Why They Should Be Repealed,* Jones quoted American legal theory and prominent public officials from the nation's past. He critiqued each section of the legislation. He sent copies to members of the state legislature, to Governor Richard Yates, and to the city's newspapers, hoping to draw public attention to the unfairness of the laws.[70] Jones was most incisive when analyzing the legislature's classification of a black or mulatto person, defined as "every person who shall have one-fourth part or more of negro blood." Blood and skin tone were not at issue. "But enough of this," Jones wrote. "It is not the complexion or shades of men that we are discussing; it is the rights of all the inhabitants of the State, that we are advocating." Residence rather than ancestry should determine an individual's citizenship. Once again, Jones drew on American history to assert that black people were American citizens "by the courage and fidelity displayed by our ancestors in defending the liberties and in achieving the independence of our land."[71]

Jones, Wagoner, Johnson, and Rev. Hall organized petition drives throughout the state. In January 1865, they submitted petitions bearing thousands of names to the Illinois House of Representatives. There was significant white support. A petition initiated by Senator Francis A. Eastman and signed by hundreds was submitted to the state senate. "Petitions continued to pour into the General Assembly from all parts of the State," the *Tribune* reported. In the meantime, a case challenging the 1853 legislation reached the Illinois Supreme Court. The justices in January 1864 ruled in *Nelson v. The People* that "the sale of a Negro" would "not reduce him to slavery." The court, however, did not address the constitutionality of the fine on free black people entering the state.[72]

In mid-January members of the state house and senate introduced bills to repeal the black laws. Jones lobbied throughout the legislative session. One legislator, Senator William H. Green of Cairo, was so impressed with Jones's rhetorical skills that he claimed he would propose a special act to enfranchise Jones but not "the entire race."[73] The Illinois state senate voted 13 to 10 and the house 49 to 30 for repeal. (The repeal votes came within days of the legislature's vote in favor of the Thirteenth Amendment banning slavery in the United States.) Jones was touted by some legislators, but it is likely that Governor Yates pushed through the repeal. In a farewell address to the General Assembly before leaving Springfield, Yates called on the legislators to "sweep the black laws from the Statute book with a swift, relentless hand." A lifelong abolitionist, Yates had that fall been elected to the US Senate and was popular statewide. A little more than two months before the Civil War's end, the General Assembly voted on February 7, 1865, to repeal the black laws, and newly inaugurated Governor Richard Oglesby signed the bill.[74]

African Americans largely attributed the victory to Jones's pamphlet and his years of campaigning. The repeal made Jones a national black leader. He was part of a delegation of black activists, including Frederick Douglass, who met with President Andrew Johnson in the White House in February 1866 to demand the vote for black men and an expansion of military protections for black southerners. The meeting was brief, since Johnson, in the words of the delegates' report, expressed "repeated intimations of indisposition to discuss or to listen" to the delegation. Claiming to represent the interests of both black people and "our country," the delegates called Johnson's views "unsound and prejudicial to the highest interests of our race, as well as our country at large." Under pressure from black and white petitioners, Congress moved in the following year to take control of Reconstruction.[75]

In the years following the war, black Chicagoans gathered frequently in the basement of Quinn Chapel, often with Jones chairing the meetings, to "devise ways and means" to win suffrage. Activists also launched a campaign for integrated public education for black children. Though the law was on their side, custom perpetuated segregated schools, while activists regularly petitioned Chicago's Board of Education. The board, though not strictly enforcing racial segregation, occasionally issued regulations barring "persons of African blood" from attending schools other than "the colored school." Jones addressed an 1864 meeting at Quinn Chapel called to protest the board's "unjust discrimination."[76]

By 1867, Chicago had become "famous" for mass meetings, noted one correspondent to the *Christian Recorder*, an African American newspaper.[77] The repeal of the state's black code lifted the threat of fines and jail time for black immigrants and permitted black men to testify in court. Black men acquired the franchise with the passage of the Fifteenth Amendment in 1870.[78] Jones would turn his voting rights, along with his carefully crafted reputation among black and white leaders, into a short-lived but significant political career.

Jones was elected to public office during the emergency after the Great Fire swept through the city. In that period of crisis, Jones's victory likely had more to do with his position as a businessman than his claim to represent his race, but that did not prevent him from promoting himself as a leader of black Chicagoans. As much of Chicago lay in ruins and the nearly one hundred thousand left homeless by the flames slept in wooden shanties and military-style barracks, the leaders of the Democratic and Republican Parties came together to form the Union Fire-Proof Party to nominate candidates for a November election. Urged on by the *Tribune*, party leaders chose a slate of candidates from outside either party's regular ranks, men considered free of the taint of corruption and incompetence that many blamed for the tragic fire. These were primarily business leaders, the *Tribune* noted, "wise and good men whose name will . . . convince the capitalists that their investments" in rebuilding the city were secure. Jones, the only black man on the Union Fire-Proof slate, likely represented business interests but also was known as a loyal Republican. *Tribune* publisher Joseph Medill, a founding member of the Republican Party who had never held public office, was elected mayor. The city's future mayor Carter Harrison had his first win in politics with election to the Cook County Board that dreary winter. Jones became the first black man elected to city or county office with his victory in the race for the Cook County Board. A year later, he was reelected on the Republican ticket to a three-year term, facing defeat with the rest of the party in 1875.[79] Jones was indicted for conspiracy with some other county commissioners in 1876 but, "there being little evidence against him," he was acquitted at trial. Jones's political career ended.[80]

Jones, as he mobilized voters in the gloomy winter of 1871, gave speeches before labor and church groups in the desolate city. He drew on the history of antebellum interracial coalitions to contend that black men, working with white Republicans, could secure fair wages for black workers, decent housing for black families, and integrated schools. He viewed his role, and that of his class of professional black men, as providing services to black laborers. While serving as a county commissioner, Jones worked on several committees, including those overseeing the county jail, the county hospital, and, in his second term, the committee for education, the poor house and paupers, and public service. The county government, financed primarily through property taxes with some state funds, was an influential institution in the 1870s. The county board managed the construction and maintenance of county roads and bridges, provided outdoor aid to the poor, and maintained a county poorhouse, hospital, and orphan asylum. Jones apparently took pride in the very local work of rebuilding the ruined city.[81]

For Jones, politics, even more than faith, would resolve the status of black people in America. Lincoln's Emancipation Proclamation had drawn Jones back to the Republican Party. "Fellow-citizens, this great party of freedom has not only given the colored man his freedom, but has set the white man free also," Jones wrote. By the time of his election, Jones was as fully partisan as any of the party's champions. In February 1876, Jones led a meeting to organize a Fifth Ward Republican Club in the Swedenborgian Church at Thirty-Third Street and Park Avenue. During a discussion of where to locate the club's headquarters, Jones commented that "if liberty was worth having, it was worth walking a little distance to advocate the cause of it." In his 1872 speech at Turner Hall, Jones reminded the crowd, "We do not owe our freedom to either the Democratic or Whig Party." Nor should black voters turn to the church: "Oh that the ministry could have sent to heaven the five million broken manacles of the slaves of this Republic. But they could not." Only the Republicans would assure civil rights to black Americans.[82]

Jones urged black Chicagoans to come together, learn about the issues of the day ("eternal vigilance is the price of liberty"), and vote. In political meetings, he concluded, "you will hear the political topics of the day discussed which will teach you on which side the truth may be found." Tucked among the pages of Jones's sparsely kept journal was a clipping of a news article titled "Importance of a Single Vote." That, surely, in the years after black men finally gained the right to vote, was among Jones's deepest beliefs.[83]

The work of the city's tiny group of antebellum activists, their integrationist vision, and efforts to establish a collective black agenda could be seen in the 1870s in the career of John W. E. Thomas, the first African American elected to the state legislature. Thomas, who owed his win to the growing number of black voters, was beholden to white Republicans and most importantly to the state's electoral system. African American activists effectively used local political structures to promote their agendas.

The system of cumulative voting could potentially double or triple the impact of a single voter. It proved a boon to African Americans. Under the system, three representatives were elected every two years from each of the state's legislative districts. Each voter had three votes to cast for the state office; the voter could cast all three for one candidate, one and a half for two candidates, or one for each of the candidates. The aim was to ensure representation from both political parties in areas where a single party dominated. But in Chicago, where growing numbers of immigrants and African Americans were demanding representation in state government, the cumulative system allowed minority groups—those who could not marshal enough votes to gain a majority in a district election—to elect their chosen candidates. Under this system, several African Americans were elected to the state house in the final decades of the nineteenth century. (None made it to the state senate until 1924, when Adelbert H. Roberts was elected.)[84]

Thomas, born into slavery in Montgomery, Alabama, on May 1, 1847, and elected to the Illinois state house in 1876, was the first black man to benefit from cumulative system. He was educated and, according to the *Inter Ocean*, taught other enslaved people to read and write. He and his wife, Maria Reynolds, arrived in Chicago in 1869 or 1870. They moved into a three-story frame house on South Fourth Street (now Federal Street) across from Olivet Baptist Church, where they became active members, and opened a grocery and, a year or two later, a school for black students. "The child and the grey-haired freedman side by side learned their letters in his home," the *Inter Ocean* reported. Thomas later studied law under the white politician Kirk Hawes and passed the bar in 1880.[85] When Thomas died in December 1899, he left an estate valued at over $100,000 and was considered the richest black man in Chicago.

Like Jones before him, Thomas used his business connections to propel his political career. He joined the largely white Second Ward Republican Club. In fall 1876, after a much-disputed vote, the Republican Party gave Thomas one of two Republican nominations for the state house from the second district. A large crowd of African Americans had attended the county convention; activists promised to bring at least fifteen hundred black votes to the ticket. The nomination came with some controversy. The Democratic *Chicago Times* called Thomas "an Ethiopian . . . wholly unfit for any legislative function" and an expression of "Republican Madness." Though there were "faint mutterings of dissatisfaction" among some Cook County Republicans, the Republican press supported the candidate. (The exclusive Republican-leaning Municipal Reform Club, led by Robert Todd Lincoln, strongly opposed Thomas's nomination, a sign that the city's white elite were not as devoted to racial equality as men like Thomas and Jones hoped.) On election day, Thomas came in second behind the sole Democratic candidate but ahead of the other Republican. Thomas's 11,532 votes amounted to well over double all the black votes in his district. Some white Republicans had supported the black candidate.[86]

Thomas's election, coming just as Republicans in Congress were retreating from their support for Reconstruction governments in the South and amid rising violence against black southerners, suggested that politics in the northern city might diverge from that of the South. Republican support for Thomas showed that at least some white Republicans were committed to African American civil rights in Chicago and that black votes in a cumulative system could influence party strategy. Political structures and a well-organized constituency, more than sheer numbers, would determine black access to government offices.

White Republican support, however, was unreliable. As early as spring 1877, Thomas "reproached the Republican party on account of its alleged neglect of the colored citizens." The party refused to back Thomas in 1878 and 1880. In 1882, when another legislative redistricting gave African American voters a stronger base, black activists demanded a black representative in the state house. Thomas served two more terms. Biracial collaboration had proved crucial to African American victories in the 1870s, but by the 1880s, activists were increasingly disillusioned with white Republicans.[87]

Chicago activists, determined to celebrate the history of the abolition-ist movement and to use the past to influence contemporary politics, or-ganized a reunion of western antislavery men in Chicago in June 1874. Jones was the only black man on the organizing committee. The four-day meeting opened with an address from Illinois governor John L. Beve-ridge and featured speeches from prominent antislavery men like George Julian and James Birney as well as "Personal Recollections and Reminis-cences, and Singing the Old Songs of Liberty." Antislavery men and women from across the nation were invited; many sent letters filled with fond memories of the long struggle for freedom. Only one, W. C. Flagg, the son of abolitionists, wrote that he could not accept the invitation "for the fact of a prior engagement in fighting the raw despotism of corporate monopo-lies." Others urged the gathering to address the continued hardship of the freed people. "Gentlemen," wrote Matthew R. Hull, "your meeting should do more than simply tell of the reunion of the fossil remains of a defunct and ostracized party."[88]

Jones, a successful businessman and real estate investor, apparently had little interest in battling "corporate monopolies." His activism was almost entirely tied to promoting the equality of black Americans; his pursuit of civil rights no doubt secured his status both as a citizen and a business leader. Unlike other former abolitionists, white and black, Jones's concern for oppressed African Americans did not translate into outrage over down-trodden European laborers. Jones's integrationist politics aimed to open opportunities for black people; he identified personally with the city's business elite, not with struggling industrial laborers. Politics and busi-ness had been mutually reinforcing activities in Jones's life, providing the interlocking social relationships that lifted him from poverty to political leadership.

Jones's faith in party politics wavered in the years that followed, but his demands for racial equality continued. After his loss in the 1875 elec-tion, Jones said, "Our colored . . . citizens have been left out in the cold."[89] Passage of federal civil rights legislation hardly erased the daily inequities and brazen incivilities suffered by black people in northern cities. Employ-ers refused to hire black men or paid them poverty wages. Black laborers sometimes faced threats on the docks or were hounded from streetcars.

"All we ask," Jones said in an 1874 speech before a "workingmen's association," "is to be paid the regular market price for our work." Fair pay was one in a list of overdue civil liberties. He concluded his speech by making a demand that was, for Jones, nearly three decades old. "We must also have our civil rights," he said. "They must not be withheld from us any longer; they are essential to our complete freedom." Freedom had long implied more than emancipation.[90]

On the thirtieth anniversary of his arrival in Chicago, Jones, at the height of his political career, opened his home to an evening of celebration, a simple and elegant instance of interracial alliance among elite Chicagoans in the 1870s. Jones welcomed "those who desired to call upon him and his most excellent wife" for an evening reception to commemorate their arrival in the city. "A brilliant, fashionable, and Thoroughly enjoyable occasion," ran the *Tribune* headline the next morning. The crowd included black and white politicians, businessmen, ministers, and journalists. Among the guests were Mahlon Ogden (a white real estate millionaire and brother of the former mayor), white abolitionist C. V. Dyer, and several county board members. Four generations of the Jones family were represented: his wife's mother, eighty-eight-year-old Mrs. Diza Richardson; Jones's daughter; and her daughter, eight-year-old Theodore Lee. A "splendid quadrille orchestra" entertained, and the young people, led "with ease and grace" by Mrs. Lee, "tripped the light fantastic till a late hour of the night."[91]

Jones's home, elaborately described in two *Tribune* articles, had long been a showplace where Jones displayed his political views and welcomed political allies. The home's interior decor was a tribute to the abolitionist cause. There was an engraving of Lincoln signing the Emancipation Proclamation, and in the front room, "against the snow-white walls were the engravings of Mr. Lincoln, John Brown, and President Grant, surrounded by those of Mr. Chase, Mr. Sumner, Horace Greeley and Joshua R. Giddings." To the left of this shrine to the cause of emancipation were oil portraits of Jones and his family. Jones's personal history and that of black America were deeply intertwined through the decor of his home and the stories he recounted of his life.[92] The aging politician had effectively answered the question facing so many black Americans. Jones and his family, his home furnishings proclaimed, would become part of a racially integrated nation.

For Jones, Waggoner, Hall, and Ford Douglas, the past, the decades before the bloody years of Civil War, shaped the political agendas of the present and gave credibility to their leadership of the postwar political community. They had become Chicago's most vocal African American leaders. Their careers spanned three decades in which a small group of black Chicagoans—with Jones and Hall at its center—built an economic foundation for a nascent urban African American bourgeoisie. The city's economy in those years hurtled from boom to ruin and back up again, building great fortunes and wrecking others. Immigrants from Europe arrived in Chicago, scrambling for industrial jobs, while this tiny group of striving black entrepreneurs and craftsmen managed to purchase real estate and launch businesses that generated steady incomes. In the 1880s, a younger generation of African American businessmen and professionals would solidify their bourgeois status through intermarriage, social organizations, and, ultimately, through a rethinking of the Civil War generation's integrationist politics. The contested politics and what might be called a late nineteenth-century black bourgeois sensibility, originated with the aspirations of a small group of urban antebellum activists.

TWO

Setting Agendas, Demanding Rights, and the Black Press

"Since our enfranchisement, we have been most foully dealt with," raged the *Conservator* just a decade after black men were granted the right to vote. "There have been more colored men murdered, butchered in cold blood, since the war, than in any battle during the war." The paper's young black editor, Ferdinand L. Barnett, railing against a lynching in Clarksville, Tennessee, and the massacre of "a few Negroes in a race riot" in Louisiana promised that black men would respond with demands for rights and, if necessary, violence. "This spirit of outraged justice" was rising across the South. The presidential election of 1880 approached, and, Barnett warned, "an outburst of an ignorant wronged minority" was likely in the polling places and the streets of southern towns and cities. Southern whites "will have to make a choice between "Blood, the Brand, and Political Liberty." Chicago, he claimed, never faced such terrible choices.[1]

Barnett drew a sharp distinction in his blazing commentaries between northern African Americans and the South's "oppressed minority." The *Conservator*, Barnett believed, contributed to the relative well-being of the city's six thousand black people. Barnett's assessment of Chicago society, perhaps a reflection of his own achievements in law and journalism, captured the views of many black Chicagoans—lawyers, laborers, and house servants—in the decades between the severe economic depressions of the 1870s and 1890s. Barnett's optimism was fueled by the growing number of political organizations and civic institutions established by black Chicagoans; by the new visibility of literary societies, church charities, and civil rights organizations; and by the increasing affluence and stability of Chicago's black elite.[2] The city's civic organizations, whose activities were chronicled in the black press, helped push through the state's first civil rights legislation, raised funds for a hospital owned by black Chicagoans, and worked with Mayor Carter Harrison, the wildly popular Democrat who served for nearly five terms. In 1886, a "colored" visitor from Kentucky noted, with some exaggeration, that the "majority" of black Chicagoans "are quite wealthy and the rest are in fair circumstances in spite of the opposition that is against them." The achievements of black Chicagoans and the contrast to African Americans living in the South were the subject of much commentary. Chicago, as Barnett observed, was home to a distinctly "educated urban" African American community.[3]

Yet beneath the sanguine tone of Barnett's comments was a sense of urgency to conserve newly acquired civil rights and to claim—and reclaim—black Americans' place within the nation. Already there were signs in Chicago and elsewhere that black Americans faced new struggles to achieve economic stability and political equality. President Rutherford B. Hayes had withdrawn federal troops from all of the former Confederate states and, in Barnett's words, "plainly told the colored people they must make peace at any cost." Though seventeen black men had been elected to Congress by 1880 and many more elected to city and county offices around the nation, prospective voters in dozens of states faced angry mobs and even in northern cities found that asserting their newly won rights could be risky. In Chicago, despite an ordinance banning racial discrimination in education, the public schools were largely segregated, and all of the city's teachers were white. The Republican Party, Barnett wrote, was at best a benign ally of black activists but had hardly fulfilled the promises of Reconstruction.[4] "We are no longer slaves," Barnett wrote. "We intend to act the part of freemen. If the Republican Party wants our suffrage it must prove worthy of it. Otherwise it may expect our tomahawk."[5] By 1890, many black intellectuals, though not Barnett, were ready to give up on the national Republican Party, some on politics all together.[6]

In the decade and a half after John Jones's election to the county board, black Chicagoans moved away from Jones's optimistic interracial politics and dedicated support for the Republican Party. Instead, activists established new and separate civic institutions designed to build a cohesive and autonomous black community. African American activists articulated a vision of a collective black identity, rooting it within social and political struggles of the industrializing northern city. Some elite black men continued to work with whites in business and to socialize with reform-minded Republicans, but well-to-do African Americans increasingly found their ambitions for social and professional advancement limited. Working-class black Chicagoans—day laborers, the unskilled, and low-waged workers—were largely left out of the social activities of the local elite. Black political activists would use new civic associations and elite social organizations to crystallize political agendas and propel themselves into leadership positions. The African American press, reporting on social events and highlighting the activities of the community leaders, framed issues, identified community leaders, provided a language for political debate, and helped to create an image of a cohesive black constituency.

On a wintry Monday evening in December 1882, Stanley Holbrook, a clerk in the mailing department of the post office, entertained friends at a "literary and musical reception" in his home at 1728 Indiana Avenue. It was one of several such gatherings publicized in the *Conservator* each week. Like those of the half-dozen literary clubs supported by black Chicagoans in the 1880s, the reception brought together successful wage laborers and aspiring professionals. Among the guests were Holbrook's coworkers at the post office, one of few employers to provide decent wages and steady work for a significant number of African Americans. Other guests included the son of one of the city's leading ministers and an editor at the *Conservator*, Abram T. Hall Jr. The evening included several piano solos, a flute solo, a recitation, and a choral performance by the Parks Quintette Club. A "substantial and elaborate supper was served by a well-known caterer," and the young people danced to the music of "Prof. Neely's Orchestra," departing at "a late hour." The notice, headlined "A Pleasing Reception," highlighted the good manners and respectable entertainments pursued by young black Chicagoans. Holbrook's reception brought together many of the new generation of leading figures in Chicago's black society, men and women who were part of a small but growing black middle class. The evening of light entertainment was among the many that cemented the networks of church and civic leaders, of social elite and political activists in late nineteenth-century Chicago.[7]

With gatherings in family homes and the formation of educational, social reform, business, and political societies, often based in churches, black Chicagoans began to establish civic institutions separate from those run by white Chicagoans. The elite of Jones's generation had formed interracial professional and social alliances and worked, sometimes uneasily, with white activists in local and national politics. That interracial elite comity began to break down in the late 1870s. Black Chicagoans did not yet face residential segregation, and although several African American enclaves formed in the wake of the fire, many well-off black families continued to know whites as neighbors, friends, and fellow congregants in local churches.

But in a city facing growing and increasingly violent conflict between white workers and their employers and where an expanding Democratic machine dispensed jobs and favors, many black Chicagoans sought to secure their status and "improve the race" through communal self-reliance.[8]

Elite black families consolidated their status through marriage and business connections, passing their social position across generations. Many were far away from the families and kin networks that had defined their communities and provided social support under slavery and Reconstruction in the South.[9] In the northern city, African Americans gradually defined themselves by building new social relationships in new urban institutions. Jones's widow, Mary, retained her relationships with white business leaders through her membership in All-Souls Church, a white Unitarian congregation. She strengthened her ties to the new black elite when her daughter, Lavinia, married the lawyer Lloyd Wheeler. A native of Ohio whose family had been active abolitionists, Wheeler managed Jones's businesses through the 1880s. Most of the city's black elite—from the family of Daniel Hale Williams, a founder of Provident Hospital, to dentist Charles E. Bentley, lawyers Laing Williams, and the Wheelers—acquired their wealth and respectability through professional education. Others, like Charles J. Smiley, who made a fortune catering the weddings, funerals, and elegant dinners of the black elite, were entrepreneurs serving African American consumers. They met at church, at private parties, and, as one old settler later recalled at the "private dancing school" owned by Etta Shoecraft Randall, "where the young people spent much of their leisure time." In leisure, business, and spiritual activities, they formed social bonds and established customs that would provide the professional elite and their children with social authority among respectable African Americans in the following decades.[10] "Until the Great Migration Chicago Negro society was excruciating in its decorum and exclusiveness," wrote Fenton Johnson of the "Chicago Negro Aristocrats" of his youth. "The old families and the professional and business element ruled."[11]

Some of the most wealthy black professionals and businessmen earned incomes that rivaled those of the white bourgeoisie; none achieved the stunning wealth of the Gilded Age industrialists, like railroad magnate George Pullman, meat-packer Philip Armour, or farm-implement manufacturers like the McCormick and Glessner families. By the mid-1880s, the physician Daniel Hale Williams listed his personal wealth at approximately $150,000, while the city's leading black lawyers and real estate investors—at most about thirty men—could claim annual incomes ranging from $25,000 to $50,000. This high society was tiny and, as the decades wore on, worked increasingly to separate itself from laboring black Chicagoans. Johnson mockingly referred to the self-consciously elite, numbering far fewer than four hundred, who might compare themselves to New York's Gilded Age aristocracy. "Actors and saloonkeepers, no matter how much money they might have were barred," Johnson wrote. "Butlers and waiters, even though they might be employed on the Gold Coast, were not considered by the Chicago Negro 400."[12]

In the 1880s, the old wealthy of John Jones's generation were gradually accepting a newer middle class: postal workers, some municipal employees, and eventually Pullman porters. Though these occupations would be considered working class among whites, among African Americans, they were what Allan Spear calls "the respectable class": economically secure, churchgoing, and often leaders of civic organizations. Middle-class status was more an expression of a "style" of life than of income. Attending elegant receptions or dance lessons, the decor of the family home, polite manners, and churchgoing marked a family as middle class. Joining social clubs and working to "improve the race" were middle-class behaviors. Newspaper accounts of dinners, literary societies, and club work made up the society pages of the black middle class.[13]

Most of the elite and some stable hourly workers owned property in the 1880s. By 1890, a growing number of black families were purchasing houses in the South Side Englewood neighborhood and in the town of Lake, which surrounded the stockyards and was later incorporated into the city. These men aimed to create a stable class of "respectables," separated geographically from the city's poorer workers and from white middle-class enclaves. Still, fewer than two hundred black men were listed as homeowners. A handful of entrepreneurs like the Wheeler and Jones families, the wealthy caterer Smiley, and the saloonkeeper Andrew H. Scott, owned commercial property. In the final decades of the nineteenth century, Chicago's black upper class was small and relatively open to newcomers who could propel themselves through work, education, and family connections into stable businesses and salaried occupations.[14]

The Colored Men's Professional and Business Directory, published by Isaac Counsellor Harris in 1885, celebrated the new generation of energetic entrepreneurs and professionals. It promoted a vision of economic independence that paralleled efforts to form autonomous social institutions (and predated Booker T. Washington's famous 1895 demand that African Americans build themselves up economically). Harris encouraged African Americans in mutual economic support, aiming to generate new wealth for black entrepreneurs by encouraging black consumers to purchase their goods and services. Even before black Chicagoans were constrained by racially segregated housing markets, Harris suggested they forge networks of economic support that crisscrossed many urban neighborhoods.[15]

Harris's directory advertised local businesses, elevating their owners to positions of influence, distinguishing employers from workers, and functioning as a social register for the nascent black middle class. Along with professionals, the directory listed forty barbershops, fifteen restaurants, and twenty saloons owned by black men and women. Saloonkeepers, often catering to white clientele, achieved wealth that rivaled those in the more respectable professions and businesses. Saloonkeepers and gamblers too would enter politics, but not until the turn of the century, and then within a more contested black political leadership. In the 1880s and into the next decade, it was primarily lawyers, doctors, undertakers, real estate entrepreneurs, and a handful of other respectable businessmen who presented themselves as the voices of Chicago's African Americans, attempting to translate their wealth and education into influence in local politics.[16]

Chicago's black elite established formal and informal networks of social support and political activism among educated professionals—"aristocrats of color"—linked through a web of business, family, and social reform connections. African American women, through their education and social reform work, often projected status on their husbands and their businesses. Elite white women, too, engaged in social reform, though many white women reformers were unmarried. African American women, like Fannie Barrier Williams, merged marriage with public careers in civic reform and race politics. Their success on the marriage market often rested more on their education and professional achievements than on their family background. Ferdinand Barnett's first wife, for example, Mary H. Graham, was the first black woman to graduate from the University of Michigan in Ann Arbor. (She likely met Barnett when his family stopped in Detroit on their way to Chicago.) She was presented to Chicago society as an "accomplished scholar, a clever musician and an agreeable lady." She died in 1890, just eight years after they were married.[17] Barnett was a longtime friend and political ally of Wheeler's. The son of a skilled slave and a free woman, Barnett had been born in Nashville, spent the Civil War in Canada, and arrived in Chicago with his parents in 1869. He went to law school in Chicago, and in the same year he established the *Conservator*, opened a law office in the business district, and launched a legal career that would take him to the district attorney's office in 1896 and later into a municipal judgeship. Fannie Barrier Williams, who was married to Barnett's law partner, was a close friend of Mary Graham Barnett and later an activist sometimes aligned with, often at odds with, Barnett's second wife, journalist and antilynching crusader Ida B. Wells-Barnett.

Before Wells-Barnett's arrival, Williams was probably the most prominent and most vocal black woman in Chicago. She and her husband, S. Laing Williams, formed a partnership that advanced each of their careers and effectively articulated an agenda for black activists that rested on the values of the urban black elite. They believed in "improving the race" through education and social reform work, advocating Christian faith and communal action, and fighting urban vice. Williams arrived in Chicago in 1887 and quickly became a well-known lecturer, prolific writer, and leader of the black clubwoman's movement. She and her husband lived in Hyde Park, on Forty-Second Place, just off Grand Boulevard among the stately brownstones owned by the newly rich Irish and German Jewish families. They were what she called "gentle folks," members of the close-knit, well-educated, and politically engaged black elite that dominated church and reform societies in Chicago and had ties to similar organizations in cities across the North. The Williamses established the Prudence Crandall Club, a literary and social club designed to promote "the highest values" among African Americans in Chicago. In the late 1880s and early 1890s, Williams devoted much energy to raising money for the construction of Provident Hospital and to fighting for educational and employment opportunities for black women. Light-skinned and well educated, Williams was "shocked" by the burdens of racial inequality—the lack of decent jobs for African American women, the poor education offered black children, and the refusal of employers to hire black men in well-paying industrial jobs. The solution, she contended, was "union and organization"—not labor unions but rather a unified black public, the banding together of black people across the city and the nation in pursuit of "race advancement."[18]

The end of the Civil War had prompted an outpouring of organizing by African American churches and northern activists determined to send assistance to the freed people. The federal government had established the Freedmen's Bureau to provide relief to white and black southerners displaced by war, while church groups across the North sent medical supplies, food, and clothing and sponsored teachers to go south to build schools for former slaves. By 1880, Chicagoans moved from assisting those recovering from war to launching their own reform and leisure organizations. Five years later, *The Colored Men's Professional and Business Directory* listed the Autumn Club (a businessmen's club), the Young People's Literary Society of Olivet Church, the Colfax Social Club, and the Eleventh Ward Social Club as well as fourteen benevolent societies. "Is this passion for organization peculiar to Negro people?" asked Fannie Barrier Williams in 1905. "Whether this be answered in the affirmative or not, it is a fact that the Negro individual does not like to be alone in good works. His bent for organization is a sort of racial passion."[19] As Williams certainly knew, the establishment of African American societies was hardly the result of "passion" but rather was a pragmatic response to politics in the late nineteenth-century urban North.

More than two decades before Williams took note of the rising number of African American civic organizations, a handful of black ministers, led by the charismatic and thoroughly "modern" Richard De Baptiste, began to forge separate African American institutions. De Baptiste, a minister, teacher, and editor, had worked with Jones's repeal campaign and in the postwar years turned his demands for statewide civil rights into a broad agenda based on racial solidarity and collective support for African American organizations. De Baptiste, born in Virginia to free parents, led the effort to organize the Olivet Baptist Church in 1862 and spurred a campaign that raised more than $30,000 for the purchase of two city lots and construction of an elegant brick church. Like Barnett and Jones, De Baptiste had personal and professional connections across the North, serving as an officer in the Northwestern Baptist Convention in 1865.[20] In the mid-1880s, De Baptiste became an editor of the *Conservator*, also contributing articles to African American newspapers in Washington, DC. Linking the spiritual with the political aspirations of African Americans, De Baptiste preached civil rights and collective solidarity from the pulpit while lecturing newspaper readers on salvation through church and social reform work. His vision, like that of Barnett, was of an urban, market-oriented black community, achieving wealth through entrepreneurship, education, and self-governing civic institutions.[21]

Social organizations, like literary societies, provided a political education to aspiring black professionals. In May 1889, John M. Langston, the US congressman from Virginia and former minister to Haiti, addressed the Colored Young Men's Library Association at Quinn Chapel. The association's president was Ferdinand Barnett, who introduced the congressman and proclaimed the group's dedication to "universal enlightenment." The Library Association, founded in 1886, was housed in "elegant, commodious rooms . . . its shelves filled with the standard works of art, science, fiction and biography." Here, education and social uplift merged with the black elite's political agenda. "This is not a white man's country . . . this is not a white man's government," Langston told his audience. "The negro has his eye on the presidency," he added, urging black Chicagoans to help build up the Republican Party across the South. The evening ended with a banquet at the Palmer House and toasts from Barnett, several ministers, and state legislator J. W. E. Thomas. Langston's toast was to "The Negro in Politics."[22]

The city's black elite, moving to augment the services provided by churches, dedicated significant time and resources to a host of fraternal societies. Through these organizations, long a source of leisure for white men, African American men established an autonomous network of social services, a counterpart, though less powerful, to the city's political parties in the final decades of the nineteenth century. The societies, solidifying the men's public connections through business and church activities, provided members with money for doctor's visits, funerals, and weddings, as well as supporting an "Old Folks' Home." Chicago was host to the National Convention of Negro Masons in 1880, an event that seemed to spur the organization of other secret societies and fraternal organizations. There were the Odd Fellows, the Knights of Pythias, the True Reformers, the United Brotherhood, the Ancient Order of Foresters, and the Elks. Most popular were the Odd Fellows and Masons, with nearly two thousand members and fourteen lodges in each. By the mid-1880s, most black men belonged to more than one secret order and many to four or five. "In no other form of organization do the terms brotherhood and mutual obligations mean so much," Williams wrote. Members gathered in homes and churches, paying monthly dues that added up to thousands of dollars in the societies' treasuries. Wives and daughters of members expanded the reach of the organizations by forming women's auxiliaries, which raised money for social events and social reform. "The lessons of right living, of charity and truthfulness," Williams wrote, "are enforced in these societies more rigidly even than in the churches."[23]

Social and civic institutions, formal and informal networks of social support and political activism, fostered educational and social reform goals, as well as furthering the political ambitions of individual leaders. The lawyer Edward H. Morris, an impoverished migrant to Chicago from Virginia in 1876, joined the United Grand Order of Odd Fellows in 1882 and rose to the office of grand master in 1888, a position he retained for fifteen years. Morris's membership in several fraternal organizations, as well as his long-standing friendship with Barnett and Williams, likely helped him get elected to the Illinois General Assembly between 1891 and 1893.[24] Similarly, the lawyer Edward H. Wright, who moved to Chicago from New

York City in 1885, quickly joined the Odd Fellows and later helped found the Appomattox Club, was elected a county commissioner in 1896. In the 1920s, Wright, who also was a Mason, served as alderman for the city's Second Ward on the South Side.[25] The biographies of all of the city's black leaders—those elected to municipal judgeships, appointed to the states attorney's office, and voted into the state legislature and the city council as well as the ministers who advised public officials and the entrepreneurs who supported political campaigns—included a brief list of memberships in fraternal societies.

Clubs and social organizations, commented Edward F. Dunne in 1898, were the "most effective way to add new pressure" to government officials. A crusader against corruption in local government, Dunne, a white Democrat who was elected mayor of Chicago in 1905 and governor of Illinois in 1912, noted in a 1903 speech that black Chicagoans had made good use of local organizations but African Americans had "been held back by race prejudice, which has placed every possible obstacle in [their] way." The sincerely optimistic Dunne believed that "the Negro will solve his own salvation as we aid him. . . . We need to extend plenty of charity to the black man. If this is done he will work out his own problem." But in the final decades of the nineteenth century, there was little white charity to help sustain African American civic institutions and social organizations. As much as civic organizations provided sustenance for black activists and sustained the "social bonds" of the black elite, it was in the newly established African American press that black writers and thinkers began to assert control over public perceptions of African Americans and to "work out [their] own problem[s]."[26]

Launched in 1878 by the energetic and ambitious Barnett and his partner, Alexander G. Clark, the *Conservator* presented a new image of black Chicago and, in many ways, of black America to its readers. The *Conservator* stood for a profound transformation in African American life. Rooted in a northern city, the paper presented a vision of black community that was urban, rights oriented, and gaining access to an increasingly industrial society. The paper and its editor were forward looking with little nostalgia for the interracial politics of past decades.[27] The paper, published weekly out of offices at 194 Clark Street in the city's commercial district, featured national and local news of black Americans. Though just four broad sheets, the *Conservator* printed announcements of church services, reports on the city's Common Council and literary and musical clubs, and a personals column, which covered weddings, births, deaths, graduations, and holidays. Readers also found comments on the work of the state legislature, reports on national politics from a Washington, DC, correspondent, and accounts of violence and the struggles of black southerners, along with the achievements of black lawyers, doctors, and writers around the nation. The paper's title, Barnett noted in an 1881 speech, referred to its mission and, in many ways, to its editor's sanguine politics as "a conservator of the rights of our race." The *Conservator*'s social agenda (although more complacent than some of its rivals) and its ambitious national coverage made it one of the most influential African American–owned newspapers in the late nineteenth century.[28]

The scores of newspapers published by African Americans during the decades after emancipation proved a crucial arena for debate among black activists and for the formation of an unruly coalition of urban and rural, laboring and elite black voters.[29] The papers helped to frame political issues and sharpen lines of argument among black leaders and presented readers with new and often disturbing visions of American society. I. Garland Penn, a journalist from Virginia and author of an 1891 history of the African American press, claimed for the "Afro-American" editor "labor [that] unites with all in building up and furthering the interest of our common country." Yet as Penn acknowledged, the weeklies and monthlies published in small towns and cities north and south revealed sharp differences of opinion among black writers, editors, politicians, and ministers. Despite their disputes, African American journalists saw the black press as a sign of progress and independence for black society. It showed, in the words of the *Austin Citizen* published in Georgia, "that we have the nerve and manhood to stand up and advocate through our own journals all priviledges [sic] for our race that are enjoyed by the white citizens of this country."[30]

"Henceforth the colored newspaper will be recognized by politicians as a power more reliable and effectual than the itinerant preacher or the school teacher," asserted the *People's Advocate* in July 1882. Though the Washington, DC–based paper's pronouncement carried a bit of hyperbole, African American editors and reporters saw the press as a new secular political base, a powerful force in black society, and a purveyor of truth as influential as the local church or schoolhouse. The editors did not suggest that newspapers would replace established churches as sources of authority and guidance. Rather, editors tended to see their work as providing another forum—another pulpit—for moral debate about black society and the social agenda of black politicians.

Newspapers, in their claims to moral authority and advocacy for "the race," were both partners of the ministry and secular counterparts to African American churches, a new civic institution aiming to guide a gradually urbanizing and increasingly educated population. Indeed, ministers, the social and moral leaders of black communities, were often editors and publishers of African American–owned newspapers. Reverdy Ransom, minister of Chicago's Institutional Church, began his career as an editor of the *Afro-American Spokesman* in Pittsburgh, and Richard De Baptiste of Mount Olivet Church was an associate editor of the *Conservator* from 1878 to 1884. De Baptiste, who dressed in the modern style of a suit and patterned necktie in the 1880s, saw himself as a progressive leader, a man who was "pastor, editor and citizen." The newspaper, he wrote, was to "discuss in a fair and liberal spirit those questions that agitate and cause an honest difference of opinion among citizens, whose aims are alike patriotic."[31] The editors used the press to circulate public images of modern African American life.

Between 1870 and 1890, the number of newspapers published by African Americans jumped from 10 to more than 150, an astonishing growth, which Penn surmised resulted from a growing readership.[32] By 1880, an estimated 20 to 30 percent of African Americans over age ten and living in the former Confederate states could read and write; more than 40 percent in the North were listed as literate in the US census.[33] Yet the audience of these weeklies was probably larger than "readership" would suggest; newspapers sometimes bridged oral and print traditions, as papers were read out loud at work sites, or friends and neighbors might gather to listen for news from beyond their town or city.

Circulation rates suggest a significant portion of black residents in northern cities—nearly one-third in mid-1880s Chicago—subscribed to a newspaper operated by black editors. Editors and publishers claimed their newspapers were "eagerly sought after and read by the best culture of the land as invariable indicators of our best thought and guides to our future action."[34] Just a few of the African American–owned papers were listed in Ayer's *American Newspaper Annual*, the yearly catalog of newspapers and their circulations published in Philadelphia and marketed to advertisers. The *Conservator* was first listed in Ayer's in 1885 with a circulation of 1,500, while the Louisville, Ohio, *Falls Express* had a circulation of 1,440 in 1881, and the *People's Advocate* of Washington, DC, had a circulation of 805 in 1885. Penn, suggesting his frustration with low readership, claimed he wrote his compendium of African American–operated newspapers to increase awareness among black readers of the black press and "to promote the future welfare of Afro-American journalism by telling to its constituents the story of its heroic labors on their behalf." Advertisements in the black press suggest marketers hoped to reach a readership of all classes and education levels, even the barely literate.[35]

In Chicago, as many as four African American–owned newspapers competed for readership, while the newsstands, shops, and saloons that sold the papers became well-known gathering places for a growing community. With the boldest promotional campaign was the *Western Appeal*, which was published in Saint Paul, Minnesota, and began distribution in Chicago in fall 1888. Cyrus F. Adams, the *Appeal*'s Chicago manager, regularly issued sworn statements (affirmed by notary public S. Laing Williams, Barnett's law partner) proclaiming the *Appeal*'s booming circulation, well ahead of its closest "Colored contemporary in Chicago," the *Conservator*. The *Appeal*'s Chicago offices, at 180 Clark Street, allowed Adams, an associate of Booker T. Washington, to keep close watch on the *Conservator* staff working less than a block away. Adams was known to report Barnett's activities to Tuskegee. Black newspapers published in other cities were distributed in Chicago; the *Detroit Plaindealer, Indianapolis World, Indianapolis Freeman,* and *Cleveland Gazette* were sold on Chicago newsstands. The editors of the *Plaindealer* and the *World* disputed Adams's claim that the *Appeal* sold four hundred more copies each week than the other three papers combined, referring to the *Appeal*'s "broad assertions and big claims that are preposterous."[36]

The *Appeal* did more than stir competition. By regularly publishing a list of where the paper could be purchased, the *Appeal* in effect fashioned a new social geography for black Chicagoans. The paper's list, which expanded each year, highlighted commercial venues welcoming black Chicagoans and charted the entrepreneurial achievements of the city's black businessmen. The paper's distribution sites were secular spaces of community life. "The Colored families that are without a Colored paper," the *Appeal* commented in December 1888, "are twenty years behind the times."[37]

Newspaper publishing was a tough business for both black and white publishers. When Barnett entered the field in 1878, Chicago boasted four morning and three afternoon papers, as well as a couple small-time broadsheets. The *Conservator*, like many of the papers owned by white businessmen, struggled to survive. Within months of the first issue of the *Conservator*, the white-owned *Post and Mail*, an afternoon paper, went bankrupt; the *Telegraph* went under two years later. The *Chicago Daily News* stumbled through the 1870s and 1880s—even with wealthy and politically influential investors—with circulation rates not much higher than those of the *Conservator*. Still, white-owned papers could call on enough capital and advertising revenue to establish themselves, purchase new presses, hire teams of newsboys, and expand in length. Most African American papers launched in the 1880s were defunct by 1900, and no black newspaper founded before 1880 was still publishing in 1914. The *Conservator* struggled until 1909 when, facing competition from the new and more widely circulating *Chicago Defender*, it closed.[38]

The African American–owned press was supported by advertising, subscription fees—usually one to two dollars per year—and private donations, typically from their founders, editors, and local political patrons. The *Conservator*, which could claim some of the highest circulation rates and most expensive advertising space of the late nineteenth-century black weeklies, regularly advertised for "job work," printing "tickets, dodgers and invitations" for additional income.[39]

Significant capital was required to launch a paper. The necessities were a hand press, a few cases of type, commercial space large enough to hold the press and a desk, and some knowledge of the printer's trade. In the late 1870s in Chicago, a four-cylinder press might run as high as $5,000. (Victor Lawson, owner of the *Chicago Daily News* estimated that such a press, formerly used by the *Post and Mail*, was worth less than $5,000 in June 1878.) In some places, typically southern towns, a group of African Americans pooled resources to start a local weekly, but newspapers frequently were personal ventures, owned and published by one person.[40] Operating costs for weekly papers were substantial. When T. Thomas Fortune started the *New York Freeman* in 1885, he estimated monthly expenses at $600, which included wages for five printers and a bookkeeper and the costs of printing and distributing the paper. Operating costs for smaller papers were much less, especially where the proprietor did much of the reporting and editorial work.[41] Black-owned papers, like many of the larger and better-financed white-owned papers, tended to reflect the idiosyncratic views, values, and politics of their primary financial backer, usually the editor.

African American leaders in the decades after Reconstruction were united in the belief that they could and should work to improve the lives of black Americans. How to do that was widely debated. Each of the newspapers highlighted the particular issues of the town or city in which it was published. But at the same time, editors took on national issues and engaged in arguments with editors around the country. Readers in Philadelphia or Athens, Georgia, were kept apprised of the views of Chicago's Ferdinand Barnett or New York's T. Thomas Fortune, as local weeklies regularly reprinted news and editorials from the Chicago and New York papers. In this respect, newspapers owned or operated by African Americans were unlike the foreign-language press or even the labor press, which tended to have largely local readerships. Black-owned papers circulated nationally, either through reprints or out-of-town subscribers. Barnett, like Jones, Bonner, and Wagoner—the generation of political leaders who preceded him—was a prominent, elite Chicagoan and a widely known national critic and opinion maker.

The editors debated in press and in person, gathering for national conventions, which further solidified the networks of allies and respected adversaries who identified issues and aimed to set the terms of political debate. Through reports on the conventions published in their weeklies and monthlies, editors and writers identified themselves as part of an interconnected, secular base of authority in African American society. Fifty editors, not including Barnett, attended the first national "colored editors" convention in August 1880. Barnett's clout was visible at the second national convention two years later. He was named president of the meeting when sixty of the nation's black editors met in the Fifteenth Street Presbyterian Church in Washington, DC, a site that revealed the editors' ambitions in national politics and their reverence for the social authority of the ministry.[42]

The four-day event, beginning on July 27, 1882, called attention to some of the major concerns and conflicts among black Americans. "The evening session was very boisterous," commented the *Christian Recorder*, about the first night. Among the topics under discussion—and, if later reports are accurate, hotly debated—was the role of "the colored churches" in America and the growth of racially segregated schools, which prompted "a speech gushing with argument against . . . Jim crow institutions." Several speakers advocated autonomous black schools. There also was debate over whether southern black people should emigrate west, how to respond to "the industrial ostracism practiced against us," and whether to call for changes in tariff and trade legislation to open new manufacturing jobs for black workers. In 1885, when the "colored press association" met in Philadelphia, the *Western Appeal* urged the journalists to "shape some line of policy" to unify black activists in a "manly and noble" pursuit of "our rights." The press, the *Appeal* claimed, was "the mouthpieces of Afro-Americans." The editors clearly saw themselves and their newspapers as setting, though hardly agreeing on, a national political agenda for black Americans.[43]

Barnett, like his editorial counterparts, was working to build a new African American constituency and, despite the limits of their influence in white America, to control how black Americans were represented in public.

He was as tough as any when he attacked his fellow editors for their positions on party politics or black society. An intense dispute erupted in the summer of 1881 after the *Conservator* proposed capitalizing the word "Negro," arguing that the initial capital was a sign of respect and "would take from our wearied shoulders a hair's weight of the burden of prejudice and ill will we bear." In Philadelphia, the *Christian Recorder* mocked Barnett, noting that his paper "wastes a vast amount of eloquence on the insignificant question." The issue, for Barnett, was not insignificant. Language was a powerful tool, he asserted, an expression of group status and identity. The lowercase "negro" was "a mark of disrespect . . . a stigma . . . a badge of inferiority" conferred by white men. To demand the "capital N" was, in Barnett's terms, an assertion by black writers—and African Americans in general—of the authority to name themselves and to demand that black people—not white—define a collective African American identity. Black leaders, Barnett believed, should pursue the "affairs of the race" whether in demanding more jobs in industry, negotiating with white politicians, or fashioning a positive public racial identity.[44]

Politics fueled the growth of newspapers operated by black Americans. At least two-thirds of the African American–owned papers listed in Ayer's *American Newspaper Annual* indicated a party affiliation; the vast majority were listed as Republican, some as independent, and a few as Democratic. In recognition of the growing importance of black voters in northern cities, political parties in New York, Philadelphia, and Chicago reportedly contributed to the papers; there is no evidence that either party helped fund the *Conservator*. Certainly the papers that survived longest were Republican papers whose owners or editors were active in politics.

Politicians and aspiring government officials found newspaper work an effective method of ministering to their constituents. Perhaps the most famous of the editor-politicians was Louisiana's P. B. S. Pinchback, who launched the *New Orleans Louisianan*, the first semiweekly paper published by an African American. Others also regularly played politics, taking government jobs to subsidize the inadequate income produced by the newspapers. The editor of Washington, DC's, first African American weekly, John W. Cromwell, was a Republican activist who was removed from his government job after Grover Cleveland's 1884 presidential victory.[45] Barnett, who moved in and out of editors' positions in the 1880s, used his connections in government to gain an appointment in the state attorney's office in 1901. For him, as for most black editors and reporters, the newspapers were both a path into government jobs and a rare opportunity to present and argue over political agendas for black Americans.

Booker T. Washington, along with those in the White House, recognized the power of the black press and moved in 1901 to control it. Not long after a meeting with President Theodore Roosevelt in which the president encouraged the man known as the nation's most powerful black leader to restrain criticism from the black press, Washington began buying some publications and subsidizing others. In October 1901, he sent his secretary, Emmett Scott, to Chicago to meet with the black editors of all of "Chicago's colored papers." Just a couple of hours after Scott arrived at Chicago's Palmer House, Washington sent a telegram noting: "Conservator has vicious editorial this week. Want to bring them in harmony if I can do so honorably." By then, Barnett and his wife, Ida B. Wells-Barnett, were part owners of the paper but Barnett no longer edited the *Conservator*.[46] Two years later, Washington was again trying to gain control of the paper, this time hoping that S. Laing Williams would influence the new editor. Washington was determined to thwart Ferdinand Barnett's career, calling Barnett "a regular sneak." The nation's most influential black activist clearly recognized a persuasive adversary.[47]

How much the *Conservator* influenced black voters in Chicago, or across the North, is difficult to determine. Black editors and journalists believed they were producing a new source of authority for black Americans, presenting new images of African American society, and setting the terms for a collective, if contentious, African American politics. Given Washington's response to President Roosevelt's request, Barnett and his colleagues in the black press had by the turn of the century effectively fashioned a powerful black civic institution.

In April 1880, Edwin Lewis, John Wagner, and J. B. Smith sent out a call for a state convention of "colored men of Illinois" to meet in Springfield, the state capital, on July 20 "for the purpose of concentrating our views upon some point as to how our claims as colored citizens" could be represented. Though most black Chicagoans would have agreed on the need for stronger representation for African Americans in state and national governments, the call for the convention sparked a notable rupture among black Republicans. Some of the "best class" of black Chicagoans felt "very aggrieved over the proposed colored men's convention," the *Inter Ocean* noted in early July, adding that the convention leaders were Masons who wanted "Masons to be the rulers in the convention." Black activists probably were not as divided as the *Inter Ocean* suggested, since 126 delegates chosen from across the state attended the Springfield convention. The publicity around the convention reveals some conflict among activists.[48]

It was the national Republican Party's growing refusal to protect black voting rights that prompted black activists to rethink their commitment to the party of Lincoln. That February, black voters in Cook County had organized an association to "concentrate the colored vote" and claimed one hundred members. (The association remained active for at least fifteen years, suggesting black Chicagoans' continued frustration with the Republican Party and determination, among association members at least, to stress race over party loyalty.) Some black activists were likely angered by the state party's refusal to support John Thomas's bid for a second term in the state house. But six months later, many among the city's elite, including Barnett, "satisfied with the Republican Convention and the nominees for State officers," were persuaded that white Republicans would act on behalf of the state's tiny black population. Still, their faith in white Republicans was faltering, no doubt a result of shifting ground beneath the Republican Party.[49]

Rapid industrialization and mass European emigration to northern US cities increasingly shaped northern politics. The Republican Party, which had united in 1880 to elect James Garfield, split into competing and incompatible factions after the president's assassination. Chester Arthur, his vice president chosen to appease the "stalwart" wing of the party, was no supporter of black civil rights. The stalwarts rejected concessions to southern Democrats; their primary goal was a highly disciplined Republican Party united by patronage and partisan loyalty, not ideology. Arthur determined, however, to strengthen the party by attracting white southerners, hoping to turn anti-Bourbon Democrats into loyal Republicans. The South did send eight Republicans and eight anti-Bourbon Democrats to the House in the mid-term 1882 election, but the strategy backfired when Republicans in Pennsylvania, Ohio, and Massachusetts either stayed home or defected.[50] It was clear to many black voters that the party's leaders were more concerned with winning over white southerners than protecting black civil rights.

The Republican Party leadership, after a close loss in the 1884 presidential election, began to concentrate on "national prosperity," heeding demands from the captains of industry for policies to promote business. Black civil and voting rights nearly dropped off the platform. Representative William D. Kelley of Pennsylvania, once a vocal advocate for black civil rights, in the 1880s earned himself the nickname "Pig Iron" Kelley for his strong support for the American steel and iron industries. The politics of race, men like Kelley contended, had been displaced by the politics of big business.[51] Republicans, Douglass wryly commented, had "made the body more important than the soul; national prosperity more important than national justice."[52]

Black voters north and south responded by attempting to hold the Republicans accountable. At a national convention of black activists and intellectuals in Louisville in 1883, a resolution endorsing the Republican Party sparked a raging conflict and was ultimately tabled. In Pennsylvania and Massachusetts, black leaders publically rejected the Republican Party. A convention of "colored voters" meeting in Des Moines, Iowa, in July 1885, urged African Americans to vote "a straight colored ticket." The group said that "they had been under the control of the Republican party long enough." African Americans in Pittsburgh organized to fight the "blind partisan aleegiance [sic] which has been to our people a veritable mockery." In New York, a small group of black activists led by Albany lawyer James C. Matthews formed the "Colored Democracy," to challenge Republican support by black voters. "A distinguished minority in the north rebelled against the Republicans," though most black activists remained within the party, August Meier notes.[53] Even in Virginia, some activists broke with the party. The *Conservator* applauded the black activists who supported the Readjusters under William Mahone in Virginia. "Although we knew [the Mahone movement] would weaken the Republican party in Virginia, we knew it would benefit the race," the paper commented.[54]

In Chicago, a group of black Republicans announced a new "Negro Party," though the group apparently was short lived. A few other black Chicagoans turned to the Democrats. "The eight colored men in the Democratic procession yesterday looked lonesome," the *Inter Ocean* commented in August 1888. "They probably felt repaid by being conspicuous."[55] Black journalist J. A. Emmerson, angered by the Republicans' neglect, commented, "Blind partisan allegiance has been to our people a veritable mockery." Writing in the *Inter Ocean* in 1884, Emmerson urged black Chicagoans to vote for "the party, without regards to its name, which shall best recognize our rights and best guard the interests of our people." Even Ferdinand Barnett, generally a devoted Republican, noted, "We are an important factor in the body politic and we know it," but if the Republic Party "counts upon us as a matter of course, and refuses to consult our wishes there will be exercised that potent influence we are known to possess and which so far we have held in peace."[56]

The 1888 presidential election was for many the breaking point, giving rise to a small but significant number of black Democrats in northern states. Four years under former Democratic New York governor Grover Cleveland, widely attacked "as a mere tool of the south," had done little to unify the Republicans.[57] As early as July 1888, "colored Democrats" held a statewide convention in Indiana. In Chicago, as in several other northern cities, there were calls for a "colored party" and efforts to organize "colored Democrats," largely funded by the city's white Democratic Party. "Neither of the two old parties do justice to the colored citizen in Chicago," the *Indianapolis Freeman* commented in 1886. Still, most black voters stuck with the Republican Party, and Republicans won control over every branch of the federal government in 1888. Perhaps the complaints of black voters were heard, however, as Harrison received more southern white votes than any previous Republican.[58]

In the North, especially, the interests of the race increasingly trumped party loyalty. The election opened a sharp debate among the nation's black editors. "Socially, morally, in private and public life," Barnett wrote, "there is no distinction between the Republicans and Democrats in their regard for the colored man." Black voters should not offer unquestioned support for the Republicans. "We are no longer slaves. We intend to act the part of free men," Barnett wrote. "That party which treats us best is the party of our choice." This proved a controversial position. The *New York Globe* agreed with Barnett. The *Appeal* was steadfastly Republican, regularly publishing articles about Chicago's Republican nominees for public office. Several southern weeklies, including the *Abbeville (SC) Journal*, the *Savannah Echo*, and the *Denver Star* said the Democrats did not deserve the African American vote. "[N]o colored man of sound political views can afford to go back on that [the Republican] party, and rally himself with the other great political party until it demonstrates its superior purity," wrote the *Star*.[59] But in northern cities, Chicago in particular, black activists were discovering that that their greatest strength lay in maneuvering among and within the major parties. This strategy would prove effective.

For Chicago's black newspapermen, ministers, and fraternal societies, politics in the 1880s was a complex game. The city's mayor through most of the decade, Carter H. Harrison, was a Democrat and a southerner who quickly expanded his power, becoming an almost singular and unstoppable force in the governance of the city. Harrison had moved to Chicago from Kentucky in the 1850s, made a fortune in real estate, and entered politics on the Fire Proof Ticket in 1871, winning his first victory to the Cook County Board along with John Jones. Political power was, in Harrison's hands, local, personal, and highly practical. He handed out jobs and favors to those who supported his administration—Republican, Democrat, or Socialist. Harrison easily won five terms in city hall, even though the city continued to fall into the Republican camp in national elections.

The mayor's great skill—some called it his flamboyant style—was his ability to gain support from seemingly competing interest groups and to draw votes from those such as German Socialists and black Republicans who would otherwise have supported his political rivals. Harrison was, writes Richard Schneirov, "a man of many contradictions." He was a respectable businessman supported by gambling king Mike McDonald, a Democrat who rarely won approval from the viscously partisan Democratic *Daily News*, and a former slave owner who appointed four black policemen and three black detectives to the police force and a company of ten black men (under the supervision of a white captain) to the fire department.[60] He left office voluntarily in 1887 only to run and win the mayor's office again, tragically as it turned out. Harrison was assassinated by an angry job-seeker just after the mayor gave the closing address at the World's Columbian Exposition on October 28, 1893.

Harrison's political genius was his recognition of the growing influence of the city's various national groups. More than any public figure in the 1880s, he recognized that nationality—as much as or more than party—would carry Chicago elections. Black politicians too gradually came to see that the competition among the city's national groups, none large enough to dominate the political scene, proved an opening for black activists. Harrison came into office following the popular Republican Monroe Heath. Harrison's victory, notes Bessie Louise Pierce, was less a result of the popularity of the Democrats than of the expanding number of smaller parties, which "scattered enough votes to provide the Democrats with a minority victory." Harrison had the support of the Greenback Party and the Socialist Labor ticket but lost in the wards where there were significant numbers of black voters.[61] Two years later, Harrison had effectively united disparate groups of immigrant voters; as the *Daily News* commented with some contempt, Harrison professed to be a descendent of Irish, Swedes, and Germans while also claiming to be "the 23rd Duke del Piazza in disguise, and . . . a descendant of Confucius."[62] Harrison, a wealthy entrepreneur, presented himself as a "man of the people," standing up to the "silk-stocking" Republican John M. Clark, a leather manufacturer and alderman. Harrison squeezed out another victory in 1884, with the same strategy of hounding the Prairie Avenue elite. That year, the Democrats, accused of corruption, were relentlessly pursued by local reformers.

Jobs in municipal government, even just a handful, were widely seen as visible recognition of black support. The *Inter Ocean* estimated that about half the black vote went to Harrison in 1884, suggesting the mayor owed his victory to black men crossing party lines. "Neither of the two old parties do justice to the colored citizen," commented a reporter for the *Indianapolis Freeman* during an 1886 visit to Chicago. "I am informed that the best out of the worst is done by the Democrats and it is nothing to brag about." As industry generally refused to hire black men, jobs in municipal government and federal agencies, primarily the post office, would become an economic foundation for a black middle class. Black voters in the North had been crucial in some local and federal elections, "yet all they have to show for it are three appointments in the diplomatic and one in the consular services," the *Inter Ocean* commented.[63] With their support for Harrison, black voters chose economic interest—and expressed an appreciation of the power of patronage—over party loyalty, though they did not get much from Harrison beyond jobs. Black voters who turned away from the Republican Party to vote for Harrison also conveyed a growing recognition that creating a cohesive black constituency would prove the path to political power.[64]

The issues that divided white Democrats, Republicans, Socialists, and labor activists were rarely mentioned in the black press. The *Inter Ocean*, operated by white Chicagoans, was largely sympathetic to African American issues and read by many black Chicagoans. It covered the leading national political issues of the decade: the controversy surrounding the tariff, monetary reform, the fight over the distribution of publicly owned land in the West, and accusations of vote buying and corrupt business practices in the White House and Congress. Black journalists addressed some of the most divisive local issues like prohibition and the growing number of gambling houses and brothels in the city. They were particularly concerned about the willingness of the city's police to allow the vice district to expand into the enclave of black families living south of the city's commercial district. Vice would remain a critical issue for elite Chicagoans, separating them from less respectable black businessmen and laborers who drew significant profits from vice trades. Yet the black press paid closer attention to issues that Harrison astutely played on: jobs in government.

The "colored citizens of Chicago [were] aggrieved" over jobs and, as the decade advanced, over civil rights. Black Chicagoans demanded in 1878 that Sheriff John Hoffman appoint someone "of their race" and pushed officials in city government—the police and fire departments primarily—to hire black men. "The colored brother does not propose to let the division

Unidentified African American policeman, ca. 1890. Courtesy of
Harold Washington Library, Special Collections.

of 'spoils' slip by without getting his share," commented the *Chicago Evening Journal* in March 1885. The *Journal*, though suggesting that black voters were corrupted by President Grover Cleveland's willingness to hand out jobs to his supporters, accurately conveyed the mood of black as well as white Chicagoans. All were determined to use whatever influence they had to acquire jobs and business from local, state, and federal officials.[65] This was precisely how white and black Chicagoans—and most Americans— understood the workings of government: a politics of personal and pragmatic relationships.

African Americans believed the politics of patronage and friendship should include them. Frederick Douglass, a devoted Republican, sent a letter of introduction for his "brother" to Mayor Harrison in June 1886. He asked the southern-born Democrat to find "a place on the staff of the police force" for his brother, who had "not been fortunate in accumulating worldly goods." [66] Most black Chicagoans did not have Douglass's national stature. Most could do little to draw the attention of the mayor or

To Colored Voters of Chicago!

The attempt is being made in this and other cities to draw a portion of the colored vote from the republican party, by using the names of a few persons who have been placed in minor official positions for party effect, to show that the Democratic party is the friend of the colored race. One A. F. Bradley is the tool they are using here, and the object is to aid Carter Harrison at the expense of honest old Uncle Dick Oglesby. But the scheme will not work. It is too thin.

Everybody knows, that knows anything, that the colored man is indebted to the republican party for every political and civil right he enjoys.

The republican party gave them their freedom and secured it by a constitutional amendment. This Oglesby was for, and Carter Harrison against.

The republican party gave them the right to vote and to hold office against the opposition of Carter Harrison and the democratic party.

The republican party have defended their rights and been their constant friend and advocate. Thus they have shown by the appointment of such men as Frederick Douglas and ex-Senator Bruce and Jno. A. Lynch to office. They honored the race by placing the last named gentleman in the high position of temporary chairman of the last Republican National Convention.

Be on your guard, fellow citizens—do not allow yourselves to be imposed upon by any such sham as, that Carter Harrison and the democratic party are your friends. NO! they would enslave your race again to-morrow if they could. See how this same democratic party treats us in the South, where every right that man holds dear is denied us.

Be not deceived ; stand by your friends, and Carter Harrison will fail in his plan of carrying Cook County—by fraud if need be——and of electing a democratic legislature, that he may go to the senate, will signally fail. No! republican success is again certain, and don't you forget it.

In behalf of the colored citizens of Chicago.

K. W. MACKAY.

J. W. POPE.   J. W. GARRETT.
W. W. SAMPSON.   ADAM CARY.

"To Colored Voters of Chicago," 1884 gubernatorial campaign broadside. Courtesy of Chicago History Museum (file iCHI-67642).

an alderman to their plight. The communal ethos of Chicago politics cemented by personal relationships largely left African Americans outside the city's multipartisan political community. Yet by 1895, the *New York Sun* approvingly noted the political skills of black activists. "The Afro-Americans of Chicago are giving the Republican managers considerable trouble by insisting upon more adequate representation in the municipal and Cook County governments," the reporter commented. "Like white Chicagoans, they are in no way modest in claiming a big slice of the earth and fighting for it."[67]

Black activists recognized the limits on their ability to win patronage jobs. Seeking an alternative to the politics of personal relationships and no longer trusting the protection of the Republican Party, activists pursued civil rights legislation at the state and local levels in the 1880s. In 1884 and 1885, Barnett and others pushed for the passage of a state civil rights bill to guarantee black residents equal access to all public spaces and employment. "Do we want social favors? Not by any means," Barnett wrote in an 1883 letter to the *Tribune*. Barnett used the pages of the *Conservator* to plead with black citizens to wield their votes as weapons in the fight for civil rights. "If the Republican Party wants our suffrage, it must prove worthy of it," Barnett wrote. Recognizing that their votes, though few, might swing elections for state legislators, activists in the 1880s began to organize "for the purpose of concentrating the colored vote," to pressure state officials to recognize black civil rights.[68]

Activists could not claim a unified constituency, but they hoped to influence officials with the presentation of a list of "100 members" who would vote in favor of their interests, despite different party affiliations. Representative John W. E. Thomas, the only African American in the state legislature, steered the civil rights bill through the legislature, where enough Chicago Republicans, and a few Democrats, were persuaded that black voters mattered. In June 1885, the legislature passed the bill, which was signed into law by Governor Richard J. Oglesby, a Republican who a year earlier had narrowly defeated Carter Harrison in a bid for the governor's office.[69] The law provided that "all persons" in the state "be entitled to the full and equal enjoyment of the accommodations, advantages, facilities and privileges of inns, restaurants, eating houses, barber shops, public conveyances on land or water, theaters, and all other places of public accommodations and amusement." It was enforced intermittently at best. Within five years, a reporter for the *Indianapolis Freeman* complained that "there are dozens of places in Chicago where on account of your color you cannot be served." Yet the law served as a symbol of a growing black political activism in Chicago in the decades after the federal government had largely turned away

Broadside for 1884 gubernatorial campaign between Carter Harrison and Richard J. Oglesby. Harrison led Oglesby in the city by 4,655 votes but lost statewide. Source: Bessie Louise Pierce, *A History of Chicago*, vol. 3, *The Rise of the Modern City, 1871–1893* (New York: Alfred A. Knopf, 1957), 359. Courtesy of Chicago History Museum (file iCHI-67643).

from the interests of black people in the South. By 1890 several lawsuits over violations of the law were pending in the courts.[70]

The city's diverse urban population and the ability of Mayor Harrison to play the varied nationalities to his advantage opened a distinct political space for astute black activists. They too began to maneuver the complex political landscape, watching Harrison respond to (and in the process encourage) the nationalist politics of varied European immigrants and increasingly using racial identity to unite and mobilize voters. African American activists achieved small but significant victories—the passage of a largely unenforced civil rights bill and a handful of jobs in city government. Those were signs of the expanding political organization among the city's African Americans and of the skills of its leading activists.

"Being convinced that the time is ripe . . . to successfully combat the denial of our constitutional and inherent rights, so generally denied or abridged throughout the republic," came the call to the first national convention of the National Afro-American League. The organization, established by New York journalist T. Thomas Fortune, included members from more than a dozen states in the North, South, and Midwest. In November 1889, Fortune announced the convention to bring together delegates from all of the state organizations, "all clubs and societies organized to secure the rights denied the race."[71] Though demanding rights, the organization would turn away from politics, a move that ultimately would leave it a marginal force at best in African American life.

Fortune, who had been born into slavery in Florida in 1856, was the most influential black journalist in the nation in the final decades of the nineteenth century. He had seen the Klan rise as Reconstruction faltered, observing savage violence against black people in his hometown of Marianna, Florida. Trained as a printer, he had moved to New York in 1879 and within a couple of years had become co-owner and editor of the *Globe*, later called the *Freeman*, and finally named the *New York Age*, and widely known "as the best Negro paper of its day." The *Age*'s editorial pages, peppered with Fortune's sharp prose and uncompromising politics, drew comment—sometimes outrage—from the white press north and south.[72] During the 1890s, Fortune published regular columns in the white-owned *New York Sun*, expanding his reputation and influence among white and black readers. He was well known among African Americans in 1887 when he promoted the first national African American civil rights organization. "The white papers of this country have determined to leave the colored man to fight his own battles," Fortune wrote in a May 1887 editorial. "We have got to take hold of this problem ourselves, and make so much noise that all the world shall know the wrongs we suffer and our determination to right these wrongs."[73] The black press proved a crucial organizing tool, reaching readers throughout the United States.

Fortune, with the support of a small group of friends and fellow "agitators," aimed to unify black activists across the nation. The constitution for the branch leagues, published in the *Freeman* in summer 1887, addressed injustices that affected the daily lives of African Americans north and south; it was not a regional document. The constitution demanded "a more equitable distribution of school funds," the inclusion of African Americans on juries, and "fair and impartial" trials, and protested the "tyrannical usage" of segregated seats on railroad and steamboat lines. The constitution, in addition, called for resistance to "mob and lynch law" and demanded "the arrest and punishment of all such offenders against our legal rights." It insisted on prison reform and the elimination of "barbarous, cruel and unchristian treatment of convicts."[74] School funding, jury trials, and prison reform had been on the agendas of northern black politicians for at least a decade. Mob violence was rising across the South and making sporadic appearances in northern towns. These were the issues—schools, travel, criminal justice, and state-sanctioned violence—that, bundled together, determined a citizen's rights.

Though the league included an array of political activists, it claimed to be nonpartisan. The league would achieve its goals, Fortune wrote, not through the ballot, but rather "by appealing to the courts of law." Fortune's strategy reflected growing African American frustration and dissatisfaction with federal policies, especially Congress's refusal to enforce the Fourteenth and Fifteenth Amendments. The Supreme Court in 1883 had ruled that the Fourteenth Amendment's promise of "equal protection" under law did not cover the actions of "private" individuals. Racial discrimination in privately owned businesses from rail lines to hotels and theaters was constitutional, an eight to one majority of the Court concluded. Outraged African Americans in northern states had responded with a push for state-level civil rights legislation. Those state laws, rarely enforced, would be the basis for the league's legal strategy. The courts would, for the moment, be the battleground.

In the half decade after its formation, the league filed several complaints in local courts, challenging racial discrimination in restaurants, theaters, and transportation. Almost all were in the North, and almost all failed. Fortune became the center of an 1890 legal battle when he refused to leave a Manhattan hotel after the proprietor maintained that the establishment served whites only. The editor's call for support generated contributions from across the nation. "Let us stand and fight," Fortune wrote.[75] The state supreme court awarded Fortune $825 in the dispute, though the editor had demanded $100,000 in damages.[76] Several civil rights cases were filed in

Chicago, though there too the strategy proved largely ineffective. It was mainly lack of funds that prevented the league from filing lawsuits.[77] The legal strategy collapsed in the wake of the 1896 Supreme Court decision permitting "separate but equal" seating on railcars and in effect legalizing racial segregation in restaurants, parks, libraries, workplaces, and schools. In the late 1880s, the courts had seemed a more welcoming forum for civil rights activism than Congress.

Fortune's strategy was less a rejection of politics than an expression of anger with the Republic Party. He demanded nonpartisan solutions to the "race problem." Fortune's call to the convention was signed by Ferdinand L. Barnett along with leading activists from across the nation. The Illinois delegation was the largest and included diverse political persuasions, with more than forty men, including Barnett, Edward Morris, Knights of Labor leader R. S. Bryan, and R. M. Mitchell. More than one hundred men from states north and south gathered for three days in mid-January in Chicago, elected Fortune president, and held meetings at the Palmer House and in Quinn Chapel. The gathering marked the "birth of the pioneer permanent colored organization in the country," the *Tribune* commented.[78] In speeches over the three-day gathering, the men denounced injustice, lectured on American history, and congratulated each other for their willingness to stand for their rights.

Fortune, in a speech that must have lasted more than two hours, placed the struggles of black Americans within a long western tradition of battling for democratic freedoms. Rather than questioning whether African Americans were part of the nation, he suggested that they, including the men gathered with him in Chicago, represented the "progress" of western history dating back to ancient Athens. To a list that included Demosthenes "thundering against the designs of Philip of Macedon," Oliver Cromwell, and Patrick Henry, he added Nat Turner and John Brown. "The arsenal, the fort, the warrior are as necessary as the school, the church, the newspapers and the public forum for debate," Fortune proclaimed. "Agitators," he said, led "the pathway of the progress of the world." The "black heroes" were part of a long line leading to the men meeting that day in Quinn Chapel. "I congratulate you that you have aroused from the lethargy of the past," he declared. "I congratulate you that you now recognize the fact that great work remains for you to do."[79] The work was to fulfill the promise of emancipation and demand the full rights of citizenship. Western history would guide contemporary struggles.

Fortune celebrated "the spirit of agitation" to argue against blind support for party politics, Republicans in particular. W. A. Pledger of Georgia, in a speech two days later, declared that black Americans were mere partial citizens. "The negro is no longer exactly a chattel, but he is in that uncertain undefinable condition of being neither a slave nor a citizen," Pledger said. Black Americans were not seeking "negro supremacy" but the "supremacy of the Constitution." The African American's "implicit obedience to the law, his undeviating devotion to the party which led him . . . out of bondage," Fortune said, "has been used against him as a crime . . . as a badge of servility." At least one speaker urged southerners to vote the Democratic ticket, hoping to mold a new Democratic Party. The convention concluded with a firm statement against party politics. The "political parties have ceased consistently to concern themselves with the importance of a denial to Afro-Americans of the rights and immunities." The Afro-American League aimed to "secure our sacred rights as citizens . . . by nonpartisan action."[80]

Fortune, in his opening-day speech, urged his listeners to shift their allegiance from party to race. Even as black activists had long fought over political agendas and convention members divided on issues large and minor, Fortune suggested that racial identity and the recognized interests of the race could unite black Americans politically. "I speak as an Afro-American first, last, and all the time," he said, "ready to stab to death any party which robs me of my confidence and vote and straightaway asks me 'what are you going to do about it?'" The local leagues might pursue party politics, but the national league represented "the race" above all. "I am now and I have always been a race man and not a party man," Fortune declared.[81]

For Fortune—and he apparently spoke for many others—black Americans could secure their rights through the creation of autonomous local civic institutions. Fortune proposed the establishment of an Afro-American bank, a bureau of emigration to resettle those seeking to move out of the South, a committee on legislation to monitor state and national legislatures, and a bureau of "co-operative industry" to purchase and sell products for an African American market. He also proposed the creation of an agency to oversee "industrial education," training artisans, farmers, and laborers. Fortune's proposals prefigured those of Booker T. Washington; the Tuskegee educator later brought the league under his control. But Fortune's proposals suggest that a militant racial stance, a warrior-like pursuit of civil rights, could coincide with industrial education and economic self-help.[82] (Fortune, who later became an ally of Washington, embodied a mix of political ideologies that did not fit neatly into the long drawn-out—and less stark than scholars suggest—conflict between Washington and W. E. B. DuBois.) With his proposals for African American institutions, Fortune urged the establishment of independent black politics.

Abandoning partisan politics, conference members advocated another method, with some sense of irony, to eliminate racial conflicts in southern states. In a petition to Congress, the convention noted that large population of black Americans in Alabama, South Carolina, Mississippi, and other southern states "makes the situation painful and uncomfortable for the small minority of white fellow citizens residing therein." The solution was for Congress to allocate $100 million to fund the emigration of white citizens "who may desire to settle in other and more favored states, free from Afro-American majorities." The funds would provide the migrating whites with "free transportation and lunch." The resolution, a play on the sixty-year-old plan by emigrationists to send black Americans to other nations, passed unanimously.[83] The resolution, with its caustic tone, signaled that black Americans, at least those intellectuals and activists attending the Chicago convention, were weary of debating whether or how they could accommodate white America. If white Republicans would not protect African American interests, then black voters would simply forge their own institutions.

Most black activists had not given up on politics. Though many called for strategies of self-help, including education and property ownership, most continued to make political activism a priority. In 1893, the *Indianapolis Freeman* published a poll of leading African American men. Just one of those queried—Booker T. Washington—did not mention political and civil rights but advised black Americans to "settle quietly down and get money and property and acquire character and education." Other black leaders spoke of education and economic concerns but also urged continued protest for civil rights. Especially among northern leaders, politics was vital, but party was in question.[84]

The final test of white Republicans, and for black support of the national party, began in Washington within months after the Afro-American League members departed Chicago. Congress took up two measures of grave concern to black activists. The outcome was deeply disappointing but probably not surprising to league members. The Blair Education Bill, proposed by Republican senator Henry Blair of New Hampshire, aimed to equalize state education funding. The legislation, which implicitly affirmed segregated schools, promised federal funds to states, which would distribute common school funds equitably among black and white schools. The Blair bill went down to quick defeat. Its companion legislation opened a lengthy Senate battle.

In July 1890, Massachusetts congressman Henry Cabot Lodge proposed a measure to protect black voting rights by funding federal supervision of polling sites. The Lodge Federal Elections Bill, or the "Force Bill" as white southerners called it, aimed to use the federal circuit courts to arbitrate complaints of election fraud or intimidation. The bill passed the House by a straight party vote in early July and was sent on to the Senate. Democrats in the Senate, led by Arthur Pue Gorman of Maryland, were determined to defeat the bill, which they insisted would "destroy the sovereign rights of the states."[85] More threatening to the legislation were Republican efforts to push through "the McKinley tariff," protectionist legislation supported by eastern business and manufacturers. Many Republicans were prepared to discard the election bill to gain support for the tariff. George F. Hoar was a Massachusetts Republican and an advocate for the Lodge bill. He denounced his fellow Republicans. The fight for the bill, Hoar stated, was "a struggle for the last step toward establishing a doctrine to which the American people are pledged by their history, their Constitution, their opinions and their interests." The elections bill was twice set aside, first for a vote on the tariff and six months later for a currency bill, when it was buried for good.[86]

African American activists were deeply disappointed. Several newspaper editors had promised Hoar petitions containing the signatures of "two to three million Negroes." Others had predicted the decline of the Republican Party. "God will not let any party prosper which will not advocate the cause of justice for all men," wrote Rev. R. Graham of Pennsylvania in the *Christian Recorder* in December 1890. The bill's demise prompted renewed outrage at both the Republican Party and Congress. "The failure of the late Congress to pass the Lodge bill settles the fact that all WHITE is more important than all Republican to the party composing the majority of that congress," the *Christian Recorder* commented. The Republicans in Congress chose their white business supporters over their African American constituents. "The error . . . of the South, in dealing with this problem is in their assumption that race hatred is the dominant passion of the human soul; that it is stronger than love of country, stronger than the principle of equality . . . stronger than justice," Hoar proclaimed. "You have tried everything else, try justice."[87]

The congressional battle over the elections bill was the final national explosion of sectional anger and bitterness over black civil rights in the post–Civil War era. The war was over, black Americans were emancipated, but their exercise of freedom was curbed by violence and restricted by politics. The battles over African American voting rights and school funding split the Republican Party, destabilizing party politics and setting the tone for major political reorganizations in the 1890s. Struggles for black civil rights would continue but largely on local terms and in northern cities. The congressional fight over the elections bill expanded the continuing debate among black Americans over whether African Americans had a place in the Republican Party or in United States.

The Afro-American League dwindled through the 1890s, lacking funds and the mass support T. Thomas Fortune had hoped for. But the desire for a national African American organization did not disappear. By 1898, the newly formed Afro-American Council counted scores of members, with Fortune, Barnett, and Chicago minister Reverdy Ransom among its leaders. "Our Plea is for Equal Rights," was its motto.[88] Its stated objectives were almost identical to those of the Afro-American League. In 1900, there was another effort to organize a "national Negro party," which drew "prominent negroes—bishops, ministers, editors and lawyers" to a meeting in Philadelphia. The short-lived group aimed to nominate candidates for state and congressional offices in every state. There was a growing recognition that though the political conditions differed from north to south, the interests of "the race" were national.[89]

National organizations like the Afro-American League and the Afro-American Council, leading to the formation of the National Urban League and the National Association for the Advancement of Colored People in the twentieth century, suggested that race, more than political party, was gradually becoming an organizing principle in American politics. The black press, more than any other civic institution, had forged this sense of collective national interests in the postemancipation decades.

In Chicago, activists used local civic organizations and church groups to establish a black constituency and position themselves as its leaders. Though education and employment status increasingly separated the "refined" from the laborer, growing numbers of black Chicagoans were engaged in political work. Several African American fraternal societies were among the labor and reform groups that supported the shift to the Australian ballot in 1891, ending the long-standing practice of each party printing its own ballot and ensuring (at least some) secrecy for the voter. With their thriving civic organizations and churches, expanding businesses and growing professional class, African American activists in the northern city continued to demand that government serve their interests.[90]

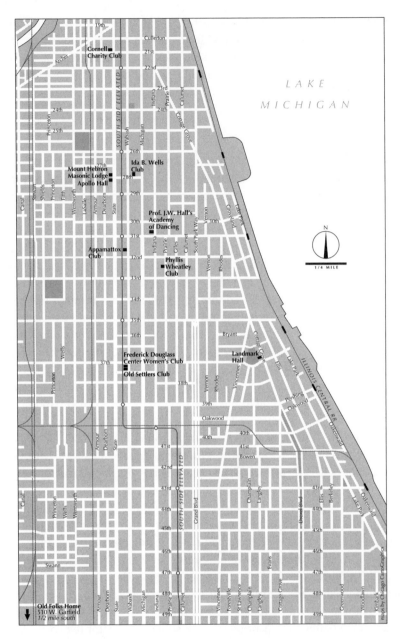

Map of Black Belt social and reform clubs, 1905, by Dennis McClendon.
(Women's clubs tended to meet at the home of the club secretary.)
Locations based on *Colored People's Blue-Book and Business Directory.*

THREE

Women's Rights, the World's Fair, and Activists on the National Stage

"In short, our women are ambitious to be contributors to all the great moral and intellectual forces that make for the greater weal of our common country," proclaimed Fannie Barrier Williams to thirty-five hundred Christians, Jews, Hindus, and Muslims gathered for the World's Parliament of Religions in Chicago in 1893. The parliament, meeting in conjunction with the World's Columbian Exposition, brought together the widest and most ecumenical assembly of religious traditions in the world. Williams was one of three black Americans invited to address the crowd and the sole black woman. Her speech in the Hall of Columbus in late September highlighted the hypocrisy of white Christians. "Religion, like every other force in America, was first used as an instrument and servant of slavery." Yet religion, if properly directed, could be a force for social justice and the improvement of "the race." The target of church work should be the family home, "the heart of every social evil and disorder among the colored people" and the domain of black women, Williams declared. "The home and social life of [black southerners] is in urgent need of the purifying power of religion."[1] Merging the influences of home and church, Williams suggested that the future of black America lay, in part, with the spiritual guidance and philanthropic leadership of educated black women.

While Williams stood within the hall delivering her speech, Ida B. Wells, the thirty-year-old journalist and antilynching crusader, was on the fairgrounds handing out a protest pamphlet. Williams and Wells (later Wells-Barnett), sometimes friends, more often rivals, represented divergent strategies and varied agendas for the struggles for African American civil rights. Williams, making her second public speech at the exposition, argued for the virtues of black womanhood and the value of women's purifying influence on African Americans. She and her husband, S. Laing Williams, would become political allies of Booker T. Washington, while Wells-Barnett, who courageously investigated lynching and issued angry public statements, was more militant and controversial.[2]

The women shared some beliefs. Both used the language of respectability and racial uplift, which permeated turn-of-the century African American reform debates. Both emphasized the family home and the role of women in improving society. Both also urged black Americans to participate in local and national politics. Some scholars contend that reforming women with their rhetoric of uplift—their focus on home, hearth, and economic stability—largely diverted attention from more aggressive public politics. But in northern cities, political activism was, in many ways, the practice of uplift; elite and middle-class activists turned the moralizing language of respectability into political engagement.[3] The World's Columbian Exposition put Wells and Williams on a national stage; in the decades that followed, each became a vocal and powerful leader of black women's organizations and African American politics broadly.

In Chicago, as across the nation, black women's clubs were important arenas for political organizing and for redrawing the political geography of the rapidly expanding city. Even before they were granted the right to vote, black women helped to expand the reach and realm of politics to include issues emerging from the industrial age: poorly constructed tenements; contagious diseases suffered by those lacking indoor plumbing; schools short on books, desks, and well-trained teachers; and widespread poverty among black children and the elderly. As they organized neighbors and friends, black women leaders, like white women reformers, politicized the distribution of municipal services and resources to residential neighborhoods. Unlike the white women who saw the city as a whole as their sphere of activity—even as many worked primarily in immigrant neighborhoods—black women worked in an increasingly racially segregated city. Racial segregation determined the physical boundaries of their work, while black women's reform campaigns gave shape to an emerging black community.[4]

Black women engaged urban politics just as mass immigration from Europe and a smaller but steady flow of people from rural America transformed urban life. Categories of social identity set in a sharp black-and-white divide in the South were expanded and revised in northern cities. By 1900, immigrants and their children constituted almost 80 percent of Chicago's population, and many immigrants, particularly those from southern and eastern Europe, were identified in government documents, sociological texts, and common parlance as members of distinct races. Race pseudo-scientists had throughout the nineteenth century classified the world's populations according to various (and arbitrary) characteristics into distinct racial groups, with the Anglo-Saxon marking the height of civilization. This classificatory system moved from pseudoscientific treatises to mundane images and daily practices in northern cities in the final decades of the nineteenth century. (The *Chicago Daily News* commented in 1891 that Italians living in Chicago were "cowardly worshippers of power as are the Chinese or any barbaric tribe.")[5] The principles of racial hierarchy—and the derogatory images of black people produced by the race scientists—were widely circulated when the world converged on Chicago in the summer of 1893. The World's Columbian Exposition put politically engaged black women on the national stage and, at the same time, sparked new contests over the place of African Americans in American history.

The World's Columbian Exposition drew the world's attention and much of the world to Chicago. The pavilions and fairgrounds stretched through the marshes in Jackson Park. The fair provided jobs for thousands of local and migrant workers. Chicago officials had lobbied aggressively in the halls of Congress for the honor of hosting the nation's second world's fair, celebrating the four-hundredth anniversary of Columbus's landing in the New World (a year late). The fair paid tribute to the nation, its growth from a humble European outpost to a dynamic industrial center. "Progress" and "civilization" were the terms guiding the fair's organizers. The organizers' decisions about how and where to represent African Americans were a powerful statement about their vision of the nation and its history—one that spurred new anger from African American activists.

The exposition plan embodied the organizers' faith in a nation reunited just twenty-eight years after a bloody civil war. Architect Daniel H. Burnham, who supervised the design of the fair, and Frederick Law Olmstead, designer of New York's Central Park, created an enchanting city within a city. A series of canals linked the lakefront to the White City, which featured seven classically inspired buildings clustered around a shallow lake, the Court of Honor. The classical architecture evoked visions of ancient Greece and Rome. The exposition buildings, covered in white paint and dramatically illuminated with electric lights, expressed America's beauty, spiritual purity, and technological advancement. Exhibits promoted American ingenuity, especially in the creation of new commercial goods. Marketing campaigns played on old racial stereotypes and fashioned new demeaning images of black Americans. Aunt Jemima, portrayed by former slave Nancy Green, became a nationally recognized figure, spurring a rash of mammy images in the arts and advertising. The White City stood in contrast to the Midway Plaisance, a mile-long strip of ethnographic exhibits interspersed with amusements, like the first Ferris wheel.[6]

Just as Chicagoans were arranging recent arrivals into a complex racial taxonomy, the exposition and especially the Midway gave race theory definite form. Fairgoers wandered through an outdoor museum of world cultures organized by Harvard University anthropologist Frederic Ward Putnam. The exhibits were designed to show the "progress of humanity." The "authentic" villages were arranged linearly, allowing the visitor to move from the "civilized German and Irish villages" to the Turkish, Egyptian, and Chinese villages and finally to exhibits of the "savage American Indians and Dahomans." Only whites were presented as civilized, as Gail Bederman notes. The Dahomans, standing in for all African people and, by implication, African Americans, represented the "animalistic origins" of humanity, commented the *Chicago Tribune*. The Midway's exhibits turned Darwinian evolution into a rigid social hierarchy that reinforced and legitimized existing social inequalities and political repression.[7]

The fair in effect transformed the city into a grand spectacle, a pleasure palace designed to educate and uplift the masses and to mask the growing social conflict in the real city. It aimed to present a new image of the nation, of Chicago, and more generally, of urban space. Exposition planners, as art historian T. J. Clark writes of Georges-Eugène Haussmann's Paris, crafted a vision of the city that was unified and, most important, guided by consumption. Labor conflict—the 1877 rail strike, the Haymarket riot in 1886, and recent local battles in Chicago's industries—worried local and national investors and threatened the inspiring image of the industrial city. Older representations of cities as sites of production and of workers valiantly building the national industrial base were increasingly accompanied by images of consumption in department stores, office towers, and restaurants. In many ways, the fair signaled this shift in representations of the city. The spectacle, Clark writes, was "not a neutral form in which capitalism incidentally happened; it was a form of capital itself and one of the most effective." The spectacular beauty of the White City, the unrivaled entertainments of the Midway, and the new consumer goods marketed at the fair were not mere distractions from social problems. Instead the fairgrounds sought to bring the nation together, to paper over growing tensions and social differences—or, as the exhibits on the Midway suggested, to explain and naturalize social inequalities—and to assure viewers that every group, no matter how different or unequal, had a place in the city.[8]

The Midway exhibits and the spectacle of the unified, consumption-oriented city sparked new challenges to white supremacy and the rise of corporate capitalism in the urban North. The *Indianapolis Freeman*, with condescension and irony, regularly referred to exposition organizers as "representatives of the civilized world," always using quotation marks around the phrase. Others in the African American press were more explicit, calling the exposition "white American's World's Fair." The exposition candidly and symbolically celebrated the triumphs of white America while diminishing the aspirations and achievements of black Americans.[9] The exposition generated widespread opposition, not just to the workings of the fair but also to what it suggested about American society.

Even before its opening, the World's Columbian Exposition had become a hub for collective political protest, prompting renewed debate over the position of African Americans in the city and the nation. The question of how African Americans would be represented at the fair merged almost seamlessly with debates about how black Americans were represented in national and local politics. No African Americans had been appointed to the fair's National Board of Commissioners in 1890. Ferdinand Barnett, T. Thomas Fortune, and other members of the African American Press Association launched a national protest to urge President Harrison to add a black man to the commission. "The Negro is surely no useless part of the great American people," the *Indiana Freeman* complained. That "no Negro is on the commission implies that no one Negro in any state of the Union had the required qualities to represent one-fourth of his state or one-eighth of the nation." Two years later, under pressure from black leaders, Harrison appointed Hale Parker, an Oberlin graduate, lawyer, and high school principal from Saint Louis as an alternate member.[10] In the months before the fair's opening, black leaders debated whether black Americans should attend at all.

African American women in Chicago were even more assertive. The fair's organizers designated a separate building for exhibits relating to women's achievements and appointed a Board of Lady Managers to oversee the exhibits. The committee named a woman architect to design the women's building. Sophia Hayden presented an Italian Renaissance–style building, which like the other neoclassical buildings in the White City signaled the achievements of Western civilization. The white women on the nine-member committee, led by Bertha Palmer, wife of one of the city's wealthiest businessmen, were not, however, prepared for the protests from black women.[11]

The exclusion of black people from the committees and from representation at the fair prompted the earliest of Chicago's black women's political organizations. The protests began when Chicago schoolteacher Lettie A. Trent petitioned Bertha Palmer for a meeting and demanded that at least two black women be appointed to work with the Board of Lady Managers. Then, on November 25, 1890, a group of African American women delivered a powerful resolution to the board meeting in Chicago. The resolution had been approved during a "mass meeting of the colored women of Chicago at Bethesda Church." A white board member, Mary Logan, presented the resolution, which began: "No provisions have as yet been made . . . for securing exhibits from the colored women of this country." The women requested, "for the purpose of demonstrating the progress of the colored women since emancipation," that the World's Columbian Commission establish "an office for a colored woman to collect exhibits from the colored women of America." The association members did not see themselves as representing black women only. They hoped to furnish "all information as to the education and industrial advancement made by the race . . . in every department of life." Black women sought to represent the interests of all black Americans.[12]

When the board sidestepped the women's demands, African American women responded with great political skill. They called for a protest meeting in Washington, DC, timed to coincide with the board's request to Congress for new appropriations for the construction of the women's building. "This matter should be attended to at once," wrote Isabel Linch, a white board representative in an October 7 letter to Palmer. "It will hurt us if they take action condemning anything we have done." Palmer responded angrily that the black women's demands were "a tissue of misquotations and untruths." She begged her friend Mary Logan, a longtime advocate for black civil rights who was in Washington that October, to "see Fred Douglas [sic] . . . and other prominent men you may know who are interested in the negro question." Palmer worried that the black women's proposed "convention" would interfere with the board's "important work."[13] Though the African American women leaders' threat hit its mark, their convention was canceled, as black women were hardly unified over the aims of the proposed meeting.

The women had divided over the goals of their protest, displaying for the white public the central issue of African American politics in the late nineteenth century: whether black Americans would integrate with or separate from white America. Lettie A. Trent had sought a separate exhibit honoring black Americans. The World's Columbian Association, a small group of Chicago women questioned her ability to represent the interests of all black Americans. Another group of black women in Chicago rejected Trent's plan entirely. In early February 1891, they established a rival organization, the Women's Columbian Auxiliary Association, which garnered support from some leading black men. The WCAA, quickly claiming one hundred "committed members," urged the inclusion of African American work among white exhibits. "Shall we have a separate exhibit or shall our work take its place in the departments in which it belongs? Upon this question the Association takes no uncertain stand," the WCAA announced. "We are American citizens and desire to draw no line that would tend to make us strangers in the land of our birth." The WCAA claimed that Dr. Daniel Hale Williams, Rev. J. L. Thompson, and Ferdinand Barnett served on its advisory board. "The ablest minds of our race are unmistakably opposed to a separate exhibit," the group asserted, listing Douglass, former senator Blanche K. Bruce, former congressmen John R. Lynch, and John M. Langston among its supporters.[14] Douglass expressed his opposition to a separate exhibit in a letter published in the *Christian Recorder*. There seemed "an unhealthy desire to exhibit the colored on this great occasion as a distinctive curiosity," he wrote.[15] The following March, the WCAA issued a statement of gratitude to Albion W. Tourgée, the white former judge and journalist who was a longtime supporter of African American civil rights. A year later, Tourgée would suggest to Ida Wells-Barnett that she protest African American exclusion from the exposition.[16]

By the fall of 1891, there were at least four organizations pushing for an African American presence at the exposition. Publicity about the battle drew the attention of African American women who had not previously lent their voices to political debates. The *Indianapolis Freeman* noted the large numbers of women who entered the fray. Naomi Anderson, a black woman living in Chicago, sent two letters to Palmer, arguing that there could be "a corner in the women's building set apart for us." She concluded, "In the name of God and humanity, open the door and bid us come in."[17] The protest had invigorated, politicized, and divided African American women.

Palmer effectively used the "quarrel" among black women activists to justify their continued exclusion, though three white members of the Board of Lady Managers urged the appointment of a black woman to the board. The *Freedman*, scolding the Chicago women, commented that conflict among black activists was hardly surprising. "It is a hellish, disgraceful and lamentable characteristic of the Negro race to be the first to pull down their own because of jealousy and envy," the paper noted.[18] "Jealousy and envy" may have been part of the problem, but the women genuinely disagreed over the goals of their protest. Should they demand the works of black artists and inventors be included among those of whites, or should they seek a separate exhibit for African American achievements? In short, was the battle for integration or separation at the fair?

The conflict over where black Americans fit into the fair—or the nation—was not resolved by the Chicago committees. None of the black organizations proved successful, though black Americans were not entirely left out of the national celebration. Several black universities sponsored booths, and at least one gallery, the New York State building, included a small African American exhibit. Several black intellectuals, including Chicago's Fannie Barrier Williams, were invited to speak during the many congresses of scholars and activists organized in conjunction with the fair. Still, the protests over the exclusion of an exhibit honoring black Americans drew attention from the national and local press to African Americans' disappointment with the fair.[19]

It was the fair and the controversy surrounding it that brought the famed antilynching crusader Ida B. Wells to Chicago in June 1893, a visit that changed the course of Wells's life and transformed local politics. Wells married Ferdinand Barnett just two years later and settled in Chicago, assisting her husband with his political career, continuing her own political work, and raising a growing family. Wells, already a well-known lecturer and writer, was incensed by the exclusion of black Americans from the exposition and called for a boycott of the fair. She was spurred to action by an open letter from a former Fisk Jubilee singer, Frederick Loudin, expressing his rage at the brutal lynching of Henry Smith in Paris, Texas. Wells had publicized the horror, writing, "Never in the history of civilization has any Christian people stooped to such shocking brutality and indescribable barbarism." Loudin proposed a protest at the fair. Wells determined to publish a pamphlet linking the struggles of black Americans in the urban North to the horrors of lynching across the South. She enlisted Douglass's support and began raising money for the publication.[20]

Before the pamphlet was even written, Wells and Douglass became embroiled in a larger debate over the participation of African Americans at the exposition or, in broader terms, which Wells and Douglass well recognized, the status of black Americans within American society. The fight, which played out in the black press and in a flurry of letters among black leaders, centered on a proposed "Colored Day" at the fair. The proposal came from a black group in Boston, which urged African Americans to raise money for what some called Jubilee Day. Fair officials had offered to subsidize similar days for other national groups. The proposal for a "Colored Day" sparked controversy among those angered by the formal exclusion of black American achievements from the fair's exhibits.

Anger turned to outrage when fair officials offered free watermelons for the jubilee. Wells called it "a mockery on its face," adding that it "showed a lack of dignity, self-respect and judgment, to say nothing of good taste." Before the watermelon controversy, Douglass had offered tepid support for the Jubilee Day and, in the weeks following, received a number of complaints about Wells's "venomous" attacks on an African American group.[21] Many elite black Chicagoans were skeptical about the proposal. The ministers at the city's three leading black churches—Olivet Baptist, Quinn Chapel, and Bethel African Methodist Episcopal (AME)—urged their congregants to boycott "Colored American Day."[22] The Colored Men's Protective Association, a civic organization, also rejected the plan.[23]

Douglass was in Chicago, staying at the Palmer House, when the fair opened. The "venerable ex-slave," as the *Tribune* described him, was by then ambivalent about the "Colored American Day." "When the matter was first proposed, I concluded it might be a good thing," he commented. "Since, however, there has been a great objection raised, and I can easily see that it may not be such a good thing after all to give my race a special day as is accorded the Indians and foreign nations." The point, he noted, was that black Americans were not foreigners but Americans struggling for a place in the national polity. "We are fighting the color line very strongly and our people think that to have a special 'colored people's day' would be to acknowledge that we are of a different class, as it were." A day devoted to black Americans suggested that the fair and, by extension, the nation were racially segregated. Douglass concluded on a gentler note. "If the day, however, is to be a day of song, I shall be pleased to do all I can to help it along and will make an address on the occasion."[24]

"Colored American Day" was more than a day of song. It was, largely to Douglass's credit, a moment for collective celebration for a people so recently released from slavery and of pragmatic contemplation of the struggles still unfinished. For many, it was not a symbol of exclusion but an assertion of the accomplishments and beauty of African American culture. "Shaking his white mane and trembling under the vehemence of his eloquence the old man [Douglass] for more than half an hour held 2,500 persons under a spell," the *Tribune* commented the next day. (The paper, though seemingly awed by Douglass's oratory, relegated its report on "Colored American Day" to page 3, despite putting most fair news on the front page that summer.) A crowd—about one-third white—gathered at 3:00 pm on August 25 in the festival hall for the program. Douglass, entering with the white abolitionist and sister of Harriet Beecher Stowe, Isabella Ward Hooker, was the first speaker. "Men talk of the negro problem," Douglass began. "There is no negro problem." As he had since antebellum days, Douglass called on white Americans to live up to the promise of the nation's founding documents. "The problem is whether the American people have honesty enough, loyalty enough, honor enough, patriotism enough to live up to their own Constitution."[25]

Douglass talked of the torture and murder of black Americans "in fourteen States of this Union" where "wild mobs have taken the place of law." "But stop," he added. Americans must recognize the "progress" black Americans had made in the thirty years since emancipation. African American history, Douglass suggested, justified black Americans' full participation in the American nation. Douglass's speech was followed by a tenor solo of the white American composer Dudley Buck's aria "The Shadows Deepen," a Verdi aria, a violin performance, and several recitations, including a poem by the young Paul Laurence Dunbar. The program was organized by Chicago's elite and designed to demonstrate African Americans' education and immersion in European culture. Black Americans, denied representation at the fair, had shown they were as civilized as white Americans, if not more so.[26]

At the Congress on Religions, where Fannie Barrier Williams made her powerful exposition debut, Williams similarly paid tribute to European culture. The Congress opened with a grand procession of religious leaders and scholars from around the globe. "There were Caucasians, Mongolians and Ethiopians," the *Tribune* noted, offering a commonplace categorization of the world's "races." They were seated on the "huge platform" of the Hall of Columbus, "the strangers from the farther points of the world with their picturesque garb." Bishop Benjamin William Arnett, the only black American invited to speak on the congress's opening day, told the crowd that he "represent[ed] on the one side the Africans in Africa and the Africans in America." In a slight jab at the European visitors, the bishop commented that an "African Jefferson" would soon appear to lead the African nations to independence.[27]

In her speech, Williams contended that black Americans, educated and

Christianized, had moved far from the "uncivilized" black Africans. Afri-cans were, in Williams's view, a separate people. "The fetishes and crudities of the dark continent have long since ceased to be a part of his [the African American's] life and character," she said. "He is by every mark, impulse and aspiration an American Christian." Drawing on the rhetoric of race scien-tists, Williams affirmed a social hierarchy, but in Williams's view "civiliza-tion" implied behavior, education, manners, and morality. Civilization was learned, a mark of the progress of humanity, not an immutable stamp of race. Williams was not alone among late nineteenth-century black activists in "commit[ting] to the myth of civilization as progress," to borrow Wil-son Moses's phrase. Alexander Crummell similarly urged black people to conform to the values of European culture. It was an elitist argument, sepa-rating well-to-do black Americans from black laborers and the rural poor, who might be more "civilized" than Africans but still required education and moral uplift. Williams was implicitly affirming the culture celebrated at the exposition, a European tradition embodied in Beaux Arts architec-ture, classical music, poetry, and art. She was placing elite black Americans within that tradition and urging all black Americans to strive to achieve the morality and manners of a European culture.[28]

Though Williams's politics would shift after 1900 to emphasizing black self-help, at the exposition before largely white audiences, Williams made a case for African American inclusion in a liberal vision of American poli-tics. Williams indirectly took up the question that had divided women activists at the fair, claiming that Christianity must be racially integrated. Christianity powerfully bound whites and blacks together. White and black Christians, moreover, had an obligation to bring the "purifying power of religion" to improve the "condition of the colored people of the South." Religion, Williams contended, should not recognize race.[29] At the World's Fair—where religious leaders celebrated the "spiritual freedom" of the United States—she reminded her audience that slavery had denigrated white Christians and blighted American society. Slavery—not biology—had caused "every moral imperfection that mars the character of the col-ored American." In speeches presented in the mid-1890s she argued for individual rights and equal opportunities for all, especially in detailing the dignity and hardships of black women workers. American history, she sug-gested, would deepen understanding of present inequalities; education, re-ligion, and dignified struggle would transform black America's future.

With Williams's speech and the black women's highly publicized battle for representation at the exposition, black women fashioned themselves as political activists and representatives of "the race." In the years that followed, African American women would face the complex questions of how to represent both their race and womanhood; they would be jeered as "unladylike" for their assertive politics while at the same time urged by black men to work for the good of the race. Black women's appearances at the fair and their debates over African American representation in the exhibits demonstrated that there was no consensus among black women—or men—over where and how African Americans claimed a place in American society.

"The Exhibit of the progress made by the race in 25 years of freedom as against 250 years of slavery, would have been the greatest tribute to the greatness and progressiveness of American institutions which could have been shown to the world," began Ida B. Wells's pamphlet that appeared that August. Titled *The Reason Why the Colored American is Not in the World's Columbian Exposition*, it was distributed from the Haitian pavilion, where Douglass, as Haiti's consul to the United States, welcomed visitors. Fundraising had fallen well short of Wells's $5,000 goal; in July she wrote to Judge Tourgée that the "outlook for the pamphlet seemed so discouraging" that it would be impossible to issue the pamphlet in languages other than English. The preface alone was published in French, German, and English.[30] The six chapters that followed, written by Douglass, Ferdinand Barnett, I. Garland Penn, and two unidentified authors (likely a combination of Tourgée's and Wells's work) traced the history of what Douglass called "race hate," discriminatory legislation, the emergence of the convict lease system, and the "injustice of lynch law." Barnett wrote of black Americans' disappointment at being left out of the World's Fair national commission and the fight for inclusion in the planning of the fair. Penn, who five years later published a history of the black press, wrote of African American achievements in art and literature, the professions, and the trades, including a list of sixty inventions patented by black inventors, which he argued could have been exhibited in the industrial pavilions. Much of the pamphlet, an effort to challenge the Midway's crude racial hierarchies, recounted African American achievements since emancipation.[31]

In her chapter "Lynch Law," Wells effectively linked the brutal murders of black men and women since emancipation to African Americans' struggles for economic stability. She provided a brief history of lynching, offered lynching statistics broken down by year and state, and in her stark prose detailed several of the brutal murders that had occurred since the opening of the fair designed to celebrate the advances of American civilization. The

Photo of Ida B. Wells-Barnett, ca. 1910. Courtesy of
University of Chicago Libraries.

irony could hardly have been lost on her readers. It was her economic arguments, though, supported by irrefutable evidence, that proved most controversial to white audiences. Lynching, Wells demonstrated, was rarely a spontaneous reaction to a rape. Rather, it was most often a well-organized mob attack on African Americans accused of breaching local customs or seeking economic mobility. It was, she demonstrated, a modern and urban phenomenon with the murderous violence common in the "so-called queen cities of the South." Wells's pamphlet powerfully demolished the image of the city as a site of benign consumption (though public lynching provided another type of spectacle). The pamphlet was widely circulated among fairgoers and publicized in the African American press.[32]

The World's Columbian Exposition proved, paradoxically, an emblem of white America's disdain for African Americans and a stage where black intellectuals and writers demonstrated their literary skills and profound understanding of American politics. The event brought together black Americans, both those who traveled hundreds of miles to visit the White City and those who read the avid reports on the fair in the black press. It sparked a collective national protest and, in the process, generated the shared experience of articulating outrage and celebrating the achievements of black Americans. For many outside Chicago, the fair made the urban North seem real and vital, a place that encapsulated the aspirations and opportunities for an expanding black nation. For black Chicagoans, the experience of the fair—of protest and amusement, of political debate and scholarly discovery—reinforced political and intellectual links to black activists around the nation, while setting Chicago on the vanguard of black culture and politics.

The fair, along with drawing national attention to Chicago, propelled Chicago's black women into local politics. Few men had adhered to T. Thomas Fortune's rejection of politics—even Fortune quickly reentered political debates; the fair experience demonstrated that race politics, broadly conceived and effectively articulated, could gain national attention. Elite and educated, a small group of black women moved to participate in urban politics. They were divided over priorities and strategies and clearly did not represent the views of all black urban women. With their protests and new national visibility, the activists made Chicago a crucial meeting place for black women's organizations and a testing ground for African American women's social reform organizations. Most important, women reformers politicized urban space, helping to make the city itself the terrain for social struggle and, despite many differences, racial unity.

Wells, hoping for more subscriptions for the pamphlet, decided to stay in Chicago for a few months after the fair closed. She also had a growing affection for Ferdinand Barnett and felt that Chicago, at least the city's black women, needed her. There was no black women's club in Chicago, though there were "Ladies' Day" meetings at the Tourgée Club, a black men's club named to honor the judge's support for the race. In the fall of 1893, inspired by a speech by British social reformer and minister W. T. Stead, Wells helped establish a new women's group. In 1894, Stead's vivid exposé of vice, poverty, and corruption in the city, *If Christ Came to Chicago*, spurred the formation of the city's leading reform group, the Civic Federation of Chicago. Wells remembered years later that Stead had said the city's black women too needed an organization to fight racist social conditions. Wells suggested that Mary Jones, widow of John Jones and one of the city's most prominent black women, lead the effort. By September 1893, the first black women's club in Illinois was established. Later chartered as the Ida B. Wells Club, the group boasted more than three hundred members the following February.[33]

Stead's speech, quickly followed by the establishment of citywide social reform organizations, marked the beginning of a new era of concern about the urban environment and a new politics that encompassed the social reform work of women and men, black and white, sometimes working inside but more often outside city hall. African American women's clubs and institutions, like those of their white peers, aimed to soften the blows of the industrializing economy on unskilled workers and to provide support and community to migrants. Chicago's population reached more than one million in 1890 and would double by 1910, drawing laborers from eastern and southern Europe and the American South. Industrial work was dangerous. Sweatshops, slaughterhouses, lumber mills, and glove, shoe, and garment factories left thousands of workers dead or severely injured each year. Housing for poor and laboring families was often unsafe. Disease raged through crowded tenement apartments, while families struggling to survive on inadequate wages sent children to work or to scavenge for food and coal. Social reform organizations provided needed services and at times advocated for the rights of the urban poor.

Women were particularly visible in the turn-of-the-century urban reform efforts. The struggles for emancipation and of the postwar rebuilding of black communities had inspired many young women activists, white and black. Chicago's most famous white woman activist, Jane Addams, like many of her generation, followed the path of her abolitionist father into social reform work. Others, like Fannie Barrier Williams and Elizabeth Lindsay Davis, had traveled south to teach in Freedman's Bureau schools. Wells, Williams, Davis, and others who moved to organize black women, quickly became part of the broader network of white and black reformers. Leading all-black organizations, they became race leaders, promoting a vision of black womanhood and adeptly articulating the central political issues facing African Americans.[34]

Chicago's African American women formed a variety of social clubs and reform institutions; sometimes the social mixed with reform work. There were literary groups that raised money for charities, though some were devoted to nothing more than "social chat and the delicacies of the occasion." Most popular among upper-class black women were clubs for playing card games such as whist and euchre. In the 1890s most clubs shifted from "diversions" to civic reform.[35] Black women, unlike white reforming women, were concerned primarily with "the social status of the race," Williams wrote. Another clubwoman commented that there may be "Afro-American women who ape the follies of this class," the leisured, card-playing elite, but "the colored woman's club is an eleemosynary organization. There may be a social feature and some attention may be given to self-culture, but these are secondary aims." The clubs' purpose was to "relieve suffering, reclaim the erring and to advance the cause of education."[36]

In July 1896, just as the nation's Supreme Court declared the racial separation of public facilities constitutional, members of Chicago's black women's clubs—just two at the time—joined African American women from across the nation in Washington, DC, to form a national movement. The National Association of Colored Women (NACW), founded by elite and educated black women, took on the task of educating the poor and improving the living conditions of African Americans, rural and urban. With its motto "Lifting as we climb," the NACW aimed to advance "the condition of the race." The organization forged a strong national network of women that paralleled and intersected with expanding networks of African American journalists and political activists. Women working with the NACW helped to create a new national black civic culture.[37]

Chicago's women's clubs and reform groups were racially segregated, developing parallel and largely similar agendas within very different political contexts. Many more white women reformers were college educated and came from families wealthy enough to support their reform work. Though some black club leaders were college graduates, many African American club members had not attended college, and many worked for wages outside the home to help sustain their families. Williams, in an uncharacteristically aggressive move, engaged in a widely publicized battle to join the Chicago Women's Club; she was the only black member for nearly thirty years. Interracial meetings were few, and biracial reform efforts tended to involve club leaders and elite black women only. Racial segregation of clubs and reform work was reinforced by racial segregation of residential neigh-borhoods; reform organizations tended to serve their neighborhoods.

Despite racial segregation of services and often of personnel, African American reform and social improvement institutions relied heavily on white philanthropy. Jessie Strong Bradley Lawson, wife of the publisher of the *Chicago Daily News*, supported Wells-Barnett's Negro Fellowship League. Louise de Koven Bowen, another wealthy white reformer, supported several black women's organizations. In the 1920s, the Julius Rosenwald Fund, launched by the president of Sears, Roebuck and Company in 1917, was the largest and most influential of white donors to African American ed-ucation and social reform work. The fund, while supporting several Afri-can American universities in the South, helped maintain two settlement houses in African American neighborhoods. White philanthropy, though welcomed by African American clubs, highlighted the economic inequali-ties between the city's black and white residents: the tiny black elite and a much wealthier, larger class of white industrialists, business leaders, and professionals able to sustain substantial philanthropic work. White sup-port raised questions about whether black women could form egalitarian alliances with whites.[38]

Many black women were inspired by church organizations to minister to the needs of the rural and urban poor. Many also sought to "uplift the race" by establishing literary clubs, educational programs, public health campaigns, and charitable organizations. Many were spurred to action by the brutal lynching of black men across the South. The first black women's clubs in the nation were organized following an 1892 meeting in New York where Wells spoke at a fund-raising rally to support her lecture tour of Great Britain. Wells's powerful investigations of lynching challenged the dominant discourses of black men's sexuality and demonstrated that rape of white women was simply an excuse for racial violence. Her published re-ports prompted some women to organize to protect the lives of black men and to defend the virtue of black womanhood.[39] While lynching generated a collective response to brutal violence, urbanization and the increasingly visible struggles of the urban poor in southern towns and northern cities prompted renewed reform efforts.[40]

Like elite black women working to assist the African American poor, many white reformers sought to aid the indigent European immigrants in northern cities. Many had become involved in the sanitary reform move-ment in the 1870s and 1880s, arguing for municipal services to improve working-class and poor neighborhoods. The sanitarians, as the reformers were known, effectively linked the material well-being of the family home to municipal services like sewer and water lines, street cleaning and garbage pickups. They argued that the health of individual households directly and literally determined the health of the city: contagious diseases caused by insanitary living conditions spread quickly from tenements to cottages and mansions. The sanitarians focused on the impact of the urban environment on the health of the family. The sanitarians, moreover, in highlighting sanitation in the urban environment, drew reformers' attention to the spatial relations of health and poverty. They, like the urban reformers who followed them, effectively made urban space a political issue.[41]

Black women also directed attention to urban sanitary conditions but, as always, with slightly different political motives. Most understood the problem as a result of racial discrimination in wages and segregation in housing, though as Michelle Mitchell argues, concerns about urban housing and public health were directly linked to broader, less tangible politics of "racial destiny," which typically merged notions of moral, material, and political progress. Black women, for example, were concerned about overcrowding caused by high rents and low wages in racially segregated neighborhoods. The practice of taking in boarders, more common among European immigrants than African Americans, worried elite reformers who believed that "lodgers" threatened the morality of the children as well as the health of the family. Chicago women launched home visitation campaigns to educate new arrivals about the moral dangers of the urban environment and about strategies to maintain health and hygiene. In the early 1910s, black women led local drives against adulterated milk. The *Defender* ran a regular column on urban health by Wilberforce Williams, a physician always urging "uplift." Health was linked to home and morality, while the well-being of the home was, it was understood, determined largely by racial segregation of housing markets.[42]

While white women's clubs and reform organizations tended to attract the wives and daughters of professionals and businessmen, black women's clubs drew from a broader spectrum of African American society. In African American clubs, the wives of lawyers, doctors, and ministers worked alongside hairdressers, teachers, and the wives of postal clerks and shop owners. Some were college educated, others not. Class and church affiliation as well as political commitments and cultural interests determined which clubs women joined.[43] There was a hierarchy among the social clubs, and often black and white women used the clubs to climb upward socially and to signify their class position. The Old Settlers Club, the Prudence Crandall Club, and the Lotus Club limited members to the city's oldest and most elite black families. But by the mid-1890s, the old settlers joined with the newer middle classes in clubs that worked to assist the poor. After the turn of the century, both the *Chicago Defender* and the *Broad Ax*, reported on the admirable work of "race advancement," though Julius Taylor, editor of the *Broad Ax*, regularly attacked well-to-do clubwomen for their "social ambitions."[44] Club membership was in and of itself an expression of middle-class status.

Not all agreed on goals or causes, and there was, as Fannie Barrier Williams scornfully noted, much jockeying for power within the clubs. But there was enough unity for the clubs to join together in the in the first statewide federation, the Illinois Federation of Colored Women's Clubs in 1899.[45] Elizabeth Lindsay Davis, a leading activist and historian of the women's club movement, listed more than thirty clubs and institutions launched and led by women. In her 1919 account of the state club movement, *The Story of the Illinois Federation of Colored Women's Clubs*, Davis noted that women's work touched all aspects of African American life, from infancy to old age, including housing, health, work, and education. Some women organized clubs to raise money to assist the ill or needy; others established institutions like the home for the aged. The women, though of diverse backgrounds and interests, were united in their desire to improve the "material, mental and moral progress made by our people," the state organization's constitution asserted. They saw themselves as improving individual lives while also boosting the status of the race in America.[46]

The Ida B. Wells Club was considered the "mother of the woman's clubs in Illinois and Chicago." The club had organized Wells-Barnett's wedding reception, as the bride was traveling across the state, "delivering addresses nightly." The club also took on more serious endeavors. It held a Christmas benefit that raised fifty dollars for the Tourgée Club, and in 1894 club members raised money to prosecute a policeman "for killing an innocent colored man" on the West Side. Wells-Barnett quit the club in the late 1890s after giving birth to her second child, but the club continued its educational and political work, raising money to establish the first African American orchestra in Chicago and, at Wells-Barnett's request, raising money for a kindergarten at Bethel Church.[47]

Black women became, in Fannie Barrier Williams's words, "civic mothers of the race."[48] The Gaudeamus Charity Club (meaning "Let Us Rejoice") was devoted to "education, charity and child welfare," while the Labor of Love Club raised money for the Home for the Aged and Infirm Colored People. In the 1910s, Ezella Mathis Carter, "aware of the alarming evil conditions and much suffering" in Chicago, organized the Chicago Hairdressers to "relieve sickness, distress, render legal advice, counsel for those needing a larger vision in life." The clubs, drawing on their founders' skills and social influence, provided services and financial support to the needy, encouraged artistic and spiritual pursuits among black Chicagoans, and sought to improve "education, the integrity of the home, the interest and support of the best women of every community."[49]

With their work in women's clubs and social reform organizations, women, white and black, effectively brought politics to bear on women's traditional realm of activity, the family home and residential neighborhood.[50] By the 1890s and early decades of the twentieth century, women activists regularly petitioned city hall for health inspections of tenements and factories, pressured politicians to pass legislation to regulate work hours and housing conditions in the city, and pushed for the establishment of hospital wards for those suffering from contagious disease. Women sanitarians and the urban reformers who continued their work contended that the cleanliness of streets, alleys, and run-down cottages and tenements was government's responsibility. The provision of government funds for sewer and water lines, hospitals, and schools quickly became hotly debated political issues, with women activists at the center of the debates.[51] Women effectively expanded the realm of municipal politics beyond the distribution of patronage jobs, saloon licenses, streetcar contracts, and street paving. By 1900, political rhetoric—if not municipal action—increasingly addressed street-cleaning contracts, tenement regulations, adulterated milk and beef, corruption among factory and food inspectors, along with women activists' greatest concerns: the vice trades—gambling, liquor sales, and brothels.

The battle to suppress vice challenged black women in ways incomprehensible to most whites. In the increasingly segregated African American South Side, business opportunities were limited, and capital for investment in property or business was almost nonexistent in the decades surrounding the turn of the century. Few white banks would lend money to black home buyers or business investors. Vice—the small-time policy rackets, brothels, and illicit liquor sales—became for some black men a primary method for raising capital for investment in licit business. (There were also plenty of white men and women profiting from the vice trades.) Vice entrepreneurs also had a forthright interest in local politics; they paid policemen to turn a blind eye and supported mayors and city council members who, though fulminating against vice, overlooked their activities. But running a gambling den did not preclude concern for African American civil rights or civic improvement. Elite black women sometimes found themselves collecting contributions from the men whose businesses they protested.[52] White reformers might face different ethical dilemmas: some white reformers who protested dangerous working conditions and low wages were linked to the city's captains of industry as family friends, husbands, or fathers.

For black women, club work had a distinctly political edge. White women could assert that reform work was simply a natural extension of their labor and identities as women. They were "municipal housekeepers." White society had long denied black women the status of "woman" and the ability to participate in the virtues of nineteenth-century womanhood. Black women were seen as capable of physical labor, while proper white women were occupied by leisure; black women were represented in public discourse as erotic and sexually active, while virtue and respectability were associated with white women's lack of sexual interest and knowledge. African American women, Williams wrote, have "had no place in the Republic of free and independent womanhood of America."[53] The black women's club movement in its practice and self-presentation challenged the dominant and demeaning discourses of black womanhood.

But black women activists also received a prickly response within their own race. Many women found their womanhood and respectability challenged by black men. For some, remaking the family home and asserting rights to property and home ownership were ways to both express women's interests and promote African American advancement.[54] But even those who were deeply sensitive to the sometimes conflicting calls of women's virtue and race politics were attacked in the press as "taking on the part of men." W. E. B. DuBois was only the most visible of the critics of women's activism. In a speech at Spelman College, DuBois called women the spiritual mothers of the race, who should not displace the public work of husbands and fathers. Unlike many middle-class black men, reforming women did not see a conflict between activism and respectability. Club work offered an opportunity to be both virtuous and political, to claim the rights of womanhood while pursuing the rights of the race.[55]

The clubs, reflecting black Americans' acceptance of dominant gender relations, affirmed women's responsibility for the family home. The Woman's Civic League, organized in Quinn Chapel in 1897 and counting more than two hundred members, distributed "Christmas cheer . . . to the children and aged of the community." The American Rose Art Club, one of the most active clubs in the state, brought together young matrons for weekly meetings to discuss "household economics and the artistic needlework they do, under the guidance of an expert instructor." The Cornell Charity Club, taking up women's nineteenth-century role in civic charity, raised money for "prompt assistance in all worthy cases." The group also donated money to support the Ebenezer Church "in its work of feeding the unemployed." Almost all the clubs listed help for the "sick and needy" among their work. The Imperial Art Club, which began as an embroidery club, became a leading fund-raiser for the "old folks home," another organization launched by black women. The club's motto captured the self-abnegating spirit of nineteenth-century middle-class womanhood. "Not Ourselves, but Others," could have applied to any of the women's organizations.[56]

African American women's clubs fostered a sense of racial identity that separated them from white reformers. They took on the causes of black civil rights and fought racial violence. The Bethel Literary and Historical Club met at Bethel Church each Sunday. In 1910, more than three hundred members attended a meeting to hear Ida Wells-Barnett report on a lynching in Cairo, Illinois. The meeting raised $13.25 to fund her investigation.[57] The Rockford Ladies Civic and Social Club took the motto "Onward and Upward," encouraging black women to work to improve "the race." That distinctive identity, and the question of whether or how African American women might ally with white reformers was a subject of much debate. Some sought to integrate with white women or at least to copy the rules, rites, and activities of white women's clubs. Others, however, questioned whether black women and white had shared interests in American society.

Fannie Barrier Williams, who left a long record of her views in magazine articles and published lectures, typified the clubwomen's ambivalence about white America. Wealthy, college-educated, reared in New England, and light-skinned, Williams bore all the characteristics of an avid integrationist. Her successful battle for membership in the elite white Chicago Women's Club reflected those politics, especially her belief that the educated elite, black and white, could and should find common cause. Yet just a few years later, Williams suggested a different vision of black club work and of black women's racial identity. In a 1904 essay, Williams deplored clubs that were "imitative and not original, in their plans of work," simply copying the work of white women's clubs. "The absurdity of this is all too obvious," she wrote. African Americans, the children and grandchildren of the enslaved, were in a unique position in American society, suffering their "own social perils." Williams's shifting politics may reflect her growing alliance with Booker T. Washington; "self-help" appeared more frequently in her early twentieth-century writing. But Williams, a native northerner married to a politically active lawyer, believed that self-help could accompany aggressive political demands. "The members of individual clubs must study the needs of the community in which they live," Williams argued.

"They must lay hold of the problems that lie nearest them and be honest enough to attempt only that which they know most about and which ought to be done in the interest of their own homes, their own families and the community in which they live." Rather than mingling with white women's clubs, African American clubwomen should work to sustain their own communities. Women's work was race work.[58]

Williams was by no means a racial separatist. Indeed, she readily boasted of her acquaintances among the white elite in Chicago. But in calling on clubwomen to work for "the benefit of the people," she acknowledged the racial segregation of civic life and the distinctive collective experiences of black people in America.[59] Williams, though described as petite and soft-spoken, was haughty and overtly elitist. Class was of critical importance in Williams's worldview, separating the cultured from the degraded rural poor. She believed the women's club movement was an "effort of a few competent in behalf of the many incompetent." She conceived of women's clubs, working where they lived, as "establishing a sort of special relationship between those who help and those who need help," creating a new African American community. It would be a community of black Americans lifted out of poverty and educated in "a finer sensitiveness as to the rights and wrongs, the proprieties and improprieties," of good citizenship.[60]

In linking notions of community to citizenship, Williams drew on the ideals of the growing settlement-house movement. Williams, who seemed to cherish her class status almost as much as she heeded the demands of her racial identity, recognized that African Americans faced limits on their citizenship rights in suffrage, fair trials, and opportunities for social mobility. A distinctive racial geography was emerging in Chicago—to Williams's growing anger and disgust. Yet she recognized that the increasingly racially segregated city could become the basis for a new multilayered African American community. Williams's views were not representative of all African American women. But she, like Wells-Barnett and Davis, increasingly articulated the clubwomen's role in constituting the new black community and, in the process, making urban housing, neighborhoods, schools, and public spaces the subjects of political struggle. They were politicizing urban space and securing a place for themselves in the political life of the city.

The city's settlement houses highlighted the distinctive geography of urban reform work. Jane Addams and Ellen Gates Starr launched Chicago's first settlement house, Hull House, on Halsted Street in 1889 amid the homes of impoverished European immigrants. It was followed by several others, including the University of Chicago Settlement established by Mary McDowell in Back of the Yards and Graham Taylor's Chicago Commons on the North Side. Each aimed to serve a particular urban neighborhood. The settlements were both homes and community centers, housing volunteers—women and men—who worked to improve urban health and education, work, and housing conditions.[61]

Amid rapid immigration from southern and eastern Europe, neighborhoods took on the national character of their new residents. Urban settlers, following the paths of previous generations, moved onto blocks and shared homes with fellow countrymen and family. There was "Little Hell," filling with southern Italians; "Smokey Hollow," home to Italians and Irish; and the largely Polish "Goose Island," along the northern bend of the Chicago River. The settlement houses increasingly identified with the cultures and needs of their neighbors: McDowell's with impoverished Lithuanian and Bohemian immigrants, Hull House with Polish and Italian West Siders. The settlements' service community, though rarely delineated, often overlapped with the contours of a newly forming ethnic community—even as most Chicago blocks contained a mix of nationalities. Generally, each settlement's domain was determined by the distance local people could walk to participate in settlement-house life.[62]

Residents of Hull House created maps, which came to represent the needs of their neighbors and functioned as a visual depiction of poverty and growing urban inequality. The maps, based on door-to-door canvassing of the neighborhood, were color coded according to residents' nationality, work type, and number of residents in each dwelling. The Hull House maps, published in a volume with essays about the settlement and its neighbors, were designed to draw the attention of well-off Chicagoans to the plight of the urban poor. The maps were publicity materials, intended to reveal areas of the city far from the homes of the white middle class. They made visible a social geography easily neglected by those who lived several miles from the immigrant West Side. Even as the maps disturbed the consciences of elite Chicagoans, or so settlement workers hoped, they made the city legible. The masses of immigrants bringing languages, beliefs, values, and customs foreign to native-born Americans were, on paper at least, lined in neat rows, visually comprehensible in the Hull House maps. The maps may have fostered some understanding and sympathy of the elite native-born for impoverished immigrants. More likely, the maps suggested that within the expanding city, there was a place for every social group.[63]

The philosophy of the settlement movement, as articulated by Addams, revolved around a notion of community that was both social and geographic. Addams's vision of community legitimized women's collective activity outside the home by defining the family home as linked through a web of mutual support to neighborhood homes. At the same time, Addams contended that the well-being of the home and the neighborhood depended on government resources, in effect politicizing women's urban reform work. Addams's vision of community—the "cooperative commonwealth," which she described so eloquently in many published articles—brought together people of diverse nationalities living in close proximity. Polish, Italian, and eastern European Jewish people might meet at Hull House and, according to Addams's argument, affirm their cultural differences while seeing themselves as part of a larger West Side community. Addams could thus justify refusing black children in the Hull House kindergarten because by the turn of the twentieth century, there were few black children living on the West Side.[64]

Just as nationality was imprinted on urban space by the immigrants who moved to Chicago and gathered in particular neighborhoods, so too were settlement-house activists remaking the city's social geography according to who gained access to their clubs, nurseries, bathhouses, employment bureaus, and education programs. The settlements' aim was to "revive" the Old World "neighborhship" destroyed by the move to the industrial city, wrote Graham Taylor: "the interests of the whole city are best promoted by cultivating this neighborhood consciousness amongst all the people of every locality."[65] Addams envisioned a diverse urban community. It was an ideal, she readily acknowledged, shattered by long-standing conflicts in American society between workers and employers, immigrants and the native-born, white and black Americans. Through Hull House, Addams created a community around collective activities and shared resources on the city's West Side. It was just one of many communities forged by turn-of-the-century activists and defined as much by collective experiences as by common social identity and shared urban geography. Settlement houses, with few exceptions, were, like the women's clubs, racially segregated.[66]

Settlement residents explicitly fostered the formation of new communities—and remapped social relations in urban space—when they helped organize neighborhood improvement associations. Addams and others, concerned about garbage-strewn alleys and dusty, unpaved streets, began to organize residents block by block. Meetings were held at the settlement houses. The groups sponsored street-cleaning events as well as protests at city hall. The aim was for residents to develop a collective interest in improving their neighborhood, to forge the bonds of community among those living in close proximity, and to use the new organizations to fight for municipal services.[67]

But community groups could easily become tools of social exclusion. In a city where community was increasingly defined by residents' race or nationality, white residents, rich and poor, sought to separate their homes and civic activities from those of black Chicagoans. Racial segregation of schools and housing, neglected by law, was increasingly enforced by white organizations and mob violence. Block clubs and neighborhood associations in the early twentieth century often turned to "indignation meetings in which hysterical protestations were registered" when a black family moved nearby. Williams was particularly incensed when her neighbors organized to bar black families from the elite Hyde Park community surrounding the University of Chicago.[68] "Many civil, social and political wrongs, and lessening of opportunities are plainly evident to people who have lived here long enough to know local conditions," commented Williams.[69]

Lines of racial segregation were hardening as a result of complex commercial, cultural, and historic forces. Black tenants, squeezed by high rents—ranging from 10 to 50 percent above those charged whites—and low wages, moved into buildings poorly maintained, often by white landlords living far away. "The consequent limited area in which the Negro is compelled to live" fueled demand for housing and spurred rent increases, wrote Monroe Nathan Work in his 1902 MA theses at the University of Chicago. "In general," he added, black Chicagoans "are compelled to rent whatever is offered, and at the price demanded."[70] Sociologist Alzada P. Comstock commented in her 1912 study of African American housing, "Colored people of all positions in life found it nearly impossible to escape the relatively small and well-defined areas" on the South and West Sides. "The explanation for this condition of affairs among the colored people," Comstock continued, "was comparatively simple." White people could not stand having "colored people living on white residence streets, colored children attending schools with white children, or entering into other semi-social relations with them."[71] It wasn't quite that simple. But the result was that race (and racism) increasingly determined where people lived, as well as where they worked and the material quality of their homes.

Black clubwomen did not create racially segregated cities, but as they identified the people they served, they recognized the newly racialized urban landscape. The always acerbic editor of the Broad Ax, Julius Taylor, accused the women's clubs of "pander[ing] to cake walks and Jim-Crowism." He was partly right. The nurseries, as well as the homes for single girls and for the aged operated by black clubwomen were designed to address the needs of the black urban poor, the people neglected by white civic organizations. In 1893, when Ida Wells proposed the creation of a kindergarten for African American children, some of the black elite accused her of "drawing the color line." As Anne Meis Knupfer comments, the color line had already been drawn by white-run nurseries that refused admittance to black children.[72] The clubwomen's political work, following the lines drawn by real estate entrepreneurs and white neighborhood organizations, traced the boundaries of black residential areas.

By working in the increasingly segregated African American neighborhoods on the South Side, black women were creating, in Jane Addams's words, the "bonds of community." The Phillis (sometimes Phyllis) Wheatley Woman's Club, among the best known of the city's black women's clubs, was organized on March 17, 1896. The club was "conceived as a neighborhood betterment organization" and targeted the South Side community rapidly becoming the heart of the city's African American neighborhoods. The club's first president was Elizabeth Lindsey Davis, a native of Peoria, Illinois, and a teacher who when she married gave up her profession to devote herself to church service and social reform. The group "began fighting saloons in proximity to the schools and succeeded in closing one that was particularly disreputable," Davis wrote. In 1904, club members opened a day nursery at Eighteenth and State Streets. Two years later, concerned about the young black women moving to the city, the club gave up its other work and established a home for single women. The nine-room house at 3530 Forest Avenue opened in 1908 and became the focus of much fundraising and organizational work among the city's black women.[73] Its location on an elite residential block marked the respectable status of the young women residents while implicitly recognizing the racial segregation of housing and work that kept them in the South Side neighborhood.

Some clubs sought to cross the color line, aiming, it seems, to use their organizations to build integrated communities, but with little success. The Cornell Charity Club, organized on January 23, 1902, near Fifty-Fourth and Wright Streets (later Normal Boulevard), sought to render "prompt assistance in all worthy cases . . . without regard to Race, Creed, Color or any other condition." The club was located on the edge of Hyde Park and likely aimed to sustain integration in the neighborhood as in the club. Its efforts were unsuccessful. The organizations helped by the Cornell club were uniformly African American. Some of Hyde Park's leading white residents formed their own neighborhood improvement association; this one aimed not at assisting neighbors but at ridding the community of black residents, including the Williamses.[74]

Even when they sought to overcome the barriers of residential segregation, black clubwomen and white clubwomen faced white hostility. In 1904, Wells-Barnett was a key force behind the city's first interracial settlement, the Frederick Douglass Center, whose location and the struggle around it typify the obstacles faced by integrationists. The settlement aimed to "promote a just and amicable relation between the white and colored people," to provide services for black families, and to study the "colored people in Chicago . . . and establish a scientific basis of inquiry and helpfulness." The center, which was launched by Wells-Barnett and Celia Parker Woolley, generated controversy from the start, especially when local papers reported on a meeting of white and black women at Woolley's home. Woolley was a white writer, Unitarian minister, and daughter of abolitionists. Both Williams and Wells-Barnett were infuriated by the reports, which apparently accused the white women of committing a "social crime" for "sipping tea while they talked" about the planned center.[75]

Controversy mounted when the women announced plans to locate the center on Wabash Avenue, just east of State Street, which was the unofficial line dividing white from black Chicago. East of State Street, houses were larger and residents were wealthier and generally white. Wells-Barnett and her family were among the first of the well-to-do black Chicagoans to move east of Wabash, having recently bought a house on Rhodes Avenue. They endured hostility from their neighbors, who often shook out rugs or slammed doors when Wells-Barnett appeared on the porch and allowed their white sons to torment Wells-Barnett's sons. Locating the settlement on Wabash had symbolic and social significance: it would mark a meeting ground for black and white South Siders. That was precisely what alarmed some white property owners. The owners of a building the women hoped to buy, apparently bowing to pressure from white neighbors, refused to sell. Wooley was finally able to purchase a three-story house at 3032 Wabash Avenue for $5,000. Despite the rocky start, the center expanded quickly. It gathered more than three hundred members in the following two years and sponsored a kindergarten, boys and girls clubs, and lectures from local professionals and scholars. It also provided meeting space for black women's clubs.[76]

As with so many race reform organizations, the center's leaders argued over aims and agendas. Wells-Barnett, always prickly, quarreled with Woolley over administrative issues, especially when Woolley supported the appointment of a white woman, Mary Plummer, as the center's president. Wells-Barnett, chosen vice president, was quickly caught up in a debate over the center's mission. Some, probably a majority of the members,

wanted the Douglass Center to serve as a "middle-class, race-relations sa-
lon of sorts." Its first charity ball in 1905 had been organized by Theodo-
cia B. Hall, wife of the well-known physician George Cleveland Hall. The
city's black elite attended the event in the Masonic Temple dressed in lavish
gowns and formal attire. Wells-Barnett had hoped to push the organization
in another direction. Her arguments for addressing the needs of the urban
poor gained some support from an unlikely source, the Broad Ax, which
published a series of searing attacks on the white women involved with the
Douglass Center. Whether Wells-Barnett was guiding the press coverage is
unclear, but the paper did note that she "was the only figure at the center
who was concerned with the poor in the Black Belt and in its red-light district." Wells-Barnett eventually broke with the Douglass Center and helped
launch the Negro Fellowship League, which provided health care, lodging,
and employment services to African American migrants and laborers.[77]

Wells-Barnett's anger at the white settlement women was not simply
over local issues. It was prompted by debates over the Atlanta riot in the
fall of 1906. The riot, the most horrifying mob violence since the burning
of Wilmington, North Carolina, in 1898, was sparked by the usual rumors
of black men attacking white women, along with a hard-fought gubernatorial race and the release of The Clansman, a play by Thomas Dixon. For four
days in late September, a mob of about ten thousand whites, aided by local
police, roamed Atlanta's streets, murdering and terrorizing black men and
women. The mobs burned and looted the African American middle-class
section of Brownsville, where Atlanta University and Clark College were
located. W. E. B. DuBois, heartbroken and outraged, wrote an impassioned
essay, "A Litany at Atlanta."[78] The destruction was a vivid demonstration
that class, education, and culture were no protection from white mobs.

Wells-Barnett's battle with her white allies was fueled by public debate
over the causes and meanings of the riot. Approximately a thousand African Americans fled Atlanta in the wake of the violence, including J. Max
Barber, editor of the Atlanta-based Voice of the Negro, which had published
essays by both Wells-Barnett and Williams. Barber made his way to Chicago, where he found temporary refuge in the home of the wealthy dentist
Charles Bentley and was invited to give an account of the violence in Atlanta at the Douglass Center. As Wells-Barnett remembered it, Barber's talk
at the Douglass Center was followed by some disturbing comments from
the center's white president, Mary Plummer. Emphasizing the threat of
sexual attacks by black men, Plummer claimed that "every white southern
woman she knew" was afraid to walk the streets at night. Wells-Barnett denounced Plummer's comments and reminded the crowd of her own lynch-

ing investigations. The scene was enough to prompt Wells-Barnett to break all ties with Woolley and Plummer. It was also a powerful reminder that the Chicago women were not isolated from or immune to the racism that permeated the white South.[79]

Ultimately, settlement-house work, with its politicization of women's concerns and careful drawing of the boundaries of racial communities, taught black clubwomen important lessons. Chicago's reform organizations, linked through national organizations as well as ties of friendship and camaraderie to other cities, became models for African American women's social reform work. Some, like Wells-Barnett, followed the Hull House example and opened African American settlements, centers for communal self-help, on the South and West Sides. Others took the model to other cities. Lugenia Hope, the Saint Louis–born wife of black educator and scholar John Hope, spent a few months at Hull House. After her marriage, when her husband became president of Morehouse College in Atlanta, Hope drew on the settlement-house ideal to found the Neighborhood Union; she presided over the community center for nearly thirty years.[80] Most significantly, the settlement model demonstrated that community was determined as much by collective interests as proximity. African Americans in Chicago might have diverse interests—influenced by their education, religion, birthplace, or previous status—but in the racially segregated city, activists recognized a common stake in the well-being of the city's expanding Black Belt.

Settlement-house life often spurred political action, especially as settlement workers recognized that municipal politics determined the resources available for their communities. African American women moved directly into politics in the 1890s. Many reforming women, African American and white, were suffragists. Black women linked their campaigns in local elections to the history of slavery, emancipation, and the unfinished work of Reconstruction. The women might have been as disappointed with the Republican Party as were the men who supported the Afro-American League. But women activists, unlike T. Thomas Fortune, saw civic institutions like settlement houses and reform organizations as spurs for political engagement, not alternatives to politics.[81]

The year after the World's Fair, black women finally got a chance to try out the ballot. Illinois women's suffrage organizations had been fighting for the vote since 1869; in 1890, they narrowly lost a battle for a state constitutional amendment to enfranchise women. A year later, in a hotly contested vote, the state legislature gave women voting rights in elections for school-related offices with the passage of the Woman's Suffrage Bill. Their first opportunity came in 1894 with statewide elections to the Illinois Board of Trustees. Women activists were determined to elect a woman to the board. They began, following the strategies of settlements and churches, by organizing their neighbors. Women met in their homes, organized ward-based clubs, and spoke at public meetings urging their neighbors and friends to take up the ballot.[82]

In August 1894, black and white women, though many more white, established the Illinois Women's Republican Educational Committee, to campaign for Republican women candidates to the board of trustees. Members of the Ida B. Wells Club were prominent supports of the IWREC. At the organization's third meeting, which drew 150 women and 6 men, the Wells Club occupied "nearly a whole row of chairs." They were "colored women all well-dressed and intelligent," the *Tribune* reported.[83] The *Tribune*, the city's leading Republican newspaper, could not help mocking the earnest "well-dressed" ladies. "Chicago women who desire the ballot have put their feet down firmly," the *Tribune* commented. "The fall styles and all the charming frippery that are so dear to the feminine heart are to be utterly forgotten." That November, women came out in large numbers to cast their first ballots.[84]

What seemed a small and even trivial election for university trustees became, in the speeches and essays of black women that fall, a campaign for voting rights and for "the peculiar interests of the colored race," as Williams wrote. The women who joined the campaign were decidedly Republican. Many were skeptical of the interracial claims of the IWREC. Some continued to distrust the Republican Party. Williams, in a November 1894 essay for the *Women's Era*, called unquestioned devotion to the Republican Party "folly and neglect of self-interest." There were a handful of Democratic black women's clubs mentioned in the Democratic press. Most women supported black Republican clubs, which were organized in the First, Third, and Twenty-Third Wards.[85]

Black women joined the boisterous crowd at the Central Music Hall in mid-October for a Republican rally. Ida Dempsey was among the black women speakers. She was born into a free black community in Indiana in 1859, married postal worker Dillard Dempsey, and devoted much of her energy to reform work, including serving on the board of the Frederick Douglass Center. Dempsey urged black women to vote. Education, she noted, was important to all women; it was an extension of their duties within the home. "What the home was, the children were, and what the children were, the state was," the *Tribune* reported of her speech. Education was a particular concern to black women. "They [black women] remembered the dark days of American slavery, when it was a crime to teach a black man to read." The election would "show how deeply interested they were" in Illinois education.[86] It also demonstrated the ways women, when they chose to, moved easily from domestic to civic life. The campaign brought together white and black women's activists for a brief and well-coordinated campaign and secured for several black women entry into local and state women's networks. It would be another two decades before Illinois women expanded their voting rights.

By 1912, suffragists, arguing that women would cleanse politics of corruption just as they cleaned their own homes, had gained support from progressives in both parties. Hull House had helped to bring immigrant women into the fight, and Wells-Barnett, long active in the suffrage cause, began organizing African American women. Grace Wilbur Trout, a white activist who had worked closely with Wells-Barnett, became the head of the Illinois Equal Suffrage Association in 1912. In January 1913, Wells-Barnett, working with white *Tribune* columnist Belle Squire, formed the Alpha Suffrage Club. The group met weekly "to study political and social questions." Members went door to door in the Second Ward, urging women "to register." The club was nonpartisan, an effort to separate itself from the tug of the Republican machine. "When I saw that we were likely to have restricted suffrage and the white women were working like beavers to bring it about, I made another effort to get our women interested," Wells-Barnett wrote. The club sought to educate black women to use their "vote for the advantage of ourselves and our race."[87] The Alpha Suffrage Club, the first black women's suffrage organization, quickly became a crucial force in Chicago politics.

On the eve of Woodrow Wilson's inauguration, the National American Women's Suffrage Association, the nation's leading women's suffrage organization, called for a parade in Washington, DC. Some five thousand suffragists arrived in the capital in early March. Dressed in white frocks and carrying banners amid carnival floats displaying the history of the suffrage struggle, women from across the nation prepared for a procession down Pennsylvania Avenue. The event would draw national attention to the women's suffrage battle and generate new hostilities between white and black activists. As was often the case, Ida Wells-Barnett found herself at the center of the controversy.[88]

The Alpha Suffrage Club had raised money to send Wells-Barnett to Washington to join a sixty-two-member delegation of Illinois women. The women were to march four abreast down the avenue. On March 3, as women gathered at the parade headquarters, it was announced that the national association demanded that the Illinois delegation be "entirely white." After much debate, the Illinois women agreed. Wells-Barnett would have to march with the black delegation at the back of the long procession. Wells-Barnett was outraged. Tears rolled down her cheeks, the *Tribune* reported, as she spoke to the group. "If the Illinois women do not take a stand now in this great democratic parade then the colored women are lost," she said. Several white suffragists asserted their support for Wells-Barnett, though the delegation's leaders supported the national association's position. Unwilling to accept a segregated parade for equal rights, Wells-Barnett found a way to join the white Illinois contingent. "Suddenly from the crowd on the sidewalk, Mrs. Barnett walked calmly out to the delegation," a *Tribune* reporter wrote. She was accompanied by two white friends, Belle Squire and Virginia Brooks, the women who had helped organize the Alpha Suffrage Club.[89]

The parade and especially the conflict between Wells-Barnett and the white Illinois delegates attracted much attention from the Chicago press. The *Tribune*, while gently mocking the suffragists, gave broad and serious coverage to the segregation fight. The *Broad Ax*, which generally opposed women's participation in politics, expressed admiration for Wells-Barnett. She "proudly marched with the . . . Ladies of the Illinois delegation showing that no Color line existed" in the parade. The *Defender* went even further. "The race has no greater leader among the feminine sex than Mrs. Ida B. Wells-Barnett," wrote one columnist, adding that National American Woman Suffrage Association officials should issue a public apology for "drawing the color line."

The conflict over Wells-Barnett's marching with the Illinois delegation not only drew attention to women's rights but also, and crucially, renewed awareness of "the color line" in politics. Black women, Wells-Barnett later told the *Defender*, were not promoting a women's agenda; she hoped, instead, to make women voters "strong enough to help elect some conscientious race man as alderman."[90] Race increasingly linked black voters across ideological differences, becoming the basis for new communities of activists and, by the 1910s, the crucial marker for representation in city government. Ultimately, conflict encouraged racial solidarity among black women, spurring even those who opposed machine politics to work for the machine's first black candidate. Black women, drawing on their experiences organizing suffrage campaigns and deeply disillusioned with many of their white comrades, became crucial campaigners for the city's first black alderman, Oscar DePriest.

The women who had helped launch the final push for statewide suffrage had been inspired and divided by the World's Columbian Exposition. Chicago's African American women had during that exhilarating summer become candid spokeswomen for the race. The new urban landscape created by rapid industrialization and an expanding urban populace became the training ground in political organizing for a generation of women activists. African American women used Chicago's women's clubs and settlement houses to expand their influence and draw new attention to the role of politics in daily life. Politics was simultaneously local in substance and national in theme. The women's clubs helped set new political agendas for the local community while cementing the bonds of national African American organizations. They were forging a new local and national civic culture that put the interests of the race over party or region.

FOUR

Challenging Urban Space, Organizing Labor

On a wintry evening in early December 1889, a group of African American men gathered at Atfield Hall to debate the political future for black Chicagoans. They would, in the words of a *Tribune* report the next day, "demand from their white brethren recognition according to the municipal strength as voters" in the First Ward. The meeting was called by Richard Smith Bryan, owner of the popular State Street restaurant Estella's and a vocal supporter of the Knights of Labor. But Bryan, who helped organize the First Ward Republican Association and whose restaurant was a meeting place for many of the ward's leading labor and political activists, did not move to the podium. Instead, lawyer and legislator Edward H. Morris, state representative John W. E. Thomas, and A. J. Saunders gave brief speeches. The final address that evening came from Berry S. Lewis, a twenty-six-year-old waiter who with his wife, Nettie, had arrived in Chicago just three years earlier. While the stated goal of the association was to "advance the interests of the colored citizens socially and politically," Lewis's agenda was more specific. He aimed to promote efforts to organize the city's waiters. In this, he would quickly gain Bryan's support, and the two men, working with several white labor organizers, would in the following half decade lead the most visible black labor organization in the city and ultimately help forge the largest biracial labor alliance in the nation.[1]

The biracial union of restaurant workers, the Culinary Alliance, was troubled from the start; it shattered after the turn of the twentieth century, spurring at least two decades of angry recriminations between the city's black and white workers. But the alliance's brief history shows that black workers were not simply subsumed in conflicts between white workers and business owners or mere tools of capitalists seeking to undermine white labor organizations. Rather, African American activists consciously linked

Map of Chicago Loop restaurants by Dennis McClendon. Locations based on *Chicago Tribune*, May 10, 1890; and *Colored People's Blue-Book and Business Directory*.

struggles over working conditions to civil rights and placed themselves within the sharp and often violent battles between labor and capital in late nineteenth-century America.[2] Labor organizing was for men like Lewis a direct path into municipal politics.

The alliance's aggressive strategies and its rancorous demise spurred a gradual though dramatic reorganization in one of the city's most visible downtown labor forces, a shift from men to women and from black to white service workers in hotels and restaurants. Labor organizing of the 1890s revealed complex status distinctions among black workers. Yet it was local employers who strategically drew lines separating higher- from lower-status waiters, black from white, men from women, and, in the wake of strikes and walkouts, effectively reorganized the service labor market. The rapid hiring of women waiters and the widespread use of multitiered wage systems in restaurants made worker unity almost impossible in the 1910s. It also brought in a new constituency of service workers, young white women, and largely cut the numbers of black waiters in Loop eateries.

Black waiters' experience in the alliance ultimately contributed to the racialized politics of the city in the twentieth century. Black Americans, always pushed to the bottom of the city's racial hierarchy, quickly recognized that their tiny but growing constituency became, during times of labor conflict, a threatening opposition to Chicagoans of European descent. In struggles over work and housing conditions, over access to government resources and political influence, native-born whites and European-born immigrants employed black Americans as both useful allies and handy scapegoats. "Color prejudice is used like any other weapon to strengthen the monopoly of the labor unions," wrote white journalist Ray Stannard Baker.[3] By the early twentieth century black laborers, largely barred from organized labor, looked to local politicians to find jobs for the city's workers. Biracial unionism—the city's sole organization of black and white, native-born and European laborers—had lasted little more than a decade.

In the 1890s, the spatial organization of the city—as well as the rapidly changing housing and labor markets—gave rise to new opportunities for political mobilization by black Americans. The alliance challenged employers in the city's downtown business district, a site that was both the symbol and material expression of the rise of corporate capitalism. Alliance organizers, in effect, made visible the conflicts that the spatial arrangement of the industrial city tended to obscure. As industrialists moved factories out of the business center, the physical and social distance expanded between employers and managers working in the new skyscrapers and wage laborers toiling in factories. Similarly, class and racial segregation of the city's housing markets left the run-down and unhealthy living conditions in slum neighborhoods almost invisible to the middle class[4] (despite efforts by women's reform organizations in the 1890s to draw attention to the growing impoverished neighborhoods). The conflict between waiters and their employers was, ironically, brought about in part by the spatial changes that distanced so many other workers from places of employment. The waiters' struggle highlights the distinctive character of the city's commercial center as a site of commerce, consumption, work, and leisure. The demise of the waiters' movement coincided with the hardening of racial segregation of neighborhoods and service and industrial work.

In the mid-1880s, northern black workers increasingly viewed the fight for the protection of labor organizations as their generation's antislavery crusade. Many who moved from the South looked for jobs in mining and manufacturing only to find that employers rejected African American workers. Vagrancy laws, poverty wages, and contract labor in the postemancipation South led many to see organized labor as a second abolitionist movement. A black man who "took the side of capital against labor," the *New York Freeman* editorialized in 1886, was like an African American who fought for the Confederacy.[5] A leader of the Knights of Labor, commenting on threats to lynch black organizers in South Carolina, compared laws aimed at banning labor organizers to the fugitive slave laws.[6]

White labor leaders typically relied on the metaphor of slavery to strengthen their demands for improved working conditions for industrial laborers. For African Americans, the rhetorical connection between slavery and the plight of free workers was historical—not metaphorical—an expression of the progressive but unfinished struggle of workers, black and white, for the rights of "free labor." As Frederick Douglass commented in 1883, "Experience demonstrates that there may be a wages of slavery only a little less galling and crushing in its effects than chattel slavery, and that this slavery of wages must go down with the other."[7]

Labor organizers, comparing themselves to abolitionists, offered a critique of racial violence that linked the struggles of northern workers to brutal attacks on black farm laborers and small-town entrepreneurs across the South. Most of the nation's newspapers accepted the claims of white southerners that mob attacks on black men were legitimate reactions to sexual assaults on white women. The labor press argued otherwise. The, New York journalist and Scottish immigrant John Swinton, who published a weekly labor-oriented paper, argued that state-sanctioned mob violence in the South was another device to control black workers and erase the economic achievements of black property owners. "I fairly warn the individual or individuals who may be caught 'spreading the light' among the pauperized field hands of Mississippi," commented *John Swinton's Paper* in February 1887, "that they will decorate pine trees in a twinkle."[8] When southern-born Ida B. Wells launched a national crusade against lynching in the mid-1880s, she offered a similar and widely publicized explanation for the steady stream of murders of black men and women. Lynching, she argued, was directly linked to systemic efforts to suppress the economic achievements of black Americans. African Americans did not—indeed could not—view workers' struggles simply as class conflict.

"All the world, as far as this country is concerned, appears to have gone mad, after the Knights of Labor," commented the *New York Freeman* in March 1886. The growth of the Knights of Labor, which reached its peak in the mid-1880s, spurred heated debate among black leaders and journalists over whether and how African American workers should join the ranks of organized labor. The Knights' stated policy called for organizing all workers—except speculators, gamblers, and liquor dealers—into one big union. Though black and white workers were organized into separate locals in some regions, the Knights of Labor was the only national labor organization to overtly recruit black workers. "We should be false to every principle of our Order," noted the Knights' official newspaper, the *Journal of United Labor*, "should we exclude from membership any man who gains his living by honest toil, on account of his color or creed. Our platform is broad enough to take in all."[9] Black workers continued to join the Knights of Labor even after the organization began to collapse. "Just as the abolitionists agitated against human slavery, so the Knights of Labor will agitate against wage-slavery," commented W. E. Turner, a Knight from Chicago, in 1891.[10] Still, the Knights hardly eliminated racial conflict, and African Americans, like journalist T. Thomas Fortune, continued to criticize them.[11]

Probably few black workers would have agreed when Turner commented: "There is no race problem, it is the wage problem. We have been bamboozled long enough with that old crie [sic] of race problem." But many were willing to join the Knights. By 1887, Frank Ferrell, the most prominent black leader of the Knights, estimated there were over four hundred all-black locals with a total of about sixty thousand members. There were two-thirds more blacks in trade assemblies in the northern states than in the South. The *New York Sun* commented, "It would not be far from right if the whole number of colored men in the Knights were estimated at 90,000 or 95,000, and they are growing at a rate out of proportion to the increase of white members." Growth took place more among black workers in cities and among those who found that no other labor organization would accept them.[12] Even after the turn of the twentieth century, liberal economists and black labor leaders credited the Knights as the labor organization most willing to accept African American members.[13]

The Knights of Labor was the first national organization to organize local assemblies of restaurant workers. In 1886, J. Ross Fitzgerald, a New York organizer for the Knights, traveled to Chicago to organize the city's first black waiters' union, the William Lloyd Garrison Colored Waiters Local Assembly 8286. The organization's name, at least, provided a symbolic link between black labor and abolitionism. Some four hundred black waiters joined. The union "braced up the colored waiters considerably," the *Chicago Times* reported. As the Knights declined in the late 1880s, some black waiters left local 8286 to form the Charles Sumner Waiters' Union, which would outlive the Culinary Alliance.[14]

The Knights of Labor was not the only organization to develop a collective agenda and build trust between black and white laborers. Contract prison labor, more than almost any other issue, unified black and white labor activists and spurred them to political action. Under the system, which was widespread in both the North and the South, entrepreneurs or "contractors" paid state governments as little as sixty-five cents per day for the labor of each convict, generally for piece work like sewing cheap garments, making bricks, or cutting stone. "The contractors have full control of state property," *John Swinton's Paper* complained in 1883. "Whatever task they set must be performed by the convicts, whether sick or well, able or not." Black activists saw the system, which did not pay the convicts, as a modern "slave system," particularly loathsome in southern states, where the majority of prisoners were African American and prison conditions were atrocious. To white workers, the system was a dangerous tactic to undercut wages. Though for different reasons, opposition to contract prison labor was one basis for a common agenda for black and white workers.[15]

Wage workers of both races joined forces in the 1880s in a broad-based political campaign to pressure state legislatures in the North—beginning with Illinois, New York, and Massachusetts—to reject the contracts and ban the contract prison labor system. In Illinois and New York, the boycott became the primary tool of protest, uniting African American activists and labor leaders in a widely promoted campaign that attracted support from nonactivists (and politicized some daily consumption choices). In Illinois, a statewide boycott of contract prison labor had the support of craft unions in shoemaking, coopering, and stonecutting. The boycott was combined with campaigns to persuade voters to oppose state legislators who had supported the system. The use of the boycott as a political strategy, with its heavily publicized attacks on contract prison labor, helped to politicize a variety of labor's demands and to spur labor activists to establish or join labor parties in several northern cities. The prison labor campaign became a model for successful biracial struggles in northern states and, like the Knights, another route to political action.[16]

Chicago was a city of expanding industries and labor organizations in the final decades of the nineteenth century. The thousands of European immigrants who flowed into the city in the wake of the fire found work in the lumber mills and stonecutting plants that lined the western banks of the Chicago River, in the meat-slaughtering and packing plants in the Union Stockyards, and scores of workshops and factories. "Now the wholesale trade is in large part supplied by the machines and manual labor in Chicago," the *Tribune* commented in 1889. "Clothing, millinery, artificial flowers, pianos, organs and jewelry may be named as near the head of a long list in which this city has come to the front."[17] Just as the city's residential areas were typically defined by particular immigrant groups, so too employers often linked jobs with workers' nationality. Higher-skilled and higher-paying work often went to northern and eastern Europeans: the skilled butchers in the packing houses, for example, were often of German descent. The lower the skill, the lower the pay and the more likely the worker was Lithuanian, Polish, Italian, or at the very lowest wage levels, African American.

Black laborers were largely excluded from industrial jobs and labor unions. There were 10,000 African Americans living in Chicago in 1885 and close to 15,000 five years later, less than 2 percent of the city's 1890 population. The 1890 US Census listed nearly 5,000 black Chicagoans working in domestic and personal service, another 1,376 working in "manufacturing or mechanical" jobs, and 474 in commercial venues. There were approximately 115 physicians, lawyers, dentists, ministers, and musicians, all grouped under the census category of "professional services." Forty-eight black Chicagoans worked in "public services," most likely the post office or the city clerk's office. Seven men worked in agriculture, and another 560 African Americans were listed as unclassified workers. The majority of black men worked as railroad porters, waiters, janitors, elevator operators and bell boys in hotels, saloon porters, dock laborers, foundry men, house servants, and coachmen. By 1905, there were three black-owned manufacturers in Chicago, one making chewing gum and two cigar-making firms.[18]

For black laborers, jobs in industry, especially with the protection of a labor union, were rare.

Sociologist Monroe Nathan Work estimated that in the mid-1890s, at the depths of a national economic depression, "a large class of unemployed negroes" numbered from several hundred to several thousand. He noted the poverty among the city's growing black population; many were living in run-down frame dwellings just south of Dearborn Station. "Of all the people dwelling in Chicago's slums, the negroes are the most neglected," Work wrote. Hard times, combined with a steady migration of unskilled rural black workers into the city, left many struggling to feed their families and a growing problem of urban crime, Work noted. By 1920, an investigation into African American workers found that black workers had for decades earned significantly less than whites and were regularly denied chances for "advancement and promotion."[19]

The final decades of the nineteenth century were tough on black workers and hard on all of the city's workers. Chicago was shaken regularly by violent battles between workers and their employers. Hostilities simmered through the economic depression of the 1870s, erupting in violence in July 1877 when the strike against the railroads reached Chicago. Hundreds of people filled West Side streets, clashing with Chicago police and state militia. At least thirteen people were killed and scores injured, and a precedent was set of neighbors taking to the streets to support the demands of striking workers.[20] Chicago's most notorious late nineteenth-century street riot came nearly a decade later in Haymarket Square on the city's West Side. A bomb exploded during a protest for the eight-hour workday, leading to the arrests of eight suspected anarchists, who were charged with conspiracy.[21] While the violence left many middle-class Chicagoans terrified of a labor uprising, the movement for the eight-hour day continued, as did regular though less deadly labor violence.

In the wake of the Haymarket riot, labor politics in Chicago was increasingly complex. Some black workers, discouraged by the Republican Party's determined support of business, turned to the newly formed and short-lived United Labor Party (ULP). The party, which tapped the existing Knights of Labor assemblies, was broadly based among laborers who had been outraged and mobilized by the use of police and state militias to attack striking workers. It was, Leon Fink contends, part of the rapid politicization of the American working class in the mid-1880s. Fink counts labor tickets in 189 towns and cities in 34 states, including the rapidly expanding party in Chicago. There were labor parties in at least 15 Illinois cities.[22] The ULP's platform opposed the use of the police and courts against organized labor and called for municipal ownership of the street railways and other utilities. The *Tribune* called the ULP and its 1887 ticket "undiluted socialism" that would break every business in Chicago. Its platform would "speedily reduce Chicago to the condition of a wilderness of untenanted houses and blasted businesses." When the ULP ticket was easily defeated in those municipal elections, labor voters dispersed among the city's other parties.[23]

Black workers had what labor historian Richard Schneirov calls "a strong presence" in the ULP. In 1886 and 1887, several African Americans ran on the ULP ticket. In 1886, William Bruce, a barber, got a ULP nomination, and a year later John W. Terry, a waiter, and James S. Nelson, a molder, were nominated for city offices. When the ULP died out, black workers, mobilized by the Knights of Labor and schooled by recent electoral experiences, turned to organizing a group that could effectively pressure local employers: restaurant workers.[24]

The tables of the First National restaurant were crowded "with hungry patrons" just past noon on May 9, 1890, when the "colored waiters put on their street clothes and deserted the establishment." The restaurant, located at the corner of Randolph Street and Wabash Avenue, was popular with merchants and businessmen working in the city's commercial center. Many had been served their entire meals "barring the checks" and "figured their own accounts" after the waiters walked out. That morning, W. C. Pomeroy, the white organizer of the waiters' union, had visited First National's owner, Mr. Stein, demanding a two-dollar increase in weekly pay, to ten dollars, and eight-hour workdays for the waiters. "My men have been treated more than fairly," Stein later told a *Tribune* reporter. "They have neither night nor Sunday work and all the breakage that has been charged up against them does not foot up more than $1." The waiters, continuing demands that had been pressed by Chicago laborers for at least a decade, fiercely disagreed. "I will close shop before one of them shall reenter my employ," Mr. Stein warned, though as the waiters recognized, closing shop would hardly prove profitable.[25]

The waiters' strike came in the wake of a citywide work stoppage on May 1 and in response to the success of an organization of white waiters. In "one of the largest and most orderly demonstrations ever held in Chicago," thirty thousand "toilers" representing nearly every labor organization in the city had joined the movement for eight-hour workdays at the usual pay for ten hours "and extra pay for overtime." White waiters had been expected to join the protest; when their employers recognized the newly formed white waiters' union, "a general strike was averted." White waiters had demanded that employers, largely the biggest restaurants and oyster houses in the city, hire "nothing but union men."[26]

Using the Knights as a model, white and black organizers had in the months before the strike established an alliance of restaurant workers as a loosely organized union of separate assemblies of different nationalities or races. The waiters were members of the eighteen-month-old Chicago Culinary Alliance, an organization launched by sixteen German waiters, meat and pastry cooks, and bartenders on January 3, 1889. The restaurant workers gradually expanded the organization to include local assemblies of waiters, cooks, and bartenders in several northern cities. Within the following year, white organizers met with African American Knights of Labor, eventually organizing gatherings of black waiters under the auspices of the Knights. The Alliance was a biracial movement of multiple nationalities, an unwieldy confederation within Chicago's carefully divided social geography.[27]

Early on, alliance leaders sought racial balance among the leadership, aiming to undermine the widely used employers' tactic of setting black workers against white. By the end of April, the *Indianapolis Freeman* reported that the Culinary Alliance had formed an executive committee, "equally divided between white and colored," of men with experience in labor organizing and in the service trades across the South and Midwest. More than 1,500 of Chicago's 3,000 to 4,000 waiters had paid initiation fees and signed membership cards. Strike leaders had moved to prevent the hotels and restaurant managers from bringing strikebreakers to the city. They telegraphed "all large cities . . . not to send any waiters," while railroad porters and dining-car workers announced they would "discourage all they can from coming to Chicago." "From the appearance of things," the *Freeman* noted, "a new man may fare hard for he will have no friends, and you can't live on wind in Chicago."[28]

The alliance committee leaders included William C. Pomeroy, a twenty-eight-year-old labor organizer from Kentucky who had successfully organized Saint Louis waiters; New York–born Knights of Labor activist R. S. Bryan; and Berry A. Lewis, who had been raised on a farm in Macon County, Georgia. Lewis, who had left the farm shortly after his father died in 1871, had, like many of the city's other waiters, lived in several southern and midwestern cities. He told the reporter for the *Freeman* that he had "successfully held positions as coachman, barber, brakeman, newsboy and waiter" in Albany, Georgia; New Orleans; Saint Louis; Saint Paul; Milwaukee; and finally Chicago. Another member of the committee and Knights of Labor member was E. B. Warwick, who was born in Richmond, Virginia, and moved to Baltimore and then Chicago, where he got a job waiting tables in July 1876. Pomeroy was the most flamboyant and controversial. He was, as Richard Schneirov writes, "a strange blend of the idealist and the cynical manipulator" with all the qualities of "a successful ward boss." He was a brilliant orator with a deep knowledge of classical literature and the author of a utopian novel, *The Lords of Misrule*. The novel, published in 1894, suggests Pomeroy's racial egalitarian views, though indirectly. (He wrote, "Mark you all mortal mothers are but the particles of a common stock.") Warwick and Pomeroy drew up the first scale of wages "ever written up for waiters," which was imposed on Chicago's restaurant proprietors. "Seeing the necessity of having the colored waiters combined with us," Pomeroy noted, they organized black and white waiters together and "fought the only successful fight of its kind ever known." They also, for the first time, came up with a wage scale that provided black and white waiters of equal status and experience equal wages.[29]

The 1890 walkout, the first of the nascent union, was organized to hit all the downtown restaurants and hotels that May morning, a strategy made possible by the enormous changes in technology, transportation, and, most significantly, the organization of business and housing in the industrializing city. Until the fire of 1871, Chicago was a walking city with twenty-five thousand of its citizens living in or near the commercial center. In the rebuilding after the fire, retailers and financiers expanded the business district, pushing wealthy Chicagoans south along Michigan and Prairie Avenues and forcing the poor into the increasingly jammed West Side. By the mid-1880s, manufacturers, seeking cheaper land and labor, had moved mills and factories west, across the Chicago River. "The different banks, churches, and municipal buildings which had been destroyed by the great fire-fiend are all re-erected in a substantial style," wrote the British novelist Lady Duffus Hardy during an 1880 visit to the city, "though with varying degrees of eccentric architecture." In her exuberant description of the "bright, bustling city," Lady Hardy extolled the city's luxurious hotels and the "tasteful" displays in the windows of the "handsome drygoods, millinery, and other stores of all possible descriptions."[30]

Skyscrapers, the ten- and soon twenty-story buildings that would mark Chicago's downtown for decades to come, were fast replacing the rows of frame buildings and low-slung brick workshops in the city's center. Manufacturing and the physically demanding work of the factory floor were

Palmer House hotel, ca. 1890. Courtesy of Harold Washington Municipal Library, Special Collections.

moving to prairie land just beyond the built-up sections of the city. In the city's center, the ten-story Home Insurance Building with steel frame and interior elevators was completed in 1885, setting off a burst of construction using the new technologies. These new buildings were hives for hundreds of office workers, young men with aspirations in business and, by the early 1890s, growing numbers of young, native-born white women taking jobs filing, typing, and moving papers for the expanding corporate enterprises that dominated the city's—and the nation's—economy.[31]

Workers, the salaried young men dressed in business suits and the hourly-paid laborers who maintained the elevators, cleaned the offices, and constructed the new buildings, traveled to work by streetcar from their homes in neighborhoods west, south, and north. Chicago's cable cars, brought to the city by a group of investors led by department store magnate Marshall Field in 1882, circled the nine square blocks of the commercial center. Cable cars largely replaced horse-drawn streetcars in the 1880s—though a few of the horse-drawn lines remained into the early twentieth century. The steam-powered cars sped travel to over ten miles per hour, transforming the ways Chicagoans shopped, worked, and experienced their city. By 1893, Chicago had the largest cable-car system in the world, with 86 miles of track, 11 power plants, and more than 1,500 cars linking far-flung neighborhoods and suburban villages to the city's commercial center. Around the turn of the century, the cable cars were superseded by the elevated railway system that established the more visible and enduring overhead loop around the business district. By then, the Loop was, by day, the most congested area of the city, a neighborhood of office workers and shoppers, almost no residences, and the city's uncontested commercial center.[32]

For Chicagoans in the 1880s, the Loop was a distinctive urban space, a place where working classes could daily see the wealth and status of employers and, as in the case of the waiters' strike, place direct and in some cases personal pressure on the city's growing middle classes. It was a site where men and women, immigrants and native-born, black and white Chicagoans might come in close contact. Though each was expected to remain within carefully circumscribed spaces—middle-class women shoppers in department stores, white women workers behind store counters, and black janitors in the basements of skyscrapers, for example—the commercial crowds of the Loop made possible face-to-face-contact that could, as in the waiters' strike, generate new social tensions.[33]

In the center of the industrializing city, commercial eateries were a modern necessity. Tearooms opened in department stores to provide comfortable spaces for lady shoppers. Restaurants and low-priced lunch counters sprung up along Wabash and Dearborn Avenues, behind the plateglass windows in street-level spaces of skyscrapers, to feed the hordes of clerks, lawyers, and other white-collar workers. The new eating places meant scores of jobs for cooks, dishwashers, janitors, and waiters. In southern towns and cities, these were jobs typically held by black men. In Chicago, white and black men were hired by restaurants, saloons, and lunch counters. German waiters were more likely found in the more exclusive hotels and oyster houses, while African Americans typically worked the counters and small tables of Loop lunchrooms, but the service workforce was hardly segregated; black and white waiters sometimes worked side by side in downtown eateries.[34] The waiters' strike, then, was made possible by changes in the social relations of work and the social geography of the industrializing city.

The waiters' strike also marked a shift from the mass strikes of the previous decade, the labor stoppages rooted in neighborhoods and supported by communities of immigrants of shared nationalities. Though typically sparked by labor grievances, mass strikes like that of railroad workers in 1877, often were sustained by neighborhood residents. Lacking strong labor organizations, workers engaged in mass strikes relied on support from neighborhood grocers, saloonkeepers, and shop owners, making the labor struggle into a communal event that linked the interests of neighborhood residents. But by the late 1880s, the experience of organizing in local assemblies within the Knights of Labor had laid the groundwork for more formal and structured labor unions. More significantly, as places of paid work were separated from residential neighborhoods—as waiters, black and white, traveled to jobs in the city's commercial center—workers turned to labor organizers rather than neighborhood leaders for support. They formed an alliance of laborers living in a variety of neighborhoods, of varied nationalities and races, with the common experience of restaurant and hotel work.[35]

The strike was carefully planned, designed to use the new commercial geography to the workers' advantage. Pomeroy, Bryan, and Lewis had been visiting eating places along with the elegant downtown hotels, the Tremont and Palmer Houses, talking with waiters, black and white, for several weeks. Some restaurants avoided the strike when the owners gave in to the demands for higher wages, shorter hours, and recognition of the union's right to negotiate for the restaurant workers. Nearly a dozen proprietors formed their own organization to fight the striking workers, a move that would become a model for the city's leading industrialists in the strike-torn years of the following decade.[36] The concentration of restaurants and hotels within the Loop combined with a growing demand for commercial eateries in the urban center strengthened the waiters' organization.

Waiters' labor was demanding and exhausting. Most, especially those employed in the large oyster houses and restaurants, worked thirteen- or fourteen-hour days. Their work included polishing silver and washing windows as well as serving food. The waiter, remembered Jere Sullivan, a leader in Chicago's white waiters assembly and a Knights of Labor member, served "as an all-around handyman who occupied the position of cook, waiter, bartender and oysterman at one and the same time." In some restaurants he was also forced "to do a singing stint" to entertain diners. As Sullivan later complained, there were no clearly defined jobs in a restaurant, no craft or trade rules.[37]

But in the more exclusive restaurants and hotels, there was a hierarchy, with headwaiters supervising captains, waiters, and water boys. The headwaiter, somewhat like a factory foreman, carried significant authority in the dining room and received respect from the larger community. Headwaiters were listed among the professionals and government workers in city directories. Pay rates suggest large and meaningful status differences among restaurant staff: headwaiters could earn as much as $75 per month, while waiters' wages ran as low as $20 per month, or $5 to $10 per week. Among African Americans, headwaiter was considered a respectable, steady occupation, similar to post office jobs. The Lexington Hotel on Michigan Avenue established one of the most elaborate systems. The hotel's fifty waiters were divided into ten ranks. The headwaiter in the 1880s was a college-educated African American, who reportedly earned $100 per month. Perry Duis notes that the ranks included a "Second Lieutenant," a "Third Man," a waiter who handed out bread and butter pats, and a "lowly water boy," who was paid just $10 per month. Crucially, headwaiters were known to stand by proprietors when their subordinates walked off the job. Proprietors apparently rewarded their headwaiters' loyalty. When the headwaiter at the Palmer House, Charles Jordan, died in Arkansas, the hotel owner, Potter Palmer, apparently paid for the embalming and shipping of Jordan's body back to Chicago for burial. Union waiters referred to the strong affiliation between headwaiters and their wealthy employers as a "vampire alliance." The waiters, angered by the headwaiters' actions, claimed that the "vampire alliance" allowed the headwaiters to draw profits from the floor workers' hard work.[38]

Waiting tables was widely considered a respectable, relatively safe occupation for black men. In the final decades of the nineteenth century, black men generally could find jobs in hotels and restaurants, especially if the prospective worker was willing to take lower pay than a European immigrant. A Missouri migrant, the son of slaves, remembered finding work easily when he arrived in Chicago in 1887. "I was a young man and soon got a job waiting table in various restaurants and hotels," he commented. "I made eighteen dollars a month." Paul Laurence Dunbar traveled from his hometown, Dayton, Ohio, to Chicago in spring 1893 in search of work at the World's Fair. He found a job "cleaning one of the big domes" and another "uncrating exhibit specimens" in a damp basement, leaving him with a hacking cough. Dunbar gave up on the fairgrounds and found a job waiting tables in a hotel.[39]

But if some black men were pleased to find the work, others complained that waiting tables simply reinforced white Americans' vision of black men as servile. "The place assigned to him [a black man] is in the lowest walks of life," commented an angry writer for the *World*, quoted in the *Christian Recorder* in 1885. "His place according to assignment is that of menial, a servant, a boot-black, waiter, a monkey." White proprietors affirmed this image. "Colored men are the best waiters by nature, and are peculiarly adapted to servitude," one restaurant owner told a *Tribune* reporter. The *Christian Recorder* published sporadic complaints and "exchanges of views" over the status of the black man waiting tables in urban restaurants.[40]

The waiters' struggle, like those of an array of craft unions in the late nineteenth century, was to set maximum hours, raise wages, negotiate trade rules, and, especially for black men, to assert the "dignity" of their work. Among their biggest complaint was the requirement that each waiter pay to replace plates or glassware he broke during service. In 1885 when a union of white waiters began negotiating with restaurant and oyster house owners, waiters demanded that employers permit them to replace the broken wares. "You will know what that means," a Boston House employee told an *Inter Ocean* reporter, "when I tell you I was compelled to pay 50 cents for plates accidently broken which at wholesale cost the proprietor 4 cents each." The waiter noted that the restaurant owners paid "8 to 9 dollars per week," but if "we broke a saucer, or goblet, or plate, we were required to pay from three to ten times its value." The waiters had "decided to fight this robbery." They also demanded "steady wages" of ten dollars per week and ten-hour days. The 1885 movement failed. Five years later, the waiters reorganized, using the Culinary Alliance to press their case. This time, among the most prominent demands was recognition of the union. Proprietors should hire "nothing but union men."[41]

The waiters won support from at least one of their employers, Henry Herman Kohlsaat, who made his fortune with a chain of low-budget lunch counters in Chicago. Kohlsaat employed unionized black waiters in his downtown eateries. He also provided his patrons, who included the staff of the *Conservator*, with a comfortable reading room that featured five hundred books. He encouraged several employers to negotiate with union leaders. "Mr. Kohlsaat," the *Tribune* noted, "made the desired increase in wages without waiting to be asked." A year later, Kohlsaat would purchase part ownership of the *Inter Ocean*, one of the few nationally distributed newspapers sympathetic to both organized labor and African American civil rights. (He also contributed to land for Provident Hospital. Wells-Barnett, impressed by his devotion to "the race," named her second child for him.)[42]

Yet conflicts between white and black workers, between skilled and unskilled, and among types of labor nearly scuttled the movement. When the waiters walked out of the First National, the restaurant's cooks, clerks, bartenders, "and the employer himself turned out" and waited on the customers. At Kinsley's, a pricey lunch spot further south on Wabash (known for serving "swell meals to swell people, or people who wanted to be known as swells"), "white-capped cooks" waited tables when the waiters walked out. The willingness of other restaurant workers to wait tables proved a short-lived obstacle to the waiters' plan. Yet tensions between black and white, English- and German-speaking workers required constant mediation. Pomeroy, Bryan, Lewis, and the other strike leaders quickly moved to resolve these differences. Waiters and kitchen staff were organized in separate but coordinated unions according to race and nationality: the German Bartenders' and Waiters' Association, Chicago Waiters' Union no. 1, Chicago Waiters' League, AF of L Local 5170, the Meat and Pastry Cooks' Union, Chicago Waiters' Association no. 7475, the Knights of Labor, the Chicago Association of Oystermen, and for African American waiters, the Charles Sumner Independent Colored Waiters' Union. Those whose allegiance lay with the Knights of Labor remained separate from those who joined the craft-oriented American Federation of Labor. Ultimately, Pomeroy and Lewis brought together all kitchen, cleaning, and wait staff in a powerful biracial federation of men and women restaurant workers, the Culinary Alliance. Separate unions reinforced social divisions of race, nationality, and skill, while the Culinary Alliance established a collective interest and experience in challenging local employers.[43]

On Monday, May 18, strike leaders "opened hostility against the hotels," reported the sympathetic *Western Appeal*. The Culinary Alliance called on the crews of waiters at the Commercial Hotel, the Tremont, the Palmer House, the Brunswick, the Grand Pacific, and the Brigges House to walk off the job. Most struck immediately, but waiters at the Tremont "for some reason or other did not pay any attention to the order." The Tremont waiters were members of the alliance, and their refusal to strike was "looked upon as rank mutiny." Pomeroy and Lewis ordered the uncooperative waiters to report to Quinn Chapel that evening. It is not known what happened at the meeting, but the newspapers later reported that "a good many of the men . . . promised to join the ranks of the strikers Tuesday morning." Proprietors' responses varied. Managers at the Commercial and the Palmer House fired "union men," while the proprietors of the Grand Pacific "took an entirely different view of the situation," signing a labor agreement Monday night. When the waiters at the Tremont House walked out, the hotel manager "pressed every employee into service," but he had "hard work of it." Chambermaids, cooks, and other servants waited tables "and grumbled not a little." By the end of May, an estimated nine hundred restaurant and hotel workers, nearly 30 percent of the workforce, were on strike.[44]

Waiters were not the city's only workers to strike that spring; the waiters, black and white, were part of a larger movement of laboring people to pressure employers for shorter hours and higher wages and a recognition of labor's right to organize. When the waiters walked out, journeymen carpenters had just settled with builders, as had employees in the sash, door, and blind factories in the lumber district with their employers.[45]

If there were black workers among the striking journeymen carpenters, Packingtown coopers, and other industrial laborers walking off the job that May, the newspapers did not mention them. Black men appeared in news accounts more often as strike breakers, brought by train from southern towns to replace striking white workers. Black workers were "easily lured to the north at wages disgustingly inadequate for white workingmen," commented *John Swinton's Paper* in 1885. "It is hard to find fault with the poor colored men but for the capitalists who have brought them to the North there would be nothing short of positive popular condemnation. . . . The imposition on the negroes is systematically carried on."[46] The Chicago papers regularly reported on the trainloads of black workers brought from southern towns to replace striking miners in southern Illinois. The press had covered in lurid detail the tense weeks in July 1886 when black strikebreakers were employed in the stockyards to crush a union in the meatpacking industry. "We have about 300 of those fellows [black men] at work now," Philip D. Armour, owner of the city's largest packinghouse, told a reporter. "When they proposed to go to work in one house we told them they would be slugged. They replied . . . all we want is work; we don't ask for protection."[47] Strikebreaking gave black workers access to jobs from which they had been previously excluded, industrial jobs that paid higher and steadier wages than agriculture and personal service.

But if some black men took advantage of strikes to propel themselves into industrial jobs, others identified with the plight of labor, white or black. Just three years before the Chicago waiters walked off the job, black workers attracted newspaper attention when they refused to scab for striking white coal miners in Peoria, Illinois. About a hundred "colored coal miners" were sent to Peoria by train in mid-March 1887. A committee of strikers met with the African Americans and "laid down their side of the case. . . . The new men had been deceived, as they were led to believe there was no trouble here." The African Americans refused to take the striking miners' jobs. This was a dramatic change from the previous year when black miners, sent from Kentucky, had worked as strikebreakers in a mining strike at Grape Creek in Vermilion County. Violence erupted as "five to fifteen Negroes arrived every other day," and that strike was defeated. Though just a tiny portion of strikebreakers, black workers stood in the white imagination as a powerful obstacle to labor unity. But in Peoria, whether out of fear of further violent attacks from white workers or a new sense of common purpose with striking miners, the well-publicized refusal of black workers to scab was a potential forerunner to the biracial alliance formed by cooks and waiters in early 1890s Chicago.[48]

The Culinary Alliance's simple and efficient tactics had generated significant support. Assistance and approbation came from many sources, from the chambermaids at the Tremont, from white labor activists like Kohlsaat, and from some of the middle-class congregants of Quinn Chapel. Hotel proprietors found their staff, even those who did not strike, fully supporting the striking waiters. "We're with the waiters every time," said the head bellboy at the Tremont House, "and we don't intend taking their places." Ferdinand Barnett published a letter in the *Inter Ocean* offering his support for the waiters. The *Western Appeal's* coverage of the strike ran under the headline: "We are With you!" The affirmation of workers' rights coming from Quinn Chapel's charismatic minister proved crucial. The church provided space for meetings and negotiations, as well as the critical backing of many of the city's black elite.[49] Of the city's major newspapers, only the *Inter Ocean* came out strongly for the waiters. "From all we can learn the waiters' strike is founded on justice," the *Inter Ocean* editorialized.[50]

Victory came on May 21, just three days after the strike had spread to the hotels. There was a celebration, a "Jubilee," at Quinn Chapel, where Lewis announced that five restaurant owners had signed the union pay scale in the previous twenty-four hours. The Tremont House, after what the *Tribune* called "a gallant fight," was forced to close its dining room and agree to the alliance demands. As waiters in one downtown hotel after another walked off the job, proprietors had been forced to negotiate with alliance leaders. The waiters won an increase in pay to nine dollars per week, though work hours would still be set by employers. Most important to alliance leaders, they had forced restaurant and hotel managers to negotiate with the union and to accept their motto: "Only union men."[51] That November, most proprietors claimed they maintained "wages proposed by the Culinary Alliance." At a mass meeting in January 1891, the German Waiters' and Bartenders' Columbia Association, the Chicago Waiters' Union Germanis, and the Charles Sumner Association of Colored Waiters Union debated forming a four-thousand-member union, ultimately deciding to retain the alliance of member unions. The alliance of German, Irish, and African American waiters would last more than a decade.[52]

The Culinary Alliance quickly became part of a national union, one of the few in the late nineteenth century to welcome African American laborers. By the time of the Chicago walkout, there were already several unions of white waiters in cities across the North. Waiters organized in local assemblies in New York, and a German waiters' union in Saint Louis had pushed Samuel Gompers, leader of the American Federation of Labor (AF of L), to include them in the new craft union in the 1880s. But it was only after the successful Chicago waiters' strike that a national waiters union was formed. The following December, at the AF of L convention in Detroit, a delegate announced plans for a "Waiters National Union" and called on the AF of L for assistance. In April 1891, during a convention in New York, the waiters wrote a provisional constitution for the new union and applied for a national charter with the AF of L. None of the Chicago leaders were listed on the charter, which was approved by Gompers on April 24, 1891. But two African American waiters were present: Richard Ellis of New York and S. K. Govern of Philadelphia. The convention ruled that local unions of any race or nationality could join the national union. Moreover, under the new charter, white workers were barred for one year from applying for jobs in a restaurant or hotel where black waiters had gone on strike.[53] The alliance had affirmed the importance of black waiters in labor's struggle.

The experience of organizing and collective victory spurred a new political consciousness among the waiters, linking them to both the white labor movement and urban black politics. Berry Lewis remained a leader of the Charles Sumner Independent Colored Waiters Union and was also elected to the board of trustees for the city's Trades and Labor Assembly, an independent labor party controlled largely by socialists and trade unionists. In March 1891, at a raucous meeting of the party members, Lewis challenged his former ally William C. Pomeroy and nominated Carter Harrison as the party's candidate for mayor. Lewis was not the only labor activist to question Pomeroy and his tactics. By 1891, Pomeroy, called by one historian a "labor hustler," had united opposition to Socialist leader Thomas J. Morgan and shoved aside the Socialists' control of the Trades and Labor Assembly. In those years, Pomeroy regularly promised and delivered labor votes to Democrats in exchange for jobs and payoffs. Pomeroy and a group of "City Hall heelers," in the *Tribune*'s words, pushed through the nomination of Dewitt Cregier, a move that divided labor activists across the city and prompted many to leave the Trades and Labor Assembly. Pomeroy and his allies were kicked out of the assembly in 1895, but the divisive battles soured many labor activists on politics.[54] Unlike many native and foreign-born white laborers who looked to labor unions for collective action, black laborers, so often rejected by organized labor, would in the early twentieth century pressure black political leaders and municipal officials for jobs and workplace rights.

In 1891, Lewis, like many other black and white labor leaders, supported Harrison. The former mayor, determined to regain his job and serve as the city's ambassador during the World's Columbian Exposition, gratefully accepted their support, blasted the "socialists and anarchists" who opposed him and went on to reelection that spring. The biracial organizing of the Culinary Alliance had propelled Lewis into the leadership of the city's labor politics and made black voters for the first time a visible, if still minor force in Chicago electoral politics.

The Culinary Alliance, the leading biracial labor organization in the city, faced its next formidable challenge when the World's Columbian Exposition opened in May 1893. That spring, as thousands of people arrived in Chicago to visit the fairgrounds, the waiters challenged not just local entrepreneurs but, in effect, the symbol of federal power and national achievement in the World's Columbian Exposition. The various waiters' organizations within the alliance issued a call for a wage increase to between eighteen and twenty dollars per week for waiters—depending on their position—in restaurants and oyster houses during the six months of the fair. Members of the "Colored Waiters' Alliance"—an estimated nine hundred black waiters—attended a meeting on April 28 in Olivet Baptist Church to "understand the scale that had been prepared by the Executive committee and adopted by the alliance." Along with pay raises, the alliance demanded ten and a half hours "to constitute a days work," six and a half days a week, with three dollars a day extra for seven-day weeks and four dollars extra for Sunday work, and "none other than union men to be employed."[55]

Two days later, on May 1, the fair's opening day, the largely white wait staff of many of the city's largest restaurants and oyster houses, walked off the job. On May 2, five hundred striking waiters met at the Culinary Alliance headquarters, Fisher's Hall on Lake Street, where they appointed a five-member committee to "induce" others to "quit work." W. C. Pomeroy, in a speech to the crowd, said he "was formerly a waiter . . . [and] had been called a labor agitator and was proud of the title." Several "colored waiters entered the hall and promised the support of their organization if needed." Though organized in separate locals, those in the alliance recognized their common interests; they had for the previous three years successfully deployed a strategy of organizing across racial lines, across differences of skill, and within workplaces of the commercial downtown. The waiters were not the only workers to take advantage of the fair. The Building and Trades Council representing workers constructing the fair's buildings walked out for a day before negotiating a settlement on April 11.[56]

"Eating places badly crippled for want of help," the *Tribune* announced on May 2. Two days later, six hundred cooks held "a secret meeting." The *Tribune*, somehow privy to the meeting, noted, "It is said that they intend to follow the example of the waiters and strike for more wages and shorter hours." It is not clear whether the cooks ever walked out. For the waiters, the strategy of mutual support, with a bit of pressure from fellow restaurant workers, proved effective. Some waiters continued working, but at least two of the city's largest oyster houses—the Lakeside Oyster House and Charles Rector's Oyster House—closed down, while several restaurant managers quickly agreed to the alliance's wage demands. The Chicago Oyster House opened "with a green crew" earning fifteen dollars per week, the *Inter Ocean* reported. The Saratoga, the American, Boston, Kinsley's, Baker & Jackson's, Chapin & Gore's, and several others were open, "running with short help."[57]

A week later, most of the leading restaurants in the city and on the fairgrounds had signed labor agreements with the alliance. "The colored waiters in Chicago are better organized and are doing better to benefit themselves," announced the *Indianapolis Freeman*, "and are getting higher wages than they ever have done before in the history of Chicago." This was, no doubt, a moment of great achievement and high hopes for Chicago's African American laborers. The agreement with proprietors had been negotiated by a committee from the Trades and Labor Assembly, fully incorporating the Culinary Alliance into the assembly.[58] Yet, the Culinary Alliance's strategy of highlighting common interests of black and white workers barely covered over the increasingly vocal and visible racial separation in Chicago.

In the decade following the fair, black workers faced expanding discrimination from white laborers and the city's employers. The summer after the fair closed, the city slipped into the economic depression that had already pummeled the rest of the nation. During the Pullman strike that July, black workers, who had been refused jobs in the plant manufacturing the luxurious Pullman cars, were, when whites walked out, willing to take the lucrative work. The strike, which in Chicago revived neighborhood-based organizing and sparked much street violence, once again drew attention to black strikebreakers.[59] When butchers, who were members of the Knights of Labor, walked out of the Chicago stockyards that summer in sympathy with Eugene V. Debs's railway workers, black men were hired to replace the strikers. "An offer was received by one of the larger packing firms," the *Tribune* reported, "to supply several hundred negroes to fill the places of strikers." The report suggested that recruiters had once again been sent south to hire black workers to break a strike. In mid-July an effigy of a black worker labeled "nigger-scab" was seen hanging from a telephone pole near the entrance to the yards, the *Chicago Record-Herald* reported.[60] By middecade, the carefully crafted pay scale that was designed to standardize waiters' wages was cracking; some of the city's proprietors were paying black waiters lower wages than those paid white men. In July 1896, black waiters, angry about "starvation wages," threatened to strike during the Democratic convention in Chicago but were persuaded by Culinary Alliance leaders to hold off, though the alliance did nothing to lift black waiters' pay. Divisions between black and white waiters in the alliance were growing.[61]

The biracial Culinary Alliance could barely be sustained against the onslaught of employers determined to use race to divide workers, European-born laborers deploying racist tactics to hold on to their jobs and homes, and black workers desperate for work. By the turn of the twentieth century, many Chicago labor leaders would affirm the racial hierarchies imposed by industrial foremen and their employers, making it almost impossible for black workers to align with white. Racial barriers in the workplace, reinforced by racial segregation in the city's neighborhoods, stamped out workers' belief in mutual, biracial support.

The Culinary Alliance shattered in 1903 when white union leaders, after a summerlong strike on restaurants, hotels, and oyster houses, refused to support equal pay for black members. The strike began on June 4 when cooks and waiters closed four of the leading downtown restaurants. The walkout spread from King's restaurant on Fifth Avenue, where, after a visit from a union committee, "men and women at the tables saw hope of luncheon vanish." Next closed was the Vogelsang on Madison Street, the Union restaurant on Randolph Street ("a favorite resort of many politicians"), and then the Bismarck. By evening, the kitchen, dining rooms, and bar were closed at the Grand Pacific and the Chicago Beach hotels. The scene at the Chicago Beach at the "dinner hour," the *Tribune* commented, "when 400 guests 'helped themselves' and each other from the kitchen, was perhaps unprecedented in Chicago." The Culinary Alliance held together in the early weeks and was successful in blocking an attempt by the restaurant managers to "get men from outside the city to assume the places of the union employees." Restaurants reported losses of between $300 and

$800 per day. The *Tribune*, in a page-one story, said the strike was "held by both employers and employees to be the beginning of a bitter struggle that may result in the closing down of all but a few of the large downtown establishments and the crippling of every hotel of importance in the city."[62]

At stake were hours and wages, but most divisive was the union's demand that proprietors hire "none but union men" and that each employer negotiate and sign an individual contract with the union. The employers, forming an association of restaurant and hotel management, called for negotiations between representatives of the union and the association. Both sides agreed to arbitration before a committee of workers and proprietors. Many waiters went back to work, and restaurants reopened. But the settlement hardly ended the dispute. Black waiters especially were angered by a wage agreement that left most black waiters, who tended to work at lunch counters and low-cost eateries, earning lower wages than white men in the city's hotels.[63]

The restaurant and hotel strike coincided with a five-week strike by the city's laundry workers, described as "the most important labor war ever waged in the west by women and children." As the *Tribune* noted on June 6, when the strike ended and commercial laundries announced they would reopen the following Monday, over 80 percent of the seven thousand striking workers were girls under twenty years of age. (A significant number were black; by 1919, the majority of laundry workers were black women, who the *Chicago Whip* claimed "were exploited and victimized by race feeling encouraged by the bosses . . . who are interested alone in profit.") In 1903, the Chicago Federation of Labor led negotiations for the laundry workers, forcing employers to "deal with the union through its proper accredited committee" but allowing the hiring of nonunion workers. The strike ended with most other issues—wages and hours regulations—headed for a board of arbitration. The *Tribune*, displaying its usual support for the city's proprietors, listed estimated losses to laundry businesses and commented, "The Chinese have taken the greater part of the trade." But the paper's reporter could not help being impressed by the determination of the young laundresses, who "stood by the union throughout the long struggle," the Tribune commented, "and last night held a dance to celebrate the settlement."[64]

The city's waiters did not see such a happy conclusion to their strike. Moreover, while young white women laundresses were portrayed as "plucky" and even fun-loving, black male waiters garnered little respect from white journalists. Indeed, black waiters had, by participating in the labor action, demonstrated they were not as servile as white employers hoped. The long-standing trope of the obsequious black servant was, under pressure from black labor organizers, giving way to a more militant image of the urban black working man. The new image might empower some black activists, but it also undermined black men's ability to hold on to their jobs in urban restaurants, among the highest-paying and most stable work available to black laborers in the industrial city. If labor activism was for black men an assertion of manhood and citizenship rights, it was to the white press a disturbing shift in a long-standing discourse of black labor. Black men would continue to hold service positions, most prominently in Pullman cars. But in the wake of the 1903 strike, the city's restaurant owners sought staff considered even more servile than black men: white women.[65]

Proprietors' moves to replace black waiters with white women were among the strikers' complaints. Waiters at H. H. Kohlsaat's lunchrooms had been among the first to walk out, angered by the firing of black waiters "on charges of inefficiency and dishonesty and the substitution in their places of white girls," Ray Stannard Baker wrote in *McClure's Magazine*. Baker contended that the waitresses were union members and that the "colored men" simply "insisted that no white girls be employed."[66]

Two days after the walkout, when the union agreed to hold a series of meetings with proprietors, most waiters and cooks returned to work. Strikes remained on several restaurants, including the Chicago Athletic and Union League clubs, while eighty-six restaurants and lunch counters had signed agreements with the union. Strangely, Kohlsaat, long a supporter of organized labor and of African American organizations, did not settle with the union but replaced his "colored men" with "girls" at 43 Dearborn Street. But on June 11, a rumor spread that "an offer had been made to settle the cooks' and waiters' strike in a way strongly suggestive of bribery." Five days later, a conservative black leader, J. T. Brewington, resigned from his position as vice president of the "colored waiters' local." Brewington, urging the union to negotiate with an association of restaurant employers, said, "I realize the radicals will attempt to crucify me because of the position I have taken, but I realize someone must suffer that the truth be heard and justice be done." That day, amid growing fear that the strike was collapsing, the union's joint board authorized lawyer Clarence Darrow "to approach some of the hotel men and open a way for peace negotiations." Though a *Tribune* headline ran "Waiters nearing a Rout," the strike was hardly over.[67]

The Chicago waiters drew attention from the national press, especially as the strike seemed to reignite the street battles that had plagued industrial cities for the previous decade. Violence erupted on streets and sidewalks outside restaurants and hotels as public space in the city's commercial center—not just the neighborhood streets surrounding industrial plants—became a site of conflict between laborers and employers. At least one waiter leaving work was attacked by striking waiters, while pickets attacked "scrubwomen" employed by the Grand Pacific Hotel. "The women fought bravely and were able to hold their own until greatly outnumbered," the *Tribune* reported. Waiters and cooks picketing Vogelsang's restaurant were supported by a raucous crowd, which dispersed only when police appeared. At strike headquarters, the "business agents" who led the strike "displayed bruised heads." No longer confined to the factory gates or the streets abutting the stockyards, striking workers and labor violence could be seen along Chicago's commercial streets.[68]

By mid-June, the strike attracted the attention of national labor leaders. Samuel Gompers, president of the AF of L, came to Chicago to meet with the union's joint board. As strikers continued to picket restaurants and hotels that had reopened with nonunion workers, Gompers met with the men representing the unions of waiters and cooks and with W. G. Schardt, president of the Chicago Federation of Labor. Gompers left Chicago with little achieved.[69] The walkout was over within a week.

That August, waiters struck half a dozen Loop restaurants, and the Culinary Alliance once again threatened a "general walk-out." Street violence escalated. At the Kensington on State Street, union men were met by the owners carrying revolvers. "When I put my head in that door to speak to the cooks they shoved two revolvers, with barrels a foot long at me," union business agent Edward Hagers said. "Did I run? Well, you see I'm still on earth." Another revolver was drawn at a restaurant on Monroe Street when the union man tried to urge the cooks to walk out, though the police forced the owner to put away his "six-shooter" and "no harm was done."[70]

This time, the leading issue was wages, especially the expanding use of a separate pay scale for black and white waiters. As one restaurant owner told the *Daily News*, "I want to go on record on this question. I believe now and have always believed that the white man is a better worker than the colored man and is entitled to more money," adding, "the colored men employed in the lunch rooms are an inferior class of waiters." The Chicago Restaurant Keepers Association, formed in 1877 and revived during the June walkout, refused to negotiate the wage "distinction."[71] The strike's conclusion, coming just a couple of days later, proved a bitter disappointment to black waiters.

On August 26, white union leaders, determined to "save their union," renounced African American waiters and abandoned their proud biracial alliance. "Waiters Beaten; Negroes To Go," ran the *Tribune* headline on August 27. The "white union men" had refused to support the "colored men," the *Daily News* noted. White restaurant workers and their employers joined in blaming African Americans for the recent labor strife. Just one member of the arbitration committee worried that black waiters "would forever be a disturbing factor in the labor movement in Chicago." Alliance representatives agreed to the separate wage scale, though threats of a strike continued for another week.[72]

As the strikers gave in, restaurant and hotel owners moved to fire all black employees from "downtown eating houses." Proprietors sent agents to Milwaukee, Indianapolis, Saint Louis, and other cities, hiring hundreds of "white girls who are willing to come to Chicago." H. H. Kohlsaat & Co. announced it was hiring only "white men and women" in its three Loop restaurants. As the union negotiated away nearly all of its demands, the president of the Restaurant Keepers Association, F. R. Barnheisel of H. H. Kohlsaat announced: "The day of the negro waiter in the downtown district is over."[73] Ending too was biracial labor organizing in Chicago, at least for several decades.

Restaurant owners in Chicago were among the first in the nation to shift from an all-male labor force to one that included women. In most parts of the country, black men maintained a disproportionate share of restaurant and hotel service jobs until around 1930. Even before the 1910s, black waiters in Chicago, Saint Louis, and other northern cities complained that only white men were hired in the most exclusive restaurants. By the mid-1910s, though, white women increasingly replaced black men as waiters in lunchrooms and cafes. The proportion of black waiters in the service work force fell by nearly 80 percent between 1900 and 1910. There may be many reasons for that drop. Among them, as Dorothy Sue Cobble notes, was the proprietors' view that women were "more compliant" than men and that employers could pay women lower wages.[74] By hiring women waiters, Chicago's downtown employers gained just a few years of labor peace. The city's long tradition of labor organizing and the aggressive actions of the Culinary Alliance spurred waitresses to organize. Several culinary unions and at least one highly publicized walkout by waitresses in 1914 were organized by the Women's Trade Union League.[75]

By then, the image of the servile black waiter held by northern employers and their white customers and linked to sentimental fictions of southern plantation life was giving way to a new version of restaurant service workers. The waitress increasingly represented the family home, performing the work of wives and mothers in the impersonal city center. In the 1910s, a new organization, the Waitresses' Alliance, financed by an association of restaurant owners, functioned as an employment service for Loop restaurants and lunchrooms, providing a place where "all types, the young and pretty, the plain and neat, the modish person, the sloven and frump" might go to find a waitressing job. "The relationship between the waitress and patron is a distinctly personal one," wrote Frances Donovan, a journalist who went undercover to waitress in a series of Chicago restaurants and lunchrooms for nine months in 1919. Her research, which resulted in a book, *The Woman who Waits*, was among a series of journalistic accounts—usually by educated middle-class "explorers"—of the new forms of urban labor published in the early twentieth century. Waitressing was, Donovan wrote, "a good deal more intimate" than other urban occupations.[76]

The white waiters' refusal to stand by African American allies helped to position women workers as rivals to men, deepening gender and racial divisions among laborers and undermining the status of urban service workers generally. Rather than finding common cause with German and Irish men, black waiters increasingly competed with white workers, especially young Irish women, for the lowest-paying restaurant work. Black waiters had proved too militant for their employers and, paradoxically, were seen by white laborers as ineffectual partners. Increasingly, it was white women who were perceived as servile, willing to accept the authority of employers, and representing a lower rung of the labor hierarchy of the expanding commercial city.[77]

Black workers, angered by the betrayal of their union, did not quickly forget. Some immediately charged the union with "bad faith." That fall, others moved to restart the strike, while at least one group of black waiters urged their coworkers to pressure proprietors to rehire them "before white waitresses take their places." But few black waiters regained their jobs. "In the matter of employment," Fannie Barrier Williams wrote in 1905, "the colored people of Chicago have lost in the last ten years nearly every occupation of which they once had almost a monopoly. . . . White men and women as waiters have supplanted colored in nearly all the fist-class hotels and restaurants." Williams's complaint came in the context of increasing racial segregation in the city. She was angered that she and her lawyer husband faced white resentment in their neighborhood, affluent Hyde Park, where they had lived peacefully for over a decade. As Williams wrote, even the "best" people were being forced out of white middle-class neighborhoods. Race, even more than class, defined the social geography of the twentieth-century city.[78]

The strike and its disheartening ending lingered in the memory of African American workers for decades. It became a point of tension between black workers and white, fostering distrust that, with slight provocation, could erupt in violence. When the Chicago Commission on Race Relations held a conference on "Trade Unions and the Negro Worker" in 1920, the waiters' strike of 1903 was still a prominent issue. The commission was charged with investigating the causes of a bloody riot in July 1919. Among the list of issues discussed at the conference was "the oft-repeated statement, 'that the negroes were double-crossed in the Waiters' Strike of 1903.'" African Americans, the conference organizers noted, had been excluded from the city's waiters' union ever since. Many considered the local assembly of sleeping-car porters "a sort of 'Jim-Crow' union." The *Chicago Whip* also noted that black labor leaders, even those who did not "know exactly what it was," reminded black workers that "something happened" to the members of a waiters' organization in 1903, which was reason to warn black workers away from the AF of L. The memory of the waiters' strike, hovering over efforts to organize black and white workers, remained a source of hostility between them.[79]

But the ruin of the Culinary Alliance and a turbulent decade of biracial labor solidarity was not all loss. Black waiters maintained their organization and continued to link their struggles in the workplace to local politics. In the years after the 1903 strike, the Charles Sumner Independent Waiters Union helped establish the Waiters Political Club of Chicago, which by 1907 claimed three thousand members. The organization sparked some controversy when it endorsed Fred Busse, a Republican and second-generation German, for mayor. Busse was well liked by black laborers for his willingness to hire black workers in city hall, particularly for increasing the number of African American police officers from about fifteen in 1905 to fifty in 1914.[80] While organized labor across the city voted in significant numbers for the Democratic candidate, black waiters returned to the party of Lincoln, the party that had opened at least a few jobs to African American workers.

The Culinary Alliance demonstrated that the rapidly industrializing city created new opportunities for labor organizing that linked the experiences of black and white, native and foreign-born workers. With their aggressive participation in at least three major work stoppages, black workers had challenged the dominant white view, perpetuated in news accounts and by employers, that black men should remain service workers because they were "by nature" servile. Black workers, participating in some of the most significant labor conflicts of the decades surrounding the turn of the twentieth century, deployed their class interests in small but viable political organizations. They were willing to support the Republican Party when it seemed to affirm their interests as workers. As black workers were betrayed by white and forced out of labor organizations, black activists turned to politics. They devoted themselves increasingly to political organizations that supported black candidates.

FIVE

Virtue, Vice, and Building the Machine

Less than a year after Berry Lewis urged support for the waiters' union at the First Ward Association meeting in December 1889, John "Mushmouth" Johnson opened a saloon and gambling house at 464 State Street, just a few doors south of Bryan's Estella Café. The saloon, which took up the ground floor of a three-story brick building, became an anchor for the new commercial district rising along with the emerging African American neighborhood south of the Loop. Though the four State Street that made up Chicago's "colored downtown" could not rival the Loop in terms of capital invested, office jobs, or retail sales, the stores, saloons, eateries, and cabarets just two blocks from Dearborn Station helped generate the investment capital that would fuel the growth of many twentieth-century African American businesses. By the 1910s, the commercial core of black Chicago, "the Stroll," as State Street was called, had moved south, becoming the heart of a growing African American neighborhood and the raucous hub of black Chicagoans' commercial leisure.

Expanding commerce along State Street became a wellspring for economic and political strength for black Chicagoans and, in many ways, transformed the structures and substance of urban politics in the early twentieth century. The saloons, dance halls, and movie theaters were new kinds of urban spaces, generating a new culture of commercial leisure and a new class of urban entrepreneurs. Those entrepreneurs, especially the purveyors of vice, gave legitimacy to the expanding political strategy of payoffs for protection and at the same time made the vice trades the subject of a rising and politically engaged reform movement. As reformers pushed local governments to regulate or eliminate vice they extended the reach of politics to these new urban spaces. State Street's commerce helped sustain another important site for African American political engagement: the

Map of selected sites in the Black Belt, 1905–10, by Dennis McClendon. Locations based on William Howland Kenney, *Chicago Jazz: A Cultural History, 1904–1930* (New York: Oxford University Press, 1993), 9–11; Cynthia M. Blair, *I've Got to Make My Livin': Black Women's Sex Work in Turn-of-the-Century Chicago* (Chicago: University of Chicago Press, 2010), 169–71; *Colored People's Blue-Book and Business Directory.*

black churches dotting the surrounding streets. Together, the churches and commercial venues, virtue and vice, set political agendas and generated capital to sustain black politics in the early twentieth century.

The commercial strip along South State Street and the rising black ministers based in South Side churches represented the emergence of a new institutionalized form of African American politics. Political scientists long conceived of black urban politics as controlled by white patrons or "patron-client politics." This was largely true until around 1900. John W. E. Thomas's career was guided by the white lawyer Kirk Hawes, just as lawyer Edward H. Morris turned to white Judge Elbridge Hanecy for his 1890 winning bid for the Illinois General Assembly.[1] After 1900, black activists began looking instead to black entrepreneurs and an increasingly organized African American constituency to sustain their political work. Black politicians were neither the puppets of ward bosses nor independent of the city's machine politics. Rather, they used the votes they influenced to promote personal ambitions and serve community interests. Their achievements came at a price.

Some of the activists and professional politicians who came of age in the early decades of the twentieth century challenged machine dominance, while others aimed to use the machine for their own ends. Neither was able to dramatically transform political power relations in the city.[2] Black Belt politics "provided a way out for some, but not a way up for the mass," Ira Katznelson writes, adding that African American "political collaboration" with the Republican machine produced "neither change nor justice." Yet such long-standing scholarly claims wrongly assume that African American politicians were mere "appendage[s]" to the machine. Instead, black politicians were part of the larger process of institutionalizing the machine; their role in the machine benefited some while delaying justice to the masses, as Katznelson rightly contends.[3] During the decades when racial segregation in housing and many public spaces hardened and outbursts of violence against black Chicagoans were increasing, activists effectively opened opportunities for jobs and political power for some African Americans. Ministers and entrepreneurs of vice gained access to the city's political machine, using it to lift them to positions of authority in the community and, at times, directing municipal resources to African American neighborhoods. The tragic paradox was that in claiming power within the machine, activists in effect legitimized the machine brand of politics and, ultimately, helped construct the gilded fortress that prevented more radical demands for social change and civil rights from gaining a foothold in city government.

The growth of the South Side neighborhood and the politics of the city's increasingly influential black ministers reflects widening divisions in African American politics nationally, particularly between northern and southern activists.[4] Booker T. Washington had by the turn of the twentieth century fashioned himself as the leader of black Americans, gaining recognition from the White House and from a coterie of black politicians who used his approval to enhance their own careers. Washington's "Atlanta Compromise" called on black Americans to improve themselves and their communities economically before challenging racial segregation laws. Washington's plea came during a decade of expanding racial terror across the South. By 1900, the promise of the compromise—physical safety and economic security—seemed empty. Northerners looked to Wilmington, North Carolina, in the fall of 1898 when whites rampaged through a black neighborhood and massacred hundreds of black people. Closer to home for Chicagoans, a riot in Springfield in August 1908 left more than $200,000 in property damage and at least two black men murdered. A year later, in November 1909, there was a lynching in Cairo, Illinois. Ida Wells-Barnett investigated the murder, delivering a brief against the Cairo sheriff to Governor Charles S. Deneen, who suspended and refused to reinstate the sheriff.[5] Providing an eloquent and sharply worded public account of the divisions among black activists, W. E. B. DuBois devoted an entire chapter of *The Souls of Black Folk* to condemning Booker T. Washington as complacent and servile. Kelly Miller, the Howard University mathematician and sociologist, who perhaps more than anyone attempted to bridge political chasm between Washington's accommodationist stance and DuBois's militant challenge to legalized racism, wrote that Washington's views were driven "by prudence."[6] Many came to believe that such prudence was not useful in the northern city.

Chicago, in part guided by Ferdinand Barnett's *Conservator*, became a hub for some of Washington's most vocal and visible critics. "In Chicago your followers may be equal in number to those arrayed against you," wrote Theodore W. Jones in a 1904 letter to Washington, "but they are far out classed by brain, tact, and influence. The opposing faction has the ear of the public and the courtesy of the press."[7] In the northern city, the simplistic conflict setting DuBois's strategies against Washington made little sense. Even Washington's devoted Chicago supporters S. Laing and Fannie Barrier Williams, participated in politics and actively sought legislative solutions to the "race problem." AME minister Archibald J. Carey, a Chicago-based Washington ally, reviving demands of 1880s activists, called for the establishment of a "black man's political party," though he also mobilized black votes for Republicans.[8]

In Chicago, supporters and opponents of Washington agreed that African Americans could advance their interests through political participation and the energetic pursuit of public office. These activists represented an increasingly urban and northern vision of the possibilities for black politics. If not working to establish a "black man's party," many were maneuvering inside the Republican Party for government jobs and representation in local and state government. It was, ironically, the growing economic strength of some black businessmen that signaled a challenge to Washington's leadership and the growth of African Americans' aspirations in urban politics.

South State Street was "a teeming Negro Street with crowded theaters, restaurants, and cabarets," wrote Langston Hughes about his first visit to Chicago in 1918. "The street was full of workers and gamblers, prostitutes and pimps, church folks and sinners." State Street developed gradually in the 1890s and then, with a burst of commercial activity and a flood of new arrivals in the 1910s, became "the Stroll," "the strip of excitement" between Twenty-Sixth and Thirty-Ninth Streets.[9] Here, the criminal world of gambling and prostitution and morally suspect saloons sat amid upstanding businesses, a convergence that bothered neighborhood respectables but was hardly coincidence.

Two decades before Hughes's arrival, State Street emerged as the commercial backbone of an expanding African American neighborhood known as the Black Belt (or Bronzeville after 1930). Racial segregation came slowly and unevenly to Chicago, leaving enclaves of African American families living among the West Side Italians and impoverished Irish immigrants through the turn of the century. Yet as the twentieth century loomed, real estate dealers and landlords, playing on the fears and prejudice of white homeowners, drew a color line around a narrow strip of land jutting south from the downtown business district.[10] "No large Northern city," wrote Richard R. Wright Jr. in 1906, "shows a greater degree of segregation."[11]

By 1910, as the city's black population jumped to forty-four thousand, the population of the Second and Third Wards, the heart of the Black Belt, were more than 25 percent African American. Most were recent arrivals: more than 80 percent of Chicago's black population in 1900 was born outside of Illinois; 77 percent were in 1910. The Black Belt expanded west, in some sections, to Halsted Street, and south to Thirty-Ninth Street, with another half-dozen blocks of African American residents running south from Forty-Seventh Street. Into the early 1910s, the *Defender* continued to express surprise and outrage over efforts to racially segregate the city. In September 1913, when an African American widow was "informed that her presence was not wanted" in a Northwest Side neighborhood, the *Defender* commented that the "neighborhood has gone so far as to advocate lynching as they do in the southern states." In 1920, the Black Belt ran south to Fifty-Ninth Street and east to the Lakefront.[12]

The Black Belt, like the city as a whole, was split into elite, poor, and middling communities. The well to do, like Rev. Carey and his wife, bought houses along Vernon Avenue east of State Street. Black lawyers, doctors, ministers, and businessmen moved into the tiny Lakefront neighborhood; some elite families, like S. Laing and Fannie Barrier Williams, lived in the largely white Hyde Park. To the west of State Street were enclaves of the "respectable working class," as DuBois labeled breadwinners with "steady remunerative work," who could maintain their families in "comfortable circumstances." These were typically postal workers, Pullman porters, and waiters in Loop hotels who lived in cottages or frame two-flats.[13]

The vast majority of black Chicagoans lived along the side streets west of State Street and south of Wabash. Most lived in one-, two-, or three-story frame buildings that contained two to six apartments. A 1912 survey found that in one four-block area of the Black Belt, just 26 percent of the dwellings were in "good repair." (European immigrants also lived in run-down tenements, though the survey found more than 70 percent of the housing in a Polish neighborhood and more than half in a Bohemian neighborhood was in "good repair.") "Colored tenants," the survey reported, "found it impossible to persuade their landlords to . . . make the necessary repairs." Municipal services like sewer and water lines and garbage pickups often did not reach these Black Belt blocks. Most families used outhouses through the 1920s. Racial segregation allowed for some class distinctions in the South Side neighborhoods but meant close proximity for elite and impoverished homes. Fannie Williams complained bitterly about the "huddling together of the good and the bad" in the segregated Black Belt.[14]

Vice was both the scourge and the financier of the Black Belt. Just as black laborers found the gates to manufacturing jobs closed, so too did black businessmen discover that commercial banks refused to lend to them. "The banks of this city, to which the colored people flock to put their money in, will not lend this same money back to colored people," the *Defender* complained in 1910, not the first or last time the paper would note the shortage of investment capital in the Black Belt.[15] The vice trades, along with the cabarets and dance halls that made up the South Side's "bright lights" district, generated quick profits, capital that could be invested in South Side real estate or in respectable businesses. The Levee, white Chicago's infamous vice district, perched on the northern border of the neighborhood, protected by payoffs to police and public officials, even through the reform years when Mayor Edward Dunne claimed to crush vice industries. It cast a long shadow across the Black Belt, lowering property values and, at least in the minds of white Chicagoans, linking the African American community to vice. More than the Levee, however, it was the lack of investment capital for new businesses—and the easy profits from vice—that drove black entrepreneurs to the vice trades.

The rise of illicit businesses was, in addition, a result of the combined history of racial segregation in working-class leisure and unequal distribution of commercial licenses among the city's local businessmen. City officials often were slow to grant licenses to legitimate saloons and dance halls on the South Side, especially to black men who lacked political influence. African American entrepreneurs in the late nineteenth century operated informal establishments, known as "buffet flats," in storefronts or private homes. These served as hotels and saloons for black visitors, barred from inexpensive hotels elsewhere in the city.[16]

By the 1910s, buffet flats had become unlicensed commercial spaces for gambling, drinking, cabarets, and sometimes prostitution. (Into the 1920s, the buffet flats apparently catered to working-class black audiences by featuring piano-based blues, rather than the jazz sought by affluent white "slumming parties" visiting Black Belt cabarets.) Some storefront spots, selling cheap drinks in tiny dark rooms, opened and closed within months. Others gained licenses or at least official sanction and, like Johnson's saloon and later Robert Motts's Pekin Theatre, the Alhambra, the Elite No. 2, and Byron's Temple of Music flourished amid the barbershops, storefront groceries, restaurants, and furniture stores along South State Street.[17] The cabarets along State Street made the Black Belt a center of African American music and culture. Harry Haywood, then a teenager and a waiter on the Chicago and North Western Railroad, remembered an older waiter taking him "to see the town." After visiting with his aunts, they headed to "the back room of a saloon at Thirty-second and State Street." There the piano man, who was playing "boogie woogie style," offered a rendition of "Those Dirty Motherfuckers." "I almost sank through the floor in embarrassment and even amazement," Haywood wrote much later. His older friend just laughed and said, "Boy, you ain't seen nothing yet!"[18]

Not all business thrived on nightlife. Entrepreneurs launched businesses that served the growing population of black residents and moved consumer capital through neighborhood stores and households. J. T. Pannell's "grocery and poultry business" was known throughout the South Side and expanded to three stores by 1909. A black business directory listed twenty-four South Side restaurants owned by African Americans in 1908, up from just fifteen black-owned restaurants along the Strip in 1901. Most offered inexpensive lunches and dinners. Shops selling housewares and furniture advertised "loans on furniture" in the *Defender* and provided jobs for black salesmen and movers. These shops, like W. A. Marshall & Co., which sold furniture and pianos, likely attracted the strivers and salaried workers hoping, through the decor of their homes and the well-trained behavior of their children, to establish themselves among the "respectable" South Side families.[19] The line separating upstanding from illicit leisure, carefully drawn by neighborhood respectables, grew murky on South Side streets where a low-slung gambling den, its windows darkened by heavy curtains, might sit beside a brightly lit barber shop, or a gentlemen's "drinking establishment" might within a couple months be transformed into a gambling saloon.[20]

The "sporting life," and the jobs it created, generated a local economy that touched almost all the households in the Black Belt, though many would have rejected any association with it. Saloons, dance halls, theaters, and gambling dens provided jobs for musicians, cooks, bartenders, and janitors. Outsiders, the whites—generally men, who frequented the brothels, black and tans, and saloons—brought money into the neighborhood, while some black men spent their earnings from the stockyards, Pullman cars, and downtown restaurants on the "sporting life." That money, filtered through neighborhood vice, purchased groceries and furniture, haircuts and flowers in the shops along black Chicago's commercial strip. In moments of crisis and joy, the earnings generated in gambling houses, saloons, and brothels paid doctor bills and undertakers, and as money moved from hand to hand, made its way, ultimately, to church coffers.

That the sporting life was intricately connected to upstanding businesses was obvious to anyone who knew "Mushmouth" Johnson, as it was visible to almost anyone who wandered down State Street. Johnson was raised in Saint Louis and with little formal education began his career as a porter in a white gambling house. "While my family went in for religion and all that," he later said, "I didn't exactly fancy so much book learning and went out to see where the money grew. Some of those who know me say that I found it." Johnson did learn to make money. His gambling emporium and brothel was known for its "voluptuous waitresses" and extravagant decor.

At his death in 1907, he left his sister Eudora Johnson more than $200,000. Johnson's unsavory reputation did not prevent him from supporting "race advancement." He contributed money to a Baptist church and through his family provided financial support for the Old Folks Home. Johnson's funeral filled Institutional AME Church with "distinguished Christian men and women," the *Broad Ax* commented under the headline "The King among the Sporting element in Chicago has Joined the Heavenly Host."[21]

Johnson, though never claiming respectability, supported his family's aspirations. He reportedly paid tuition for his sister Cecilia Johnson to attend the University of Chicago. Johnson's nephew, Fenton Johnson, became a leading figure among the city's intellectuals and social elite and a member of the Appomattox Club, a political organization formed by black politicians in 1900. Johnson's brother, Elijah, used the gambling proprietor's legacy to open the Dreamland Ballroom, later the famous Dreamland Café. Mushmouth Johnson's most significant contribution to civic life was through his sister Eudora, who in 1912 married Jesse Binga, who used his wife's inheritance to expand a real estate firm and launch the city's first African American–owned bank.[22]

Binga's marriage to Eudora Johnson revealed the blurring of moralizing distinctions between respectable and unsavory Chicagoans. Binga, who had been raised in Detroit, arrived in Chicago in 1893 with the crowds attending the Columbian Exposition. He later offered several versions of his early years in the city. In one, he peddled coal; another account had him running a fruit stand at the corner of Twelfth Street and Michigan Avenue. The tale of his humble beginnings was the prelude to his Horatio Alger story, an account likely intended to cover up his ties to vice and his pragmatic use of Mushmouth Johnson's gambling fortune. Whatever the source, Binga managed to invest his earnings in real estate, becoming one of the richest black men in Chicago, a symbol of race advancement and the economic expansion of South State Street.[23]

The South Side's most famous venue was the Pekin Theatre at 2700 South State Street, which opened as a beer garden serving black and white customers. It was remade into a "Cabaret better known as a music hall" in 1904 and, two years later, under the ownership of Robert T. Motts, reopened as a twelve-hundred-seat "theater for the Colored People of this City." It was the first club to employ musicians associated with ragtime and prejazz popular music, writes jazz historian William Howland Kenney. Motts, who was born in Washington, Iowa, in 1861, moved at age twenty to Chicago, where he and two partners reportedly ran a gambling club at 480 South State Street.

Photo of Pekin Theatre, ca.1920. Courtesy of University of Chicago Libraries.

Like Johnson, Motts invested his gambling profits in South Side real estate. Though he never lost his reputation as a gambling boss, Motts claimed he went "respectable" with the opening of the theater.[24]

Motts's most significant contribution to Black Belt life was to cement ties between the Stroll's businessmen and ward politicians. He quickly recognized that business, legal or otherwise, depended on the goodwill of ward bosses and local police captains. "Police corruption," in the words of vice reformer and Chicago Commons founder Graham Taylor, was "infamous."[25] Yet, as every South Side businessman knew, payoffs to police and ward leaders were the cost of commerce, as much as were rent and taxes. The exchange of cash and votes for protection, "tribute money," forged distinct alliances in the Black Belt. Motts was known to pay his customers five dollars per day to help white Second Ward alderman George F. Harding register black voters. Mushmouth Johnson also paid tribute to local politicians. One of Johnson's friends told political scientist Harold Gosnell that when a "mayoralty campaign came around he would give $10,000 to the Democrats and $10,000 to the Republicans so that no matter who won, he'd be protected." (If the dollar amount is close to accurate, Johnson was among the richest men on the South Side.) While Johnson's politics served his business interests, Motts apparently used politics to "advance the race." Motts's political workers were expected to vote for Republican candidates; the ward boss was expected to secure jobs for black South Siders. The *Defender* later credited Motts with getting jobs for at least forty women in the recorder's office.[26]

Motts's willingness to enter partisan battles reveals a subtle but significant shift in South Side politics. "Patron-client politics" characterized the ascent of some black politicians in the 1890s.[27] After 1900, black activists found they could secure jobs for their supporters and gain some limited benefits for the Black Belt. Motts became a leading force in Black Belt politics when he sponsored the successful legislative race of Edward H. Morris, a former slave widely known as the "dean of black lawyers" in Chicago. Motts took the place of Morris's white patron, Judge Elbridge Hanecy, a powerful figure in the Republican machine. Morris, however, quickly lost Motts's support, and therefore his job, when he apparently misread the interests of his new patron. Within a year after taking office, Morris introduced a bill to legalize the playing of "policy," a form of gambling popular in South Side joints. Motts fought the effort to legalize those who might compete with his illicit but lucrative enterprise. He shifted his money to Edward D. Green, a lifelong bachelor who had organized Pullman porters during the 1896 presidential election and won a legislative seat representing the first district in 1904.[28]

African American civic organizations, despite the growth of black businesses, remained beholden to the city's white businessmen. George Pullman and his daughter Florence were leading contributors to Provident Hospital, which opened in 1891 and was the first hospital in the United States to accept black and white patients and to train black doctors and nurses. The Pullman Company, along with employers like Swift, Armour, and International Harvester, contributed to the Wabash Avenue YMCA and to the Urban League. Yet, as St. Clair Drake and Horace R. Cayton note, five of the city's most prominent industrialists, white men who had taken a "paternalistic interest in the Negro community," had died by 1907, leaving black Chicagoans to place greater emphasis on "racial self-reliance." And white-supported civic organizations like the YMCA urged on young black men a passive attitude of racial uplift and respectability, warning them away from machine politics. It was African American entrepreneurs who, along with the Republican machine, were the primary contributors to black political campaigns.[29]

Southside entrepreneurs, working with white ward bosses, walked a tricky line between racial self-help and economic necessity. Motts was the most outspoken—and most self-promoting—of the Black Belt cabaret owners. He, like the owners of the Monogram Theatre and the Grand, the South Side's largest vaudeville and later movie theater, appealed to racial pride while serving a mixed clientele. The *Defender* regularly highlighted this difficulty. The newspaper in April 1910 touted Motts for providing high-quality vaudeville acts of both races but added that the proprietor "caters much at present to white people." Motts made the Pekin into a self-consciously black entertainment institution. He encouraged race-oriented productions and presented legitimate plays like *Tallaloo* and *Carib* with African American themes. But ticket sales came largely from white audiences. Motts's business was one of the few venues to put white dollars into the pocket of a black businessman, strengthening the urban black economy.[30]

White immigrant entrepreneurs quickly saw the profits to be gained from State Street entertainments. In a 1912 *Defender* column titled "Union Is Strength," Minnie Adams scolded readers for spending time in white-owned theaters. Adams demanded that "the race" show "our pride and loyalty by patronizing" the Pekin. By 1915, an angry writer in the *Defender* complained that white men owned most of the theaters and "places of cheap amusement" along the Stroll, "with just here and there a struggling little Negro business venture." Other reports suggest the writer overstated the losses of black businesses. *Defender* columns reported a race consciousness among business and civic leaders, just as similar campaigns urging black consumers to support black-owned businesses emerged in other cities.[31]

South State Street was by the 1910s considered the heart of African American Chicago. The blocks surrounding the *Defender* office at Thirty-First Street were in many ways a biracial strip, particularly at night, when vaudeville houses were open and ragtime spilled into the crowded street. The appearance of white thrill seekers and music lovers did not prevent Motts and his sometime advocate *Defender* editor Robert Abbott from celebrating the Stroll. Black Chicagoans were barred from most of the city's commercial amusements, like skating rinks and amusement parks. No large commercial dance hall welcomed African Americans until the Savoy Ballroom opened in 1927. Yet Abbott wrote that African Americans had no fear of "racial embarrassment" in the cabarets, vaudeville houses, and smaller dance clubs along South State Street. He regularly published articles on the restaurants and hotels along the street, and columns guiding readers along the Stroll. Among his favorite spots was Thirty-First and State Streets, where the Defender's offices were located, and where "every man of color in Chicago, young or old . . . [could] meet all of his friends and . . . talk 'shop' to his 'hearts content.'" The Stroll was a "Mecca for Pleasure," comparable to world capitals as lively as Rome, Athens, and Jerusalem. The Stroll, Abbott suggested, was as much a state of mind as a place. It was a symbol of racial pride where "everything [was] up to date" and "Afro-Americans maintain[ed] the best decorum."[32]

The rise of commercial leisure spurred black entrepreneurs to seek political influence to protect their businesses, either through legal licensing or extralegal payoffs. Black entrepreneurs like Motts and Binga, along with the politicians they supported, powerfully influenced both the form and substance of local politics. As politics and business and legal and extralegal moneymaking intersected in the First and Second Wards, payoffs by and protection of entrepreneurs who mobilized voters and influenced electoral outcomes became not just common but the accepted method for participating in municipal governance. Entering the vice trades was, in many ways, a political choice, a means to create the collective financial muscle to engage local politics.[33]

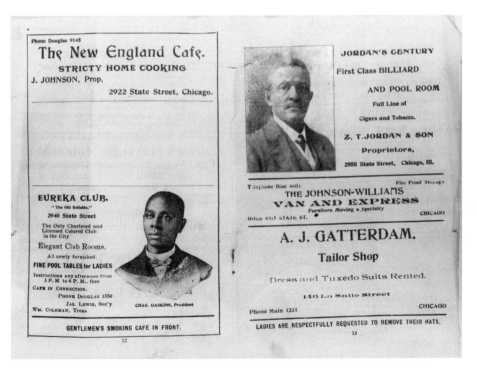

Ads for State Street clubs, *Chicago Defender*, n.d. Courtesy of University of Chicago Libraries.

Vice and the "bright lights" leisure that lined South State Street helped to generate a new movement of reformers who worked to shape government policy, becoming another force in local politics. Vice and the reformers who fought it then produced new issues of contention in civic life, new political language, and new public policies—whether the strategy of segregating vice or of sending police inspectors into brothels and gambling dens.[34] Many of the Black Belt's upstanding businessmen started out in the vice trades, and many successful politicians, especially those who launched careers before World War I, found their strongest financial backers among the entrepreneurs of vice. While vice generated capital to sustain black politicians, local churches gathered a constituency and brought politics into the daily lives of black Chicagoans.

———————————

The church had long been a central institution in African American communities. But at the turn of the twentieth century, as growing numbers of African Americans were moving to northern cities, black ministers grew increasingly concerned with guiding their congregants through the urban scene and making the church into a civic center viable and relevant to the demands of the twentieth century.[35] In Chicago, while Baptist churches grew and Catholic and Episcopalian churches attracted black congregants, two ministers of the AME Church emerged as the most vocal and visible religious leaders in the first decade of the twentieth century. Both men— Reverdy C. Ransom and Archibald J. Carey—were well educated, charismatic, and connected to the national Republican Party. The Reverends Ransom and Carey were also rivals, competing for influence in the AME hierarchy, for congregants, and for clout in local politics. Both used the pulpit and the press to advocate for civil rights for African Americans and to urge their supporters to participate in local and national politics. Both charted a new moral and political terrain in the city—a map of areas that accommodated black residents, of sites that threatened virtue, and of new urban spaces that remained racially contested, such as theaters, schools, and department stores. Most significantly, in linking church, community, and social struggles of urban black congregants, they in effect called into being a new political force constituted by the increasing concentration of black voters on the city's South Side.[36]

Chicago had approximately thirty-two churches open to African Americans in 1903 when Monroe Nathan Work and W. E. B. DuBois completed a survey of the black churches in Illinois for the eighth annual conference for "the Study of Negro Problems" at Atlanta University. There were a reported 8,000 church members in the city but only 4,969 "active members." Some black Chicagoans attended churches run by white ministers with largely white congregations. Racial segregation of the faithful occurred gradually in the 1910s and 1920s and was likely most pronounced among the city's Catholics. African American congregations ranged from fewer than a hundred members to more than a thousand, from rented rooms to the neo-Gothic buildings owned by Quinn Chapel, Olivet Baptist Church, and Bethel AME.[37] Until the 1910s, when tens of thousands of black southerners moved to Chicago, the AME churches were the city's most prominent black churches. During World War I, however, Baptist churches began to challenge the AME churches, with ministers like Rev. E. J. Fisher of Olivet gaining prominence. By 1915, the Baptists were the largest denomination, with more than twelve thousand members. Some churches were associated with established Chicago residents; others were quickly organized by new arrivals from the South.[38] In either case, churches attracted sinners and saints alike, those searching for social interaction and those seeking salvation.

The buildings housing the city's largest African American churches, typically neo-Gothic emblems of status, were designed to evoke European traditions. "A larger number of these churches are of the first order of architectural beauty and magnificence," said AME bishop Moses B. Salter during the 1904 AME conference hosted by Rev. Carey in Quinn Chapel.[39] The Gothic revival style arrived in the United States from Europe in the 1830s and was popularized in American pattern books, women's magazines, and fiction. For mid-nineteenth-century white Americans, the Gothic revival, promoted by writers like John Ruskin and landscape architect Andrew Jackson Downing, was a romantic turn away from stark neoclassicism and, with its ornate carvings, a celebration of both nature and preindustrial craftsmanship. The Gothic revival style signaled a cultural link to European Christianity.[40]

But the imposing neo-Gothic church buildings erected in late nineteenth-century cities by black and white congregations served other cultural purposes as well. The neo-Gothic church aimed to separate the church visually from the dirt and strife of industrial capitalism. Church buildings summoned images of domestic architecture, expanded versions of the Victorian cottage with their elaborate ornamentation, peaked roofs, and gabled interiors. For black congregations packed into racially segregated neighborhoods where vice and virtue were forced to live side by side, the Gothic revival church represented a break, a sharp separation, from the crass and often illicit commerce nearby. Congregations and their ministers regularly

Photo of Institutional Church, n.d. Courtesy of Chicago History Museum (file DN-0000554).

expressed pride in their church buildings, advertising the church alongside images of the building in city directories. Many also worried about the financial burdens of such signs of respectability and status.[41]

Nearly all of Chicago's black churches were in debt, mainly with mortgages for church property, which put pressure on ministers to raise money and at times limited the ability of the churches to respond to congregations' needs. The debt on "imposing edifices" sparked criticism of the ministers. Work and DuBois published comments from unnamed congregants interviewed in Chicago. "The primary idea seems to be to get the most good-paying members," commented one church member, referring to the ministers' need to raise money. "The building of large and imposing edifices . . . makes morals and religion serve as bell-ringer merely to call the congregation in order to cajole, importune or brow-beat interest money and pastor's salary," said another. Others noted, with regret and some bitterness, class differences among congregations. "The larger churches are largely attended by fashionably dressed people," a congregant said. "The smaller ones have a hard struggle to exist."[42]

While the "character" of the ministers was debated—with assessments ranging from "character good" to "charged with drunkenness and immorality"—a greater worry was whether or how the churches addressed "matters of charity and reform." Ministers and church members commented on life in the northern city: black Chicagoans struggled for wages and decent housing and to maintain respectable households despite the temptations of urban vice. These proved the greatest burden for the churches. "Poverty," answered one minister when asked about "their especial difficulties." Another responded, "How to secure sufficient means to prosecute the work in my district, which is the 'Slum District,' and how to treat and deal with the influx now migrating here from the South."[43]

Work and DuBois, in their expressly empirical study, were engaging and expanding a debate over the role of the churches and the status of ministers in urban centers. The authors—two educated northerners—revealed their own anxiety about the "ignorant" masses arriving in northern cities. Howard University sociologist Kelly Miller warned that unless African American churches addressed the problems of black southerners, "the last state of the race would be worse than the first." The black northerner "knows what this migration costs," commented DuBois in 1916.[44] Northern scholars like Miller, DuBois, and Work hoped churches and schools would "raise the moral standards" of migrating southerners. The survey questions about the ministers' character and comments on church services suggest that DuBois and Work were at best skeptical of less educated ministers and deeply critical of those who might see the ministry as a way to earn a living rather than a spiritual calling. "I do not know of any specific cases of immorality such as you make mention of here," one congregant responded to their leading question. Other interviewees did comment on the rumors of "sexual immorality and drunkenness" among ministers. Incompetent or ignorant ministers, the survey implied, were undermining the churches' chances for remaking rural migrants into upstanding urban residents.[45]

The function of the church mattered; so did the form and rhetoric of worship services. DuBois and Work were uneasy when "much emotion was displayed" in the delivery of the sermon. For them, emotionally charged sermons were signs of a backwardness, of a rural culture that needed to be transformed in order to succeed in modern urban society. Other black commentators linked excessive emotion to femininity, suggesting that a fervent and expressive spirituality was stripping black men of manhood. Emotional spirituality, said Rev. J. D. Brooks, impeded "a spirit of manhood." Brooks, who later became the secretary-general for Marcus Garvey's Universal Negro Improvement Association, considered the "singing and shouting" at some black churches an obstacle to the advancement of the race. Brooks's views tended to feminize black clergy—later a tactic of Garveyites attacking their opponents—a view not widely held in Chicago. His rejection of emotive preaching was common among the urban middle classes. Some white ministers offered a similar critique of "excessive" emotionalism. Though the rhetoric—the attacks on "primitism"—was similar, white church leaders and intellectuals apparently were more concerned with reconciling religion with science. African American intellectuals were distinguishing themselves from southern migrants, aiming to lift rural black congregants into the "modern" church.[46] "There are few positions in which a young man can do more harm than in the leadership of a church which is the exponent of nothing better than a mere emotional religionism," said Washington Gladden, president of the American Missionary Association, in 1903.[47] Carey repeatedly urged ministers to present themselves with "proper decorum."[48] By the late 1930s, the conceptual linkage of ministers' preaching style to the social class of the congregation was assumed by many church visitors and encoded in studies of African American religious life.[49] The critique of unrestrained emotion captured the tensions between rural and urban congregations, between uneducated migrants and well-to-do residents of the industrializing North.

The mission and character of ministers—frequently portrayed as charlatans—often lay at the core of concerns about the "ignorant" masses newly arrived from the rural South. In fiction and scholarly studies, black intellectuals expressed a new anxiety over who best to lead black Americans through the struggles of adjusting to and gaining influence in the industrializing city. Novelist and filmmaker Oscar Micheaux was widely known in the 1920s for his depictions of unscrupulous ministers in films like *Body and Soul*, a melodramatic tale of a corrupt minister played by a young Paul Robeson and released in 1925.[50] In their dry social science language, DuBois and Work's survey effectively drew on and reinforced an increasingly common caricature of the miscreant preaching with excessive fervor, grasping donations and leading congregants toward emotional outbursts. "There are few ministers with college and theological training," they wrote, "and the debt-ridden conditions of the churches call for men with ability to raise money rather than for men intellectually and morally strong."[51] The church was the place where ambitious young men might acquire influence—free of white pressure—in black neighborhoods. If they were not the right men—educated, moral, and respectable—then the ministers would not be prepared to guide their congregants through the dangers and challenges of life in the city.

The problem was not simply that ministers might be corrupt or uneducated. Even more, the city posed new dangers. Migration north broke up established communities and disrupted long-standing patterns of authority. Families might migrate together, and many sought to rebuild their old communities as they searched for friends and neighbors from home when they arrived in the city. Most black families, like European immigrants, reached Chicago with little money and little education. Black men, unlike European men, rarely got jobs in industry. The 1900 census found that almost 65 percent of African American men and over 80 percent of women worked as domestic and personal servants. A decade later, over 45 percent of employed black men worked in just four occupations—porters, servants, waiters, and janitors—and over 63 percent of women were domestic servants or laundresses. Black workers earned significantly less than white workers, and most faced regular layoffs. If they came north seeking stable jobs in rising industries, most found instead a new experience of urban poverty, run-down housing, and high mortality rates from contagious diseases.[52]

Southerners brought their own ideas about and experiences of worship services, sermons, ministers' roles, and community involvement in church activities, which often were at odds with the practices of established northern churches. Southerners, writes Wallace Best, were used to a preaching style that was "unschooled, emotional and theatrical."[53] By the 1910s, as migrants streamed into the city, many would try out several churches before settling on one; some, after a brief stay at a large old-line church, might split off and start a new one. These new institutions worried established church and community leaders. Storefront churches, "with their untrained pastors" and "unwholesome quarters," were often blamed for social ills in black neighborhoods.[54] Even worse were the "Negro spiritualists, advisers, mediums, and consultants," wrote Robert Sutherland in his 1930 study of black churches in Chicago. "These latter resemble churches only in the slightest degree." The "unscrupulous advisers" who took "large fees through the use of questionable methods" threatened to undercut the strength of the South Side's religious communities and the authority of the local black elite.[55] The city, filled with strangers, new temptations for the weak of character, and swindlers ready to cheat the ignorant, posed a host of dangers to susceptible new arrivals.

Debates over the role of the church often reflected differences in class, region, and denominational practices. The new arrivals placed new demands on established churches; many moved into inadequate housing, found little but low-paying jobs, and struggled to sustain themselves in the city. The church frequently was the sole agency able or willing to assist impoverished black families. Debates quickly emerged over whether and how to extend the church's spiritual mission to secular needs. Ultimately, with their social reform campaigns and political activism, some of Chicago's ministers would blur distinctions between the secular and the spiritual, putting local politics at the center of the ministers' concerns.

Archibald J. Carey Sr. was, in the first decade of the twentieth century, Chicago's most powerful politician who did not hold public office, certainly the most powerful black politician in or out of office. Born in Atlanta, the child of former slaves, Carey arrived in Chicago in 1898 with a strong education in theology and politics. He had graduated from Atlanta University in 1888 and immediately became a minister in the AME Church. Carey attributed his lifelong interest in politics to his childhood; at age ten, he became the secretary of the "Negro Republican organization of Atlanta" as he and his father, the organization's president, were the only members able to read and write. Carey's enthusiasm for politics likely was enhanced by his future wife, Elizabeth Hill Davis, the daughter of Reconstruction legislator Madison Davis.[56] The Careys moved to Jacksonville, Florida, where Carey served the state's largest AME church, Mount Zion. In 1898, saying he wanted to provide his children with "a fine education," Carey moved his wife and children to Chicago, to a comfortable house at Twenty-Fourth and Dearborn Streets. (The Careys later moved to the elegant Vernon Avenue.)[57] They arrived in a city rapidly filling with immigrants from eastern and southern Europe and in a neighborhood increasingly identified as the heart of black Chicago.

Carey's move to Chicago marked the expansion of a political education already begun with his work in the church. The AME Church, established in Philadelphia in 1816, had long been active in northern politics and would continue to claim authority in local issues. The church, as Carey's Chicago experience would show, was a deeply political institution, regularly split by internal rivalries and ideological disputes. The church was a highly structured, hierarchal institution. Bishops handed out church assignments and protected protégées. The denomination's conventions often were scenes of polite but hard-fought contests for promotions and prominent ministries. To gain the plum assignment to Quinn Chapel, considered the city's elite

Photo of Archibald J. Carey at the White House with President Calvin Coolidge and other black leaders, 1920. Courtesy of Chicago History Museum (file iCHI-31006).

black church, Carey surely had to maneuver around tough adversaries and demanding patrons. Carey's experiences within the church hierarchy prepared him well for Chicago's treacherous politics.[58]

Carey built his reputation as a sound businessman and an influence peddler with his first appointment in Chicago at the venerable Quinn Chapel, home to the city's oldest black congregation and, in 1898, a victim of the recent economic depression and poor management. When Carey arrived, the church was near financial ruin. The brick and gray stone building at the corner of Twenty-Fourth Street and Wabash Avenue, which the congregation had built in 1891, was slated for sale to pay off construction debts. In the following six years, Carey managed to clear nearly two-thirds of the $30,000 debt while completing several improvements on the building.[59] As he would in all endeavors, Carey raised money by drawing on personal connections and political favors. Well-known figures like poet Paul Laurence Dunbar, Rabbi Emil G. Hirsch, and social reformer Jane Addams were invited to speak at Quinn. Booker T. Washington gave a speech from Quinn's pulpit. It was also Carey's dramatic style, his eloquent sermons and explicit politics, that drew crowds on Sunday mornings. Carey doubled the Quinn congregation in just a few years, reportedly preaching to capacity crowds twice each Sunday. Carey's "fight for the race in the pulpit and on the public rostrum is one grand chapter in Chicago life," a reporter commented in the *Half-Century Magazine* in 1919.[60]

During Carey's first years in Chicago, the church's most auspicious guest was President William McKinley, who was invited by Carey to speak at Quinn while on a brief visit to Chicago in October 1899. McKinley's speech enhanced Carey's status among black leaders and sparked new tension with Ransom, who had invited the president to Bethel Church.[61] As African American leaders expressed disappointment with the Republican Party, McKinley openly courted northern black votes. McKinley's visit to Quinn Chapel suggested the rising influence of northern black political leaders. Men like Carey, McKinley implied, could be counted on to get out the black vote. A former governor of Ohio, McKinley won strong support from African American leaders, including the Barnetts, for his endorsement of antilynching legislation, which subsequently passed in Ohio. McKinley's campaign, run by Republican operative Mark Hanna, was headquartered in Chicago, where Hanna astutely established the Afro-American Bureau, a branch of the Republic National Committee. The bureau, reflecting Republican concern about black votes, was run by Ferdinand Barnett, who used the black press to get out the vote. It was enormously successful in bringing disillusioned black voters back to the Republican ticket.[62]

McKinley beat the free-silver Democrat William Jennings Bryan in 1896 and in his inaugural speech paid tribute to the black men who had supported him with an announcement that lynching would not be tolerated in the United States. Two years later, the new administration's intervention in Cuba had strong support from black Chicagoans who backed the Cuban independence struggle against Spain, the island's colonial ruler. In 1896, Spain crushed a rebellion and then "concentrated" the population in heavily guarded camps where thousands died of hunger and disease. Chicagoans, led by the Barnetts, had gathered at a mass meeting at Bethel church to "demand freedom for the Cubans." For his antilynching stance and apparent support of Cuban insurgents, McKinley remained personally popular among African Americans.[63]

McKinley's visit to what the *Tribune* called "the most pretentious church of the colored people of Chicago" drew a crowd of two thousand and bolstered Carey's claim to the status of a political insider. "The word 'welcome' in large letters was suspended over the pulpit," the *Tribune* enthused, "and the front of the church was draped with red, white, and, blue bunting."

As the president entered the church, the "congregation began singing 'My Country, 'Tis of Thee.' The President joined them." In attendance were members of the Eighth Illinois Volunteers who had fought in Cuba. McKinley praised black Americans for their "love of country." "The black men of the United States have shown their patriotism and valor. They not only fought in Cuba, but they are fighting valiantly in the Philippines, upholding the flag in that distant land," McKinley said. For Carey, it was an opportunity to demonstrate black patriotism to white Chicago and to display his own influence in national politics to local white and black officials.[64]

Carey found other ways to gain influence among black Chicagoans and, in the process, helped to expand the role of the church in the growing African American neighborhood. Drawing on a tradition of social activism at Quinn, Carey pushed the congregation to support an array of social services based in the church and financed by the minister's fund-raising. In 1901, a group of women church members formed a "Kindergarten Association" and began raising money for the "poor children in the neighborhood of the church." His church sponsored women's clubs, men's clubs, literary associations, and discussion groups on political topics of the day.[65]

In his social reform work, Carey was likely influenced by his charismatic rival at Bethel AME, Rev. Reverdy C. Ransom. A free-born Ohioan who had attended Oberlin College and Wilberforce University, Ransom was deeply affected by the social gospel movement of the late nineteenth century. He was, according to his close friend and ally Ida Wells-Barnett, "a tall, spare stranger" with "a musical voice, a pleasant smile and a winning manner."[66] After serving as Bethel's pastor for four years, Ransom, in 1900, founded the Institutional Church and Social Settlement, where he stayed until 1904, when he left Chicago under pressure from Carey and his supporters. Ransom moved first to a church in New Bedford, Massachusetts, became a founding member of the NAACP, ran unsuccessfully for Congress from upstate New York, and in 1924 was elected bishop of the AME Church. Ransom married three times and published six books and scores of articles and poems in Christian and secular journals.[67] Ransom, throughout his life, openly and confidently, merged his spiritual mission with seemingly secular pursuits.

Ransom's most innovative and influential work in Chicago was to found the Institutional Church and Social Settlement, a new kind of organization designed to help the church address the challenges of the modern city. With approval from AME bishop Benjamin Arnett and $34,000 from the national AME Church, Ransom purchased a former Presbyterian church building on Dearborn near Thirty-Ninth Street in 1900.[68] The neo-Gothic

Photo of Reverdy and Emma Ransom on the steps of Institutional Church, ca.1904.
Courtesy of Chicago History Museum (file DN-0000555).

brick building contained sixteen rooms, including an auditorium, dining room, kitchen, and gymnasium. Reverdy and Emma Ransom moved into three rooms at the rear and opened the building to the public on July 24. Ransom had been impressed with the work of Jane Addams, who in 1889 opened Hull House on the city's West Side. Her aim, she said, was to live among the poor and provide services and education for European immigrants. Ransom also drew on an older African American tradition of self-help, the work of northern evangels traveling south after the Civil War to help remake southern society. The missions, or "proto–settlement houses," as Frank Luker calls them, were built in rural communities and, by the 1870s, in northern cities. They served as churches, schools, and settlement houses, organized to help recent migrants and immigrants rebuild rural communities or make new lives in cities. Ransom's settlement house was the first owned and operated by African Americans for African Americans. Its direct tie to the church made it a mix of the new and old, European and American strategies for addressing urban social problems.[69]

With Institutional Church, Ransom stepped fully into the social reform movements that spread throughout Chicago society at the turn of the twentieth century. Though Ransom aimed to operate the church as an autonomous black institution, its links to the settlement-house movement, both in theory and practice, put the black ministers in regular contact with white reformers. Many white Chicagoans—including Jane Addams, Mary McDowell, Graham Taylor, lawyer Clarence Darrow, and Jessie Strong Bradley, the wife of Victor Lawson, owner of the *Chicago Daily News*—donated money and provided "active sympathy and cooperation."[70] Institutional Church and Social Settlement was also a reaction to the refusal of white settlement houses to address the needs of black Chicagoans. Ida B. Wells-Barnett was outraged to learn in 1900 that white-owned settlement houses were turning black children away from their kindergartens. She opened a kindergarten at Bethel Church and later launched a settlement house.[71]

Ransom saw Institutional Church as the "future church," less concerned with denominational doctrine than with the social struggles of black urban residents. His program was ambitious and comprehensive. "We know no creed and no race," Ransom told the *Inter Ocean*. "Anybody who needs help can come here." Ransom added that the settlement's primary aim was to assist the "young men and women from the Southern states and help them to get work in Chicago." It provided an employment bureau and kindergarten, classes on black history and literature, music, sewing, and "domestic arts" courses. The church sponsored men's and women's clubs. The social settlement, the first "in the world for the race," aimed to thwart the pull of neighborhood vice. Ransom was concerned about the growing number of women and men in "Joliet Penitentiary. . . . This is . . . because nobody takes an interest in them," the *Inter Ocean* noted. "He [Ransom] hopes to get out of the saloons and gambling places, Negro boys from 18 to 20 and the girls from 14 years who are a community problem."[72]

Ransom's church and settlement worked to create a sense of community, of black Chicagoans bound together in need and assistance. As with white settlement houses, the racially segregated neighborhood determined the boundaries of church work. The church sponsored "a dozen deaconesses" who canvassed the neighborhood, "seeking strangers, visiting the sick and feeding, clothing and making warm the poor and needy." They served the community and the church.[73]

Ransom opposed Booker T. Washington and was outspoken in his attacks on the Tuskegee leader. Disgusted by Washington's refusal to challenge southern disfranchisement of black voters, Ransom was among the first black leaders to openly criticize Washington. At a meeting of the Afro-American Council in Chicago in August 1899, Ransom proclaimed, "No such man ought to claim to be our leader. We want the country to know he is nothing to us." Even DuBois thought Ransom had gone too far and urged him to send a note of apology, which Ransom did. Others among Ransom's opponents labeled him a socialist, claiming he was more concerned with finding jobs for black workers than with saving their souls. Ransom ultimately found an ally in DuBois and some AME bishops, all the while stirring conflict among Chicago's black ministers.[74]

Ransom's vision was of racial uplift through self-help, education, and political engagement. There were lectures on politics, philosophy, and the arts at Institutional Church. Men and women each had important tasks in lifting up "the race." The girls club featured instructions "in hygiene, morals, deportment and direction in the choice of reading matter." Black women were to be trained to raise healthy, moral children, not simply in the drudgery of household service. Ransom also offered support for a group that was largely rejected by Chicagoans, black and white: interracial couples. In his autobiography written nearly fifty years later, Ransom described the Manasa Society, a group of married couples of black and white partners who were "shunned by the Negro churches." He welcomed parents and children to the church so they might come "under a Christian influence." "Not only in its narrower sense [was] the religious life developed in Institutional Church, but humanity in all its breadth [was] taught," commented a 1901 article in the *Chicago American*.[75]

It was that breadth of services, apparently, that sparked controversy among the South Side ministers and, ultimately, prompted Ransom to leave Chicago. Carey reportedly complained to Bishop Abram Grant about the church's shift away from customary religious programs. Bishop Henry McNeal Turner backed Ransom while the Chicago ministers continued to attack. His fellow ministers, some possibly envious of his growing congregation, saw Ransom as stripping the church of its religious purpose and denominational distinctiveness. "Most of the preachers of Negro churches of that day strenuously opposed it [Institutional Church]," Ransom wrote years later. "It was entirely beyond their conception of what a church should be. . . . Going out into the street and highways, bearing a message of social, moral, economic and civic salvation they did not believe to be a function of the church." Under a steady stream of criticism, Ransom abruptly quit Institutional Church and moved to New England in 1904.[76] Some, like Wells-Barnett and Richard R. Wright, saw the controversy as scandalmongering among Ransom's opponents and a victory for the more conservative and self-promoting Carey. Five years later, Carey was appointed pastor of Institutional Church and though he had been among Ransom's leading critics, Carey maintained much of the church's social mission.[77]

Despite spending just a decade in Chicago and despite his controversial departure, Ransom proved a crucial force in directing black churches to address the social and secular problems of twentieth-century urban congregants. The Institutional Church and Social Settlement was, DuBois wrote, "the most advanced step in the direction of making the church exist for the people rather than the people for the church."[78]

Even as Carey, Ransom, and other ministers argued over the role of the church in the industrializing city, they were, in many ways, drawing a map of the modern city, highlighting the color line and denouncing pockets of vice. Their sermons and published speeches detailed scenes of vice and sites of danger, identified places of friendship and those of bigotry. The racial segregation of urban space, by law or custom, was a growing concern. At a 1908 General Conference in Norfolk, Virginia, the AME bishops denounced "class legislation. . . . This ostracism is inhuman, anti-Christian, and barbarous, and should be buried—hastily so—in the grave side by side with that infamous institution, slavery."[79] In Chicago, where racial segregation of public spaces was widely recognized but not set in law, ministers reminded new arrivals that Jim Crow thrived in the North. AME ministers urged congregants to avoid places where "discriminations are practiced," including "hotels, cafes, restaurants, soda fountains, ice cream parlors, barber shops, etc."[80] The ministers warned newly arrived urban residents away from embarrassing (or worse) encounters in public even as they aimed to protect them from the temptations of State Street leisure.

As urban congregations grew, ministers offered increasingly explicit exhortations against the dangers of city life. Archibald Carey, following AME bishops, attacked local saloons and gambling halls. Robert Motts was condemned as "the keeper of a low-gambling dive." In a highly publicized break with the Barnetts in 1905, Carey savaged Ida Wells-Barnett for holding a fund-raising ball for the Women's Club of the Frederick Douglass Center at the newly renovated Pekin Theatre. What most incensed Carey was that the theater sat across the street from Olivet Baptist Church. Wells-Barnett recalled later that Olivet's Rev. Elijah J. Fisher denounced the theater, proclaiming that "he hoped his tongue would cleave to the roof of his mouth and its right hand lose its cunning" if he ever entered the Pekin Theatre. Carey and Fisher stirred up enough controversy that some of Wells-Barnett's elite friends refused to attend the ball. For Carey, the controversy may have been part of a larger plan to discredit Wells-Barnett, especially after her alliance with Ransom. He viewed her as a threat to his political ambitions. (Wells-Barnett later reported that Elijah Fisher came to see the Pekin Theatre as a respectable venue and agreed to address a political meeting there. Wells-Barnett, remembering Fisher's pious attack on the Pekin, mischievously noted that as he approached the stage, he was struck with a paralysis from which he never recovered.)[81] Carey and Fisher, preaching against vice from pulpits within walking distance of "the Stroll" generated a series of intersecting and overlapping maps—rhetorically at least—guiding their parishioners (and those who read about the controversy) through the expanding and increasingly chaotic Black Belt.

Carey may well have seen the gambling bosses and saloonkeepers, men like Motts and Johnson, as challenging his political strength. At the same time, he believed the church must call attention to sites that threatened the community's virtue. Neither stance, political or moral, was incompatible. During Carey's first year as an AME bishop, the Kentucky conference, over which he presided, issued a blunt warning against the dangers of urban life. "There is, in the social order to-day certain influences, as deadly to the moral, mental and spiritual welfare of the young, as was the deadly saloon," stated the bishops' speech in 1921, "namely the public dance hall, with its 'Jazz' music, and immoral dances." After denouncing urban dangers like gambling dens and saloons, the bishops declared, "We further believe, it is the duty of all churches to do all in their power to stamp out every influence which leads to intemperance."[82]

In listing the dangers posed by the city, the ministers, in effect, defined the city as a challenge to the sacred space of the church and made cleansing the city an extension of saving the souls of their neighbors. In their hands, the urban environment called on committed churchgoers to improve city life. To travel along an urban street, choosing which doors to enter and which commercial sites to protest, was both an expression of moral commitment and a political choice.[83] For Carey, it was this new city, freighted with danger but populated with an increasingly mobilized black constituency that would transform both urban and national politics. "Teach your people," he admonished the AME ministers in a 1922 lecture, "God gives them the privilege and opportunity for helping themselves and their race along through our church."[84]

Carey moved from Quinn Chapel to Bethel and then to Ransom's old pulpit at Institutional Church in 1909. He quickly turned Institutional into what his biographer Joseph Logsdon calls "the town hall," though it was more like headquarters for an increasingly engaged and militant African American electorate. As he had at Quinn, Carey invited famous activists and intellectuals, black and white, to lecture at the church. During election time, candidates—usually but not always Republican—were invited to speak from the pulpit.[85]

The ballot, Carey commented, "is his [the African American's] only weapon of defense, his only means of protection against injustice and oppression." Discussions of civic and community affairs were regular features of Carey's church work. There were forums almost every Sunday evening and most weeknights, often advertised in the *Defender*. One 1913 call to a political forum announced a "special meeting" to discuss "opposition to 'Jim Crow Legislation'" before the state legislature in Springfield. Ida Wells-Barnett and the Honorable G. W. Ellis were among the announced speakers. "Because Dr. Carey so frequently" discusses "current events and recent openings in his discourses," he attracted large crowds, the *Defender* commented. "None were disappointed."[86]

Most of the city's black churches attended to secular issues; there were few other agencies assisting struggling black families living in the South Side neighborhoods. But especially after he left Quinn Chapel, Carey's churches were probably the most overtly and directly political. Carey drew new attention to city hall's neglect of black Chicagoans by employing church staff to challenge city policies. While leading Institutional Church, Carey hired a staff of trained social workers to assist church members in

finding housing and jobs and petitioning health inspectors or fighting purported violations of local health codes.[87] Most important, Carey launched
an employment service, which effectively linked the minister to powerful
white employers and generated for him a growing and grateful constituency of black voters. The service found jobs for parishioners as domestic
workers in the homes of wealthy white Chicagoans and sent black men to
the Pullman Company and the firms in the stockyards. Carey's daughter,
Annabelle, later recalled that some of the city's wealthiest industrialists had
been important benefactors for the church and that Carey used those connections to set up jobs for his congregants.[88] On some Sundays, Carey even
announced available positions from the pulpit, simultaneously offering
spiritual and economic succor.

Carey was a vocal opponent of organized labor. In the first two decades of the twentieth century, labor unions largely rejected black workers; Carey's attitude toward labor organizing may well have been forged
by labor's own racism and was not that different from the views of most
black activists in the city. In 1905 during a bloody teamsters strike, he led
a mass meeting and, along with other ministers, signed a letter protesting
the way "certain newspapers . . . inject the race issue" into the strike. Ida
Wells-Barnett and the well-known physician George Cleveland Hall spoke
to the crowd in the church. Like the ministers, they "deplored the attitude
taken toward the colored workmen" by the union and the press. But by
the 1920s, ministers at other churches, particularly at Olivet and Ebenezer
Baptist, allowed organizers to speak on Sundays and unions to hold meetings in their churches. Carey's position did not change. He opposed the
race-conscious efforts of black organizers to build the Brotherhood of
Sleeping Car Porters, aligning himself instead with their white employer.
The Pullman Company gave money to black organizations, in particular
to Institutional Church. Elite and educated, Carey, though promoting African American political interests, identified with the status and concerns of
white industrialists. He argued for a collective approach to politics while
affirming the individualist ethos of capitalism. "The interest of my people
lies with the wealth of the nation and with the class of white people who
control it," he commented.[89]

Carey's opposition to labor unions may have been fueled by the AME
Church's official position, which was largely to ignore labor conflict in the
North. The "labor question," which had disrupted and divided American
cities since Reconstruction, did not prompt official statements from the
church until 1920, when the General Conference, meeting in Saint Louis,
appointed a "Labor Commission" to "collect data and facts" on labor in

general and "Negro labor in particular." Carey, who became a bishop in 1920, helped to shape church policy. He imposed his antilabor views on all Chicago area churches, barring leaders of the Brotherhood of Sleeping Car Porters from AME churches. Church officials through the 1920s seemed more concerned with helping migrants learn about the "nature of work" in factories than with addressing their conflicts with employers.[90] Some black Chicagoans, particularly those who supported the Pullman porters' organizing campaigns in the 1920s, considered Carey's approach conservative, if not altogether thwarting the interests of black workers.

With his employment service, Carey took on the role of the ward captain or political boss, handing out jobs in exchange for steadfast dedication. During the 1910s and 1920s, ministers in poorer storefront churches often augmented their income by serving as informal employment services for local industrialists. Carey, in the first decades of the century, ran fairly large and financially stable churches. He used his connections to wealthy industrialists to enhance his own position with his congregants, while strengthening his church with large donations. Carey's ability to provide for his congregants in the secular and the spiritual realms expanded his popularity among grateful congregants, though by the 1920s, his opposition to labor unions fueled new criticism.[91] Merging the provision of jobs and other services with the church's mission of spiritual salvation, Carey made the church into a civic institution with an increasingly robust and politically engaged group of supporters.

Carey's introduction to Chicago politics, and to the man whose career would be entwined with his, came a couple of years after his arrival in the city. The minister met and befriended William Hale Thompson, future mayor and future leader of the city's Republican machine, in 1900 during the aldermanic campaign in Chicago's Second Ward. Thompson, heir to a fortune in Chicago real estate, lived in the Metropole Hotel, at Twenty-Third Street and Michigan Boulevard, the "silk-stocking" district of the Second Ward. At six feet tall and recently returned from running a ranch in the West, Thompson was an athlete and a gambler. On a bet from a friend at the Chicago Athletic Association, he decided to run for alderman, challenging the Democratic incumbent Charles F. Gunther. Carey quickly became Thompson's champion among black voters. Carey took the candidate from "door to door throughout the Negro neighborhood," introduced him to his congregants, and urged their support. Though Carey's sermons from 1900 (a collection of which were in his son's possession) contain no mention of the campaign, Thompson credited the minster with getting out the vote and swinging the election to the Republican.[92]

With the campaign, Thompson faced several major hurdles that would continue to divide black activists and complicate efforts to form a cohesive black electorate for the following decade. The city's Republican Party was split into two hostile factions; the Second Ward was largely Democratic, divided among working-class black voters, elite whites along the eastern edge, and a growing red-light district that angered black and white voters. While Carey helped swing the election Thompson's way, Thompson owed his victory to the powerful and corrupt aldermen of the First Ward, John Coughlin and Michael Kenna, better known as "Bathhouse John" and "Hinky Dink," who together protected and profited from the Levee district's gambling and prostitution. As the Levee expanded south from the First into the Second Ward, Coughlin and Kenna sought to protect their interests, and Second Ward alderman Gunther refused to cooperate. The two retaliated by handing Thompson the "flop house vote," and Thompson beat Gunther by four hundred votes. It was therefore vice and virtue, the minister and the flophouse, that gave Thompson his first political victory and, not coincidentally, lifted Carey to kingmaker among black voters in the Republican Party.[93]

Thompson's victory and the rapid conclusion to his aldermanic career were likely Carey's first lessons in northern machine politics. Coughlin and Kenna, determined to expand their vice empire, convinced the novice and largely uninterested alderman to support a redistricting plan in 1901, which extended the First Ward to include all the vice district and Thompson's home, thus forcing Thompson from office. Before he left, Thompson pushed the city council to allocate $1,200 for the construction of a playground in the Second Ward—apparently in appreciation for his black supporters. The playground was built directly across the street from Quinn Chapel. This cemented Thompson's friendship with the politically astute minister. Carey had effectively drawn his congregants' attention to the benefits of participation in local elections, and the result was visible: a playground in a neighborhood without parks. The church could and would provide many social services, but if black Chicagoans would join the give and take of ward politics, they might garner further benefits.[94]

Thompson's greatest gift, and perhaps liability, to Carey was to introduce the minister to influential white politicians, putting the ambitious minister in the midst of the Republican Party's early twentieth-century interparty battles. Carey quickly became an ally of William J. Lorimer, a US representative and later senator, the "placid blond boss, whose name aroused conflicting emotions and animosities." Lorimer, as Harold Gosnell writes, "played the game of politics that is based upon personal loyalties. . . . He was faithful to his friends and ruthless in his attacks upon his enemies." He handed out jobs and favors in exchange for support at the polls. Lorimer's strength came from the West Side, but when he combined with Thompson and Representative Martin B. Madden, the Lorimer faction, as it was known, amassed considerable support from black voters. The English-born Madden, a representative for the First Congressional District on the South Side, had been courting black politicians and voters since his election as alderman in 1889.[95]

There was little reason Lorimer should have appealed to black Chicagoans. He was known to make racist comments from the floor of the Senate and did little for black civil rights. But he seemed to support the fight against lynching, appearing at a protest meeting at Institutional Church in 1897. His brand of politics, a pragmatism that brought needed jobs and cash to struggling South Siders, appealed to black political leaders. Moreover, Lorimer's opponent within the Republican Party, Charles S. Deneen, was widely seen as cold and aristocratic. Deneen, who served as governor from 1905 to 1913 and US senator from 1925 to 1931, portrayed himself as a reformer. He won some support from well-to-do black Chicagoans like Wells-Barnett and her husband when as governor he backed a state antilynching bill. He appointed several black leaders to political offices, though his appointment of Ferdinand Barnett to the state attorney's office came only after pressure from Edward Wright, then president of the county board. The political scientist Charles Merriam, himself a devoted reformer, wrote that the Lorimer faction "developed a powerful organization all over the city, and in general built upon patronage, graft, privilege, and all sorts of political alliances of whatever character seemed useful for the moment." Merriam considered such activity corrupt, as did many others. "Senator Lorimer represents a school of politics which every intelligent American citizen knows is rotten to the core," wrote one journalist in 1912. But for Carey and many South Side black voters, patronage, corrupt or not, proved a powerful tool.[96]

Machine politics—the delivery of jobs and services in exchange for support at the polls—expanded and further entrenched the work of the church. The machine provided a path for ambitious black men to win local office or influential and relatively high-paying municipal jobs. It was, generally, the only entity willing to support employment for black men in city hall or in local industry. Though machine leaders hand-picked candidates, it was the black constituency—voters, congregants, club members—who bestowed political clout on their African American leaders. Black leaders garnered neighborhood support by bringing jobs and services to the community; they proved their worth to the machine by delivering votes, collected through corrupt or legal means.

The tiny band of black activists who allied themselves with Lorimer came together, at least initially, in 1901 to promote the mayoral candidacy of Judge Elbridge Hanecy, who had lost a race for governor the previous year. Hanecy expressed (probably false) surprise when a group of Second Ward Republicans visited his offices in February 1901 and urged him to run for mayor. The group included Robert Motts's personal lawyer and former state legislator Edward H. Morris along with Carey and a dozen other white and black community leaders. "Demand of Second Ward committee gets judge's consent to be candidate," ran the *Tribune* headline, adding the group claimed to be "wholly independent of Lorimer influences." That claim rang hollow. Hanecy was a longtime Lorimer supporter, and his candidacy marked a challenge to Lorimer's opponent, the Republican reformer John M. Harlan. "Judge Hanecy is the fittest man in the city for the Mayoralty," Carey told a *Tribune* reporter, openly aligning himself with Lorimer.[97]

Carey used his alliance with the Lorimer faction effectively and strategically. He made it clear that Lorimer could not simply assume his support. Carey's biographer portrays him as an "ambassador" to white Chicago, while other scholars describe early twentieth-century black politics as "white clientage."[98] Black political work was undoubtedly deeply entwined in the intrigues of white factions. But the agendas pursued by black leaders and their constituencies were hardly determined by or dependent on white politicians. Carey, with a base of supporters and salary independent of politics, was able to navigate networks of white politicians to achieve at least some of his goals. He did not always support Republicans. Indeed he was vilified by the Democratic African American newspaper the *Broad Ax* for his willingness, when convenient, to shift his support between Democratic and Republican candidates. Though publically extolling Hanecy, Carey backed Democrat Carter H. Harrison II for mayor. After Carey's vocal support for Harrison's reelection in 1911, the mayor appointed Carey to the Motion Picture Censor Board, where Carey led a protest against the overtly racist film *The Birth of a Nation*. Harrison, who appointed several black men to city hall jobs, reportedly said, "The Negro will divide his vote if the proper intelligence is displayed in seeking it." That was Harrison's experience. Similarly, Carey's support for Democratic governor Edward

Dunne led to Carey's appointment to head the committee to celebrate the fiftieth anniversary of the Thirteenth Amendment. Carey's church served as the committee headquarters, winning some of the $25,000 appropriated by the state legislature for the event. Yet it was Carey's alliance with Lorimer that gave Carey a regular voice in municipal politics; even when he was attacked for the alliance in the black press, his views were read by thousands of black Chicagoans.[99]

Carey's opposition to Deneen and the coalition of reformers who supported him may have furthered his own ambitions but was also calculated to serve African American interests. Carey, along with many black politicians, opposed legislation considered "progressive" by white activists. They opposed the introduction of the initiative, referendum, and recall measures touted by progressives as bringing greater democracy to the state and moving legislative decisions out of what many perceived as corrupt, machine-run city halls. But many black leaders believed the initiative and referendum threatened black civil rights. The measures, the *Chicago Defender* asserted, were "simply a dose of disfranchisement, sugar coated, albeit, with high sounding and illusive verbiage for the consumption of the northern Negro." The paper said that "in the broad light of day" black people had a "chance for justice" but with these progressive measures "the civil rights of the Negro will be decided in the silence and seclusion of the voting booth, where his enemies may stab him in the back and none be the wiser."[100]

Similarly, Carey and other black leaders opposed legislation to establish direct nominations by voters for candidates in primary elections. Activists contended that direct nominations would draw greater publicity to the candidates' race and likely eliminate black candidates from consideration. The activists believed the machine system, with ward bosses choosing candidates based on the candidates' contributions to the party, gave black politicians a stronger chance of getting on the ballot. Gosnell suggests that passage of the law requiring nominations of candidates by voters in 1910 proved the activists right; fewer black candidates were elected to the Cook County Board of Commissioners, which required a citywide vote, after passage of the law.[101] Carey's aim was to assure that black voters continued to have access to the political process and that black politicians, particularly those loyal to him, got elected. Support for the party bosses and the backroom deals they represented seemed to serve the interests of his church, his supporters, and Carey himself.

Not all black activists agreed with Carey. Some strongly supported reform candidates, in particular the University of Chicago political science professor Charles E. Merriam, who served as alderman for the Hyde Park neighborhood and made two failed runs for the mayor's office. Merriam was a vocal enemy of the Republican machine, arguing to ban patronage and for a government assault on South Side vice. He won support from a number of influential white Chicagoans.[102] Some elite black Chicagoans favored Merriam, as did some waiters, Pullman porters, and respectable churchgoing families. Merriam spoke at a "mass meeting" of progressive Republicans at the Pekin Theatre in April 1912. The Negro Fellowship League, founded by Ida Wells-Barnett in 1908, supported Merriam's mayoral bid in 1911 and again in 1919. The league included forty to fifty young men, mostly recent migrants from the South and churchgoers seeking "friendship" in the city. Wells-Barnett in a handwritten letter appealed "to my race throughout the city to work and vote for Chicago's best interests" by voting for Merriam. Allying herself with those progressives who believed that partisan politics had corrupted urban governance, Wells-Barnett promoted Merriam as an "expert in civic affairs," an incorruptible manager who could "deal with every phase of the city's complex life."[103]

Politics did not cut seamlessly across class lines, but in the 1910s, some among the educated and elite found a white reformer preferable to a machine candidate. African American support for Merriam seemed to increase in the winter of 1919 when he announced he would challenge Mayor William Hale Thompson for the mayor's office. There was a "Young Colored Men's Merriam for Mayor Club" run by Wells-Barnett's oldest son and including two other Barnetts, as well as several black lawyers, dentists, and doctors. They backed Merriam despite rumors that he had worked with a neighborhood organization that sought to bar black families from Hyde Park, an accusation Merriam denied. The machine, they argued, was the enemy of the "the race." A statement from the "Second Ward Merriam for Mayor Club" in 1919 urged voters to "redeem this ward from the clutches of bossism and debauchery." Merriam's support among black Chicagoans appeared to come largely from the well-off and educated.[104]

Carey, when he needed to, could work effectively with the progressive faction of the Republican Party. His work, particularly an effort to free a black laborer in 1910, revealed the complex lines of political influence and ethnic and racial hatred cutting through Chicago. Carey, spurred by a plea from Wells-Barnett, worked with gambling boss Dan Jackson and lawyers Edward Wright and W. G. Anderson to save Steven Green, a black farm laborer, from lynching. After a shootout on an Arkansas farm, Green had fled to Chicago, where, according to the *Defender*, "a dirty set of Irish policemen at Harrison Street police station" arrested him and threatened to send him back to Arkansas, where a mob attack and lynching likely awaited him. Carey and Green urged Governor Deneen to reject extradition for Green, and Anderson persuaded a judge to order the Harrison police to turn Green over to the county sheriff's office. When asked by Judge Tuthill if he was willing to return to Arkansas to face charges in the shooting death of a white farmer, Green answered, "No, your honor, because I knows the nature of that country." The judge, after a hearing before a packed courtroom, freed Green.[105]

The alliance between church and politics, Carey and the machine branch of the Republican Party, was perhaps most visible November 1911 when Carey celebrated the twentieth anniversary of his ordination at Institutional Church. Among the "distinguished guests" celebrating the "noted divine" were William J. Lorimer and Martin Madden. The event brought "out a larger number of prominent men of both races than has been seen in Chicago in a long time," the *Defender* commented. Madden and Lorimer were "stalwart friends . . . always at home" wherever "the race gathers." Speakers that evening were ministers, politicians (including Madden), and local dignitaries like George C. Hall. No one who attended the celebration or read about it in the *Defender* the following week could have missed the point that politics was part of the church's mission and that the city's white machine politicians were in many ways beholden to its black ministers.[106]

Carey did more than collect favors and promote African American candidates, though he did quite a bit of both. He also proved a powerful voice for black civil rights, both within the church and at secular public gatherings. "We ask nothing more than a fair chance and will be satisfied with nothing less," Carey proclaimed in a 1913 speech.[107] Even as the increasingly rigid racial segregation in housing provided Carey and the black politicians he supported with a steady voter base, the minister railed against racial segregation. "This nation cannot live on injustice," he proclaimed. In 1906, Carey helped organize a "peace rally" to protest a speech by Senator Ben Tillman in Orchestra Hall. Tillman, a South Carolina Democrat, was an outspoken racist. Carey, then minister at Bethel Chapel, worked with a group of elite black Chicagoans, including the dentist Charles S. Bentley and *Broad Ax* editor Julius F. Taylor, to pressure Mayor Busse to "call the affair off" with a "sensational 'tongue lashing.' " They appealed to "liberty loving Negroes to rise up and drive Tillman from Chicago." Tillman's speech went forward as planned but without an introduction from the mayor; Carey had demonstrated his devotion to the race and willingness to take on at least some white politicians.[108]

"I may have been represented to you as a 'political preacher,' " Carey wrote in an angry 1914 letter to the *Defender*. "I do not deny that." Proudly defending his record as a voice for the more than "70,000 colored people in Chicago" as well as those in Illinois and the nation, Carey announced that he sided with "the white men in this city who were disposed to give the Negro fair play." These were, of course, the leaders of the Lorimer (by then Madden) faction and the powerful Democrats Carter H. Harrison and Edward F. Dunne. "I have never voted for nor advocated any man whom I did not feel was interested in civic betterment, in the community's uplift, and was disposed in his heart," Carey wrote, "to give my people fair play."[109] Carey could hardly have believed that Lorimer, Madden, or Thompson had the rights of African Americans at heart. But he was well aware that those machine politicians, steeped in the fine art of quid pro quo, might offer something in exchange for the support of the city's most vocal black minister. A new playground, some jobs for black laborers, some state and municipal revenue tossed to the Black Belt church: all were signs that he was effectively ministering to his people.

Carey remained loyal, if somewhat distant, when the "blond boss," William Lorimer, was booted out of Washington. Lorimer had been elected to the US Senate in 1909 and, after three years of bitter attacks by a hostile Chicago press and two investigations of bribery charges, was unseated by the Senate in 1912. It was a humbling defeat for the formerly powerful machine leader, who in the following years became a banker. He was never convicted on the bribery charges, though his career with the LaSalle Street Bank was cut short in 1916 when he was charged with and acquitted of embezzling bank funds. Lorimer's removal from the Senate spurred reformers who had long argued that state legislatures, which until then appointed US senators, were susceptible to bribery for Senate seats. A year later, a constitutional amendment gave the voters of each state the right to elect their senators.[110]

Carey was in the crowd that greeted Lorimer when he returned to Chicago, as was William Hale Thompson, who had cemented the bond between the minister and the machine. Lorimer's fall only strengthened Thompson and left Carey with a new opportunity: the chance to direct South Side black votes Thompson's way in the mayoral election in 1915.

Carey's ties to the Lorimer organization were just one piece of an expanding and complex political system in the Black Belt. The policy kings, cabaret owners, and storefront saloonkeepers with their payoffs to local police and contributions to South Side candidates made up another, sometimes intersecting power base. The vice trades spread money throughout the community, creating an economic infrastructure for African American politicians and reinforcing the reciprocal relations of municipal politics. The ministers rallied their congregations with promises of jobs and services, building on the rigid planks of racial segregation that concentrated black voters in South Side wards. Cash and favors moved through official coffers, State Street businesses, Black Belt churches, and neighborhood homes.

Robert Motts's funeral in July 1911 was an elaborate exhibit of the complex lines linking licit and illicit businesses, the spiritual to the earthly delights of Black Belt politics. The event was held at Quinn Chapel, where "a waiting throng" spilled into the street. Three ministers presided over the ceremony, which interspersed scriptural readings with "solos by some of our most prominent artists." The *Defender* listed distinguished men in the crowd including Dr. Daniel Hale Williams and nightclub owner Henry "Teenan" Jones, as well as lawyer and future alderman Louis B. Anderson. Jesse Binga was an honorary pallbearer. The *Tribune*'s obituary reminded readers of Motts's early career in gambling, subtly disparaging the achievements of a leading Black Belt entrepreneur and, in all likelihood, aiming to tie all black entrepreneurs to vice. The *Defender* never mentioned Motts's illicit activities, instead honoring him as the "owner of the first race theatre in America."[111] Motts was, in the *Defender*'s account, a model of African American success and a symbol of black Chicago's unity and self-sufficiency. Neither report captured the complexity of affiliations and obligations binding black entrepreneurs, ministers, and politicians along the Stroll.

Motts had well understood the political imperatives of debts and favors, legal and extralegal reciprocity. He had pioneered a powerful strand of black politics, linking black business, the illicit and the respectable, to African American political power. Within a few years after his demise, Motts's close friend Henry "Teenan" Jones took up the political aims of the Stroll. Jones, who had worked in white-owned restaurants in Hyde Park, was a part owner of the Elite Café at 3030 South State Street, a bar and restaurant with a small music hall. In 1915, he opened Teenan Jones' Place, also known as Elite No. 2, at 3445 South State Street, a cabaret where he sold "fine wines, liquors and cigars" and advertised as "the most elaborate emporium on the Stroll." He was widely known as a political force on the South Side; Jones, following Motts's business tactics, raised significant funds for the Oscar DePriest's run for alderman in 1915.[112]

SIX

Representation and "Race Men"

"My Country, 'Tis of Thee" rang through Archibald Carey's Institutional Church on a spring Sunday in April 1915. It was less than a month after the election that gave the city its first African American alderman and put William Hale "Big Bill" Thompson in the mayor's office. The crowd was so large and so boisterous that a fire lieutenant "was on the scene" to see "that the fire ordinance was kept intact and the safety of the people was perfectly secure," the *Broad Ax* noted. "Many disappointed persons came too late to get in," ran the May 1 headline. The newly elected alderman, Oscar DePriest, sat on a platform beneath the altar. Beside him were "prominent representative citizens," including African American lawyers Edward Morris, Edward Wright, and S. Laing Williams; the white senator Samuel Ettelson; and *Defender* editor Robert S. Abbott. Finally, Rev. Carey moved to the rostrum and announced that the mayor-elect had arrived. As the crowd rose, "flags were waving, hands clapping. Voices singing in harmony." As Thompson made his way down the aisle, his six-foot frame visible from the far corners of the hall, the crowd continued to sing, "giving the declaration," the newspaper commented, "to a full expression of this being our country and the sweetness of a land with every corner permeated with liberty." It was an extraordinary show of support for the white playboy mayor and a rare sincere declaration of fealty to the nation—and a Republican— from the usually acerbic *Broad Ax*.[1]

Thompson, introduced by Carey and rising amid roaring applause, promised the crowd his full devotion and, in the process, revealed the close relationship between the white Republican machine and the city's black politicians. "My very good friend," Thompson addressed Carey. "When Dr. Carey calls for me," he continued, "it matters not where I am or when it is made, I will come." To more applause, he added, "You supported me loyally and I believe in reciprocity." Thompson's speech, with his boast of a re-unified Republican Party and promises of dedication to black Chicagoans, was printed in full in the black press. Brief speeches from the other distinguished guests were mentioned in the news coverage the next day. The celebration ended with DePriest and Thompson, "both athletic in their manly development, clasping hands" in friendship. "It would have taken an artist to have portrayed vividly to you this scene," the *Broad Ax* concluded. "I leave it to your imagination."[2]

Thompson's victory and his appearance at Institutional Church that Sunday night was an expression of a mutually beneficial alliance between black leaders and the Republican machine. The relationship between Thompson and Carey was crucial and revealing: the Republican machine

Photo of William Hale Thompson, n.d. Courtesy of
Chicago History Museum (file iCHI-67641).

and a cadre of powerful black politicians had emerged simultaneously. Carey and Thompson had known each other for at least fifteen years; each man had worked to promote himself while, almost unnoticed, giving credibility to the other in the urban political scene. The handshake between Thompson and DePriest cemented the alliance between Carey's followers and Thompson's wing of the machine. The triumph of Thompson and DePriest was framed as a victory for black "manhood," as the vivid description of the two "athletic" men implied. This was an expression of the new maturity of black voters and of their political strength.

Neither DePriest nor Thompson (nor Carey, for that matter) represented all voters of his race. The city's leading black-owned newspaper, the *Defender*, had supported DePriest's opponent in the Second Ward primary. Some African American activists, like the Barnetts and Williamses, already questioned the deal: the pragmatic alliance of African American leaders with the Thompson arm of the Republican machine. Yet many others believed the new mayor, already indebted to his Black Belt constituency, would serve African American interests. This, men like Carey argued, was how urban politics worked. Black activists—who a generation earlier were debating whether to participate in the nation's political life—had placed a representative in local government.

The election of a black alderman legitimized African Americans' place in the urban polity. DePriest's victory in particular signified that black Chicagoans, whether residents of the Second Ward or not, had gained a voice, had gained representation in city government. "Representation" was the key term, appearing in political speeches and newspaper editorials throughout the campaign season. The term reveals much about black Chicagoans' vision of politics, as black voters came out strongly for DePriest. Though representation, in theory, was defined by geography (a public official represented a specific section or region), it was, in the immigrant city, increasingly defined by social identity (Polish immigrants, for example, demanded a Polish official). In a city filling with immigrants and migrants, geography tended to reflect social identity; this was particularly true for African Americans constrained by racial segregation; most black voters lived in two South Side wards. For most, representation was concrete and visible: a "race man" who brought material benefits to his constituency. Crucially, just as race was the primary feature defining urban real estate markets, race would, as black activists predicted, become the core of urban political struggles in the twentieth century.[3]

In the spring of 1915, many still hoped that political victories in the mayoral and aldermanic elections would bring sustained change. It was a time of uncertainty, of idealism and threats of brutal violence in the city and the world. War had erupted in Europe; by April, reports of bloody atrocities in Belgium and fighting across northern France had appeared in the *Defender* and the major white-owned newspapers. At home, a southern Democrat was in the White House and in Chicago fire bombings of black homeowners and random attacks on black workers were increasingly common. The Great Migration was beginning; already the newly formed Urban League, the city's leading social service provider for black Chicagoans, worried about a housing shortage and complained that black workers were hired only as strikebreakers and low-wage laborers. Black Chicagoans placed much hope with the new mayor and Alderman DePriest.

Representation in city hall and the reciprocity of Chicago machine politics would, many later observed, prove a partial, even Pyrrhic, victory.[4] Though Thompson, in his first term at least, fulfilled some promises to black voters, his record over three terms in city hall was inconclusive at best and deeply corrupt according to many observers. Thompson's popularity, like DePriest's, lay primarily with laboring black voters, those who believed the Republican machine might help them find work. (There are no reliable data on the number of jobs provided by the machine.) Most of those jobs were likely low paying and short term.

In the 1910s, both men responded to some demands of black voters while overlooking the growing poverty and deteriorating living conditions in the Black Belt. DePriest, one of Thompson's closest allies on the city council, moved only rarely to demand enforcement of black civil rights and faced repeated charges of graft. Black Chicagoans built a political machine, Allan Spear writes, and "dealt with white politicians not as party retainers seeking favors, nor as spokesmen for a special interest group, but as political powers in their own right." But working with the machine meant that black leaders were less likely to support organized labor, at least until the late 1920s, and much less likely to challenge local government's refusal to protect black families breaking the "color line." Indeed, enforcing segregation in housing was part of the unstated deal. Allying with the Republican machine gave black politicians greater visibility and influence while simultaneously stifling demands for social changes in African American neighborhoods and the city at large.[5]

Chicago's political organizations and its governmental structures were, in the early twentieth century, unstable, susceptible to pressures from new immigrant groups, well-organized activists, and shrewd deal makers.

This instability contributed to the rise of the political machines while simultaneously creating opportunities for new social groups—like African Americans—to organize, enter politics, and gain influence in city hall. The concentration of new social groups, most pronounced in the racially segregated South Side wards, strengthened their claims in the city's ward-based polity. The machine ultimately proved a strategy for managing cultural differences. The chaotic political scene, volatile and rapidly changing, helped to legitimize the demands of varied urban constituencies for representation in government while in many ways undermining the legitimacy of city government itself.[6]

Scholars and activists have long debated the benefits and harm of machine rule: some see the machine as cushioning government from the demands of more radical popular movements, others conceive it as an extralegal system that stripped communities of resources and wrecked the democratic process, and still others claim urban machines provided services to communities lacking economic and civic resources.[7] Charles M. Merriam and Harold Foote Gosnell were leading scholars of Chicago politics and, by extension, of political machines in the first three decades of the twentieth century. Seeing themselves as benign reformers, the two political scientists considered the machine a damaging but almost inevitable outgrowth of the unruly structures of urban governance. The machine, in handing out favors to varied and often competing interests, helped stabilize northern cities split among diverse ethnic, racial, and class interests. It gave an economic foothold, serving as a means for upward social mobility, to recent immigrants and African Americans, and it legitimized their engagement with government. Yet the machine, both scholars emphasized, blunted struggles for more radical social change. It was a fair conclusion for a student of early twentieth century Chicago to draw.

Formally, Chicago's city government consisted of a mayor, aldermen representing the city's wards, and the heads of various administrative agencies. The mayor's term was extended from two to four years in 1907. From his office on the fifth floor of city hall, the mayor was the city's "chief personnel agent . . . its city manager . . . chief lawmaker, its chief financier, its diplomat, its leader, all in one," Merriam wrote, "or he should be, if he did all that is expected of him." Among his most important jobs was appointing heads of administrative agencies: health, fire, police, public works, finance, and law, as well as members of special boards or commissions. These appointments, and those of the workers within each agency, were part of the much-vaunted and regularly denounced patronage system, giving the mayor and his allies the ability to reward supporters and punish opponents. The mayor could present legislation and veto acts of the council "and through his patronage and prestige control" the aldermen.[8]

There were two aldermen from each ward, each elected for two-year terms, with the terms staggered so that there was an aldermanic election every year. The number of wards jumped to thirty-five in 1901. Aldermen were concerned primarily with the infrastructure of their wards, with street improvements, street cleaning, lighting, policing, and schools. Any of these might provide jobs on the city payroll for loyal supporters. Aldermen guided constituents through the maze of city hall agencies and bureaucratic requirements, securing building permits, licenses for saloon owners (and others), "adjusting disputes with the health department and police," and intervening in tax conflicts and quarrels with the gas, electric, and telephone companies. "Aldermen," Merriam wrote, bustled "about seeking to satisfy their constituents by fair means or by foul, and often their constituents [were] highly unreasonable in their demands."[9]

Chicago was divided into wards, which often, though not always, coincided with neighborhood boundaries. The ward system meant that geography influenced political careers and determined access to city hall. Each ward included a variety of social groups. Yet as immigrant groups tended to cluster in neighborhoods and the city's housing market tended to separate rich from laboring households, wards tended to be identified by the ethnicity and class of residents. As demographics shifted, as they always did, new residents put new pressure on local political organizations to nominate candidates representing their interests. Voters did not always vote their ethnicity, but the small size of the city's wards gave the city's varied social groups—immigrants, African Americans, and old-stock whites—a chance for representation in city government and a chance to benefit from representation. The system was simple and direct, noted Grace Abbott, director of the Immigrants' Protective League in the 1910s. She quoted, for example, a letter written by Alderman John Powers for an Italian resident of the Nineteenth Ward: "This is a neighbor and a friend of mine. Please give him work." Abbott added that the Italian worker, "in his gratitude" would vote for Powers and "the machine." Chicago's ward system was the "institutional feature" that gave the city's immigrant groups "a political base," writes Ira Katznelson. "The politics of Chicago were the politics of boundary management and direct ethnic bargaining."[10]

The lines separating ethnic and racial groups, reinforced by ward boundaries, were in constant flux in a city whose population was growing rapidly, where, especially after 1900, immigrants from southern and eastern Europe were moving into areas previously housing northern and western Europeans and where African Americans from Mississippi, Missouri, Arkansas, and other southern states were competing with old settlers and immigrants for homes in South Side neighborhoods. Politics was an expression of urban geography as much as it was a struggle over neighborhood identities and boundaries and for municipal power among newly mobilized social groups.[11]

In the early decades of the twentieth century, Chicago's political scene was volatile, and electoral outcomes, particularly for the mayor's office, were unpredictable. Neither Democrats nor Republicans dominated the city, which distinguished Chicago from New York and Philadelphia. Between 1897 and 1915, the mayor's office swung from Democrat Carter Harrison II to Republican Edward Dunne and then to a Republican representing another faction in the party, Fred Busse, then back to Harrison, and then to Republican Thompson. The city council too was divided among Democrats, Republicans, Progressives, and Socialists. The political parties were themselves divided internally among factions. Recognizing the dangers of constant internal struggles, Roger Sullivan, longtime leader of a faction of West Side Democrats, moved in 1910 to put together a "harmony ticket" for the fall elections. The alliance, which was widely discussed in the daily press, fractured within days, only to be reconfigured after a marathon conference at the LaSalle Hotel in mid-July. Unity paid off—the Democrats carried all important city offices that fall—but unity did not last. The Democrats, like the Republicans, continued their internal squabbles through the 1910s, creating a politics that, though representing many competing interests, was shifting constantly.[12]

For African American activists, the ward system combined with constant struggles between Democrats and Republicans and, within each of the parties, provided crucial political opportunities. Increasingly rigid racial segregation of the city's housing markets, enforced with racial covenants, threats to white homeowners considering black buyers or renters, and outright mob attacks on black families living outside the Black Belt, generated a concentration of black voters with an growing sense of racial solidarity. "The Negroes formed this community as an accommodation to the northern urban environment," Gosnell wrote, blithely ignoring the white violence that produced this "environment." He added, however, that the segregated "community" became the base for African American political power. Neither Democrats nor Republicans had a "built-in majority." Unlike those of New York, Philadelphia, Milwaukee, or Boston, Chicago's party leaders relied on "pivotal minorities," including black voters, to win in city and state elections. Even more, Chicago's labor activists and its tradition of third-party challenges to the dominant parties left open the possibility that small, well-organized groups of voters could swing citywide elections.[13] This was precisely what happened in the mayoral election of 1915. As black voters were increasingly concentrated in the Black Belt, African American leaders could more effectively mobilize black voters to pressure ward leaders to nominate black candidates.

City hall was just one among many seats of power in a complex and chaotic urban government. Chicago, as Merriam noted, had "many city halls and many governments." Chicago's government was decentralized, with a series of overlapping agencies sometimes representing municipal voters and other times representing Cook County (which included Chicago), which oversaw an array of services and distributed resources. There were at least eight separate taxing bodies within the city, including the Cook County Board of Commissioners, the Chicago Board of Education, the Chicago Public Library Board, the three park boards, and the Metropolitan Sanitary District. There were, in addition, more than fifty elective judges in the circuit, superior, municipal, and county courts. This bureaucracy, the child of a timid and small nineteenth-century urban regime, was in part created by downstate legislators who resented the city and refused to address its changing social needs with state resources. Springfield, dominated by rural interests, simply created new public agencies funded largely by city and county taxes or bond issues. Chicago government grew over just two generations into a complex, multilayered bureaucracy controlled by a handful of powerful politicians.[14]

The problem was widely recognized. But reorganizing and streamlining municipal governance required a revision of the city's charter, set by the state's 1870 constitution. There were several efforts at charter reform in the first decade and a half of the century. The revised charters were approved by the state legislature but went down in municipal votes. City governance was, in Gosnell's words, "decentralized, chaotic, and inadequate."[15] The system duplicated services and nurtured corruption. Equally significant, it established multiple power bases within government and encouraged competing blocs within and among the established political parties.

"There is in Chicago as in other great cities of the United States an inner organization directed against the great Organization known as the Law," wrote Merriam in his 1929 study of Chicago politics.[16] Merriam referred to the machine, though no single machine dominated the city in the early decades of the twentieth century. There were, instead, rival bosses leading factions, "often more hostile to each other than the parties themselves."[17] Until the mid-1910s, the factions vied for power, each based in a section of the city, each identified with an immigrant group, and each struggling to form alliances that would give it control over wider sections of the city. The machines, with their ability to control electoral outcomes, were cursed by reformers, even those who sometimes found common cause with machine bosses. "Any political faction which holds power for a considerable length of time," Gosnell wrote, "is likely to be called a machine by the opposing forces."[18] It was this instability—the rise and fall of machines, the competing factions facing constant challenge from opponents—that created openings for smaller, well-organized groups to gain influence and ultimately sway elections.

Entry to the system came at the ward level, where the city's aldermen stood at the levers of the machines. Along with serving on the city council, the aldermen controlled a web of party functionaries. A committee person was responsible for each precinct, expected to deliver the precinct's four to six hundred votes, and for appointing precinct captains. Some precincts covered just two city blocks; others ran to six or eight blocks. In the Second Ward, which elected DePriest in 1915, there were more than fifty precincts, comprising a population of about sixty-three thousand. The precinct captains ran their own organizations, which included a president, vice president, secretary, treasurer, and block workers. These were the foot workers who knew each constituent personally; were familiar with the neighborhood's fraternal organizations, women's clubs, and churches; and knew how to flatter and cajole voters on election day.[19] "Precinct captains were the back-bone of any metropolitan political organization, since upon them rests the responsibility for seeing and winning the voters," Gosnell wrote. By the 1920s, voters were well aware that successful precinct captains received "some political job or favor" and often handed jobs to friends and supporters. "Their zeal for their party cause," Gosnell noted, "would thus be closely tied up with their bread and butter."[20]

Above the precinct captain was the ward committeeman, who "had to be constantly alert to weed out inefficient precinct captains and discover new ones who [would] carry their precinct." Turnover among precinct captains was high. In wards where populations were changing, turnover became an opportunity for ambitious activists representing newer groups. The number of black precinct captains in the Second Ward grew from none to several (though the *Defender* does not list exact numbers) by 1915, a mark of the instability of the machine system during a period of dramatic population growth and increasing organization among black Chicagoans.[21]

Though the system did not lead inevitably to corruption, it often did. Precinct captains promised assistance and protection in return for votes;

when votes were not enough, cash changed hands. The "Kingdom of Graft," ranged from the small cash exchanges for help with getting a city permit to the payoffs to police and other officials to overlook explicit lawbreaking or to protect thriving brothels, gambling houses, and unlicensed saloons. The "Big Fix" was the term used to describe the links between the city's underworld and the politicians who "[gave] it immunity from the law." Without overt protection from all levels of government—from the aldermen down to the policemen walking the beat—the city's vice district could not have survived. The graft flowing to First Ward aldermen "Bathhouse" John Coughlin and Michael "Hinky Dink" Kenna, was an open secret. The "Big Fix" protected the gambling houses, cabarets, and illicit saloons that, to a large extent, were the mainstay of the Black Belt economy.[22]

The Kingdom of Graft included more than the city's vice trades. As Merriam observed, "The lords of the Kingdom of Graft . . . know magnates and powers in the world of efficiency and organization, and they do business with them from time to time." Business leaders, especially those running the utility companies that so angered reformers, used their influence "where graft might take the politer form of extortion or blackmail or the sweeter term of 'legal expense.'" Well-placed payoffs allowed industrialists to rely on police protection against striking workers or city council votes for contracts for city business. "We calculated that one-third of the members [of the city council] were on the market," Merriam wrote. "One-third were not for sale; and one-third were watching the press and the public, with wavering impulses."[23]

Corruption had been part of the city's political lexicon for decades. It gave rise to another institutional feature of Chicago's governance: the civic reform organizations that hovered at the edges of government. The Citizens' Association, a group of elite white men, had been investigating "election frauds" and pursuing "rascals" in government since its founding just after the Great Fire.[24] A broad, organized political reform movement emerged in the 1890s, following a visit by William T. Stead, a British magazine editor. Stead wandered the streets of the Levee and the back alleys of immigrant neighborhoods, collecting tales of vice, depravity, and brutal poverty in the grimy industrial city. Stead's book, *If Christ Came to Chicago*, was a best seller; among its most popular sections was a chapter on public officials, "The Boodlers and the Boodled." Stead estimated that of the sixty-eight aldermen then serving on the city council, only ten were honest "enough to have saved Sodom, but [they were] not sufficient to save City Hall from . . . the domain of King Boodle."[25] Responding to Stead's call, a group of business and labor leaders formed the Civic Federation of Chicago in 1894, determined to "discover and correct the abuses in municipal affairs, and to increase the interest of citizens in such affairs." Two years later, some of the group's members established the Municipal Voters' League, which targeted politics specifically.[26]

By the early twentieth century, there were a host of other civic organizations, which along with business and labor groups made up what Merriam called the "visible and invisible" governments. These groups relied on publicity, usually the press, to pursue their agendas. Most did not endorse candidates but instead promoted public policies, "commend[ed] or criticize[d] the conduct of officials," and in many cases, took on the typically governmental function of initiating ordinances, policies, and urban programs. By funding, studies of urban problems, publishing articles, and sponsoring conferences, these groups put issues into public debate. With the exception of organized labor, the city's civic organizations tended to be "recruited from, and largely supported by the middle class and the benevolently minded well-to-do." These groups attempted to fill space left open by ineffective or corrupt governance. The class interests of their members limited their impact. Groups aggressively attacked brothels and gambling houses but remained silent during strikes and violent battles between labor and employers.[27]

Most prominent issues concerning reformers in the early decades of the twentieth century fit under the umbrella of "efficiency": efficient governance, efficient transportation, efficient commerce. Waterways, or the swift movement of vehicles on rivers, canals, and the lake, were the Civic Federation's leading topic of study and advocacy in the first decade of the twentieth century. Urban infrastructure—public transportation, or the traction issue, as Chicagoans called it—drew much public attention. White reformers were dedicated to fighting streetcar magnate Charles Tyson Yerkes, who had claimed a virtual monopoly and was widely hated for providing poor service at ever-higher fees. Even after Yerkes was indicted, demands for municipal ownership persisted. Traction wars helped elect reform mayor Edward Dunne in 1905, who after fighting with the city council for two years, watched as "private carriers" gained twenty-year extensions on existing franchises. Dunne lost the next election to Republican Fred Busse, a North Sider who promised to end the constant fighting with the city council, a promise that could not be kept. Even Merriam, a strong advocate for civic reform groups, criticized their narrow and timid agendas.[28]

Black Chicagoans, largely excluded from white civic reform, formed their own organizations. African American civic groups typically were controlled by elite and middle-class black Chicagoans. Racial solidarity was a priority, though that was not necessarily in opposition to working-class interests. Ida B. Wells-Barnett's Alpha Suffrage Club, organized in 1913, worked to help laboring women and fought for women's suffrage. Even the Appomattox Club, with its membership of black political elite, advocated for black workers. Some black reformers, like Wells-Barnett and Fannie Barrier Williams, were deeply critical of machine corruption and black politicians' links to vice, yet most activists willingly worked with the city's political factions when such alliances served their interests. Black activists, even the most respectable, saw the political machines as an opportunity, not a blight on urban politics.[29]

The major issues concerning black reformers in the 1910s, aside from the growing violence against black families living outside a carefully policed African American neighborhood, centered on racial segregation of public spaces, primarily public schools. (The traction issue apparently attracted little activist attention.) Jim Crow, many worried, was moving north. Wendell Phillips High School became a flashpoint of protest in the spring of 1914 and again the following fall, when "the dean of the school," a white woman, Fanny R. Smith, attempted to separate black and white students during school-sponsored social events. The high school, which opened in 1904 at Thirty-Ninth Street and Prairie Avenue, had a predominantly white student body, including many students from the elite white neighborhood nearby. There were a growing number of black students at Wendell Phillips, however. "Miss Smith, who espoused the discriminating act, is only a public servant and has no right to inflict her prejudice and narrowness on a public institution," the *Defender* said.[30] Parents of black students at Englewood High School had complained about a similar effort to separate their children from white students' social activities, the *Defender* reported. The black press regularly demanded integrated schools, which proved increasingly elusive as white families moved further away from the Black Belt.

The one organization explicitly concerned with abuses in the electoral process was the Municipal Voters' League, a nonpartisan, generally white group, aiming for "honest and efficient municipal government." The league promoted a version of representative government that ran counter to the methods of the machine and to the views of most of the city's residents. Representation, in the league's view, had nothing to do with shared interests or experiences and certainly did not mean a shared social identity. Instead, the league held up an abstract "people," who would be represented by men of "character and capacity." There were no competing interests or legitimate social conflicts among those noble men. Rather, men with the proper "qualities will faithfully represent the people, treat justly all private interests and dispose of every public question on its merit."[31] By the 1910s the league was promoting "nonpartisan" elections, in which party affiliation would not be listed on the ballot. For black Chicagoans and for recent immigrants, especially laboring men, this version of representation likely lacked credibility. The city's captains of industry—the men held up by the Municipal Voters' League as the models for representative government—would hardly seem to represent the men who were denied jobs in their factories or who fought and generally lost bloody street battles for safer working conditions, shorter hours, or higher wages. Reform, then, meant different things to different groups. There was not even wide agreement that the machine threatened democracy.

Black activists generally ignored the league or openly rejected its principles, while the league regularly attacked black officials. After DePriest's election, the alderman was denounced in the league's yearly report. "No alderman in Chicago's history piled up a more notorious record in so short a time," the report commented, noting that DePriest had been "implicated with a graft syndicate in his neighborhood." (DePriest would ultimately be acquitted of those charges.) The league also condemned white aldermen like the notorious Michael "Hinky Dink" Kenna of the First Ward, who was listed as "utterly unfit." League reports complained that African American public officials lacked "independence." That, of course, meant that the aldermen were allied with the Republican machine. The league's comments on black officials and on the machine, whether accurate or not, came to dominate public views of urban politics and those of many later scholars.[32]

The Illinois electoral system benefited both the major political parties and minority groups like African Americans. Illinois established a system of cumulative voting in 1870. This meant that a voter could spread his votes among several candidates or cast one, one and a half, or three votes for a representative, depending on whether the Republican convention had nominated three, two, or one candidates. Before 1891, only party ballots were issued in Illinois. The Australian Ballot Act of 1891 included a straight-ticket device as well as a secret ballot. Under the new law, any person who voted the straight Republican ticket in a senatorial district where a black man was nominated for another office automatically cast one, or as many as three, votes for the black representative. The system allowed a group that sought representation while lacking a majority of voters in a particular district or ward to compete and even gain office. It also helped to strengthen and discipline party organizations.[33]

The machine was itself a product of the industrial city and came of age just as black activists began to claim influence in governance. Accusations of corruption, which were rife in early twentieth-century Chicago, raised a host of questions, issues that pressed at the shifting meanings of democracy and of pluralistic governance. What, for example, did an elected official owe his constituency? What could a voter fairly demand in return for his or her vote? What did representation mean? Whether the machine system served the interests of constituents, especially poor and laboring people who often had little direct access to government officials, was widely debated. Gosnell posed the problem succinctly: "The party philanthropist acts in direct and human fashion which appeals to the individual in distress. Thus a voter receives some immediate concrete service in return for which he is willing to support the candidates sponsored by his benefactor." Warning of the system's dangers, Gosnell added: "These candidates, however, may be racketeer unionists or gangster-politicians who prey upon the community and who oppose constructive social welfare legislation."[34] Black Chicagoans' alliance with the machine helped to legitimize both the machine and ambitious black politicians. Some black activists may have recognized that this path to self-governance came at the cost of narrowing strategies for improving living conditions in the Black Belt, but in the 1910s, few mentioned it, and few saw better alternatives.

The second decade of the twentieth century marked a dramatic expansion of African American participation in northern politics. No city experienced this change more than Chicago.[35] The new political activism resulted in part from the Great Migration, the mass movement of African Americans from the rural and small-town South to northern cities during and just after World War I. Many black migrants moved north to escape the brutal sharecropping system and racial violence across the South. Many hoped that with the onset of war in Europe, northern industries would begin to hire black workers; they hoped for better housing and better schools for their children, for civil rights and voting rights in northern cities. The migration began slowly in the 1890s and increased to a flood of new arrivals in the late 1910s.[36]

Yet the sudden growth of the urban black population is not the only nor even a primary explanation for the increasing visibility and influence of black activists in municipal politics. Indeed, Oscar DePriest, a symbol of the new African American political might, was elected in 1915, just as the migration was expanding and before the city's black population hit new highs. African American influence was not about numbers alone. It was,

crucially, a consequence of effective organization, inspiring political leaders, and the specific social conditions and political structures found in the
urban North.

In Chicago, as in New York, Philadelphia, and Cleveland, activists like
the Barnetts and the Williamses, Edward Wright, and Edward Morris had
formed social clubs and political organizations; ministers, women reformers, and labor leaders had worked to forge a sense of common purpose
among black Chicagoans. That black Chicagoans rarely found common
ground hardly mattered when growing numbers of the city's black residents came to see their interests, their working and living conditions, their
spiritual lives and daily aspirations, as influenced, at least in part, by the
mechanisms of government. The city's numerous social and political organizations generated competing agendas, divisions separating the educated
from the less educated, new arrivals from old settlers, Booker T. Washington's supporters from those of the newly formed National Association for
the Advancement of Colored People, among other lines of disagreement.
Still, organization bred a sense of broader purpose, a vision that individual
hardship was linked to larger social issues and political structures. Though
living in a nation where the majority of African American citizens were denied the right to vote, where government at all levels sanctioned brutal violence against black citizens, and where visible and organized opposition to
racial discrimination was relatively recent, black activists and many silent
voters were convinced that they could use the ballot to make a difference.

By the early 1910s there were at least eight black political organizations,
not including groups of black Democrats, which formed around election time, then disappeared from the political scene. Whatever the number of members regularly attending meetings—and no membership lists
are extant—at least six political clubs were prominent enough to be listed
in the *Colored People's Blue-Book*.[37] Several advertised meetings in the *Defender*. Undoubtedly many more black Chicagoans joined social clubs and
"secular societies," than attended political meetings, but *Defender* articles
and advertisements suggest that turnout for political meetings was on the
rise in the early 1910s. Wells-Barnett's Alpha Suffrage Club was the leading
black women's political organization. Calling itself the "mother suffrage
club," the Alpha Suffrage Club boasted of its ability to train women in precinct work and to win "political appointments" for its members. The club,
though nominally opposed to the machine effectively used machine strategies to serve its members' interests. It sponsored social events, like a Christmas dance at the Odd Fellows Hall, and trained women in the fine art of
politics. Its members united "their strength for their own advancement."[38]

The National Association for the Advancement of Colored People, which quickly became the preeminent national organization for black Americans, did not directly engage municipal politics. The organization did win enormous support among Chicago's white and black reformers, linking the city's activists to a new and increasingly aggressive band of activists across the nation. The *Defender* tended to highlight the NAACP's campaigns against lynching but also noted its calls for aggressive action for civil rights in the courts and in the ballot box. "The Passive Days of the Negro Race are Past," announced the *Defender* in a 1912 article on the organization.[39] Jane Addams and Ida Wells-Barnett were among the group's founding members and on the host committee when it held its fourth national meeting in Chicago in late April 1912. Among the topics addressed were "Disfranchisement" and "Problems of Urban Segregation of the Negro." With a front-page photograph of the distinguished guests gathered in front of Hull House, the *Defender* called the event "the most significant and important gathering for race welfare since the days of abolition."[40] Dr. George Cleveland Hall, lawyer S. Laing Williams, and Dr. Charles E. Bentley were members of the local committee, which received significant financial support from Sears president Julius Rosenwald. In Chicago, the NAACP helped to fund lawsuits against theater and hotel owners who discriminated against black patrons.[41] Most of the local committee's members campaigned for candidates or ran for office, but the organization was not directly involved in local elections.

Chicago politics was a wide-open game; where to enter the system was not always clear. Black voters nationally had long supported the Republican Party. But in the urban North, activists, angry at Republican neglect, had since the 1880s urged voters to reconsider, to force the major parties to court black voters, and to punish Republicans who did not promote African American rights.[42] In Chicago, the question of party loyalty was further complicated by splits within the Republican Party. Many among the black elite had questioned Rev. Carey's early alliance with the Lorimar (and later Thompson) branch of the Republican machine. There also were some African American Democrats: the *Broad Ax*, published by the abrasive Julius Taylor, typically supported Democratic candidates (and likely received some funding from the Democratic Party). Ninety members of a black Democratic club endorsed Democratic mayoral candidate and reformer Edward F. Dunne in 1907. Some among the black elite, like many of the city's white middle classes, hoped to replace the city's internecine ethnic squabbles with efficient and honest governance.[43] Black activists, however, soon learned that the pursuit of efficiency and integrity were nearly always trumped by white racism.

The experience of Ferdinand Barnett during his campaign for a municipal court judgeship silenced some of the machine critics and drew new attention to the potential benefits of working with a powerful ward organization. Mayor Dunne, a Democrat and avowed reformer, came into office in 1905 determined to implement municipal ownership of the transit system, tax equity, education reforms, and a rewriting of the city charter. He lost the fight for municipal ownership and his bid for mayor two years later. But in 1906, Dunne established a municipal court, widely considered the first modern and, at the time, most progressive court system in the nation. It consolidated specialized divisions like juvenile and domestic relations before a single municipal bench. African Americans saw the new court as an opportunity to seat black judges. That June, some black leaders met at Quinn Chapel to pick a candidate for one of the twenty-seven new municipal judgeships. They settled on Barnett, whom even his old nemesis the *Broad Ax* praised for his integrity and experience in the courts. Yet when Barnett announced he would run in the countywide race, the white press erupted in race-baiting and bigotry. The *Chicago Chronicle* (a nominally Republican paper) published a crude cartoon of a courtroom scene with a white woman clutching a child before a black judge and jury. The caption ran: "Vote the white man's ticket." Cards bearing a similar image were circulated around the city. When the city's bar association announced its endorsements, Barnett, who had spent a decade as an assistant state's attorney, was "found wanting." A week before the election, the "Afro American Republican club . . . issued leaflets" urging support for Barnett. After a prolonged recount, Barnett lost, the victim of "color prejudice," in the *Tribune*'s words. [44]

"Is this Christianity?" asked his wife, Ida Wells-Barnett, commenting on the hateful election cards. "We might have expected something of the kind in Atlanta but this is a city that holds itself the stronghold of democratic opinions. The appeal against us has been to race prejudice, not to principle." Barnett eventually put the loss down to election fraud, which the *Tribune* reported was widespread. But as his wife suggested, political ideology, even party loyalty, were easily swept aside by racial prejudice.[45]

Barnett's loss, announced during a mass meeting at Bethel Church, came amid growing black anger at President Theodore Roosevelt. Rev. Carey presided over the meeting called to protest the president's discharge of "three companies of colored troops" involved in a race riot near a military base in Brownsville, Texas. Black leaders, including Carey and Barnett, had endorsed a personal letter to the president and a petition to the War Department denouncing the president's action, which came without a court-martial or official investigation. The *Tribune* reported that more than two thousand people gathered at Bethel that November evening. "The verdict of dismissal of these soldiers is illegal and unjust and amounts to executive lynching," attorney B. F. Mosely told the crowd. The audience was treated to speeches denouncing the planned Chicago appearance of racist senator Ben Tillman. Roosevelt's "unjust" treatment of black troops, Tillman's planned speech, and Barnett's electoral loss were interspersed in fiery speeches, linking local to national concerns and creating a sense of urgency among black activists.[46]

Just as racial segregation in housing generated a geographic community, racist attacks in city politics fostered political unity, as unruly as it was. Barnett's loss and the ugly racial attacks might have soured black Chicagoans on local politics. Instead, activists renewed their organizing efforts at the ward level. Barnett's defeat, in Paula Giddings's words, "heightened black political determination." In 1910, the *Defender*, still admonishing, "remember F. L. Barnett," threatened that the "colored man [would] clean house at the next election" if local Republicans did not offer "more recognition" and more and better-paying jobs at the post office.[47] Barnett's defeat, along with Roosevelt's apparent disregard for black soldiers' civil rights, strengthened claims that fights among black activists, divisions based on "principle" or political beliefs, needed to be overcome to gain representation in government.

The black Republican Club already affirmed this goal. It had in 1906 supported Barnett's bid for a judgeship and DePriest's run for the county board, which was not surprising, since both men were Republicans, but they were also ideological and professional opposites. While Barnett presented himself as an educated professional and reform-minded politician, DePriest was a former housepainter turned real estate investor who had worked with the Lorimer faction of the Republican Party. For the political organization, however, both candidates presented an opportunity for representation of "the race" in municipal government. White Democrats and Republicans, including Barnett's reform-minded friends, had turned on him, just as white Republicans ignored black protests against the Brownsville discharges. Barnett "could not have been treated much worse in the south," wrote S. Laing Williams in a letter to Booker T. Washington.[48] Representation was linked to the election of black men and was increasingly viewed as crucial to the "advancement of the race." Activists began to focus on the city council and to fix their hopes on the Second Ward.

Black activists had been moving into Second Ward politics since at least 1901. There were, of course, the saloonkeepers, cabaret owners, and gambling bosses who saw politics as a protection game, paying workers to canvas for friendly candidates. There also were "respectables" who began inserting themselves into the party, hoping to gain access to city hall for black Chicagoans. Republican leaders, hardly champions of black civil rights, recognized they needed black precinct workers to channel the South Side's growing black population into the Republican Party. Lucy McNiell Miller, an "old settler" and wife of the first black janitor at the University of Chicago, remembered the white animosity when she became the first "Negro clerk" on her precinct board, serving with four white men. "When these men saw me coming into the polling place they were so astounded that the white gentlemen with whom I was to canvass the precinct refused to work with me." The men complained to the board of commissioners; the commissioner "that listened to his complaint told him that he would either work with me or go to jail," she remembered in an interview twenty years later. "And like a fairy tale, we worked happily together."[49] Those events may have grown rosier in Miller's memory. Clearly, an African American woman working the precinct marked the beginning of a dramatic, often rocky change for the ward workers.

The party's enlistment of Mrs. Miller as a precinct worker was an expression of another significant shift in the structure of Chicago politics: in 1913, the Illinois General Assembly granted women limited suffrage. Women could vote for presidential electors and all municipal officeholders. Women black and white had been active in politics long before gaining the franchise; women organized meetings, campaigned around social issues and for candidates, and helped set the public agenda for local government. Many had fought hard for women's suffrage, gaining significant experience in the workings of state and local politics. Gosnell estimated that as many as one-quarter of precinct captains in the Second and Third Wards were women. "These women leaders . . . were thoroughly familiar with their local neighborhoods," Gosnell wrote, "and they had demonstrated their abilities as canvassers and organizers."[50]

Black Chicago's fight for an African American alderman came during the administration of the first southern-born president since Reconstruction and amid a systemic effort to establish racial segregation in federal offices. Within a month after his inauguration, Woodrow Wilson agreed to suggestions from his cabinet to "segregate white and negro employees in all Departments of Government." The administration determined to limit the hiring of black workers for federal jobs. Soon, all applicants for civil service jobs were required to submit photographs with their applications, and black leaders complained that evaluators were tampering with test scores on civil service exams. How else, the *Defender* asked, to explain the unusually low number of African Americans who passed the city's post office exam in 1913, just 6 out of 260 who took the test.[51]

Post office jobs, stable and well paid, were crucial to the small African American middle class. In response to Wilson's policies, black postal workers in Chicago helped establish the National Alliance of Postal Employees, a black organization formed in Syracuse, New York, in 1913.[52] It was clear that public officials from the president down could disrupt the economic viability of African American communities; at the same time, threats to, or promises of, jobs for black workers could mobilize voters in local elections.

African Americans were outraged by the White House's new policies. Many black leaders, including W. E. B. DuBois and Booker T. Washington, had voiced support for Wilson's candidacy, hoping that the "cultivated scholar," as DuBois called him, would bring "farsighted fairness" to Washington. But within a year after Wilson's inauguration, they were railing against him. That November, a delegation headed to Washington, led by Ida B. Wells-Barnett and Monroe Trotter, the Boston newsman whose National Independent Political League had campaigned for Wilson. The effort was fruitless; Wilson refused to respond to questions about segregation and remained standing during the brief meeting.[53] The president's obvious disdain further focused African American fights for representation in local government.

For black Chicagoans, the municipal elections of 1915 really began in 1910 and ended in 1917. The fight for the city's first black alderman, an aspiration of black activists since at least the 1880s, took visible shape in 1910, when Edward Wright ran as an independent. Wright and others had pressured the Republican organization to back a black candidate for the Second Ward, where the voting population was about 27 percent African American in 1910. Republican leaders refused, but just days after George F. Harding, a white real estate investor known to rent to black families, won the Republican nomination for Second Ward alderman, black politicians formed an independent party and nominated Wright as an aldermanic candidate. A former Cook County commissioner, Wright devoted much of his energy to politics. The campaign was spurred by *Defender* correspondent W. A. Wallace, who goaded black Chicagoans by noting that Cleveland had just elected a black alderman. He urged "good people of color, men of influence, apostles of civil rights and advocates of political liberty" to "get together and get together quickly and nominate and elect a Negro alderman." Whether they liked Wright or not, Wallace urged Second Ward black voters to vote for the man "capable of representing you. . . . Men, if you have any race pride, show it now." Wright lost that April, receiving just 18 percent of the vote.[54]

Wright's campaign convinced at least some white Republican leaders that black men could be organized and that black votes might matter. Two years later, when Wright made another unsuccessful run for alderman, the *Daily News*, expressing concern over Wright's apparent links to former senator Lorimer, refused to support him. This time Wright managed to carry 16 of 52 precincts and lost by just 672 votes. Just a few years later, he became a Second Ward committeeman, campaigned for DePriest and Thompson, and was appointed by Thompson to be an assistant corporation council.[55]

Wright's near win inspired some activists. But it was debates in the Illinois State Legislature that provoked renewed efforts among Chicago's black politicians to gain local representation. The legislature, following the national trend, debated a stream of discriminatory bills in 1913. Among the proposals was a Full Crew Bill, which would allow white transportation unions to replace nonunion African Americans in positions such as train flagmen, brakemen, switchmen, and porters. Several antimiscegenation bills also made it to the house floor. Members of the Appomattox Club and of the Alpha Suffrage Club headed to Springfield, where they lobbied legislators and were joined by black club members from around the state. Years of organizing had created the local networks to mount a significant lobbying effort. The *Defender* chronicled the campaign, noting that after defeat of the Jim Crow railroad bill, the bill's author "declared that he had never met so many brilliant persons of color."[56] The rest of the bills were also voted down. Growing anger at the Wilson administration combined with the victories in the state legislature led many to believe the time was right to push for an African American alderman.

Opportunity came in 1914. The aldermanic race that year, a victory in the long run but a defeat for black activists, demonstrated the vitality of the black voting bloc and the energy and political skills of black women activists. The campaign began in the winter of 1913 when Wright, who had previously run as an independent, announced his support for William Randolph Cowan in his challenge to the regular Republican organization's white incumbent, Hugh Norris, in the February 1914 primary. Cowan, a prominent real estate broker who had arrived in Chicago in 1880, was new to urban politics. Wright believed he would appeal to the newly enfranchised women voters, as well as the reformers who were fighting the machine. The Municipal Voters' League supported Cowan's bid, as did Victor Lawson's *Daily News*, a reform paper, and the *Defender*.

Wells-Barnett's Alpha Suffrage Club went all out for Cowan, gaining its first experience at street-level campaigning. Members faced daunting rebukes from men who said the women should stay at home and stop trying to "wear their [men's] trousers." The women, going door to door across the Second Ward, registered an astonishing number of voters. In the Second Ward, 7,290 women and 16,327 men were registered. Wells-Barnett boasted in her autobiography that registration numbers for the Second Ward were the sixth highest among the city's thirty-five wards. "Women to show loyalty by casting first ballot for Cowan," ran the *Defender*'s February 21 headline. The paper stressed their primary allegiance to their race, clearly recognizing divisions among white and black suffragists.[57]

Days later, Cowan lost the Republican primary. The loss was by a slim margin—Cowan received 2,704 votes to Norris' 3,056. Many observers, including machine leaders, realized that politics in the Second Ward had shifted dramatically.[58] Cowan's strong showing highlighted the pull of race loyalty and demonstrated the strength of the organizing and registration campaigns of Wright and the Alpha Suffrage Club. Official precinct returns showed that many of the precincts that went for Wright in 1910 and 1912 went for Cowan in 1914 (though, as Charles Branham notes, precinct lines were redrawn after elections, making it difficult to track voting numbers from 1910 to 1914). A 1914 ward map shows that in the largely black precincts around State Street, Cowan took almost twice as many votes as Norris. Cowan also carried the generally middle-class 25th, 26th, 33rd, 34th, and 35th precincts. Cowan's strength, as Branham notes, was not necessarily a rejection of the Republican machine or an expression of absolute unity among black voters. Norris won in at least six precincts with significant black voting populations. But Cowan's ability to draw support from affluent and laboring sections of the Black Belt was a mark of the success of his—as well as Wright's and the *Defender*'s—appeals for racial solidarity and of the *Defender*'s regularly repeated claim that African Americans deserved "recognition" or "equal representation."[59] Cowan decided to run as an independent in the regular election but lost that bid also. Politicians had learned that black voters could be organized and would come to the voting booth to assert their racial interests. "The political complexion of the ward has changed," the *Defender* proclaimed.[60]

They also learned that it was difficult if not impossible to beat the machine. With Lorimar's departure from the Senate, his ally, Martin B. Madden, had become the chief distributor of jobs and political favors for the South Side wards. Madden had expressed support for Carey early on. A US congressman from the First Congressional District, which included the Second Ward, Madden had provided some services to his African American constituents. He had helped defeat Democratic-sponsored discrimination legislation in Congress and pressured Wilson administration officials to hand some patronage jobs to black workers. Perhaps most important, Madden, a member of the House's Post Office Committee, claimed responsibility for the jobs of hundreds of black postal workers, who through their organization, the Phalanx Forum, were a leading black political force. Nearly all of Illinois's black state representatives and political appointees were beholden in some way to Madden. Even the Alpha Suffrage Club had honored Madden for his "fight against race discrimination."[61]

Madden and the machine had learned a lesson too. Shaken by the primary results and recognizing the growing influence of Wells-Barnett and the women activists, Madden's organization sent Oscar DePriest and Samuel Ettelson to a meeting of the Alpha Suffrage Club. DePriest, who had been moving through the Republican organization for nearly a decade, began by congratulating the women on their successful registration campaign. Then he urged them to support Norris in the regular election. He assured them that the organization finally grasped the need for a black alderman and affirmed that a black man would be nominated at the "next vacancy." Ettelson, a white state senator and president of the ward organization, nodded in agreement. Norris won the general election. The Second Ward's black activists had won another important victory: the machine's support for a black candidate.[62]

Still, the 1914 elections had not gone smoothly for black politicians. Black Belt struggles surrounding the elections and the gossip and scandal-mongering in the black press revealed persistent divisions among activists. In the regular election, many black activists had abandoned Cowan and backed another independent candidate for alderman, Charles Griffin, an ambitious young newcomer. Wright, who endorsed Griffin, may have believed the younger man had a better shot than Cowan, though it's not clear why Wright turned on the candidate he had so energetically promoted in the primary. Carey too expressed support for Griffin, though he was, once again, vilified by the *Broad Ax*, which claimed he was just trying to split the black vote and assure the Republican machine candidate's victory. A pamphlet circulated through the Second Ward asserted that "colored men owe it to themselves and the race to support the organization candidate." The *Defender* attacked the "supposed Afro-American leaders" who came out for Norris, including Oscar DePriest, Edward Green, and the two African American state representatives, Robert R. Jackson and Adelbert Roberts.[63] Second Ward leaders might have agreed on the goal of getting a black man on the city council; they could hardly agree on who or how to do that. Their opportunity came in the winter of 1914–15 when the ward's white alderman, George F. Harding, announced he would step down to run for a seat in the state senate.

The Republican organization was determined to hold on to the city council seat; for white machine leaders, party unity proved more important than race that campaign season. The organization clearly needed to appeal to its black constituency. In a sign of their respect for DePriest and deference to black voters, Madden and his allies gathered in DePriest's real estate offices on South State Street in mid-November 1914 to officially nominate DePriest. Along with Madden, the gathering included Ettelson and "white and colored men representative of all the party's factions," the *Tribune* reported. The men, well aware of the historic significance of the event, commented to a reporter, "It is the first time a regular party organization in any Chicago ward has indorsed a colored man for alderman." DePriest was born in Florence, Alabama, where he learned early the dangers of political activism; he was the son of a farmer who had reportedly hidden a well-known black politician from a lynch mob. The family had moved to Salinas, Kansas, before settling in Chicago. DePriest, who had little formal education, was known for his shrewd dealings in politics and business.[64] If elected, DePriest would be the first African American on the city council.

DePriest's nomination was not linked to Thompson's, but the afternoon before the meeting at DePriest's offices, the party regulars had gathered to discuss mayoral candidates. They could, the *Tribune* reported, "see a chance to elect a mayor in April" but had not yet settled on a candidate. Thompson would emerge as the organization's choice in the following weeks. Some white voters in the Second Ward, however, were unhappy with the party's choice for aldermanic nominee. In January, the ward's "Young Men's Republican club" endorsed a white candidate, Max J. Schmidt. Though black Chicagoans were certain they wanted a black alderman, they were not decided on DePriest; the Republican organization's endorsement hardly settled the issue.[65]

In 1915, the city's political system had been unstable for more than a decade, swinging from stiff-nosed reformers to colorful thugs. There were two or three factions within each party, creating an obvious opening for black activists to leverage their constituency. On the Democratic side, the former unskilled laborer Roger Sullivan was preparing to vanquish his longtime opponent Carter Harrison II, a former mayor and the son of a mayor. Sullivan had been raised in the farming town of Belvidere, Illinois, and, after arriving in Chicago in his teens, worked his way through patronage positions to become the leader of the West Side Irish just after 1900. By the 1910s, he was moving to attract Polish voters and to consolidate the Democrats under his control. Harrison, the city's mayor from 1897 to 1905, was reelected in 1911 but lost the Democratic primary in 1915. He gained support from reformers by fighting traction magnate Yerkes but also won the loyalty of the First Ward bosses, Coughlin and Kenna, when he enacted the policy of segregating vice south of Eighteenth Street. His faction represented the flophouses and middle classes.[66] Thompson, a product of the Republican Lorimer faction, was moving, with Martin Madden at his side, to solidify a Republican machine that could trounce both the Democratic machine and the progressives, led by Merriam, within the Republican Party. With the help of black activists who saw an opening for themselves amid the clashes of white politicians, Thompson won the Republican nomination. But even Thompson's newly empowered machine could not pull black politicians together.

Black activists began in December 1914 to try to build unity. Just five days before Christmas, there was a mass meeting at the Fellowship Club "in the interest of arousing" black voters "to the danger of a multiplicity of candidates for Alderman being prejudicial to the chances of procuring the nomination for one of the race." The three announced black candidates were invited, each giving a speech to a crowd that filled the club rooms "to the utmost capacity." A few days later, Ferdinand Barnett called the three candidates—Louis B. Anderson, Charles Griffin, and Oscar DePriest—to a meeting with a committee of black leaders at the Douglass Center on Monday evening, December 28. The committee, which included Edward Wright and a woman, Kizzie Bills, urged the candidates to agree to a "pre-primary for colored voters" in the predominately black precincts in the Second

Ward. The winner of that pre-primary would be declared "the choice of the colored people in the regular primaries." The committee would attempt to raise money to pay for the pre-primary, but most of the cost would be borne by the three contestants, each of whom, as "evidence of good faith," would deposit one hundred dollars with the committee. Anderson agreed. Griffin apologetically rejected the proposal, saying that his political organization, the Political Equity League, "would not permit him to enter into any agreement." The Political Equity League, reflecting another strand of antimachine activism in the Second Ward, was started by Griffin to promote his candidacy and challenge the machine. The *Defender* had supported his campaign against Norris, claiming Griffin was "not obligated to the bosses." DePriest, of course, was backed by the bosses. He "flatly refused" Barnett's plan. He was, he said, the choice of the Republican organization and "that it was the duty of all voters to . . . abide by the organization's choice." With no agreement, Barnett and his committee stepped aside and let the *Defender* take up the task of uniting black voters behind one African American candidate.[67]

African American politicians saw the election of the city's first black alderman as a symbolic victory. Symbols mattered. Though many, like Griffin and the Political Equity League, hoped a black alderman would bring substantial improvements to the Second Ward, they also recognized that a black representative on the city council—whoever was elected—would establish that African Americans were a vital part of the urban polity, unlike the disenfranchised citizens in the rural South. Especially in an urban political scene of multiple ethnic loyalties, a black alderman marked a newly empowered constituency. The city's first black alderman would, the *Defender* noted, represent "the best interests of 70,000 Afro-American people of Chicago" whether they lived in the Second Ward or not. Representation was not tied to a geographic unit but rather to social identity. Though voters writing to the paper and the paper's columnists surely wanted an "honest man," race was paramount. A black alderman, by virtue of his race in and of itself, would represent the city's black population. This view of representation was not unique to black Chicagoans. It was precisely the vision of representation promoted by machine leaders in both parties who sought to pull together coalitions of immigrant voters, especially those "amenable to voting the right way."[68]

Representation was visible and direct: it meant someone who looked and talked just like the voter, regardless of whether the candidate and constituent shared economic interests or views of vice or of municipal ownership of public utilities or any of the other issues that stirred Chicago politics. Representation meant "a man to lead us," in the *Defender*'s words. "Mr. Rosenwald is the recognized leader for the Jews of Chicago," the paper noted about the philanthropic head of Sears, Roebuck and Company. Black Chicagoans needed someone "who [would] not lick any man's paw because that man has more money . . . or because he is white and has a better opportunity to get favors." Representation meant claiming a place within the reciprocal networks of urban politics.[69]

With the three black candidates entering the race, the *Defender* sought to become a voice for unity and an obstacle to Madden's organization. Robert Abbott and his columnists came out full bore for Anderson. Stories ran recounting the "hundreds of letters regarding his platform, pledges . . . and generally in relation to the sentiment of the voters toward him." The danger, of course, was that if the three black candidates split the African American vote, then a white Democrat would win the city council seat. One large cartoon ran above the phrase "Foolish, futile, puerile, personal, revengeful and utterly hopeless candidacies often work to ruin and destroy the chances of a good man and prevents race representation." The four panels depicted the three candidates arguing over who should lead the race, with Anderson as the only rational voice.[70]

But "platforms and pledges" were hardly discussed. The candidates never debated issues and never appeared to disagree on anything tangible except who should hold a seat on the city council. None of the three candidates distinguished himself from the others. Anderson, recognizing the influence of the Republican organization in the ward, assured voters that he was a "regular Republican." The primary, Anderson told a *Defender* reporter, was designed to choose the party's candidate, and the party should "under no circumstances insist that the voters must be limited in their choice to the one of their own choosing." Anderson did not oppose the machine; he just did not want the "regular Republicans" to dictate who the ward's candidate should be.[71]

Women were seen as a particularly influential voting bloc, perhaps as a result of the hard work of the Alpha Suffrage Club. The paper claimed the "newly emancipated citizens" favored Anderson. There was even a front-page column about Anderson's wife under the headline "A Good Husband should make a good alderman." Explicitly linking home and work, or private and public life, the column stated that Anderson "would bring to office all of the virtues that so conspicuously characterize his life at home." It was an affirmation of the argument that women activists had made for years: that women would bring the virtues and purity of the home to the polity. Anderson's wife, identified only as "Mrs. Louis B. Anderson," claimed to know "nothing of the political game." The *Defender* aimed to win over both those who supported the suffrage movement and those women who opposed it.[72]

Yet it was women activists who most clearly distinguished between Anderson and DePriest. As many as seventy-five women attended a meeting in the home of "Mr. and Mrs. Adolph Tervalon" to hear a speech from Anderson. Other women throughout the ward opened their homes to gatherings of women to meet with Anderson. "Mr. DePriest has the preachers, Mr. Anderson the congregation," one woman was quoted in the *Defender*, "Mr. DePriest the doctors, Mr. Anderson, the patients; Mr. DePriest the ward healers, and Mr. Anderson the voters." Though Anderson was a lawyer, had worked as an assistant county attorney for nearly seventeen years, and was, in Gosnell's words, "thoroughly familiar with the methods of political organization," women activists reportedly perceived him as representing ordinary people, not the elite or professional politicians.[73]

There were political gatherings in all of the major venues across the ward, secular and spiritual. Two events garnered widespread attention, one at the Odd Fellows Hall and the other at Olivet Baptist Church. Both the church and the men's club had publicized open debates among the candidates; both drew large crowds. There is no record of the candidates' speeches, but the *Defender*, ever promoting Anderson, reported "a subterfuge" at the Olivet event, claiming DePriest "was favored." At the Odd Fellows Hall a week later, there was nothing but "mud slinging," a reporter commented. Despite the *Defender*'s best efforts, unity in the Second Ward was elusive.[74]

Though the candidates refused to participate in a "pre-primary," the *Defender* held its own "straw ballot." Readers were instructed to clip the ballot from the paper, check a box, and send the ballot back to the Defender's office. Each week, the paper announced results "in order that the sentiment of the Afro-American people in the Second Ward may be expressed."[75] The well-placed ballots no doubt also helped to stir excitement about the election and spark political debates among Second Ward voters. By January 23, with 1,152 ballots returned, Anderson was nearly 400 votes ahead of DePriest and more than 600 ahead of Griffin. The *Defender*'s page-one headline that Saturday ran "Louis B. Anderson logical man for alderman." The article issued another plea for unity, noting that the "white citizens agreed that we should have an alderman." If the three-man race lead to the election of a white alderman, then black voters, the paper suggested, would once again be stuck as outsiders in politics, supplicants making requests with "resolutions and petitions." Representation meant not having to resort to petitions but having a voice in the council chambers and a vote in city governance.[76]

The "Great Three Cornered Battle for Nomination" ended with a celebration of African American unity, of women's activism, and a victory for DePriest. Of the 7,268 votes cast in the Second Ward primary, DePriest took 3,194 to Anderson's 2,632 and Griffin's 1,432. "Throughout the day" and across the ward, voters lined up at the polls and debated the outcomes. "At any time and at any place could one hear within the territory where the 'brethren and sisters' to any considerable extent reside," the *Defender* said, "three different arguments, all equally forcible, in favor of the three respective candidates representing this group of people." Women activists were widely heralded; the women's vote, despite the *Defender*'s claims, came out heavily for DePriest. (Women voted 1,093 for DePriest, 762 for Anderson, and 500 for Griffin.) Some may simply have followed the votes of their husbands or fathers. But some may also have chosen to reward the Republican "organization" for finding jobs for black women in city hall. Madden sent his congratulations almost immediately; DePriest's win was seen as a triumph of the Republican machine.[77] The *Defender* clearly was not as powerful as the machine.

In the following weeks, the *Defender*, with much less enthusiasm, urged its readers to support DePriest in the regular election, "since the winner is a member of our race all differences must be brushed aside," the paper editorialized. DePriest represented all black voters. "The success of any individual is the success of every individual," the paper's editorial noted, highlighting the long-held view that every achievement of a black American was an achievement for the race. Anderson too came out for DePriest. Quoting Lincoln—"With malice toward none, with charity for all"—he issued a self-important letter noting his dedication to "race uplift" and his "duty" to support the "race's representative in this fight."[78]

Divisions remained within the Black Belt. There were rumors that William Randolph Cowan had "tossed his Old Kentucky Hat in the Ring" with the support of several leading white politicians, including Harding. Cowan's candidacy, if it was serious, was portrayed as a challenge to Madden's control of the Republican Party. A defeat of DePriest would, the *Broad Ax* noted, lessen Madden's "influence and power in local and national politics." That did not happen. Instead, DePriest closed his campaign with "a grand street parade and a monster mass meeting at the Eighth Regiment Armory" at Thirty-Fifth Street and Forest Avenue.[79]

On April 6, 1915, DePriest was elected Chicago's first African American alderman. DePriest's win showed the combined power of the black vote and the Republican organization. The new alderman secured support from nineteen of twenty black precinct captains and all of the ward's white Republican captains. Even the nominally Democratic *Broad Ax* proclaimed DePriest a "great credit on the Afro-American race" who would "make a dandy alderman." The official count in the general election that April gave DePriest 10,599 votes, more than 4,000 more than his closest competitor, the white Democrat Al Russell, and well ahead of the Socialist and Progressive candidates.[80]

Three days after the election, "a Brilliant Affair" at the Appomattox Club cemented the alliance between the Madden-Thompson machine and the city's leading black politicians. The banquet in the club's "spacious parlors" drew two hundred members and guests. The "jolly crowd" was served a seven-course dinner. "It was a feast for the gods," commented a *Broad Ax* reporter. After coffee and "toasted crackers, the last course," had been served, a slew of speakers were introduced. The first commemorated the victory at Appomattox, the formal cause for the gathering. Then came the politicians, black and white: Edward H. Wright, Louis B. Anderson, Major R. R. Jackson, and the newly elected Alderman Oscar DePriest. The final speaker was Martin Madden, who told the crowd they could depend on him to "battle with all his might and main for equality before the law for all mankind whether black or white, rich or poor." To tremendous applause, the congressman toasted to the "wonderful progress" of "the American Negro."[81] The machine's achievement went unmentioned, though hardly unnoticed. The 1915 election was a crowning moment for the Republican machine and, as the honors bestowed on both Madden and DePriest suggested, a vivid confirmation of the interdependence of the machine and the city's leading African American activists.

DePriest was not the only winner in 1915. Thompson won the mayor's office. Second Ward voters took great pride in news reports asserting that black voters had turned the election and handed the office to the white mayor. Ida Wells-Barnett's Alpha Suffrage Club had stumped for Thompson before Chief Municipal Court Judge Harry Olson, a friend and strong supporter of the Barnetts, announced his candidacy for the Republican ticket. Then Wells-Barnett backed off, but the club had already generated women's support for Thompson. Rev. Carey and Edward Wright too had put their political muscle behind the new mayor. But black voters made up just a small percentage of Thompson's total votes. He won wide support from immigrants, especially in areas where "rents were low." Thomp-

old Gertrude Fowler, who would receive a salary of $1,020 a year.
ipson appointed several others to well-paying positions in the cor-
e council's office.

ie mayor was also touted for his opposition to racial segregation.
i the Republican national convention was held in Kansas City in 1928,
ipson, according to some accounts, demanded that black delegates
ated with white. He had reportedly made a similar demand during a
uet for Republican officials in Chicago in the late 1910s. Whether the
r actually challenged racial segregation in hotels and restaurants is
ar—he did not move to enforce legislation banning segregation—but
d allow the stories of his battles against segregation to circulate in the
By apparently challenging Jim Crow and providing jobs to black con-
nts, Thompson, many contended, was an important representative of
Chicagoans.[83]

ompson's inaugural celebration, a parade of fifty thousand people
l nationalities," highlighted the diversity of the city's population and
nstrated the influence of African Americans in city politics. It was also
pression of the transformation of Chicago from a nineteenth-century
f muddy streets and horse-drawn wagons to a twentieth-century me-
lis of sleek, modern automobiles and elaborate floats. From each
came Chicagoans "with their multi-colors, tongues and costumes."
)efender estimated that three hundred thousand Chicagoans partici-
. The Second Ward was represented by an "inter-racial section of au-
biles." There were twenty automobiles, all carrying signs celebrating
ling's Heroes," a reference to state senator George F. Harding, an oration man who had helped get out the vote for Thompson. All of the
s leading politicians, black and white, were carried in the automobiles
gh Loop streets and past the reviewing stand at city hall, "where they
heered by the occupants and appropriately referred to by the mayor
he statement, 'There goes my boys.'"[84]

at spring and summer, Mayor Thompson moved quickly to show his
ciation for the Second Ward's support. The new mayor's first act in
was an expression, both symbolic and financial, of gratitude to black
. The mayor signed into law an ordinance proposed by DePriest that
August 23, 1915, a legal holiday commemorating the fiftieth anniver-
f emancipation. The state legislature had already allocated $25,000
e Lincoln Jubilee and National Half Century Anniversary Exposi-
f Negro Freedom scheduled for August and September in Chicago.
pson, according to the Defender, would send a significant portion of
funds to Carey and other supporters. Later that spring, Carey was

son was reelected in 1919 but stepped aside in 192:
Dever, a Democrat with some support from the Re
moved into city hall. Thompson was elected again i
mayor's office were widely linked to patronage, pe
pay-rolls," gangsters, and "buffoonery in public of
Thompson retained significant support from black l
primaries in which he was a mayoral candidate, T
80 percent of the Republican primary vote cast in tl

The mayor appreciated African American loya
repaid it. For black Chicagoans, the mayor provi
organized labor refused: steady work. Thompson a
can Americans to municipal offices that his Repul
city hall "Uncle Tom's Cabin," an epithet Thomp
tage when campaigning in the Black Belt. Thomp
some of the leading businesses in the Black Bel
nore the payoffs that kept illicit saloons and gamk
helped keep the South Side economy afloat throu
you people the best opportunities you've ever h
promised an African American audience in 1915
jobs, and any of you want to shoot craps go ahea
kept those promises. By August 1915, he had alre
rican Americans to the city attorney's office; the f

Broadside, "Think—Fight for Chicago." Courtesy of Ch
(file iCHI-06418).

year
Tho
pora
Whe
Tho
be s
ban
may
uncl
he d
city.
stitu
blac
of "z
dem
an e
city
trop
warc
The
pate
tom
"Hai
gani
ward
thro
were
with
appi
offic
voter
mad
sary
for
tion
Tho
thos

given a position in the corporate counsel's office, and Edward Wright was hired as an assistant corporate counsel at a salary of $5,000.[85] Black Chicagoans had reason to celebrate.

In the years just after the 1915 election, Thompson and DePriest, two tall, charismatic figures, would often be seen at Black Belt events, joking, back-slapping, and professing concern for their constituents. Thompson, unlike so many white politicians, was perceived as respecting black Americans. He appeared often on the South Side at political rallies, community gatherings, and funerals, including the 1931 funeral of Bishop Carey. Thompson was known to proclaim to black audiences that he would not regale them with tales of his "dear old mammy." He announced instead that he appointed black men because they were the most qualified for the job and because he was grateful to his black supporters. DePriest often served as Thompson's floor manager for city council debates, a sign of the political interdependence and trust between the two men.[86]

Though on most ordinances DePriest fell in line with his machine colleagues, the alderman did move to represent his race directly in at least one instance. DePriest found himself without Republican support in the spring of 1916 when he introduced an ordinance prohibiting discrimination in restaurants, hotels, public accommodations, and amusements. Even if it had passed, the ordinance would have been meaningless without enforcement, and Thompson never expressed a willingness to enforce it. But the *Tribune* warned that the ordinance would frighten white customers from the city's hotels and restaurants. "If the law protected Negroes completely," the paper editorialized, "and if they insisted upon exercising all privileges theoretically there would not be a hotel in the city." Better to protect the city's business interests than to challenge what the *Tribune* considered "human nature." DePriest's bill emerged from committee a year later and was voted down. The failure to pass the ordinance, Branham notes, "was a dramatic demonstration of both the possibilities and limitations of black political power in 1916."[87]

Not all African American activists supported the new mayor, and his popularity in the Second Ward, though always strong, declined the longer he was in office. Even in 1915, some African Americans had voted for the Progressive candidate, Charles Merriam. After the election, some complained about the continued racial segregation in the fire department, despite the hiring of black fire fighters. Thompson did little to halt the attacks on black families who sought to move beyond the carefully policed color line on the South Side. Many people were angered by his weak response to the racial violence in the summer of 1919. During the riot, which began on a hot July afternoon in 1919, the police force moved slowly and inadequately. By the winter of 1919, some activists who previously supported the mayor considered the Thompson administration corrupt and poorly managed. Ida Wells-Barnett, along with more than a dozen black professionals, led an effort to throw Thompson out of office. Supporting Merriam, they argued for "clean politics, good government and fair dealing and representation to all citizens without regard to race or creed."[88] Their rejection of Thompson was an implicit critique of the black politicians who continued to work with the machine. For this small group of progressive professionals, representation increasingly meant more than the quid pro quo of jobs for votes. A representative of "the people" needed to address a wide array of social problems, especially those associated with life in the Black Belt.

By the 1920s, a growing number of black activists were angered by the mayor's neglect of Black Belt vice. Sharp increases in gangland violence—much expanded by prohibition and the criminals, black and white, who trafficked in alcohol—endangered the lives of Black Belt residents and lowered property values for middle-class homeowners. Thompson, some complained, might have provided city hall jobs to his supporters, but he had done little to improve the daily living conditions in the Second and Third Wards, where most black Chicagoans lived. "Some individuals get a chance to make money through methods by which the race as a whole is held back and discredited," wrote Junius Wood in the *Daily News*.[89]

DePriest's triumph was short lived. In 1917, the alderman was indicted, the victim of the commercial forces that had financed his rise in politics. State's attorney Maclay Hoyne charged DePriest with accepting payoffs from gambling kings and accused him of making "vassals and pawns" of Black Belt police officers. Hoyne, a Democrat determined to discredit the Republican administration, called DePriest "King of the Black Belt." In August 1916 DePriest had issued a public statement denying a report that he accepted a bribe to use his connections in city hall to help open a notorious cabaret, the Panama Café. In January, Hoyne announced that the grand jury had indicted DePriest and others for conspiracy to "keep open saloons, bar rooms and tippling houses" after legal closing hours, for "keeping houses of ill fame . . . and divers gaming houses." Among the twenty-two defendants named in the "graft syndicate," were police officers, "alleged gamblers," saloonkeepers, and Republican ward workers. When the case went to trial that June, DePriest was represented by Edward Morris, a leading African American lawyer, and Clarence Darrow, the white lawyer who at fifty-nine was known for defending labor activists and had recently turned his attention to racial injustice. Though DePriest was eventually acquitted, his aldermanic career was over. Republican leaders had pressured him to withdraw from the primary that spring.[90]

The indictment and the trial proved a lively display of the close ties among the city's African American politicians and entrepreneurs of vice. When DePriest surrendered to court officials, Elijah Johnson, brother of the "well known gambler" "Mushmouth" Johnson, paid $110,000 of his bond. Among his coconspirators were Henry "Teenan" Jones and Arthur Codozas, owner of the Elite No. 1.[91] Jones, in a widely publicized day on the witness stand, testified against DePriest, claiming he had given the alderman $2,500 to protect his cabaret from police interference. A day later DePriest took the stand before a courtroom packed with African American observers. DePriest, under questioning from Darrow, asserted that he had received just $1,000 from Jones and most important, that the cash was a campaign donation. Employees of a couple of cabarets testified, as did a handful of the city's leading politicians. DePriest admitted helping several cabarets and "notorious" black and tans to get licenses from city hall, which he implied was simply work for his constituents. DePriest also claimed that he had sent $300 to Harry Miller, a candidate for state's attorney running against Hoyne in 1916. Though a check made out to Miller was presented at trial, Miller denied receiving the money. The effort to fund Hoyne's opponent may have prompted the indictment, though Hoyne was a known enemy of commercial vice.

After more than seven hours of deliberations, at 1:30 a.m. on June 9, the jury returned a verdict of not guilty. "I expected acquittal," DePriest told reporters. "There could have been no other result." Several jurors told reporters that they had been divided on the verdict, but an agreement was reached when those for acquittal convinced the others that DePriest could not have been powerful enough to control such a vast bribery scheme. "I believe the power attributed to DePriest came from someone higher up," a juror was quoted in the *Tribune*. The implication was that a black man, even an influential alderman, was unlikely to be powerful enough to control a gambling syndicate and police officers.[92] The jurors' racism saved DePriest, The trial showcased the intricate web of alliances linking State Street's commercial vice to city hall.

Gradually, the story of DePriest's indictment and acquittal became a tale of racist attacks on a hard-fighting "race leader." Hoyne, who used

Thompson's alliance with black Republicans to challenge Thompson in the 1919 mayoral election, was portrayed as aiming to crush black political achievements. Rather than a battle between vice and virtue, or legal and illicit methods of fund-raising, DePriest's trial was cast as a struggle for black representation against a powerful white conspiracy. DePriest promoted this image, a reputation that would propel him back into politics in the 1920s.

DePriest's 1915 win set a precedent; in the following years, black Chicagoans expanded their hold on representation on the city council. That spring, when DePriest was under indictment, Louis Anderson was elected to represent the Second Ward, a position he would hold for the next sixteen years.[93] In 1918, the Republican organization nominated Major Robert R. Jackson, a former state legislator, to serve as the ward's second alderman. "The genial and pleasant" Jackson was a lifelong Chicagoan, a former postal worker, and a member of the Masons, the Odd Fellows, the Knights of Pythias, and at least fifteen other clubs. He had served as a major in the Eighth Illinois Infantry during the Spanish-American War.[94] Both men were supported by Madden and the regular Republican organization. When ward lines were redrawn in 1923 on a fifty-ward plan with one alderman from each ward, the council, under pressure from the Republican organization, carved out two wards, one each for Anderson and Jackson. Black voters held a majority in each of the two new wards. Black politicians had secured their influence with the Republican organization and mobilized their voters to demand representation on the city council.[95]

Film, History, and the Birth
of a Black Political Culture

In late March 1915, the producers of *The Birth of a Nation* petitioned Chicago's municipal board of film censors for permission to show the film at the Illinois Theater in the Loop. The request set off a huge protest, which brought together white and black activists and was probably the largest interracial movement since the founding of the NAACP six years earlier. "Pernicious caricature of the Negro race," was how Hull House founder Jane Addams described the film when it opened in New York. The film, a full-length feature by director D. W. Griffith, presented a version of southern life after the Civil War. Its portrayal of black men as violent and uncivilized was, as Addams proclaimed, "both unjust and untrue."[1] William Hale Thompson quickly took advantage of the protest to strengthen his support among black voters, declaring, "If Any Part of [the] Film is hurtful to [the] Race It can Not be Exhibited in This City." The film had been approved by Mayor Carter Harrison II in the waning days of his administration after his wife, in a highly publicized and perhaps exaggerated private viewing, approved the film. But the film did not open as scheduled. Instead, "Big Bill listened to a complaint from Negro voters," the *Tribune* reported. Thompson announced on the day of his inaugural, "*Birth of a Nation* will not be shown in Chicago."[2]

The fight over *The Birth of a Nation* signaled the rising power and political confidence of urban black activists. It was, in many ways, the culmination of a local mobilization of black voters and of efforts to link black and white activists across the North. Chicago was not the only city to generate opposition. Activists in New York, Milwaukee, Des Moines, Minneapolis, and Oakland protested the film. In Boston and Philadelphia, there were near riots when police battled protesters. That fall, several black women were arrested during demonstrations against the film in Boston. The film

censor board in Kansas City banned the film, as did Cleveland's city council. In Illinois, the movement against *The Birth of a Nation* brought together
social reformers and professional politicians and forced Chicago's city hall
and the state legislature to address a cultural form that had previously been
targeted by just a small group of white women reformers.[3]

Defender editor Robert Abbott left little doubt that the film involved
much more than racist propaganda. For Abbott and his allies, the battle
against *The Birth of a Nation* was a fight for control of images of African
Americans in politics, public culture, and American history. To the activists,
the public circulation of images and the ability to produce new knowledge
about America's past was directly linked to political power. The fight to
ban the film erupted amid expanding attacks on African Americans, particularly the city's black entrepreneurs and stable working-class families.
The home of Jesse Binga, the prominent banker and real estate entrepreneur, was firebombed in 1914, while black homeowners living in white
neighborhoods faced regular threats and often violence. In the pages of the
Defender, demands for a ban on the film appeared alongside articles about
southern lynching and rising northern urban violence. The conclusion of
the fight against the film would leave African Americans once again embit-
tered by the weakness of white allies, newly determined to forge autonomous sources of black popular culture and politics, and facing expanding
mob violence.

———————————

The fight against the film extended the reach of politics to new urban
spaces. Film, the new medium of the industrial age, spurred the construction of new sites for commercial leisure along urban streets. By 1915, there
were more than six hundred movie houses in Chicago. Movie houses provided new opportunities for separating the races and for politicizing public
spaces. The *Defender* reported in 1910 on the struggle of Mrs. Monroe L.
Manning, who refused a seat in the Globe Theater's "Jim Crow section they
have for Negroes that go to their theatre." She complained to the manager, received a better seat, and told a *Defender* reporter, "The reason our
people are treated like they are [is that] they do not enforce their political rights." Mrs. Manning was not the only black Chicagoan to challenge
Jim Crow in movie houses, though most theaters already separated black
from white viewers simply by their locations in the city. Most were owned
by recent immigrants and were little more than storefronts with folding
chairs, showing silent shorts for immigrant laborers. There were a handful of storefront movie houses in the Black Belt, crammed alongside the

beauty shops, laundries, grocery stores, and dance clubs lining South State Street. Not until the 1920s would large chain movie palaces appear in the city, but even then, neighborhood theaters continued to attract the bulk of the city's working-class immigrant and African American audiences.[4]

Both the content of film and the experience of attending a movie house were subject to political debate in newspapers, in city council meetings, and on the floor of the state legislature. Film had sparked opposition among some women reformers in the century's first decade. Activists, seeing film as a threat to customary sources of authority like the family and church, pushed for censorship laws. Children, they argued, spent more time in theaters than they did in their homes. In 1906, Chicago's city council passed the nation's first movie censorship law, which gave police the authority to review and reject any film showing nudity or sexual innuendo.[5] Censorship, they argued, was needed to preserve the morals of the next generation. Vigilant reformers also moved to alter the experience of watching films: in 1912, the city council approved an ordinance requiring that theaters remain lighted during all performances to prevent "familiarity among patrons."[6]

Some activists, recognizing the power of the moving image, began to consider film as a tool for reform. In the 1910s the city's public health department sponsored films about public hygiene, and Jane Addams starred in a suffragist movie titled *Votes for Women*. Addams had begun to see movies as extensions of settlement houses, capable of educating recent immigrants living in Chicago slums.[7]

The fight over *The Birth of a Nation* drew new attention to the political influence of film and to the growing authority of black politicians. For many, the battle over the film was itself a mark of the achievement of years of political organizing by African Americans. Edward Wright remembered how activists had hoped to bar theatrical productions of *The Nigger* and *The Clansman*. Wright complained that when "the colored people of the city held meetings and sent delegations to the mayor" in 1912, their efforts failed "because we had no representative in the City Council to plead our cause."[8] The *Defender*, recognizing the ability of film to shape public attitudes and politics, had launched a campaign to gain representation on the film censor board. The paper's editors noted that the city's varied national and religious groups had won representation on the board. "The object of the Jew, Irish, German and other nationalities is obvious," the paper commented, suggesting that board members would have the authority to influence popular images of their national group. The paper noted the expanding number of "objectional" films appearing in Chicago's theaters, suggesting that a black representative would effectively bar such "insult." Harrison, responding to the *Defender*'s demands, appointed Rev. Archibald J. Carey to the three-member film censor board in March 1914. A year later, under pressure from the newly elected Oscar DePriest, Thompson appointed another African American, A. J. Bowling, to the board. Representation in governance then meant control over public perceptions—public representations—of national groups.[9]

After a brief court fight, *The Birth of a Nation* opened at the Illinois Theater on June 5. Judge William Fennimore Cooper, following a similar case in New York, issued an injunction barring the city from interfering with the showing of the film. *The Birth of a Nation*, the judge contended, would not generate "race hatred." To the corporate council's argument that *The Birth of a Nation* would provoke "racial animosity," Judge Cooper responded that the city's lawyer assumed viewers would not realize the film depicted people of "two or three generations ago. . . . In the succeeding time, the negro race has advanced almost immeasurably." The city filed an appeal in early July; Louis Anderson, DePriest's opponent in the aldermanic race that spring, was an assistant corporate council and wrote much of the city's brief. The Illinois Supreme Court, citing a missed deadline for filing a second brief, threw out the appeal the following February. During the summer and fall of 1915, the film received rave reviews in the white press, drew large audiences in downtown theaters, and continued to spark protest among black and white activists. Despite his promise, Thompson did little more to fight the film.[10]

As Judge Cooper's ruling suggested, the battle over *The Birth of a Nation* was in many ways a contest over the remembering and writing of American history. Three days after the film opened, amid reports that the city would appeal the judge's ruling, the director, D. W. Griffith, appeared at the theater. He thanked Judge Cooper, who was in the audience that evening, and proclaimed the accuracy of the film. "We should be able to portray the wrongs of the past in order that we may be able to avoid errors in the future," Griffith said.[11] To the outrage of the *Defender*'s publisher, the *Chicago Tribune*, the city's leading white-owned newspaper and the voice of the business-oriented Republican Party, editorialized that the film "is in all essential episodes grounded in historical fact." But the paper's film critic, W. Allison Sweeney, joined the opposition, blasting the film as "grotesque, insolent, and absolutely barren of plausibility." For many, both those who favored and those who opposed the film, the central issue was whether the film told "the truth" about America's past.[12]

How America's past was represented on screen profoundly affected the lives of African Americans. The *Defender*'s pages, which regularly included lurid accounts of lynchings of black men and women, linked the murderous attacks on black people to *The Birth of a Nation*. "Where Birth of a Nation was conceived too often the popular chord is a hideous, monstrous medley of mob law and the bay of bloodhounds," the *Defender* announced. One report on a multiple lynching in Texas featured a photograph of four men, hands bound behind their backs, nooses taut around their necks, hanging from a tree. "This," the story noted, "is the lesson that is being taught by the 'Birth of a Nation.'" Highlighting the "genuine" dangers posed by the film, the report continued, "Remember that any paper that carries the ad of that photo play you should not buy. Any moving picture house that uses any of Griffith's plays should be boycotted."[13] By midsummer, the *Defender* had linked the battle over *The Birth of a Nation* to growing violence on Chicago's South Side. Abbott published a series of editorials expressing outrage over white fears of black home buyers. Local whites "fuss and fume because members of our race have the audacity to buy homes in white neighborhoods, thereby 'depreciating property values,'" he commented.[14] The film only reinforced those beliefs.

The fight to ban *The Birth of a Nation* marked the culmination of black Chicagoans' long struggle for representation in city government and, at the same time, suggested the limits of African Americans' political achievements. Representation on the city council, even on the film censorship board, could not outweigh the interests of a powerful film industry, even during a period when film censorship was widely considered a legitimate way to protect public morals. The film, which reinforced and widely circulated an inaccurate (and racist) history, proved a more powerful explanation of America's past than any of the arguments made by black politicians or the biracial band of protestors against the film. The film presented the divisive and derogatory images of black Americans and Reconstruction so long challenged by black activists and so dangerous to all black Americans. In the debate over the meaning of American history, *The Birth of a Nation* won.

Four years and a little less than two months after the film opened in Chicago theaters, a bloody race riot erupted on the city's South Side, leaving twenty black and fifteen white Chicagoans dead. The riot was attributed to many changes in the city. Chicago's black population had nearly tripled over the decade of the 1910s, increasingly restrictive racial segregation had led to a severe housing shortage in African American neighborhoods, the end of World War I had brought home white servicemen who competed for jobs with black workers, and many who had fought in the war were newly trained in the use of firearms. There were enough tensions and fissures in the city's social fabric to explain the outburst of violence on a hot July day.[15] Yet film somehow entered African American accounts of the street battles.

In the fall after the riot, a young black novelist and filmmaker, Oscar Micheaux, wrote and directed a response to *The Birth of a Nation. Within Our Gates* deliberately aimed to provoke black moviegoers to respond to white hypocrisy and racial violence. As Micheaux told a *Defender* reporter, the film "is a bit radical, it is withal the biggest protest against race prejudice, lynching and concubinage that was ever written or filmed." The *Defender* reporter agreed, writing, "The author has not minced words in presenting the facts as they really exist." Most shocking to the censor board and most "thrilling and gripping" to the *Defender* was a scene of a black woman nearly raped by a white man, an image that clearly challenged the long-standing justification for lynching, the widely held white view that black men regularly raped white women. The film aimed to correct the historical record. As its title suggested, the film was, in addition, a call to racial solidarity and a plea for African Americans to turn inward, to build political and cultural communities "within our gates."[16]

Over the following decade, a score of black directors, writers, actors, and investors produced films depicting African American life. Some were based in Chicago, others in Kansas City, New York, and Los Angeles. Micheaux, among the best known, left Chicago for New York City in 1922 and continued to be a leading force in the new genre of race films. *The Birth of a Nation* succeeded in producing a powerful and dominant image of race relations in America. But the organized opposition to the film and African American outrage over its popularity among whites helped to give life to another nation, an increasingly black-centered urban culture. As Davarian Baldwin writes, *The Birth of a Nation* gave birth to two nations.[17]

Despite the horrors of the 1919 riot and the obvious conclusion that political representation could not protect them from brutal violence, black Chicagoans did not turn away from politics. Indeed, many reinvigorated efforts to use politics to transform urban society. There were some Garveyites in Chicago—as many as eighteen hundred showed up for a mass meeting in 1920—but the Universal Negro Improvement Association did not sustain wide support in Chicago. Perhaps this was because, as Spear suggests, Chicago's activists, unlike those in New York, had city council representation, weakening Garvey's appeal.[18] By the 1923 aldermanic race, black

Chicagoans had asserted their right to at least two seats on the city council. Many continued to work within the Republican machine. Yet in the late 1910s, a small, but growing number of activists, arguing that city council representation was not enough, began to demand African American control over South Side politics. Once again, Oscar DePriest, the political trickster and self-promoter, led the way.

On January 11, 1918, during a meeting at the Odd Fellows Hall, DePriest formed the People's Movement, the only independent African American political organization in the city's history. With the organization, DePriest confirmed his political skills and the growing independence of black voters. The People's Movement, especially as it expanded during the 1920s, reflected a heightened race consciousness in urban politics. Its first platform, issued in 1918, challenged the machine's control over politics in the largely African American Second and Third Wards. "We denounce and deny the right of a few men to name the candidates for the greatest or the smallest place," the platform announced. "We are Republicans who are seeking to purify the party." Though it initially fought for little more than DePriest's reelection, the movement became an expression of African American resistance to white control over South Side wards, particularly to machine politicians. The machine, the party platform said, "thwarted the people in securing their representation and power." The movement's leaders demanded control over the racially segregated communities: "Our campaign is for political supervision of the territory in which we live, by the group most numerous therein." The movement's leaders called for black political autonomy.[19]

DePriest initially used the organization to run for his old seat against Major R. R. Jackson, a former state legislator and black candidate supported by the machine. DePriest had been abandoned by the Republican machine and lost the 1918 primary. Breaking all the rules of the political organization, DePriest refused to drop out of the race and instead ran as an independent backed by the People's Movement. The campaign was ugly, with accusations of abandoning black Chicagoans shooting from both sides. DePriest lost by just 498 votes out of 8,600 cast, coming in ahead of both the Democratic and Socialist candidates. (The battle over *The Birth of a Nation* may have sustained Jackson, who had pushed through legislation to ban the film in 1915.) A year later, DePriest ran and lost by a slim margin again. Both runs suggested the strength of DePriest's reputation as a race leader and the power of his independent organization.[20]

DePriest, running against two black alderman, was fighting not for race representation but, as Charles Branham argues, "under the banner of black control of the Second Ward." In a close analysis of the election returns in the 1918 and 1919 aldermanic races, Branham shows that DePriest ran well, especially in 1919, among voters in the southern and eastern ends of the ward, areas where the ward's more affluent black residents lived. These also were areas where the color line was pushing into white-controlled blocks, where black homeowners and renters faced renewed white violence, and where a vote for DePriest might be an assertion of anger and resentment toward white politicians.[21] The polls suggested DePriest might finally have gained support from middle-class progressives, especially those whose class position was undermined by white mob attacks on their homes. The movement also suggested a subtle shift in black political attitudes: rejection by some recent migrants and longer-term black Chicagoans of the Republican machine's hold on black politics.

The machine remained powerful in the Second and Third Wards, and black politicians continued to use the machine to propel themselves into office. *Defender* editor Robert Abbott never forgave DePriest for tarnishing the image of the race and refused to support his movement. But the People's Movement remained a visible force in Chicago politics through the 1920s and attracted some political radicals, like Joseph R. Bibb, an editor of the *Chicago Whip*. The editor's anger over the white machine's continued interference in Black Belt politics apparently overcame his long-standing hostility toward DePriest. The *Whip*, "a sharp-tongued gadfly," goaded machine politicians, calling leaders of the Second Ward Republican organization "big-fake politicians who for a 'mess of pottage' have preached submissiveness to the black masses"; called Edward Wright a "demagogue"; and attacked banker Jesse Binga. It became the voice of Chicago's "New Negroes" and a vocal supporter of the People's Movement.[22]

"I wish this country would show more interest in the black man," DePriest was quoted, with some mockery and distain, by the German-language press in 1929. "In my opinion," DePriest continued, "the people of my race should have the right to self-determination." As the news account noted, DePriest had effectively taken on the rhetoric deployed by Woodrow Wilson as he led the nation into World War I. The People's Movement, drawing on political strands of black self-reliance and the vocabulary of independence movements challenging European powers, appeared as a small but visible challenge to the old pragmatic alliance between black politicians and the Republican machine.[23]

DePriest ended his career in Washington in 1934, a nationally known politician and a symbol of African American achievement. Through the 1920s, DePriest maneuvered between and among factions, even across party lines. DePriest's old rival, Edward H. Wright, had become committee-man for the Second Ward, repeatedly opposing DePriest's efforts to regain office. Still, the "blundering, blustering schemer," as the *Whip* called him, maintained his ties to Madden and Thompson, even when Thompson left office in 1923. In 1928, a year after Thompson again won a mayoral race, Madden died just days after winning the Republican primary for reelection. DePriest, who was vacationing at a summer resort in Indiana, immediately sent telegrams to the other ward committeemen, who had the legal power to fill the vacancy. By the time DePriest returned to the city, he had secured support for his own candidacy. The general election, however, did not go smoothly. Just days after DePriest's nomination was announced, Assistant Attorney General William H. Harrison, a prominent Democrat, entered the race as an independent. Then, a couple of months before the election, DePriest was indicted for "aiding, abetting, and inducing" South Side entrepreneurs to run gambling houses and brothels and protecting them from the law. The charges were later dropped, but DePriest's win was unusually narrow, especially in a district that was reliably Republican. Voters had given Madden a 14,000-vote plurality in 1926; two years later, DePriest won by just 3,800 votes. With that victory, DePriest became the first black man elected to the House of Representatives since Reconstruction, more than half a century earlier. He presented himself as standing not just for his district but as "the official representative of 12,000,000 people," all African Americans.[24]

DePriest, not a distinguished legislator, devoted much of his time in office to speaking tours across the nation, bargaining for appropriations for African American colleges and universities, and eventually to supporting federal relief to Depression-plagued black communities. "To the race, Congressman DePriest has become the National idol," wrote a reporter in the *Washington Tribune*. "His months in Washington have given the Negro new hope, new courage, new inspiration."[25] DePriest had become a representative of a new national political constituency, black Americans, and an emblem of the racial struggle that would both unify and divide Americans for the rest of the twentieth century.

In Chicago, black politics meant much more than DePriest's stormy career. DePriest won a pair of firsts—first black alderman and first black post-Reconstruction congressman. His achievements resulted from years of struggle, organizing, speechmaking, and door-to-door canvassing by black Chicagoans. DePriest's campaigns divided the black electorate and were tainted by corruption, demonstrating the complexity of black politics. His victories emerged out of a larger arena of urban black politics convulsed by internal debates over ideology and agendas, split among aspiring activists, and fueled by South State Street's "bright lights" entrepreneurs.

DePriest's 1915 victory fulfilled African American demands for representation in urban politics. His defeats just a few years later signaled the strength of the Republican machine he had helped build. For better or worse, DePriest and the long line of activists who had made his 1915 election possible gave rise to the powerful black machine that would become a crucial ally to white machine Democrats from the late 1930s through much of the twentieth century. DePriest's continuing career in politics suggested an expanding and powerful pull of racial solidarity, a movement that demanded not just representation but also African American control over politics in African American neighborhoods. Activists had moved from nineteenth-century demands for full inclusion to using white violence and racial separation as tools in political struggles.

The activists and career politicians of the late nineteenth and early twentieth centuries had created an aggressive and organized black political culture; they made race the defining feature of twentieth-century American urban politics. From John Jones through the Barnett and Williams families and Edward Morris, Edward Wright, Archibald J. Carey Sr., and even the wily DePriest, they were courageous, pragmatic and able politicians who knew their history. They compromised when necessary and, drawing on their understanding of the past, built new alliances and institutions. Their achievements, tainted, compromised, and hard won, were limited both by personal ambition and the racial structures of the American polity. And yet the northern activists who overcame the defeats of Reconstruction and repeatedly demanded representation in late nineteenth- and early twentieth-century urban governance forged a powerful new racial solidarity that would become the foundation for continuing the struggle.

ACKNOWLEDGMENTS

Several colleagues and friends read drafts of chapters or bits and pieces of this manuscript. Thanks especially to Elizabeth Blackmar, Eric Foner, Iver Bernstein, Maureen Flanagan, Daphne Spain, Leigh Schmidt, Paula Lupkin, Clarissa Hayward, Jean Allman, Eric Mumford, David Suisman, Wallace Best, Andrea Friedman, Charly Coleman, Will Winter, Harold Platt, James Grossman, C. S. Adcock, and Nic Sammond. Sections of the manuscript received thoughtful and helpful comments from audiences, panelists, and commentators at conferences, university workshops, and public talks over the past few years. I am grateful to all, especially members of the Newberry Library's Labor History Seminar, the wonderful crowd at the Illinois State Historical Society dinner in 2008, and my colleagues at the Washington University History Department Writing Workshop.

For reading and offering detailed comments on the entire manuscript, I thank Eric Arnesen, Peter Dimock, and an anonymous reviewer for the University of Chicago Press. Arnesen provided the kind of generous and meticulous reading most authors can only dream of.

I had research assistance from a remarkable group in Chicago. Thanks to Kali Cleary, Maggie Hanson, Jack Hanson, Becca Bernstein, and Mike Hines and to Madelyn Silber in Saint Louis. Financial support for the research on this book came from a Newberry Library summer fellowship, the American Philosophical Society, the Gilder Lehrman Institute of American History, and Washington University.

I am grateful for two editors, Robert Devins and Timothy Mennel, who offered crucial advice at key moments in the writing and editing of this book. Thanks to George Roupe for truly attentive copyediting, and to Russ Damian for steering the manuscript through the editorial process with great care.

Thanks to the archivists and librarians at the Newberry Library, the Chicago History Museum, the Harold Washington Library Special Collections, the Vivian Harsh Research Collection at the Woodson Regional Library, the Schomburg Center for Research in Black Culture, the New York Public Library, the Special Collections Research Center at the Joseph Regenstein Library at the University of Chicago, and to the librarians at the Washington University Olin Library, especially the staff of the interlibrary loan department. Dennis C. Dickerson kindly guided me through the AME Archives in Nashville, even as he was completing his own important study of Archibald Carey.

This book builds on the work of a number of important studies of Chicago and African American history. Charles Russell Branham's unpublished dissertation, "The Transformation of Black Political Leadership in Chicago, 1864–1942," was crucial.

My friends in Chicago and New York were kind and patient enough to listen to me talk about black politics in Chicago over many years. Thanks to Sarah Hanson, Gerry Cleary, Betsy Farrell, Babs Davey, Miles Harvey, Rengin Altay, Chris Kasamas, Rich Cohen, Sonia da Silva, Willie Thaler, Kamala Mantha-Thaler, Amelia McDonnell-Parry, Charly Coleman, and Bahareh Rashidi.

As always, I thank my teachers Eric Foner and Elizabeth Blackmar for their brilliant work and continuing kindness, generosity, and friendship.

Emily Garb, Kevin Ohlinger, and Charlie and Janie Garb contributed love and support, especially at the saddest moments. It is my great sorrow that my parents are not alive to read this book.

Freedom's Ballot is dedicated with love and gratitude to my two favorite people: Mark Gregory Pegg and Eva Scott Garb.

African American Political Leaders in Chicago, 1870–1920

Name	Birth date	Birthplace	Occupation	Highest office	Party
Robert S. Abbott	1870	GA	Publisher		R
Cyrus F. Adams	1851	KY	Editor	Asst. registrar, (A)	R
Louis B. Anderson	1870	VA	Lawyer	Alderman (E)	R
Julius Avendorph	1868	AL	Asst. pres., Pullman Co.	Asst. to county clerk (A)	D
Ferdinand Barnett	1859	TN	Lawyer, editor	Asst. state atty. (A)	R
Ida B. Wells-Barnett	1862	MS	Journalist	Adult probation officer (A)	R
James Bish	. . .	. . .	Major, National Guard	State rep., 2 yrs. (E)	R
James T. Brewington	. . .	MS	Realtor (worked for George F. Harding)	. . .	R
Richard Smith Bryan	. . .	NY	Restaurant owner, organizer of 1st Ward Republican Club	. . .	R
John C. Buckner	. . .	IL	Waiter	State rep., 4 yrs. (E)	R
Archibald Carey	1858	GA	AME minister	Civil service commissioner (A)	R
Alexander Clark	. . .	. . .	Editor	. . .	R

(*continued*)

Name	Birth date	Birthplace	Occupation	Highest office	Party
James Cotter	1880	TN	Lawyer	Asst. US atty. (A)	R
William R. Cowan	1858	KY	Realtor	. . .	R
Elizabeth L. Davis	1855	IL	Teacher, writer	. . .	R
Richard De Baptiste		VA	Minister, editor	. . .	R
Ida Dempsey	1859	IN	Frederick Douglass Center board member	. . .	R
Franklin A. Denison	. . .	TX	Lawyer	Asst. state atty. (A)	R
Oscar DePriest	1871	AL	Contractor, lawyer	Congressman (E)	R
H. Ford Douglas	1831	VA	Lecturer	. . .	R
Warren B. Douglas	1886	MO	Lawyer	State rep. (E)	R
George F. Ecton	. . .	KY	Waiter, baseball player	State rep. (E)	R
George W. Ellis	1875	MO	Lawyer	Secy. to US legation, Liberia (A)	R
Elijah J. Fisher	. . .	TN	Minister	. . .	R
Albert George	1873	. . .	Lawyer (Washington, DC)	State rep. (E)	R
Edward D. Green	1865	TN	. . .	State rep., 4 yrs. (E)	R
Charles Griffin	1884	OH	Insurance sales	State rep., 4 yrs. (E)	R
Abram T. Hall	ca. 1822	PA	Minister	. . .	R
George C. Hall	1864	MI	Physician	Chicago Public Library Board (A)	R
Daniel H. Jackson	1870	TN	Undertaker	2nd Ward committee-man (A)	R
Robert R. Jackson	1870	IL	Publisher	Alderman (E)	R
John M. Johnson	1853	MO	Saloon owner	. . .	R
Henry T. Jones	1860	AL	Saloon owner	. . .	R
John Jones	1816	NC	Tailor, employment service provider	County board member (E)	R

Name	Birth date	Birthplace	Occupation	Highest office	Party
John G. Jones	. . .	IL	Lawyer	State rep., 2 yrs. (E)	R
Theodore W. Jones	. . .	Canada	Businessman	. . .	
George T. Kersey	1865	. . .	Undertaker	State rep. (E)	R
Alexander Lane	1857	MS	Physician	State rep., 4 yrs. (E)	R
Jennie Lawrence	1890	NC	Social worker	3rd Ward committee- man (A)	R
Berry Lewis	1863	GA	Waiter	. . .	
Morris Lewis	1875	IL	Personal secretary	Secy. to Cong. DePriest (A)	R
Benjamin Lucas	1879	IL	Insurance sales	State Rep. (E)	R
J. Gray Lucas	. . .	TX	Lawyer	Asst. state atty. (A)	D
John R. Marshall	1859	VA	Colonel, US Army	Deputy sheriff (A)	D
William L. Martin	. . .	MO	Lawyer	State rep., 2 yrs. (E)	R
Robert M. Mitchell	1853	AL	Waiter	. . .	R
Edward H. Morris	1858	KY	Lawyer	State rep., 4 yrs. (E)	R
Beauregard Moseley	. . .	GA	Lawyer	. . .	R
Robert T. Motts	1861	IA	Theater owner	. . .	R
Lawrence A. Newby	1868	IN	Lawyer, editor	Asst. prosecuting atty. (A)	R
Adam E. Patterson	1880	MS	Lawyer	Asst. state atty. (A)	D
Adelbert H. Roberts	1867	MI	Lawyer	State senator (E)	R
Julius F. Taylor	1859	VA	Editor	. . .	D
John W. E. Thomas	1847	AL	Teacher	State rep., 6 yrs. (E)	R
Lettie A. Trent	. . .	. . .	Teacher	. . .	
Sheadrack B. Turner	1869	VA	Lawyer, publisher	State rep.	R
Henry O. Wagoner	. . .	MD	Editor	. . .	R
S. A. T. Watkins	1869	TN	Lawyer	Asst. state atty. (A)	D

(*continued*)

Name	Birth date	Birthplace	Occupation	Highest office	Party
Daniel Hale Williams	1856 or 1858	WI	Physician	IL State Board of Health (E)	R
Fannie Barrier Williams	1855	NY	Writer, lecturer	. . .	R
S. Laing Williams	1860	GA	Lawyer	Asst. US dist. atty. (A)	R
Edward Wright	1864	NY	Lawyer	2nd Ward committee-man (E)	R

Sources: Harold Foote Gosnell, *Negro Politicians: The Rise of Negro Politics in Chicago* (1935; reprint, Chicago: University of Chicago Press, 1967); Charles Russell Branham, "The Transformation of Black Political Leadership in Chicago, 1864–1942," (PhD diss., University of Chicago, 1981); Christopher Robert Reed, *Black Chicago's First Century*, vol. 1, *1833–1900* (Columbia: University of Missouri Press, 2005).
Note: E = elected; A = appointed; R = Republican; D = Democrat

Election Results for Mayoral and Aldermanic Candidates in the First, Second, and Third Wards, 1900–1920

Candidate	Party	Ward 1 total votes	Ward 2 total votes	Ward 3 total votes
		1900 (Aldermanic)		
John J. Coughlin	Democrat	2,665 *(uncontested)*		
William H. Thompson	Republican		2,519	
Charles F. Gunther	Democrat		2,113	
Thomas J. Dixon	Republican			3,292
D. Van Ness Person	Democrat			1,061
Henry S. Fitch	Independent			1,012
William H. Rexroat	Cit.			6
		1901 (Mayoral)		
Elbridge Hanecy	Republican	3,223	4,939	4,061
Carter H. Harrison	Democrat	6,710	3,842	3,921
Avery E. Hoyt	Prohibitionist	80	70	75
Gus Hoyt	Social Democrat	20	35	18
John R. Pepin	Socialist Labor	9	15	19
Thomas Rhodes	Single Tax	41	11	25
John Collins	Socialist	33	43	65
		1901 (Aldermanic)		
Michael Kenna	Democrat	6,395		
Edward E. Everett	Prohibitionist	463		
John F. Sheppard	Single Tax	245		
Charles Alling	Republican		5,558	
Joseph M. Wineman	Democrat		3,077	
S. F. Welbasky	Prohibitionist		59	
C. H. Hartman	Single Tax		23	
Reiss Wasbrough	Socialist		40	
John Cordingly	Independent		101	
Milton J. Foreman	Republican			4,474
Samuel H. Hoffheimer	Democrat			3,587
A. J. Rosier	Prohibitionist			40
George Hazel	Single Tax			12
Louis Dalgaard	Socialist			48

Candidate	Party	Ward 1 total votes	Ward 2 total votes	Ward 3 total votes
		1902 (Aldermanic)		
John J. Coughlin	Democrat	5,361		
David L. Frank	Republican	2,808		
Carl Gezelius	Prohibitionist	81		
John Conzlemann	Socialist	51		
John F. Sheppard	Single Tax	20		
Thomas J. Dixon	Republican		3,813	
Stephen F. Welbasky	Prohibitionist		79	
Rice Wasbrough	Socialist		84	
William H. Williamson	Independent Republican		99	
J. W. Davis	Single Tax		88	
William S. Jackson	Republican			2,740
Arthur J. Rosier	Prohibitionist			66
George Hazel	Single Tax			226
		1903 (Mayoral)		
Graeme Stewart	Republican	3,150	4,861	4,540
Carter H. Harrison	Democrat	6,368	3,661	3,511
Thomas L. Haines	Prohibitionist	60	55	43
Charles L. Breckon	Socialist	78	75	135
Daniel L. Cruice	Independent Labor	156	134	249
Henry Sale	Socialist Labor	30	20	13
		1903 (Aldermanic)		
Michael Kenna	Democrat	6,153		
Frank A. Morton	Prohibitionist	219		
J. Laughton	Socialist	110		
Edward V. Davis	Independent Labor	282		
Hans A. Nielson	Socialist Labor	40		
Charles Alling	Republican		5,242	
John V. Ryerson	Prohibitionist		76	
Stanley Kleindienst	Socialist		119	
L. J. W. Bim	Socialist Labor		40	
Milton J. Foreman	Republican			4,918
August Larson	Prohibitionist			65
Sidney C. Yeomans	Socialist			237
Thomas S. Stevenson	Independent Labor			492
George Hazel	Single Tax			55
		1904 (Aldermanic)		
John C. Coughlin	Democrat	4,729		
Oscar Odelius	Prohibitionist	591		
C. W. Goldman	Socialist	291		
Thomas J. Dixon	Republican		3,521	
Robert Greer	Prohibitionist		100	
Robert Kurth	Socialist		315	
Morris Wheeler	Independent Cit.		653	
William J. Pringle	Republican			3,268
William H. Craig	Prohibitionist			68

Candidate	Party	Ward 1 total votes	Ward 2 total votes	Ward 3 total votes
Frank Bohlman	Socialist			234
Louis J. Behan	Independent Republican			806
Edwin F. Masterson	Independent			1,486
1905 (Mayoral)				
John Maynard Harlan	Republican	2,508	4,773	4,352
Edward F. Dunne	Democrat	6,307	4,023	3,953
Oliver W. Stewart	Prohibitionist	80	85	51
John Collins	Socialist	165	286	304
1905 (Aldermanic)				
Michael Kenna	Democrat	6,001		
Rollo H. McBride	Prohibitionist	423		
Fred Scholl	Socialist	250		
Isaac W. Lillis	Independent Republican	52		
Geo F. Harding Jr.	Republican		?	
S. F. Welbasky	Prohibitionist		58	
Robert Kurth	Socialist		302	
W. H. Williamson	Independent		240	
Henry S. Fitch	Independent Republican		2,494	
Henry W. Peterson	Independent		73	
A. W. K. Downes	Independent Democrat		1,209	
Milton J. Foreman	Republican			4,735
Thor J. Benson	Democrat			2,911
James Ritchey	Prohibitionist			45
Frank Bohlman	Socialist			281
Maxwell Edgar	Independent			479
1906 (Aldermanic)				
Frank Norton	Republican	1,397		
John J. Coughlin	Democrat	5,293		
Oscar Odelius	Prohibitionist	110		
Fred Scholl	Socialist	372		
Marcus Pollasky	Independent	55		
Thomas J. Dixon	Republican		2,902	
A. B. Perrigo	Democrat		2,902 (?)	
W. C. Benton	Socialist		312	
William J. Pringle	Republican			3,793
Louis E. Hamburg	Democrat			2,464
C. P. Hard	Prohibitionist			51
Louis Dalgaard	Socialist			340
1907 (Mayoral)				
Fred A. Busse	Republican	3,310	6,038	5,296
Edward F. Dunne	Democrat	4,173	3,474	3,530
William A. Brubaker	Prohibitionist	98	133	131
George Koop	Socialist	105	165	151

Candidate	Party	Ward 1 total votes	Ward 2 total votes	Ward 3 total votes
		1907 (Aldermanic)		
Michael Kenna	Democrat	4,309		
Robert S. Wood	Prohibitionist	135		
Louis F. Hemse	Socialist	194		
C. W. Espey	Independent Labor	314		
Vito A. Taglia	Independent Republican	195		
Geo F. Harding Jr.	Republican		6,183	
Samuel B. Lingle	Prohibitionist		535	
A. Corking	Socialist		257	
Milton J. Foreman	Republican			5,292
Frank Halbeisen	Democrat			3,259
William S. Baird	Prohibitionist			106
Louis Dalgaard	Socialist			177
		1908 (Aldermanic)		
William A. Brush	Republican	1,329		
John C. Coughlin	Democrat	4,514		
Robert S. Wood	Prohibitionist	110		
C. W. Espey	Independent Labor	246		
Thomas J. Dixon	Republican		3,275	
William F. Kellett	Prohibitionist		155	
Robert Kurth	Socialist		324	
H. Bond	Independent Labor		1,068	
William J. Pringle	Republican			3,847
William S. Newburger	Democrat			2,199
William S. Baird	Prohibitionist			211
Owen Brown	Socialist			195
		1909 (Aldermanic)		
Michael Kenna	Democrat	3,897		
George G. Pendell	Prohibitionist	214		
Henry Cramer	Socialist	137		
Scattering		4		
G. F. Harding Jr.	Republican		5,184	
Richard N. Noland	Democrat		829	
William F. Kellett	Prohibitionist		68	
Henry Kohl	Socialist		120	
Milton J. Foreman	Republican			5,311
M. A. Mergentheim	Democrat			1,916
John F. Johnson	Prohibitionist			127
M. Winberg	Socialist			122
		1910 (Aldermanic)		
John C. Coughlin	Democrat	3,736		
John S. Townsend	Republican	1,147		
George G. Pendell	Prohibitionist	198		
Axel Gustafson	Socialist	172		
Wilson Shufelt	Republican		3,619	
J. M. Montgomery	Democrat		2,375	
Samuel B. Lingle	Prohibitionist		86	

Candidate	Party	Ward 1 total votes	Ward 2 total votes	Ward 3 total votes
Robert Kurth	Socialist		128	
Harry Snow	Independent Republican		20	
E. C. Wentworth	Independent Republican		1,081	
Ed H. Wright	Independent Republican		1,587	
William J. Pringle	Republican			*3,420*
James D. Marshall	Democrat			2,880
John F. Johnson	Prohibitionist			206
Owen Brown	Socialist			155
	1911 (Mayoral)			
Charles Merriam	Republican	1,549	4,157	*4,591*
Carter H. Harrison	Democrat	*5,193*	*4,341*	4,414
William A. Brubaker	Prohibitionist	46	75	50
William E. Rodriguez	Socialist	179	260	247
Anthony Prince	Socialist Labor	14	16	21
	1911 (Aldermanic)			
Michael Kenna	Democrat	*5,096*		
Simeon W. King	Prohibitionist	199		
Thomas Beebe	Socialist	227		
G. F. Harding Jr.	Republican		*5,400*	
George Hagenauer	Democrat		2,749	
C. E. Ostergren	Prohibitionist		54	
Charles W. Kven	Socialist		270	
Milton J. Foreman	Republican			3,581
Albert R. Tearney	Democrat			*4,912*
Oscar Larson	Prohibitionist			62
F. W. Kramer	Socialist			181
John H. Fitch	Independent Republican			510
	1912 (Aldermanic)			
Joseph Semans	Republican	1,413		
John J. Coughlin	Democrat	*5,827*		
Simon W. King	Prohibitionist	49		
Rice Wasbrough	Socialist	352		
Hugh Norris	Republican		*5,356*	
Raymond T. O'Keefe	Democrat		1,603	
George W. Doolittle	Prohibitionist		113	
A. C. Harms	Socialist		328	
P. P. Jones	Independent		476	
Joel F. Longenecker	Republican			5,092
Si Mayer	Democrat			*5,140*
Leroy Veazey	Prohibitionist			63
W. J. Standley	Socialist			198
	1913 (Aldermanic)			
Andrew Donovan	Progressive	713		
Michael Kenna	Democrat	*4,458*		

Candidate	Party	Ward 1 total votes	Ward 2 total votes	Ward 3 total votes
Rice Wasbrough	Socialist	203		
Alfred Tonser	Progressive		440	
Thomas F. Ennis	Democrat		1,808	
George F. Harding Jr.	Republican		*5,193*	
Samuel Block	Socialist		261	
W.W. Mitchell	Progressive			2,338
Thomas D. Nash	Democrat			*4,013*
Sanford K. Huston	Republican			1,625
Michael J. DeMuth	Socialist			163
1914 (Aldermanic)				
Miss Marian Drake	Progressive	2,786		
John C. Coughlin	Democrat	*6,667*		
Philip I. Orme	Republican	623		
Charles M. Leffler	Socialist	279		
William F. Kellett	Prohibitionist	18		
Simon P. Gary	Progressive		1,664	
Thomas T. Hoyne	Democrat		2,358	
Hugh Norris	Republican		*6,925*	
August C. Harms	Socialist		418	
Charles A. Griffin	Independent		2,934	
John H. Quinchett	Prohibitionist		3	
Joel F. Longenecker	Progressive			2,170
Jacob Lindheimer	Democrat			*7,552*
William J. Pringle	Republican			6,979
Robert H. Howe	Socialist			750
1915 (Mayoral)				
Robert Sweitzer	Democrat	*8,470*	6,345	7,691
William H. Thompson	Republican	5,075	*15,715*	*15,309*
Seymour Stedman	Socialist	293	422	500
John H. Hill	Prohibitionist	40	113	147
1915 (Aldermanic)				
Michael Kenna	Democrat	*8,594*		
Winfield S. Troupe	Republican	3,910		
Lester Phillips	Socialist	574		
W. A. R. Mitchell	Progressive	73		
Al Russell	Democrat		6,893	
Oscar DePriest	Republican		*10,599*	
Samuel Block	Socialist		433	
Simon P. Gary	Progressive		3,697	
Thomas D. Nash	Democrat			9,457
Edward J. Werner	Republican			*12,844*
Robert H. Howe	Socialist			394
1916 (Aldermanic)				
J. J. Coughlin	Democrat	*6,033*		
W. H. Schrader	Republican	1,233		
Rice Wasbrough	Socialist	230		
Harry Hildreth Jr.	Democrat		4,212	

Candidate	Party	Ward 1 total votes	Ward 2 total votes	Ward 3 total votes
Hugh Norris	Republican		6,055	
Arther E. Holm	Socialist		243	
Ulysses S. Schwartz	Democrat			9,756
F. W. Patterson	Republican			6,887
Rowland Shelton	Socialist			377
1917 (Aldermanic)				
Michael Kenna	Democrat	5,484		
G. T. Royer	Socialist	246		
Fred Wenig	Democrat		3,991	
Louis B. Anderson	Republican		6,369	
Frederick W. Hack	Socialist		209	
George F. Iliff	Democrat			7,282
Frederick W. Patterson	Republican			6,055
Joseph F. Greer	Socialist			262
1918 (Aldermanic)				
John J. Coughlin	Democrat	6,706		
Walker E. Whitley	Republican	1,037		
P. H. Geluk	Socialist	224		
Clem Kuehne	Democrat		3,187	
Robert R. Jackson	Republican		6,669	
Arthur E. Halm	Socialist		312	
Oscar DePriest	Independent		6,021	
Ulysses S. Schwartz	Democrat			8,360
Felix A. Narden	Republican			5,537
Joseph H. Greer	Socialist			409
1919 (Mayoral)				
Robert M. Sweitzer	Democrat	6,526	3,323	7,166
William H. Thompson	Republican	3,469	15,569	10,360
John M. Collins	Socialist	463	474	330
Adolph S. Carm	Social Labor	9	10	16
John Fitzpatrick	Labor	414	496	944
Maclay Hoyne	Independent	1,028	1,644	5,677
1919 (Aldermanic)				
Michael Kenna	Democrat	6,861		
John J. Kennedy	Independent	499		
A. L. Davidson	Democrat		3,870	
Louis B. Anderson	Republican		14,730	
George F. Iliff	Democrat			8,484
John H. Passmore	Republican			10,870
Isadore Gordon	Socialist			312
Joe Winkler	Labor			48
O. T. Reilly	Independent			2,517
1920 (Aldermanic)				
Guy C. Van Alen	Republican	508		
John C. Coughlin	Democrat	4,881		
Robert R. Jackson	Republican		5,025	

Candidate	Party	Ward 1 total votes	Ward 2 total votes	Ward 3 total votes
A. B. Perrigo	N/A		710	
R. E. Westbrooks	N/A		1,025	
Ulysses S. Schwartz	N/A			3,727 *(uncontested)*

Sources: *Chicago Daily News Almanac,* 1900–1902; *Chicago Daily News Almanac and Yearbook,* 1903–1921.
Note: Italicized vote totals indicate election winners.

NOTES

INTRODUCTION

1. In 1900, 17 percent of southern African Americans lived in cities, making up about 31 percent of the region's urban population. Most studies of the South in this period focus on rural and small-town life. Some work has focused on black community development in southern cities. See, for example, John W. Blassingame, *Black New Orleans, 1860–1880* (Chicago: University of Chicago Press, 1973); Howard N. Rabinowitz, *Race Relations in the Urban South, 1865–1890* (New York: Oxford University Press, 1978); George C. Wright, *Life behind a Veil: Blacks in Louisville, Kentucky, 1865–1930* (Baton Rouge: Louisiana State University Press, 1985); Michael W. Fitzgerald, *Urban Emancipation: Popular Politics in Reconstruction Mobile, 1860–1890* (Baton Rouge: Louisiana State University Press, 2002); David Goldfield, *Region, Race, and Cities: Interpreting the Urban South* (Baton Rouge: Louisiana State University Press, 1997).

2. William P. Jones, *The Tribe of Black Ulysses: African American Lumber Workers in the Jim Crow South* (Urbana: University of Illinois Press, 2005); Jones, "Black Milwaukee, Proletarianism, and the Making of Black Working-Class History," *Journal of Urban History* 33 (2007): 544. Jones's study of southern lumber workers and other recent works have gone a long way toward overturning the traditional narrative. But in much of the literature on African American life influenced by the 1920s and 1930s studies of Howard W. Odum and his students, black Americans were long portrayed, at best, as a prepolitical peasant class. See for example, Lynn Moss Sanders, *Howard W. Odum's Folklore Odyssey: Transformation to Tolerance through African American Folk Studies* (Athens: University of Georgia Press, 2003). Among the important recent challenges to this view are Jones, *The Tribe of Black Ulysses*; Leslie Brown, *Upbuilding Black Durham: Gender, Class, and Black Community Development in the Jim Crow South* (Chapel Hill: University of North Carolina Press, 2008); Adele Oltman, *Sacred Mission, Worldly Ambition: Black Christian Nationalism in the Age of Jim Crow* (Athens: University of Georgia Press, 2008); Steven Hahn, *A Nation under Our Feet: Black Political Struggles in the Rural South from Slavery to the Great Migration* (Cambridge, MA: Harvard University Press, 2003).

3. See, for example, Daniel Letwin, *The Challenge of Interracial Unionism: Alabama Coal Miners, 1878–1921* (Chapel Hill: University of North Carolina Press, 1998); Eric Ar-

nesen, *Waterfront Workers of New Orleans: Race, Class, and Politics, 1863–1923* (New York: Oxford University Press, 1991); Tera W. Hunter, *To 'joy My Freedom: Southern Black Women's Lives and Labor after the Civil War* (Cambridge, MA: Harvard University Press, 1997); Peter J. Rachleff, *Black Labor in the South: Richmond, Virginia, 1865–1890* (Philadelphia: Temple University Press, 1984).

4. In one of the very few efforts to compare African American life in southern and northern cities, Howard N. Rabinowitz writes, "In general, the differences in patterns of race relations between northern and southern cities in this period are striking." Rabinowitz, "A Comparative Perspective on Race Relations in Southern and Northern Cities, 1860–1900," in *Race, Ethnicity, and Urbanization: Selected Essays* (Columbia: University of Missouri Press, 1994), 219. Studies of African Americans in northern cities before the Great Migration include Stephen Kantrowitz, *More Than Freedom: Fighting for Black Citizenship in a White Republic, 1829–1889* (New York: Penguin, 2012); Gilbert Osofsky, *The Making of a Ghetto: Negro New York, 1890–1930* (New York: Harper and Row, 1966); Marcy S. Sacks, *Before Harlem: The Black Experience in New York before World War I* (Philadelphia: University of Pennsylvania Press, 2006); Leslie Schwalm, *Emancipation's Diaspora: Race and Reconstruction in the Upper Midwest* (Chapel Hill: University of North Carolina Press, 2009).

5. US Bureau of the Census, *Negro Population, 1790–1915* (Washington, DC: Government Printing Office. 1918), 90–92.

6. Nancy J. Weiss, *Farewell to the Party of Lincoln: Black Politics in the Age of FDR* (Princeton, NJ: Princeton University Press, 1983).

7. Kelly Miller, "Negro Politicians," *Washington Post*, Sept. 8, 1935, 8.

8. Harold F. Gosnell, *Negro Politicians: The Rise of Negro Politics in Chicago* (1935; reprint, Chicago: University of Chicago Press, 1967). Charles Russell Branham's unpublished dissertation, "The Transformation of Black Political Leadership in Chicago, 1864–1942," (University of Chicago, 1981) is a crucial guide for this study. In addition, no scholar of black Chicago can do without Christopher Robert Reed's exhaustive study of nineteenth-century African American life in Chicago, *Black Chicago's First Century*, vol. 1, *1833–1900* (Columbia: University of Missouri Press, 2005).

9. Much has been written in recent years about the importance of global or transnational studies. Here I want to make a case for the local as global, or in Carlo Ginsburg's very specific phrase, microhistory. Ginsburg writes that the prefix *micro* refers "to the microscope, to the analytic gaze, not to the dimensions, alleged or real, of the object under scrutiny." Microhistory aims for big conclusions, or "general implications," from close analysis of local conditions. He contends that microhistory, through a detailed analysis of local history, can and should subvert "political and historiographic hierarchies." Carlo Ginzburg, "Our Words, and Theirs: A Reflection on the Historian's Craft, Today," in *Historical Knowledge: In Quest of Theory, Method and Evidence*, ed. Susanna Fellman and Marjatta Rahikainen (Newcastle upon Tyne, UK: Cambridge Scholars, 2012), 114–16. On the importance of urban space in shaping and being shaped by political struggles, see Henri Lefebvre, *The Production of Space*, trans. Donald Nicholson-Smith (Cambridge: Basil Blackwell, 1991), 73, 17–18; Helmuth Berking, "Contested Places and the Politics of Space," in *Negotiating Urban Conflicts: Interaction, Space, and Control*, ed. Helmuth Berking et al. (London: Transaction Publishers, 2006), 30–31; Manuel Castells, *The City and the Grassroots: A Cross-Cultural Theory of Urban Social Movements* (Berkeley: University of California Press, 1983), esp. 313–14; Dolores Hayden, "Urban Landscape History:

The Sense of Place and the Politics of Space," in *Understanding Ordin*
ed. Paul Groth and Todd W. Bress (New Haven, CT: Yale Universit₁
111–33.

10. US Census reports, 1850–1920. There were just a few immigrants fr₁
Asia, despite organized labor's vocal complaints about Chinese ν
New York City in the teens and twenties, which drew black people ſ
bean, Chicago drew blacks mostly from the rural South.

11. David Harvey, quoted in Hayden, "Urban Landscape History," 133
ing work on the social construction of ethnic identities in immiɟ
hoods includes Donna R. Gabaccio, *From Sicily to Elizabeth Street: H₁*
Change among Italian Immigrants, 1880–1930 (Albany: State Univerſ
Press, 1984); Deborah Dash Moore, *At Home in America: Second Gen*
Jews (New York: Columbia University Press, 1981); Humbert S. N
grants to Ethnics: The Italian Americans (New York: Oxford Univers
Nelli, *Italians in Chicago, 1880–1930: A Study in Ethnic Mobility* (N
University Press, 1970); Dominic A. Pacyga, *Polish Immigrants α*
South Side, 1880–1922 (Columbus: Ohio State University Press, 1
Guglielmo, *White on Arrival: Italians, Race, Color, and Power in Ch₁*
(New York: Oxford University Press, 2003). For a theoretical stat₁
work see Andreas Wimmer, "The Making and Unmaking of Ethɪ
Multilevel Process Theory," *American Journal of Sociology* 13, no. ₄
970–1022.

12. Michael C Dawson, *Behind the Mule: Race and Class in American I*
NJ: Princeton University Press, 1994); Lizabeth Cohen, *Making a*
trial Workers in Chicago, 1919–1930 (Cambridge: Cambridge Univ₁
Michelle R. Boyd, *Jim Crow Nostalgia: Reconstructing Race in Bronze*
University of Minnesota Press, 2008); Thomas Lee Philpott, *The S*
Immigrants, Blacks, and Reformers, 1880–1930 (Belmont, CA: Wadɪ

13. Wallace D. Best, *Passionately Human, No Less Divine: Religion aɪ*
Chicago, 1915–1952 (Princeton, NJ: Princeton University Press, 2
man, *Land of Hope: Chicago, Black Southerners, and the Great N*
University of Chicago Press, 1989); Branham, "Transformatioɪ
Leadership"; Robin F. Bachin, *Building the South Side: Urban Spa*
in Chicago, 1890–1919 (Chicago: University of Chicago Press, 2₀

14. Eric Foner, *Reconstruction: America's Unfinished Revolution* (Nev
Row), 122–23; Kate Masur, *An Example for All the Land: Emancipι*
over Equality in Washington, DC (Chapel Hill: University of N₁
2010), 86–112. Foner notes "the 'politicization' of everyday li
demise of slavery." Masur, however, highlights the "politicizatiₒ
the struggles over who would have access to public spaces in ¹
also Kirt H. Wilson, *The Reconstruction Desegregation Debate: T*
and the Rhetoric of Place, 1865–1875 (East Lansing: Michigan S
2002). There is a vast literature on the rise of racial segregatiₒɪ
ture of segregation, Grace Elizabeth Hale, *Making Whiteness: T*
tion in the South, 1890–1940 (New York: Vintage Books, 1998)

15. On the complexity of segregation see Carl H. Nightingale, *Seg*
tory of Divided Cities (Chicago: University of Chicago Press, 20¹

16. Herman Clayton, "The Game Policy," unpublished manuscɪ
Papers, box 35, folder 13, Illinois Writers Project, Vivian G. ŀ

tion, Woodson Regional Library, Chicago (hereafter IWP). On the rise and economic influence of brothels, cabarets, gambling houses, and dance halls in the Black Belt, see Cynthia M. Blair, *I've Got to Make My Livin': Black Women's Sex Work in Turn-of-the-Century Chicago* (Chicago: University of Chicago Press, 2010); William Howland Kenney, *Chicago Jazz: A Cultural History, 1904–1930* (New York: Oxford University Press, 1993); Nathan Thompson, *Kings: The True Story of Chicago's Policy Kings and Numbers Racketeers: An Informal History*, rev. ed. (Chicago: Bronzeville, 2006).

17. Lefebvre, *Production of Space*, 286. See also Yi-Fu Tuan, *Space and Place: The Perspective of Experience* (Minneapolis: University of Minnesota Press, 1977); Doreen Massey, *For Space* (New York: Sage, 2005). On the similar histories of concepts of race and urban space, see Penelope Edmonds, *Urbanizing Frontiers: Indigenous Peoples and Settlers in 19th-Century Pacific Rim Cities* (Vancouver: University of British Columbia Press, 2010), 10–11.

8. Hanna Fenichel Pitkin, *The Concept of Representation* (Berkeley: University of California Press, 1967), 81. Political theorists call this version of representation "descriptive representation," "a politics of presence," or "self-representation." This view, which parallels the arguments made by early twentieth-century immigrants and African Americans, contends that in a deeply hierarchical society, politically subordinate groups should be represented by those who share their social position and group experiences. Jane Mansbridge, "Should Blacks Represent Blacks and Women Represent Women? A Contingent Yes," *Journal of Politics* 61, no. 3: 628–57; Suzanne, Dovi, "Preferable Descriptive Representatives: Will Just Any Woman, Black or Latino Do?" *American Political Science Review* 96, no. 4: 1–22; Robert R. Preuhs, "Descriptive Representation as a Mechanism to Mitigate Policy Backlash: Latino Incorporation and Welfare Policy in the American States," *Political Research Quarterly* 60, no. 2 (June 2007): 277–92. On the failure of the liberal vision of representation to adequately represent the interests of African Americans and white and black women, see Melissa Williams, *Voice, Trust, and Memory: Marginalized Groups and the Failings of Liberal Representation* (Princeton, NJ: Princeton University Press, 1998). For critique of this view of representation, which argues that it is static and, in many ways, essentializing, see Clarissa Rile Hayward, "Making Interest: On Representation and Democratic Legitimacy," in *Political Representation*, ed. Ian Shapiro et al. (Cambridge: Cambridge University Press, 2009); Iris Young, "Deferring Group Representation," in *Ethnicity and Group Rights*, ed. Ian Shapiro and Will Kymlicka (New York: New York University Press, 1997), 354. I do not intend to enter this debate among political theorists over how best to represent the interests of disadvantaged groups. Rather, my aim is to detail historically how a vision of representation tied to social identity emerged in the early twentieth century.

Dawson, *Behind the Mule*; Hanes Walton and Robert C. Smith, *American Politics and the African American Quest for Universal Freedom* (New York: Longman, 2000); Walton, *Black Political Parties: An Historical and Political Analysis* (New York: Free Press, 1972).

John Jones, untitled published speech pasted in scrap book, Jones Collection, folder 3, Chicago History Museum (hereafter CHM); Michael C. Dawson, *Black Visions: The Roots of Contemporary African-American Political Ideologies* (Chicago: University of Chicago Press, 2001).

Allan H. Spear, *Black Chicago: The Making of a Negro Ghetto, 1890–1920* (Chicago: University of Chicago Press, 1967), 23–25. On conflict and differences among black

activists, see Cathy J. Cohen, *The Boundaries of Blackness: AIDS and the Breakdown of Black Politics* (Chicago: University of Chicago Press, 1999); Preston H. Smith II, *Racial Democracy and the Black Metropolis: Housing Policy in Postwar Chicago* (Minneapolis: University of Minnesota Press, 2012); Kimberle Crenshaw, "Mapping the Margins: Intersectionality, Identity Politics, and Violence against Women of Color," *Stanford Law Review* 43, no. 6 (July 1991): 1241–99.

22. On Merriam, see Barry D. Karl, *Charles E. Merriam and the Study of Politics* (Chicago: University of Chicago Press, 1974). Gosnell's papers, including reviews of *Negro Politics* and letters and speeches about his Chicago research are housed in the Merriam Collection at the Special Collections Research Center, University of Chicago Library.

23. My understanding of politics relies on the pioneering work of feminist scholars who expanded our understanding about how power operates, demonstrating that politics was often marked by gender and racial hierarchies even when women and people of color were excluded from formal politics. See Joan Wallach Scott, *Gender and the Politics of History* (New York: Columbia University Press, 1988); Elsa Barkley Brown, "Negotiating and Transforming the Public Sphere: African American Political Life in the Transition from Slavery to Freedom," in *The Black Public Sphere: A Public Culture Book*, ed. Black Public Sphere Collective (Chicago: University of Chicago Press, 1995), 111–50; Evelyn Nakano Glenn, *Unequal Freedom: How Race and Gender Shaped American Citizenship and Labor* (Cambridge, MA: Harvard University Press, 2002).

24. Elizabeth Jones Lapsansky, "Friends, Wives and Strivings: Networks and Community Values among Nineteenth-Century Philadelphia Afro-American Elites," *Pennsylvania Magazine of History and Biography* 108, no. 1 (Jan. 1984): 5–6.

25. A thoughtful new biography argues persuasively that Dawson was a pragmatic and progressive politician. Christopher Manning, *William L. Dawson and the Limits of Black Electoral Leadership* (DeKalb: Northern Illinois University Press, 2009).

26. Allan H. Spear, *Black Chicago: The Making of a Negro Ghetto, 1890–1920* (Chicago: University of Chicago Press, 1967). See also St. Clair Drake and Horace R. Cayton, *Black Metropolis: A Study of Negro Life in a Northern City* (New York: Harcourt, Brace, 1945); Grossman, *Land of Hope*; William H. Tuttle Jr., *Race Riot: Chicago in the Red Summer of 1919* (New York: Atheneum, 1970); Davarian L. Baldwin, *Chicago's New Negroes: Modernity, the Great Migration, and Black Urban Life* (Chapel Hill: University of North Carolina Press, 2007); Timuel D. Black Jr., *Bridges of Memory: Chicago's First Wave of Black Migration* (Evanston, IL: Northwestern University Press, 2003); Arvrarh E. Strickland, *History of the Chicago Urban League* (Urbana: University of Illinois Press, 1966).

CHAPTER ONE

1. John Jones, untitled published speech pasted in scrapbook. Jones Collection, folder 3, CHM; *Chicago Tribune*, Jan. 2, 1874.

2. John Jones, untitled published speech; *Chicago Tribune*, Jan. 2, 1874.

3. Oil painting by Aaron E. Darling, ca. 1865, owned by CHM. A reproduction of a small photograph of Jones, which was exhibited along with photographs of other leading Chicagoans at the Philadelphia Centennial Exposition of 1876, appears in Joseph Kirkland, *The History of Chicago* (Chicago: Dibble, 1892), 105.

4. Benjamin Quarles, *Black Abolitionists* (New York: Oxford University Press, 1969),

148; Arna Bontemps and Jack Conroy, *Anyplace But Here* (New York: Hill and Wang, 1966), 41; St. Clair Drake and Horace Cayton, *Black Metropolis: A Study of Negro Life in a Northern City* (New York: Harcourt, Brace, 1945), 40–41.

5. Steven Hahn, *A Nation under Our Feet: Black Struggles in the Rural South from Slavery to the Great Migration* (Cambridge, MA: Harvard University Press, 2003), 15.

6. The classic work on black abolitionism remains Quarles, *Black Abolitionists*. Several recent works also highlight African American activism, for example, Bruce Laurie, *Beyond Garrison: Antislavery and Social Reform* (New York: Cambridge University Press, 2005); David M. Jacobs, ed., *Courage and Conscience: Black and White Aboli-tionists in Boston* (Bloomington: Indiana University Press, 1993); Paul Goodman, *Of One Blood: Abolitionism and the Origins of Racial Equality* (Berkeley: University of California Press, 1998; Richard S. Newman, *The Transformation of American Abolition-ism: Fighting Slavery in the Early Republic* (Chapel Hill: University of North Carolina Press, 2002).

7. On black activists in other northern cities, see Leon Litwack, *North of Slavery: The Negro in the Free States, 1790–1860* (Chicago: University of Chicago Press, 1961); James Horton and Lois Horton, *Black Bostonians: Family Life and Community Struggle in the Antebellum North* (New York: Holmes and Meier, 1979); Leslie M. Harris, *In the Shadow of Slavery: African Americans in New York City, 1626–1863* (Chicago: University of Chicago Press, 2003); Margaret Hope Bacon, *But One Face: The Life of Rob-ert Purvis* (Albany: State University of New York Press, 2007); Julie Winch, *Philadel-phia's Black Elite: Activism, Accommodation, and the Struggle for Autonomy, 1787–1848* (Philadelphia: Temple University Press, 1988); Keith P. Griffler, *Frontline Freedom: African Americans and the Forging of the Underground Railroad in the Ohio Valley* (Lex-ington: University Press of Kentucky, 2004).

8. Rufus Blanchard, *Discovery and Conquests of the North-west, with the History of Chi-cago* (Wheaton, IL: R. Blanchard, 1881), 242–43; Christopher Robert Reed, *Black Chicago's First Century*, vol. 1, *1833–1900* (Columbia: University of Missouri Press, 2005), 51–54; *Chicago Journal*, Aug. 5, 1853; William Cronon, *Nature's Metropolis: Chicago and the Great West* (New York: W. W. Norton, 1991), 28–30. Bryant quoted in Donald Miller, *City of the Century: The Epic of Chicago and the Making of Amer-ica* (New York: Simon and Schuster, 1996), 63, 87. An 1845 city census lists 140 people designated "Colored" living in the city. Reed, *Black Chicago's First Century*, 1:489n33.

9. Joseph Kirkland, *The Story of Chicago* (Chicago: Dibble, 1892), 181; Blanchard, *Dis-covery and Conquests of the North-west*, 445–48; Blanchard, *History of Illinois, to Ac-company an Historical Map of the State* (Chicago: National School Furnishing, 1883), 68–69.

10. Kirkland, *The Story of Chicago*, 184–85; Miller, *City of the Century*, 93.

11. "Chicago in 1856," *Putnam's Monthly Magazine*, June 1856, 606–13, reprinted in Bessie Louise Pierce, ed., *As Others See Chicago: Impressions of Visitors, 1673–1933*, (Chicago: University of Chicago Press, 2004), 151.

12. Kirkland, *The Story of Chicago*, 255.

13. Harris, *In the Shadow of Slavery*; Eric Arnesen, "The Quicksands of Economic In-security: African Americans, Strikebreaking, and Labor Activism in the Industrial Era," in *The Black Worker: Race, Labor, and Civil Rights since Emancipation*, ed. Arnesen (Urbana: University of Illinois Press, 2007), 45–47; Kimberley L. Phillips, *Alabama-North: African-American Migrants, Community, and Working-Class Activism in Cleve-land, 1915–45* (Urbana: University of Illinois Press, 1999), 39–41.

14. Joseph Kirkland, "The Poor in Great Cities IV: Among the Poor of Chicago," *Scribner's Magazine*, July 1892, 25.

15. Drake and Cayton, *Black Metropolis*, 40–41; Reed, *Black Chicago's First Century*, 1:191–99; Kirkland, "The Poor in Great Cities IV," 23, 26, 5.

16. Bessie Louise Pierce, *A History of Chicago*, vol. 3, *The Rise of a Modern City, 1871–1893* (New York: Alfred A. Knopf, 1957), 21–22; US Census, 1850; local census 1848; Reed, *Black Chicago's First Century*, 1:48. Miller writes that the city's population was just 14,000 in 1846. Miller, *City of the Century*, 85.

17. Drake and Cayton, *Black Metropolis*, 32.

18. Ibid., 35.

19. Miller, *City of the Century*, 77; Bessie Louise Pierce, *A History of Chicago*, vol. 1, *The Beginning of a City, 1673–1848* (New York: Alfred A. Knopf, 1937), 322–25. In 1837, the city was divided into six wards; that number increased to nine under an 1847 general amendment to the city charter, with two aldermen to represent each ward. In 1847, tenure in office for aldermen was extended from one to two years. Pierce, *A History of Chicago*, 1:325.

20. Blanchard, *Discovery and Conquests of the North-west*, 235; Samuel Edwin Sparling, "Municipal History and Present Organization of the City of Chicago," *Bulletin of the University of Wisconsin* 23 (1898): 21; Miller, *City of the Century*, 74–75.

21. Miller, *City of the Century*, 77.

22. Sparling, "Municipal History," 29; Drake and Cayton, *Black Metropolis*, 41; Robin L. Einhorn, *Property Rules: Political Economy in Chicago, 1833–1872* (Chicago: University of Chicago Press, 1991).

23. Article 6 of the Northwest Ordinance of 1787 banned slavery in the Northwest Territory, yet the Illinois constitution permitted slavery in some forms long after statehood in 1818. Toi K. Hatcher, "The Meaning of Freedom: Work and Lives of 'Free Persons of Color' in Antebellum Illinois," unpublished paper, Dec. 2012, in the author's possession. In 1842, a candidate for mayor, Henry Smith, ran on a platform of abolishing slavery and repealing the black laws. Reed, *Black Chicago's First Century*, 1:88.

24. Stephen Middleton, *The Black Laws in the Old Northwest: A Documentary History* (Westport, CT: Greenwood, 1993), 272–74; Charles A. Gliozzo, "John Jones and the Repeal of the Illinois Black Laws," Social Science Research Publications (Duluth: University of Minnesota, 1975), 4. Other midwestern states passed similar laws. See, for example, Schwalm, *Emancipation's Diaspora*; Litwack, *North of Slavery*, 72.

25. John Jones, *The Black Laws of Illinois, and a Few Reasons Why They Should Be Repealed* (Chicago: Chicago Tribune Book and Job Office, 1864), 15–16; "Colored Children in the Public Schools," *Chicago Tribune*, Oct. 6, 1864, 4; Drake and Cayton, *Black Metropolis*, 40–41.

26. Henry O. Wagoner (Denver) to Hon. S. H. Kerfoot (Chicago), Sept. 27, 1884, Henry O. Wagoner Manuscript Collection, CHM; Willard B. Gatewood, *Aristocrats of Color: The Black Elite, 1880–1920* (Bloomington: Indiana University Press, 1990), 135–36; Reed, *Black Chicago's First Century*, 1:54. Reed spells Hall's name Abram.

27. Drake and Cayton, *Black Metropolis*, 43; R. Nathanial Scott, "What Price Freedom? John Jones, a Search for Negro Equality" (master's thesis, Southern Illinois University, 1971), 31; Perry J. Stackhouse, *Chicago and the Baptists: A Century of Progress* (Chicago: University of Chicago Press, 1933), 15, 29–32; St. Clair Drake, *Churches and Voluntary Associations in the Chicago Negro Community* (Chicago: Work Projects Administration, 1940).

28. Advertisements for Jones & Bonner's ran in *Frederick Douglass' Paper* in the mid-1850s. See for example *Frederick Douglass' Paper*, Apr. 14, 1854, Dec. 7, 14, 1855; *Chicago Tribune*, Mar. 12, 1875, May 22, 1879.

29. *Report of the Proceedings of the Colored National Convention Held at Cleveland, Ohio, September 6, 1848*, in Howard Holman Bell, ed., *Minutes of the Proceedings of the National Negro Conventions, 1830–1864* (New York: Arno Press, 1969), 5; Nell Painter, "Martin R. Delany: Elitism and Black Nationalism," in *Black Leaders of the Nineteenth Century*, ed. Leon Litwack and August Meier (Urbana: University of Illinois Press, 1988), 149–71. On the debate about domestic servants see Harris, *In the Shadow of Slavery*, 232–33.

30. *Chicago Tribune*, Mar. 12, 1875, May 22, 1879. Bruce Laurie describes a similar paternalistic relationship between white and black abolitionists in Massachusetts. Laurie, *Beyond Garrison*, 98–100.

31. Harman Dixon, "Negro in Illinois: The Attitude of Illinois toward Negro Suffrage," box 29, folder 2, IWP.

32. Scott, "What Price Freedom?" 31; Stackhouse, *Chicago and the Baptists*, 15, 29–32; Reed, *Black Chicago's First Century*, 1:89. Reed writes that the meeting to select Jones occurred at Quinn Chapel AME Church; most other sources mention Second Baptist.

33. Pierce, *A History of Chicago*, vol. 2, *From Town to City, 1848–1871* (New York: Alfred A. Knopf, 1940), 364; Alfred Theodore Andreas, *History of Chicago*, 3 vols. (1884–86; reprint, New York: Arno, 1970), 1:332, 428.

34. Bell, *Minutes of the Proceedings of the National Negro Conventions*, 14–15; Patrick Rael, *Black Identity and Black Protest in the Antebellum North* (Chapel Hill: University of North Carolina Press, 2002), 29–31. As Rael notes, northern black people, in part, "constructed black identity through self-conscious acts of public political speech." This, he adds, was primarily "an elite process" (45).

35. James Brewer Stewart, *Holy Warriors: The Abolitionists and American Slavery* (New York: Hill and Wang, 1976), 134–37. Martin R. Delany issued the call for a national convention in Cleveland in 1848 with the explicit aim of bringing black residents of Ohio, Illinois, Indiana, and Michigan into the movement. *North Star*, July 28, 1848; Bell, *Minutes of the Proceedings of the National Negro Conventions*, 269–70; Charles A. Gliozzo, "John Jones and the Black Convention Movement, 1848–1856," *Journal of Black Studies* 3, no. 2 (Dec. 1972): 228–29.

36. Gliozzo, "John Jones and the Black Convention Movement," 230. Along with Douglass's autobiographies, biographies of Douglass include Phillip S. Foner, *Frederick Douglass: A Biography* (New York: Citadel, 1964); Benjamin Quarles, *Frederick Douglass* (Washington, DC: Associated Publishers, 1948); David Blight, *Frederick Douglass and Abraham Lincoln: A Relationship in Language, Politics, and Memory* (Milwaukee: Marquette University Press, 2001); Waldo E. Martin Jr., *The Mind of Frederick Douglass* (Chapel Hill: University of North Carolina Press, 1984).

37. Frederick Douglass, "An Address to the Colored People of the United States," *North Star*, Sept. 29, 1848; *North Star*, Aug. 11, 1848.

38. Douglass, "An Address to the Colored People of the United States." On the networks of people linked to Seneca Falls convention and to abolition see Judith Wellman, *The Road to Seneca Falls: Elizabeth Cady Stanton and the First Woman's Rights Convention* (Urbana: University of Illinois Press, 2004).

39. *Liberator*, Oct. 20, 1848; *North Star*, Sept. 29, 1848; Gliozzo, "John Jones and the Black Convention Movement," 230–31; Bell, *Minutes of the Proceedings of the National Negro Conventions*, 100–10.

lumbia: University of South Carolina Press, 1
Century, 1:117, 118.

68. Reed, *Black Chicago's First Century,* 1:143; Chica
1863.

69. Resolution quoted in Reed, *Black Chicago's First*

70. Jones, *The Black Laws of Illinois;* Scott, "What P
Jones and the Repeal of the Illinois Black Laws,'

71. Jones, *The Black Laws of Illinois,* 14, 4.

72. Gliozzo, "John Jones and the Repeal of the Illin
390; N. Dwight Harris, *The History of Negro Ser*
Clurg, 1904), 120, 137.

73. *Chicago Tribune,* Jan. 6, 15, 1865; *Chicago Time*
and Conroy, *Anyplace But Here,* 49; Gliozzo, "J
linois Black Laws," 6–7.

74. *Journal of the House of Representatives,* Jan. 2, 186

75. *Christian Recorder* (Philadelphia), Feb. 17, Mar.
Radical and the Republican: Frederick Douglass, A
Antislavery Politics (New York: W. W. Norton, 20
tionist sentiment after Reconstruction see Mich
African Americans and the Politics of Racial Desti
University of North Carolina Press, 2004), 16–5

76. "Colored Children in the Public Schools," *Chi*
Times, Apr. 5, 1869; Scott, "What Price Freedom

77. *Christian Recorder* (Philadelphia), Jan. 5, May 18

78. Black women were granted the right to vote un
1920.

79. *Chicago Tribune,* Oct. 20, 24, 1871, Mar. 12, 18
Politicians: The Rise of Negro Politics in Chicago (1
Chicago Press, 1967), 85–86; Pierce, *A History of*
and years in office see Karen Sawislak, *Smoldering*
1871–1874 (Chicago: University of Chicago Pres
"Joseph Medill: Chicago's First Modern Mayor,"
Tradition, ed. Paul M. Green and Melvin G. Ho
University Press, 1995), 1–15; Richard Schnein
Conflict and the Origins of Modern Liberalism in C
sity of Chicago Press, 1998), 49–52.

80. Jones apparently was indicted in connection wi
on Public Charities and Hospitals and the distril
charities. *Inter Ocean,* Oct. 7, 1874; *Chicago Tribu*

81. Cook County Commissioners Records, Dec. 1
I. C. Harris, *The Colored Men's Professional and*
cago, 1885–86), 13–62; St. Clair Drake, *Church*
Chicago Negro Community (Chicago: WPA, 1940)
120–27.

82. "Fifth Ward Republicans," *Inter Ocean,* Feb. 4, 1
IWP; Jones, untitled published speech, *Chicago Tr*

83. Jones, untitled published speech pasted in scrap
CHM.

84. Gosnell, *Negro Politicians,* 65; Branham, "Transfo"

40. Sean Wilentz, *The Rise of American Democracy: Jefferson to Lincoln* (New York: W. W. Norton, 2005), 623–31; Eric Foner, *Free Soil, Free Labor, Free Men: The Ideology of the Republican Party before the Civil War* (New York: Oxford University Press, 1970).

41. Charles Merriam, *Chicago: A More Intimate View of Urban Politics* (New York: Macmillan, 1929), 18; Wilentz, *The Rise of American Democracy,* 623–31; Foner, *Free Soil, Free Labor, Free Men.*

42. Elizabeth R. Varon, *Disunion! The Coming of the American Civil War, 1789–1859* (Chapel Hill: University of North Carolina Press, 2008).

43. *Chicago Daily Journal,* Oct. 3, 1850; Drake and Cayton, *Black Metropolis,* 34; Quarles, *Black Abolitionists,* 202.

44. When Frederick Douglass sent out a call for a "Colored National Convention" in Rochester, New York, to address the issues raised by the Fugitive Slave Act, Jones, Bonner, and Wagoner were chosen to represent Chicago, though Bonner announced he would not be able to attend. *Frederick Douglass' Paper,* June 10, 1853.

45. Quarles, *Black Abolitionists,* 211–13; Thomas P. Slaughter, *Bloody Dawn: The Christiana Riot and Racial Violence in the Antebellum North* (New York: Oxford University Press, 1991).

46. *Frederick Douglass' Paper,* Jan. 8, 1852; *Chicago Daily Times,* Dec. 29, 1852. Though Albert Pettit disappeared from Chicago, his daughters apparently lived with Jones's family in 1860. US Manuscript Census, 1860, schedule 1, pp. 454–55; "Slavery in Chicago: The Underground Railroad Which Helped Slaves to Freedom in Canada . . . An Interesting Interview with LCP. Freer," *Inter Ocean,* June 28, 1891; Reed, *Black Chicago's First Century,* 1:103.

47. *Frederick Douglass' Paper,* Nov. 11, 1853, Jan. 14, 1854.

48. Martin R. Delany, "Political Destiny of the Colored Race, on the American Continent," in *Proceedings of the National Emigration Convention of Colored People, Held at Cleveland, Ohio, August 24, 1854* (Pittsburgh: A. A. Anderson, 1854), reprinted in *Pamphlets of Protest: An Anthology of Early African-American Protest Literature, 1790–1860,* ed. Richard Newman, Patrick Rael, and Philip Lapsansky (New York: Routledge, 2001), 238; Quarles, *Black Abolitionists,* 215; Jane Rhodes, *Mary Ann Shadd Cary: The Black Press and Protest in the Nineteenth Century* (Bloomington: Indiana University Press, 1998).

49. Mary Ann Shadd, *A Plea for Emigration; or, Notes of Canada West, in Its Moral, Social, and Political Aspect; with Suggestions Respecting Mexico, West Indies, and Vancouver Island, for the Information of Colored Emigrants* (Detroit: George W. Pattison, 1852), reprinted in Newman, Rael, and Lapsansky, *Pamphlets of Protest,* 199. Howard Holman Bell argues that opponents of emigration were more likely to be people with an "economic as well as an idealistic interest in keeping the American Negro community stable." These men were ministers, lawyers, and self-made businessmen whose livelihood was drawn from black consumers or who depended on black workers. Bell, *Minutes of the Proceedings of the National Negro Conventions,* 112.

50. Martin R. Delany, *Condition, Elevation, Emigration, and Destiny of the Colored People of the United States* (1853; reprint, Baltimore: Black Classic Press, 1993), 2–3; Quarles, *Black Abolitionists,* 216. In 1860, Douglass suggested he was rethinking his stance on emigration when he accepted an invitation to visit Haiti. The trip was canceled when South Carolinians fired on Fort Sumter and war was declared in the United States.

51. Quarles, *Black Abolitionists,* 219.

52. Jones, *The Black Laws of Illinois,* 4; *Douglass Monthly,* May 1859. Jones's views of

interracial status may have been influenced by
black person as anyone with "one-eighth negro
'twas true, could not draw one drop of blood ir
oath, must lose an eighth." *Chicago Daily Time*
"John Jones and the Repeal of the Illinois Blac
53. Robert L. Harris, "H. Ford Douglas: Afro-Amer
nal of Negro History 62, no. 3 (1977): 217–34; (
Black Chicago's First Century, 1:104–5.
54. *Proceedings of the State Convention of Colored Cit
City of Alton, Nov. 13th, 14th, and 15th, 1856* (C
3. Frederick Douglass suggested that he, Ford
lies when he recalled an evening with Dougla
Janesville, Wisconsin, during an "anti-slavery t
*Life and Times of Frederick Douglass: His Early Li
and His Complete History to the Present Time* (Ha
55. *Western Citizen*, Feb. 22, 1853, Mar. 1, 1853.
56. *Christian Times*, Aug. 31, 1853; *Western Citizen*,
in Gliozzo, "John Jones and the Repeal of th
Black Laws of Illinois, 13.
57. *Proceedings of the State Convention*, 3, 4, 5, 13.
58. Ibid. Thanks to Iver Bernstein for drawing my
stein, "Securing Freedom: The Challenges of F
Slavery in New York, ed. Ira Berlin and Leslie M.
289–324; *Proceedings of the State Convention*, 6–
59. *Proceedings of the State Convention*, 9–10.
60. Ibid., 6, 19. On politics and black manhood in
*Reforming Men and Women: Gender in the Antei
versity Press, 2002); James Oliver Horton and
and Identity: Black Manhood in Antebellum A
the African American Community, ed. James Oli
sonian Institution Press, 1993), 80–97.
61. *Proceedings of the State Convention*, 17–18, 11
1:78.
62. *Proceedings of the State Convention*, 18; Leon F. I
the Free States (Chicago: University of Chicago
app, *The Origins of the Republican Party, 1852–
Press, 1987).
63. *Proceedings of the State Convention*, 17–18; Jam
*struction of Slavery in the United States, 1861–18
On the millenarian tone of black politics in th
*Hearts of Men: Radical Abolitionists and the Tra
Harvard University Press, 2002).
64. *Frederick Douglass' Paper*, July 22, 1853.
65. *Christian Recorder* (Philadelphia), May 18, 186
1:136–37; Drake and Cayton, *Black Metropolis
New York Times*, Mar. 12, 1865.
66. Quoted in Reed, *Black Chicago's First Century*, 1
67. US Manuscript Census, 1860, schedule 1, p.
*Civil War Soldiers of Illinois: The Story of the Ti

ship," 17; B. F. Moore, *A History of Cumulative Voting and Minority Representation in Illinois* (Urbana: University of Illinois Press, 1909).
85. *Chicago Tribune*, Oct. 16, 1876; *Inter Ocean*, Dec. 19, 1899; David A. Joens, "John W. E. Thomas and the Election of the First African American to the Illinois General Assembly," *Journal of the Illinois State Historical Society* 94, no. 2 (Summer 2001): 200–216. See also Joens, *John W. E. Thomas: A Political Biography of Illinois' First African American State Legislator* (Carbondale: Southern Illinois University Press, 2009).
86. *Inter Ocean*, Nov. 6, 1876; *Illinois Election Results, vol. 4, 1873–1882*; Joens, "John W. E. Thomas," 209, 212; Gosnell, *Negro Politicians*, 66.
87. *Inter Ocean*, Mar. 20, 1877; *Conservator*, Dec. 23, 1882.
88. "The Great Anti-Slavery Reunion," undated pamphlet, CHM. Letter dated May 26, 1874, from W. C. Flagg, letter dated Apr. 24, 1874 from Matthew Hull, in Zebina Eastman Collection, box 1, folder 4, CHM; Zebina Eastman, *Historical Sketches of the Anti-Slavery Movement* (Chicago: W. B. Keen, Cooke, 1874) vii–ix.
89. Quoted in Scott, "What Price Freedom?" 137.
90. *Chicago Tribune*, Jan. 2, 1874.
91. *Chicago Tribune*, Mar. 12, 1875. The paper listed Ogden as M. K., but his middle initial was D.
92. Ibid.

CHAPTER TWO

1. *Conservator* quoted in Ralph Nelson Davis, "The History of the Negro Newspaper in Chicago" (PhD diss., University of Chicago, 1939), 11–12. Davis had access to a scrapbook kept by Barnett of articles published between 1878 and 1882. The scrapbook was "a valued family possession," which apparently has disappeared. Davis writes that Barnett stated that "Chicago was a pretty fair place for Negroes to live and that there was little friction between the races." Davis, "The History of the Negro Newspaper in Chicago," 13.
2. Davis, "The History of the Negro Newspaper in Chicago," 13–14; St. Clair Drake, *Churches and Voluntary Associations among the Negroes of Chicago* (Chicago: Works Progress Administration, 1940), 14.
3. *Indianapolis Freeman*, Aug. 28, 1886; *Conservator* quoted in Davis, "The History of the Negro Newspaper," 11–12, 18.
4. Eric Foner, *Freedom's Lawmakers: A Directory of Black Officeholders during Reconstruction* (Baton Rouge: Louisiana State University Press, 1996); Christopher Robert Reed, *Black Chicago's First Century, vol. 1, 1833–1900* (Columbia: University of Missouri Press, 2005), 222.
5. *Conservator* quoted in *Christian Recorder* (Philadelphia), July 27, 1882. Barnett also wrote: "The Republican Party need not fear a loss of our votes so long as a due regard is paid to our acknowledged rights." Davis, "The History of the Negro Newspaper," 11.
6. Stanley P. Hirshson, *Farewell to the Bloody Shirt: Northern Republicans and the Southern Negro, 1877–1893* (Chicago: Quadrangle Books, 1962); Lawrence Grossman, *The Democratic Party and the Negro: Northern and National Politics, 1868–92* (Urbana: University of Illinois Press, 1976), 60–106; Paul Frymer, *Uneasy Alliances: Race and Party Competition in America* (Princeton, NJ: Princeton University Press, 1999), 49–81.
7. *Conservator*, Dec. 23, 1882. On post office work see Henry W. McGee, "The Negro in the Chicago Post Office" (master's thesis, University of Chicago, 1961); Philip F.

40. Sean Wilentz, *The Rise of American Democracy: Jefferson to Lincoln* (New York: W. W. Norton, 2005), 623–31; Eric Foner, *Free Soil, Free Labor, Free Men: The Ideology of the Republican Party before the Civil War* (New York: Oxford University Press, 1970).

41. Charles Merriam, *Chicago: A More Intimate View of Urban Politics* (New York: Macmillan, 1929), 18; Wilentz, *The Rise of American Democracy*, 623–31; Foner, *Free Soil, Free Labor, Free Men*.

42. Elizabeth R. Varon, *Disunion! The Coming of the American Civil War, 1789–1859* (Chapel Hill: University of North Carolina Press, 2008).

43. *Chicago Daily Journal*, Oct. 3, 1850; Drake and Cayton, *Black Metropolis*, 34; Quarles, *Black Abolitionists*, 202.

44. When Frederick Douglass sent out a call for a "Colored National Convention" in Rochester, New York, to address the issues raised by the Fugitive Slave Act, Jones, Bonner, and Wagoner were chosen to represent Chicago, though Bonner announced he would not be able to attend. *Frederick Douglass' Paper*, June 10, 1853.

45. Quarles, *Black Abolitionists*, 211–13; Thomas P. Slaughter, *Bloody Dawn: The Christiana Riot and Racial Violence in the Antebellum North* (New York: Oxford University Press, 1991).

46. *Frederick Douglass' Paper*, Jan. 8, 1852; *Chicago Daily Times*, Dec. 29, 1852. Though Albert Pettit disappeared from Chicago, his daughters apparently lived with Jones's family in 1860. US Manuscript Census, 1860, schedule 1, pp. 454–55; "Slavery in Chicago: The Underground Railroad Which Helped Slaves to Freedom in Canada . . . An Interesting Interview with LCP. Freer," *Inter Ocean*, June 28, 1891; Reed, *Black Chicago's First Century*, 1:103.

47. *Frederick Douglass' Paper*, Nov. 11, 1853, Jan. 14, 1854.

48. Martin R. Delany, "Political Destiny of the Colored Race, on the American Continent," in *Proceedings of the National Emigration Convention of Colored People, Held at Cleveland, Ohio, August 24, 1854* (Pittsburgh: A. A. Anderson, 1854), reprinted in *Pamphlets of Protest: An Anthology of Early African-American Protest Literature, 1790–1860*, ed. Richard Newman, Patrick Rael, and Philip Lapsansky (New York: Routledge, 2001), 238; Quarles, *Black Abolitionists*, 215; Jane Rhodes, *Mary Ann Shadd Cary: The Black Press and Protest in the Nineteenth Century* (Bloomington: Indiana University Press, 1998).

49. Mary Ann Shadd, *A Plea for Emigration; or, Notes of Canada West, in Its Moral, Social, and Political Aspect; with Suggestions Respecting Mexico, West Indies, and Vancouver Island, for the Information of Colored Emigrants* (Detroit: George W. Pattison, 1852), reprinted in Newman, Rael, and Lapsansky, *Pamphlets of Protest*, 199. Howard Holman Bell argues that opponents of emigration were more likely to be people with an "economic as well as an idealistic interest in keeping the American Negro community stable." These men were ministers, lawyers, and self-made businessmen whose livelihood was drawn from black consumers or who depended on black workers. Bell, *Minutes of the Proceedings of the National Negro Conventions*, 112.

50. Martin R. Delany, *Condition, Elevation, Emigration, and Destiny of the Colored People of the United States* (1853; reprint, Baltimore: Black Classic Press, 1993), 2–3; Quarles, *Black Abolitionists*, 216. In 1860, Douglass suggested he was rethinking his stance on emigration when he accepted an invitation to visit Haiti. The trip was canceled when South Carolinians fired on Fort Sumter and war was declared in the United States.

51. Quarles, *Black Abolitionists*, 219.

52. Jones, *The Black Laws of Illinois*, 4; *Douglass Monthly*, May 1859. Jones's views of

interracial status may have been influenced by Illinois black laws, which classified a black person as anyone with "one-eighth negro blood." Jones wrote, "Poor Shylock, 'twas true, could not draw one drop of blood in taking his pound, but we, to take an oath, must lose an eighth." *Chicago Daily Times*, Dec. 29, 1852, quoted in Gliozzo, "John Jones and the Repeal of the Illinois Black Laws," 4.

53. Robert L. Harris, "H. Ford Douglas: Afro-American Antislavery Emigrationist," *Journal of Negro History* 62, no. 3 (1977): 217–34; Quarles, *Black Abolitionists*, 228; Reed, *Black Chicago's First Century*, 1:104–5.

54. *Proceedings of the State Convention of Colored Citizens of the State of Illinois, Held in the City of Alton, Nov. 13th, 14th, and 15th, 1856* (Chicago: Hays and Thompson, 1856), 3. Frederick Douglass suggested that he, Ford Douglas, and Jones were political allies when he recalled an evening with Douglas and "my old friend John Jones" in Janesville, Wisconsin, during an "anti-slavery tour in the West." Frederick Douglass, *Life and Times of Frederick Douglass: His Early Life as a Slave, His Escape from Bondage, and His Complete History to the Present Time* (Hartford, CT: Park, 1883), 552.

55. *Western Citizen*, Feb. 22, 1853, Mar. 1, 1853.

56. *Christian Times*, Aug. 31, 1853; *Western Citizen*, Mar. 1, 1853; *Chicago Tribune* quoted in Gliozzo, "John Jones and the Repeal of the Illinois Black Laws," 5; Jones, *The Black Laws of Illinois*, 13.

57. *Proceedings of the State Convention*, 3, 4, 5, 13.

58. Ibid. Thanks to Iver Bernstein for drawing my attention to this point. See Iver Bernstein, "Securing Freedom: The Challenges of Black Life in Civil War New York," in *Slavery in New York*, ed. Ira Berlin and Leslie M. Harris (New York: New Press, 2005), 289–324; *Proceedings of the State Convention*, 6–7.

59. *Proceedings of the State Convention*, 9–10.

60. Ibid., 6, 19. On politics and black manhood in the antebellum era see Bruce Dorsey, *Reforming Men and Women: Gender in the Antebellum City* (Ithaca, NY: Cornell University Press, 2002); James Oliver Horton and Lois E. Horton, "Violence, Protest, and Identity: Black Manhood in Antebellum America," in *Free People of Color: Inside the African American Community*, ed. James Oliver Horton (Washington, DC: Smithsonian Institution Press, 1993), 80–97.

61. *Proceedings of the State Convention*, 17–18, 11; Reed, *Black Chicago's First Century*, 1:78.

62. *Proceedings of the State Convention*, 18; Leon F. Litwack, *North of Slavery: The Negro in the Free States* (Chicago: University of Chicago Press, 1961), 275; William E. Gienapp, *The Origins of the Republican Party, 1852–1856* (New York: Oxford University Press, 1987).

63. *Proceedings of the State Convention*, 17–18; James Oakes, *Freedom National: The Destruction of Slavery in the United States, 1861–1865* (New York: W. W. Norton, 2012). On the millenarian tone of black politics in the 1850s, see John Stauffer, *The Black Hearts of Men: Radical Abolitionists and the Transformation of Race* (Cambridge, MA: Harvard University Press, 2002).

64. *Frederick Douglass' Paper*, July 22, 1853.

65. *Christian Recorder* (Philadelphia), May 18, 1867; Reed, *Black Chicago's First Century*, 1:136–37; Drake and Cayton, *Black Metropolis*, 43; *Chicago Tribune*, July 15, 1864; *New York Times*, Mar. 12, 1865.

66. Quoted in Reed, *Black Chicago's First Century*, 1:117; *Chicago Tribune*, Apr. 4, 6, 1861.

67. US Manuscript Census, 1860, schedule 1, p. 454; Edward A. Miller Jr., *The Black Civil War Soldiers of Illinois: The Story of the Twenty-Ninth US Colored Infantry* (Co-

lumbia: University of South Carolina Press, 1998), 20; Reed, *Black Chicago's First Century*, 1:117, 118.

68. Reed, *Black Chicago's First Century*, 1:143; *Chicago Tribune*, Jan. 21, Mar. 20, Apr. 15, 1863.

69. Resolution quoted in Reed, *Black Chicago's First Century*, 1:127.

70. Jones, *The Black Laws of Illinois*; Scott, "What Price Freedom?" 101; Gliozzo, "John Jones and the Repeal of the Illinois Black Laws," 5.

71. Jones, *The Black Laws of Illinois*, 14, 4.

72. Gliozzo, "John Jones and the Repeal of the Illinois Black Laws," 6; 33 *Illinois Reports* 390; N. Dwight Harris, *The History of Negro Servitude in Illinois* (Chicago: A. C. Mc-Clurg, 1904), 120, 137.

73. *Chicago Tribune*, Jan. 6, 15, 1865; *Chicago Times*, Jan. 4, 1865. See also Bontemps and Conroy, *Anyplace But Here*, 49; Gliozzo, "John Jones and the Repeal of the Illinois Black Laws," 6–7.

74. *Journal of the House of Representatives*, Jan. 2, 1865; Dixon, "Negro in Illinois," 13.

75. *Christian Recorder* (Philadelphia), Feb. 17, Mar. 10, 1866. See also James Oakes, *The Radical and the Republican: Frederick Douglass, Abraham Lincoln, and the Triumph of Antislavery Politics* (New York: W. W. Norton, 2007), 247–55. On the rise of emigrationist sentiment after Reconstruction see Michele Mitchell, *Righteous Propagation: African Americans and the Politics of Racial Destiny after Reconstruction* (Chapel Hill: University of North Carolina Press, 2004), 16–50.

76. "Colored Children in the Public Schools," *Chicago Tribune*, Oct. 6, 1864; *Chicago Times*, Apr. 5, 1869; Scott, "What Price Freedom?" 105.

77. *Christian Recorder* (Philadelphia), Jan. 5, May 18, 1867, Mar. 10, 1866.

78. Black women were granted the right to vote under the Nineteenth Amendment in 1920.

79. *Chicago Tribune*, Oct. 20, 24, 1871, Mar. 12, 1875, May 22, 1879; Gosnell, *Negro Politicians: The Rise of Negro Politics in Chicago* (1935; reprint, Chicago: University of Chicago Press, 1967), 85–86; Pierce, *A History of Chicago*, 3:48. On Medill's election and years in office see Karen Sawislak, *Smoldering City: Chicagoans and the Great Fire, 1871–1874* (Chicago: University of Chicago Press, 1995), 129–35; David L. Protess, "Joseph Medill: Chicago's First Modern Mayor," in *The Mayors: The Chicago Political Tradition*, ed. Paul M. Green and Melvin G. Holli (Carbondale: Southern Illinois University Press, 1995), 1–15; Richard Schneirov, *Labor and Urban Politics: Class Conflict and the Origins of Modern Liberalism in Chicago, 1864–97* (Chicago: University of Chicago Press, 1998), 49–52.

80. Jones apparently was indicted in connection with his service on the Committees on Public Charities and Hospitals and the distribution of county contracts to local charities. *Inter Ocean*, Oct. 7, 1874; *Chicago Tribune*, Mar. 12, 1875.

81. Cook County Commissioners Records, Dec. 14, 1871, Jan. 15, May 13, 1872; I. C. Harris, *The Colored Men's Professional and Business Directory of Chicago* (Chicago, 1885–86), 13–62; St. Clair Drake, *Churches and Voluntary Associations in the Chicago Negro Community* (Chicago: WPA, 1940), 60; Scott, "What Price Freedom?" 120–27.

82. "Fifth Ward Republicans," *Inter Ocean*, Feb. 4, 1876, typed copy, box 29, folder 1, IWP; Jones, untitled published speech, *Chicago Tribune*, Jan. 2, 1874.

83. Jones, untitled published speech pasted in scrapbook, Jones Collection, folder 3, CHM.

84. Gosnell, *Negro Politicians*, 65; Branham, "Transformation of Black Political Leader-

ship," 17; B. F. Moore, *A History of Cumulative Voting and Minority Representation in Illinois* (Urbana: University of Illinois Press, 1909).

85. *Chicago Tribune*, Oct. 16, 1876; *Inter Ocean*, Dec. 19, 1899; David A. Joens, "John W. E. Thomas and the Election of the First African American to the Illinois General Assembly," *Journal of the Illinois State Historical Society* 94, no. 2 (Summer 2001): 200–216. See also Joens, *John W. E. Thomas: A Political Biography of Illinois' First African American State Legislator* (Carbondale: Southern Illinois University Press, 2009).

86. *Inter Ocean*, Nov. 6, 1876; *Illinois Election Results*, vol. 4, *1873–1882*; Joens, "John W. E. Thomas," 209, 212; Gosnell, *Negro Politicians*, 66.

87. *Inter Ocean*, Mar. 20, 1877; *Conservator*, Dec. 23, 1882.

88. "The Great Anti-Slavery Reunion," undated pamphlet, CHM. Letter dated May 26, 1874, from W. C. Flagg, letter dated Apr. 24, 1874 from Matthew Hull, in Zebina Eastman Collection, box 1, folder 4, CHM; Zebina Eastman, *Historical Sketches of the Anti-Slavery Movement* (Chicago: W. B. Keen, Cooke, 1874) vii–ix.

89. Quoted in Scott, "What Price Freedom?" 137.

90. *Chicago Tribune*, Jan. 2, 1874.

91. *Chicago Tribune*, Mar. 12, 1875. The paper listed Ogden as M. K., but his middle initial was D.

92. Ibid.

CHAPTER TWO

1. *Conservator* quoted in Ralph Nelson Davis, "The History of the Negro Newspaper in Chicago" (PhD diss., University of Chicago, 1939), 11–12. Davis had access to a scrapbook kept by Barnett of articles published between 1878 and 1882. The scrapbook was "a valued family possession," which apparently has disappeared. Davis writes that Barnett stated that "Chicago was a pretty fair place for Negroes to live and that there was little friction between the races." Davis, "The History of the Negro Newspaper in Chicago," 13.

2. Davis, "The History of the Negro Newspaper in Chicago," 13–14; St. Clair Drake, *Churches and Voluntary Associations among the Negroes of Chicago* (Chicago: Works Progress Administration, 1940), 14.

3. *Indianapolis Freeman*, Aug. 28, 1886; *Conservator* quoted in Davis, "The History of the Negro Newspaper," 11–12, 18.

4. Eric Foner, *Freedom's Lawmakers: A Directory of Black Officeholders during Reconstruction* (Baton Rouge: Louisiana State University Press, 1996); Christopher Robert Reed, *Black Chicago's First Century*, vol. 1, *1833–1900* (Columbia: University of Missouri Press, 2005), 222.

5. *Conservator* quoted in *Christian Recorder* (Philadelphia), July 27, 1882. Barnett also wrote: "The Republican Party need not fear a loss of our votes so long as a due regard is paid to our acknowledged rights." Davis, "The History of the Negro Newspaper," 11.

6. Stanley P. Hirshson, *Farewell to the Bloody Shirt: Northern Republicans and the Southern Negro, 1877–1893* (Chicago: Quadrangle Books, 1962); Lawrence Grossman, *The Democratic Party and the Negro: Northern and National Politics, 1868–92* (Urbana: University of Illinois Press, 1976), 60–106; Paul Frymer, *Uneasy Alliances: Race and Party Competition in America* (Princeton, NJ: Princeton University Press, 1999), 49–81.

7. *Conservator*, Dec. 23, 1882. On post office work see Henry W. McGee, "The Negro in the Chicago Post Office" (master's thesis, University of Chicago, 1961); Philip F.

Rubio, *There's Always Work at the Post Office: African American Postal Workers and the Fight for Jobs, Justice, and Equality* (Chapel Hill: University of North Carolina Press, 2010.)

8. Black civic organizations in Chicago, with the exception of church groups, were mostly started in the 1880s.

9. Steven Hahn argues that kin networks became the basis for political alliances and actions in the rural South in the late nineteenth century. Those ties were not a given in the urban North, where individuals and families settled far from extended family. Hahn, *Nation under Our Feet: Black Political Struggles in the Rural South from Slavery to the Great Migration* (Cambridge, MA: Harvard University Press, 2003).

10. Drake, *Churches and Voluntary Associations*, 71.

11. Fenton Johnson, "Chicago Negro Aristocrats," unpublished manuscript dated June 18, 1941, 5, box 9, folder 14, IWP; Willard B. Gatewood, *Aristocrats of Color: The Black Elite, 1880–1920* (Bloomington: Indiana University Press, 1990), 120.

12. Johnson, "Chicago Negro Aristocrats," 5.

13. Bart Landry, *The New Black Middle Class* (Berkeley: University of California Press, 1987), 18–66; Willard B. Gatewood, *Aristocrats of Color: The Black Elite, 1880–1920* (Bloomington: Indiana University Press, 1990); August Meier, "Negro Class Structure and Ideology in the Age of Booker T. Washington," *Phylon* 23, no. 3 (1962): 258–66; Deborah Gray White, *Too Heavy a Load: Black Women in Defense of Themselves, 1894–1994* (New York: W. W. Norton, 1999), 70.

14. Monroe Nathan Work, "Negro Real Estate Holders in Chicago" (master's thesis, University of Chicago, 1903); "Chicago," *Appeal*, June 9, 1888; *Indianapolis Freeman*, Nov. 19, 1990; Reed, *Black Chicago's First Century*, 1:262. For a similar argument about the consolidation of the white bourgeoisie through marriage, business connections, and leisure activities, see Sven Beckert, *Moneyed Metropolis: New York and the Consolidation of the American Bourgeoisie, 1850–1896* (New York: Cambridge University Press, 2001).

15. Isaac Counselor Harris, *The Colored Men's Professional and Business Directory and Valuable Information on the Race in General* (Chicago, 1886), Vivian Harsh Collection, Woodson Library, Chicago.

16. Harris, *Colored Men's Directory*. Barnett too encouraged black consumers to purchase from African American–owned businesses. *Conservator*, Dec. 16, 1882. See also Reed, *Black Chicago's First Century*, 1:256–60; Meier, "Negro Class Structure," 258–66.

17. Undated newspaper clipping, scrapbook of Ferdinand F. Barnett, Ida B. Wells Collection, University of Chicago Library; *Conservator*, Nov. 18, 1882; Patricia A. Schechter, *Ida B. Wells-Barnett and American Reform, 1880–1930* (Chapel Hill: University of North Carolina Press, 2001), 177.

18. Fannie B. Williams, "The Intellectual Progress of the Colored Women of the United States since the Emancipation Proclamation," in *The World Congress of Representative Women*, ed. May Wright Sewall (Chicago: Rand McNally, 1894), 703–7; Williams, "Religious Duty to the Negro," in *The World's Congress of Religions*, ed. J. W. Hanson (Chicago: W. B. Conkey, 1894), 893–97. Allan H. Spear argues that after the turn of the century Williams's politics shifted away from demands for equal opportunities and toward the doctrine of racial self-help and solidarity. He suggests that her speaking tours on behalf of Booker T. Washington may have been an effort to promote her husband's career. Spear, *Black Chicago: The Making of a Negro Ghetto* (Chicago: University of Chicago Press, 1967), 69–70.

19. Fannie Barrier Williams, "The Social Bonds in the Black Belt in Chicago," *Charities*

15, no. 1 (1905): 41; Harris, *Colored Men's Directory*; Drake, *Churches and Voluntary Associations*, 64–66.

20. Drake, *Churches and Voluntary Associations*, 53–54; Miles Mark Fisher, "History of Olivet Baptist Church" (master's thesis, University of Chicago, 1922).

21 "Iola," unpublished manuscript, box 28, folder 1, IWP.

22. *Inter Ocean*, May 2, 1889. 6.

23. Williams, "Social Bonds of the Black Belt," 42; Drake, *Churches and Voluntary Associations*, 64–65. W. E. B. DuBois also considered fraternal societies as crucial mechanisms of social support for black Americans. See W. E. B. DuBois, *Philadelphia Negro: A Social Study*, (1899; reprint, Philadelphia: University of Pennsylvania Press, 1996), 224. In some cities, fraternal organizations established savings and loans and sometimes commercial banks, becoming the basis for business growth in, for example, Richmond and Hampton, Virginia, and Newbern, North Carolina. Arnett G. Lindsay, "The Negro in Banking," *Journal of Negro History* 14, no. 2 (Apr. 1929): 172–76.

24. Reed, *Black Chicago's First Century*, 1:247, 259.

25. James N. Simms, *Simms' Blue Book and Negro Business and Professional Directory* (Chicago: J. N. Simms, 1923), 100; *Broad Ax*, Dec. 27, 1902; *Chicago Defender*, Feb. 17, 1912.

26. Edward F. Dunne, "On the Race Problem," speech before the Monticello Club, Oct. 2, 1898, reprinted in *Dunne: Judge, Mayor, Governor*, ed. William L. Sullivan (Chicago: Windermere, 1916), 143–44.

27. For a similar argument about the urbanization of newspapers by white journalists and editors, see David Paul Nord, *Communities of Journalism: A History of American Newspapers and Their Readers* (Urbana: University of Illinois Press, 2001), 108–28.

28. Barnett's speech printed in *Christian Recorder* (Philadelphia), Sept. 15, 1881; Davis, "The History of the Negro Newspaper." 8–13. Just four copies of the *Conservator* remain. But Davis quotes widely from stories in a now lost scrapbook owned by Barnett. In addition, other newspapers published by African Americans regularly reprinted articles from the *Conservator*, demonstrating the paper's broad influence in the nineteenth century and providing contemporary scholars with examples of the *Conservator*'s articles. The *Conservator* was one of the longest-surviving of the black-owned papers published in the nineteenth century.

29. There were also a handful of general interest magazines owned and operated by black editors after Reconstruction. See Penelope L. Bullock, *The Afro-American Periodical Press, 1838–1909* (Baton Rouge: Louisiana State University Press, 1981), 64–149.

30. I. Garland Penn, *The Afro-American Press and Its Editors* (1891; reprint, New York: Arno, 1969), preface; *Austin Citizen* quoted in *Conservator*, Dec. 18, 1886. There were a few newspapers published by African Americans before the Civil War, notably John B. Russworm's *Freedom's Journal* and the papers published by Frederick Douglass. See S. N. D. North, "History and Present Condition of the Newspaper and Periodical Press of the United States," in US Bureau of the Census, *Tenth Census* (1880), vol. 8; Vilma Raskin Potter, *A Reference Guide to Afro-American Publications and Editors, 1827–1946* (Ames: University of Iowa Press, 1993); Emma Lou Thornbrough, "American Negro Newspapers, 1880–1914," *Business History Review*, 40, no. 4 (Winter 1966), 467–90; Roland E. Wolseley, *The Black Press, USA* (Ames: Iowa State University Press, 1971), 17–29.

31. *People's Advocate* quoted in *Christian Reporter* (Philadelphia), July 27, 1882; Penn,

The Afro-American Press and Its Editors, 148–49, 262–64, 110; Calvin S. Morris, *Reverdy C. Ransom: Black Advocate of the Social Gospel* (New York: University Press of America, 1990), 102–15; St. Clair Drake and Horace R. Cayton, *Black Metropolis: A Study of Negro Life in a Northern City* (New York: Harcourt, Brace, 1945), 52–54.

32. Penn, *The Afro-American Press and Its Editors*, 112–15. Thornbrough cites several studies with higher numbers of African American newspapers in this period. Charles A. Simmons claims there were 115 newspapers operated by African Americans published during the Civil War. The discrepancies are likely because some papers survived less than a year and were not counted by Penn. Thornbrough, "American Negro Newspapers," 467–68; Simmons, *The African American Press: A History of News Coverage during National Crises, with Special Reference to Four Black Newspapers, 1827–1965* (Jefferson, NC: McFarland, 1998), 15.

33. The 1880 federal census presents data on the number of African Americans over the age of ten (and in various age categories) who were unable to write, thus exaggerating the extent of illiteracy, since some of those who were unable to write were able to read. See Department of the Interior, *Compendium of the Tenth Census* (Washington, DC, 1883), 2:1650–53.

34. *Austin Citizen* quoted in *Conservator*, Dec. 18, 1886.

35. Thornbrough, "American Negro Newspapers, 1880–1914," 468, 475; N. W. Ayer and Sons, *American Newspaper Annual 1881* (Philadelphia: N. W. Ayer and Sons, 1881), 155; *American Newspaper Annual 1885* (Philadelphia: N. W. Ayer and Sons, 1885), 218; *American Newspaper Annual 1884* (Philadelphia: N. W. Ayer and Sons, 1884), 63, 115; Penn, *The Afro-American Press and Its Editors*, preface.

36. *Western Appeal*, June 23, Dec. 1, 1888, Feb. 23, 1889. The *Indianapolis World* was quoted and disputed in the *Appeal*, Dec. 1, 1888.

37. *Western Appeal*, Dec. 1, 1888, Feb. 23, 1889, Dec. 29, June 23, 1888.

38. *Conservator*, Dec. 16, 1882; Thornbrough, "American Negro Newspapers," 473–74; Charles H. Dennis, *Victor Lawson: His Time and His Work* (Chicago: University of Chicago Press, 1935), 12–18, 32, 48–49. Chicago's newspapers were the morning *Times*, *Tribune*, *Daily News*, and *Inter Ocean* and the afternoon *Journal*, the *Post and Mail*, and the *Telegraph*.

39. Thornbrough, "American Negro Newspapers," 473–74; *Conservator*, Dec. 16, 1882.

40. Dennis, *Victor Lawson*, 48–49; *Conservator*, Dec. 16, 1882; Thornbrough, "American Negro Newspapers," 473–74. In 1904, when Booker T. Washington considered establishing a paper in Boston, his prospective editor, Charles Alexander, estimated the initial investment at $5,000. Washington was shocked, agreeing to advance much less.

41. *New York Freeman*, Jan. 28, 1904; Roland Edgar Wolseley, *The Black Press, USA* (Ames: Iowa State University Press, 1990), 33. As with the African American-owned press, thousands of white weeklies, including the foreign-language press, were founded by individuals who were proprietor, editor, and printer.

42. *Christian Recorder* (Philadelphia), Sept. 9, 1880, July 6, 13, 1882.

43. *Christian Recorder* (Philadelphia), July 6, 13, 1882; *Western Appeal*, July 11, 1885. These networks of editors were further solidified when correspondents trained in the offices of one press went off to start their own papers. The *Conservator*'s Washington correspondent, J. E. Bruce, launched the *Norfolk (VA) Republican* in fall 1882. *Christian Recorder* (Philadelphia), Sept. 14, 1882.

44. Davis, "The Negro Newspaper in Chicago," 13; *Christian Recorder* (Philadelphia), Sept. 15, 7, July 27, 1882. Debate over the issue continued for the following half

century. See Monroe N. Work, *The Negro Year Book, 1931–32* (Tuskegee, AL: Negro Year Book Publishing, 1932), 21–26.

45. Penn, *The Afro-American Press and Its Editors*, 156; Thornbrough, "American Negro Newspapers, 1880–1914," 479–80.

46. *Booker T. Washington Papers*, 14 vols., ed. Louis R. Harlan (Urbana: University of Illinois Press, 1972–89), 6:234.

47. Washington to Timothy Thomas Fortune, Dec. 27, 1903, *Washington Papers*, 7:380; Washington to Charles William Anderson, June 16, 1904, *Washington Papers*, 7:533.

48. *Inter Ocean*, Apr. 24, July 9, 21, 1880.

49. *Inter Ocean*, Apr. 24, July 9, 21, Feb. 5, 1880, Feb. 16, 1894.

50. Xi Wang, *The Trial of Democracy: Black Suffrage and Northern Republicans, 1860–1910* (Athens: University of Georgia Press, 1997), 184–201; George Frederick Howe, *Chester A. Arthur: A Quarter-Century of Machine Politics* (New York: Frederick Ungar, 1935), 100–104; Steven Kantrowitz, *More Than Freedom: Fighting for Black Citizenship in a White Republic, 1829–1889* (New York: Penguin Books, 2012). Wang argues that Garfield stressed programs for African American education in the south and diverted attention from voting rights. Wang, *The Trial of Democracy*, 206.

51. Wang, *The Trial of Democracy*, 206; Hirshson, *Farewell to the Bloody Shirt*, 145–48; Heather Cox Richardson, *The Death of Reconstruction: Race, Labor, and Politics in the Post–Civil War North, 1865–1901* (Cambridge, MA: Harvard University Press, 2001).

52. Frederick Douglass, "Address Delivered at the Twenty-Third Anniversary Celebration of the Emancipation of Slaves in the District of Columbia," Apr. 16, 1885, in *The Frederick Douglass Papers*, vol. 5, ed. John W. Blassingame and John R. McKivigan (New Haven, CT: Yale University Press, 1979–91), 178.

53. *Western Appeal*, July 4, 1884; *Inter Ocean*, Mar. 13, 1884; *New York Globe*, Sept. 29, 1883; *People's Advocate*, Oct. 6, 1883; *Washington Bee*, December 1, 1883; *New York Freeman*, Apr. 4, 1885; *Washington Bee*, Feb. 10, 1883; *New York Freeman*, Dec. 12, Apr. 4, 1885; August Meier, *Negro Thought in America, 1880–1915: Racial Ideologies in the Age of Booker T. Washington* (Ann Arbor: University of Michigan Press, 1963), 26–30.

54. *Conservator*, Sept. 8, 1883. On the Readjuster movement see Jane Dailey, *Before Jim Crow: The Politics of Race in Post-Emancipation Virginia* (Chapel Hill: University of North Carolina Press, 2000).

55. *Inter Ocean*, Aug. 26, 1888; Hirshson, *Farewell to the Bloody Shirt*, 144. See also Douglass, "Address at the Twenty-Third Anniversary Celebration," 178; Wang, *The Trial of Democracy*, 206.

56. *Inter Ocean*, Mar. 13, 1884; *Conservator* quoted in Davis, "History of the Negro Newspaper," 32. In the 1870s and early 1880s, black activists in Cincinnati had urged black voters to reject party and vote instead for local officials who offered jobs. David A. Gerber, *Black Ohio and the Color Line, 1860–1915* (Urbana: University of Illinois Press, 1976), 233.

57. Allan Nevins, *Grover Cleveland: A Study in Courage* (New York: Dodd, Mead, 1932), 323, 332.

58. L. P. Morton to John Edward Bruce, July 9, 1888, John Edward Bruce Papers, reel 1, Schomburg Center for Research in Black Culture, New York; *Inter Ocean*, June 7, 1900; *Indianapolis Freeman*, Aug. 28, 1886; Paul Frymer, *Uneasy Alliances: Race and Party Competition in America* (Princeton, NJ: Princeton University Press, 1999), 79.

59. All quoted in *Christian Recorder* (Philadelphia), July 27, 1882; *Western Appeal*, Mar. 30, 1889.

60. Richard Schneirov, *Labor and Urban Politics: Class Conflict and the Origins of Modern Liberalism in Chicago, 1864–97* (Urbana: University of Illinois Press, 1998), 88–89; Claudius O. Johnson, *Carter Henry Harrison I, Political Leader* (Chicago: University of Chicago Press, 1928), 196; Pierce, *A History of Chicago*, vol. 3, *The Rise of a Modern City, 1871–1893* (New York: Alfred A. Knopf, 1957), 305; *Indianapolis Freeman*, Aug. 28, 1886.

61. *Chicago Tribune*, Mar. 9, 10, 13, 30, 1879; *Chicago Times*, Mar. 13, 1879; Claudius O. Johnson, *Carter Henry Harrison*, 137; Pierce, *A History of Chicago*, 3:351–52.

62. Pierce, *A History of Chicago*, 3:356; *Chicago Daily News*, Mar. 26, Apr. 19, Aug. 20, 1884; *Chicago Tribune*, Apr. 2, 1881.

63. *Inter Ocean*, Jan. 17, 1895.

64. *Inter Ocean*, Oct. 9, 1885; *Chicago Tribune*, Mar. 15, 25, Apr. 5, 8, June 25, 1885; *Chicago Council Proceedings, 1884–85*, 672–75; Johnson, *Carter Henry Harrison*, 196; *Indianapolis Freeman*, Aug. 28, 1886; Pierce, *A History of Chicago*, 3:360–65. In 1887, another widely publicized corruption scandal among Democrats on the county board combined with furor over the Haymarket bombing to undermine Harrison's support on almost all sides. He refused to run again, leaving his party without a candidate and opening the election to victory by Republican lawyer John Roche.

65. *Inter Ocean*, Dec. 9, 1878, Feb. 5, 1880; *Chicago Evening Journal*, Mar. 10, 1885; Andreas, *A History of Chicago*, 3:624. See also *Inter Ocean*, Feb. 5, 1886.

66. Frederick Douglass to Carter Harrison, June 13, 1886, Harrison Collection, box 20, folder 988, Newberry Library, Chicago.

67. *New York Sun*, Apr. 14, 1895, from the scrapbook of T. Thomas Fortune, Schomburg Center for Research in Black Culture, New York.

68. *Chicago Tribune*, Nov. 5, 1883; Barnett quoted in *Christian Recorder* (Philadelphia), July 27, 1882.

69. *Inter Ocean*, Feb. 5, 1880; Howard W. Allen and Vincent A. Lacey, eds., *Illinois Elections, 1818–1990: Candidates and County Returns for President, Governor, Senate, and House of Representatives*, (Carbondale: Southern Illinois University Press, 1992), 21. Other northern states passed civil rights bills in the late nineteenth century: Connecticut, Iowa, New Jersey, and Ohio in 1884; Indiana, Massachusetts, Michigan, Minnesota, and Rhode Island in 1885; Pennsylvania in 1887; New York in 1893; Washington in 1890; and Wisconsin in 1895. See Donald G. Nieman, "The Language of Liberation: African Americans and Egalitarian Constitutionalism, 1830–1960," in *The Constitution, Law, and American Life: Critical Aspects of the Nineteenth-Century Experience*, ed. Nieman (Athens: University of Georgia Press, 1992), 82–83.

70. *Inter Ocean*, Feb. 5, 1880; *Chicago Tribune*, Nov. 5, 1883; *Indianapolis Freeman*, June 21, 1890. On challenges to discrimination in public spaces, see Elizabeth Dale, " 'Social Equality Does Not Exist among Themselves, nor among Us,': *Baylies vs. Curry* and Civil Rights in Chicago, 1888," *American Historical Review*, 102, no. 2 (Apr. 1997): 311–39.

71. *The Birth of the Afro-American National League Organized in Convention of Afro-Americans, Held at Chicago, Ill., January 15, 16, & 17, 1890. Official Certified Compilation of Proceedings* (Chicago: J. C. Battles and R. B. Cabbell, 1890).

72. Emma Lou Thornbrough, "The National Afro-American League, 1887–1908," *Journal of Southern History* 27, no. 4. (Nov. 1961): 494–95; Cyrus Field Adams, "Timothy Thomas Fortune: Journalist, Author, Lecturer, Agitator," *Colored American Magazine* 4 (Jan.–Feb., 1902): 224–28; Michael L. Goldstein, "Preface to the Rise of Booker T.

Washington: A View from New York City of the Demise of Independent Black Politics, 1889–1902," *Journal of Negro History* 62, no. 1 (Jan. 1977): 81–99.

73. *New York Freeman*, May 28, 1887; Thornbrough, "The National Afro-American League," 495.

74. *New York Freeman*, May 28, 1887.

75. *New York Age*, May 1, 1890; Goldstein, "Preface to the Rise of Booker T. Washington: A View from New York City of the Demise of Independent Black Politics, 1889–1902," 84.

76. *New York Sun*, n.d. (1891), T. Thomas Fortune scrapbook, vol. 1, Schomburg Center for Research in Black Culture, New York.

77. *Indianapolis Freeman*, June 21, 1890; Thornbrough, "The National Afro-American League," 500–501. On a case not brought by the league that narrowly upheld integrated seating in a Chicago theater, see Dale, "Social Equality Does Not Exist."

78. *Chicago Tribune*, Jan. 12, 1890.

79. *The Birth of the Afro-American League*, 9–10; Thornbrough, "The National Afro-American League," 498–99.

80. *The Birth of the Afro-American League*, 22, 12, 36.

81. Newspaper column, no newspaper title, n.d. (1896), Fortune scrapbook, Schomburg Center for Research in Black Culture, New York.

82. *The Birth of the Afro-American National League*, 17–18.

83. Ibid., 28.

84. *Indianapolis Freeman*, Nov. 25, 1893; Meier, *Negro Thought in America*, 82.

85. "To Amend and Supplement the Election Laws of the United States and to Provide for the More Efficient Enforcement of Such Laws, and for Other Purposes," H.R. Report No. 2493, 51st Cong., 1st Sess., June 19, 1890; Henry Cabot Lodge and T. V. Powderly, "The Federal Election Bill," *North American Review* 151, no. 406 (Sept. 1890): 257–73; Richard E. Welch Jr., "The Federal Elections Bill of 1890: Postscripts and Prelude," *Journal of American History* 52, no. 3 (Dec. 1965): 514; Lisa G. Materson, *For the Freedom of Her Race: Black Women and Electoral Politics in Illinois, 1877–1932* (Chapel Hill: University of North Carolina Press, 2009), 40–41.

86. George F. Hoar, "The Fate of the Election Bill," *Forum* 11 (Apr. 1891): 136; Welch, "The Federal Elections Bill of 1890," 518–19; Frymer, *Uneasy Alliances*, 80–81.

87. *Christian Recorder* (Philadelphia), Dec. 25, 1890, Mar. 19, 1891; Hoar quoted in Welch, "The Federal Elections Bill of 1890," 519.

88. John Edward Bruce to W. Ting Tang, May 1898, Bruce Papers, reel 1, Schomburg Center for Research in Black Culture, New York.

89. *Inter Ocean*, June 7, 1900.

90. *Chicago Tribune*, Nov. 5, 1883; Pierce, *A History of Chicago*, 3:369.

CHAPTER THREE

1. Fannie Barrier Williams, "Religious Duty to the Negro," in *The New Woman of Color: The Collected Writings of Fannie Barrier Williams, 1893–1918*, ed. Mary Jo Deegan (DeKalb: Northern Illinois University Press), 73–77; *Chicago Tribune*, Sept. 12, 1893.

2. There are several excellent biographies of Ida Wells-Barnett: Mia Bay, *To Tell the Truth Freely: The Life of Ida B. Wells* (New York: Hill and Wang, 2009); Patricia A. Schechter, *Ida B. Wells-Barnett and American Reform, 1880–1930* (Chapel Hill: University of North Carolina Press, 2001); Paula J. Giddings, *Ida: A Sword among Lions: Ida B. Wells and the Campaign against Lynching* (New York: HarperCollins, 2008); Linda O.

McMurry, *To Keep the Waters Troubled: The Life of Ida B. Wells* (New York: Oxford University Press, 1999); James West Davidson, *They Say: Ida B. Wells and the Reconstruction of Race* (New York: Oxford University Press, 2008); Ida B. Wells, *Crusade for Justice: The Autobiography of Ida B. Wells*, ed. Alfreda M. Duster (Chicago: University of Chicago Press, 1991).

3. Much of the scholarship on racial uplift focuses on southern African Americans. See for example, Kevin K. Gaines, *Uplifting the Race: Black Leadership, Politics, and Culture in the Twentieth Century* (Chapel Hill: University of North Carolina Press, 1996); Michelle Mitchell, *Righteous Propagation: African Americans and the Politics of Racial Destiny after Reconstruction* (Chapel Hill: University of North Carolina Press, 2004); Leslie Brown, *Uplifting Black Durham: Gender, Class, and Black Community Development in the Jim Crow South* (Chapel Hill: University of North Carolina Press, 2008). On uplift in Chicago see James R. Grossman, *Land of Hope: Black Southerners and the Great Migration* (Chicago: University of Chicago Press, 1989). Activists in Boston similarly spoke of uplift while engaging in politics. See Stephen Kantrowitz, *More Than Freedom: Fighting for Black Citizenship in a White Republic, 1829–1889* (New York: Penguin, 2012).

4. Paula Baker, "The Domestication of Politics: Women and American Political Society, 1780–1920," *American Historical Review* 89, no. 3 (June 1984): 620–47; Kathryn Kish Sklar, *Florence Kelley and the Nation's Work: The Rise of Women's Political Culture, 1830–1900* (New Haven, CT: Yale University Press, 1995); Rebecca Edwards, *Angels in the Machinery: Gender in American Party Politics from the Civil War to the Progressive Era* (New York: Oxford University Press, 1997).

5. *Chicago Daily News*, May 25, 1891, quoted in Thomas A. Guglielmo, *White on Arrival: Italians, Race, Color, and Power in Chicago, 1890–1945* (New York: Oxford University Press, 2003), 24.

6. Gail Bederman, *Manliness and Civilization: A Cultural History of Gender and Race in the United States, 1880–1917* (Chicago: University of Chicago Press, 1995), 31–41; Robert Rydell, *All the World's a Fair: Views of Empire at American Expositions, 1876–1916* (Chicago: University of Chicago Press, 1984); James Gilbert, *Perfect Cities: Chicago's Utopias of 1893* (Chicago: University of Chicago Press, 1991); Christopher Robert Reed, *All the World Is Here! The Black Presence at White City* (Bloomington: Indiana University Press, 2000); David F. Burg, *Chicago's White City of 1893* (Lexington: University Press of Kentucky, 1976); Reid Badger, *The Great American Fair: The World's Columbian Exposition and American Culture* (Chicago: Nelson Hall, 1979); Grace Elizabeth Hale, *Making Whiteness: The Culture of Segregation in the South, 1890–1940* (New York: Vintage Books, 1999), 151.

7. Bederman, *Manliness and Civilization*, 35; Rydell, *All the World's a Fair*, 61–62.

8. T. J. Clark, *The Painting of Modern Life: Paris in the Art of Manet and His Followers* (London: Thames and Hudson, 1984), 36; David Harvey, "The Political Economy of Public Space," in *The Politics of Public Space*, ed. Setha Low and Neil Smith (New York: Routledge, 2006), 23. On the shift from representations of workers to emphasis on consumption, see Hale, *Making Whiteness*, 151–68.

9. *Indianapolis Freeman*, May 27, 1893; *Cleveland Gazette*, Mar. 25, 1893.

10. F. L. Barnett to Mrs. Potter Palmer, Dec. 20, 1891, Wells Papers, box 10, folder 7, Special Collections Research Center, University of Chicago Library; *Indianapolis Freeman*, Dec. 27, 1890; *Washington Bee*, Nov. 15, 1890; *New York Age*, Feb. 21, Mar. 28, 1891; Mrs. N. F. Mossell, *The Work of the African American Woman* (1894; reprint, New York: Oxford University Press), 113; Elliot M. Rudwick and August Meier, "Black

Man in the 'White City': Negroes and the Columbian Exposition, 1893," *Phylon* 26 (1965): 254.

11. Jeanne Madeline Weimann, *The Fair Women* (Chicago: Academy Chicago, 1981), 148–50.

12. Chicago World's Columbian Exposition, 1893 (hereafter WCE), Board of Lady Managers Official Record, Nov. 19, 1890–Sept. 3, 1891, 96, 109–10, CHM; Mrs. J. C. Roberts to Bertha Palmer, Dec. 16, 1891, folder Nov. 13–Dec. 17, 1891, CHM; *Chicago Tribune*, Nov. 16, 1890; Rudwick and Meier, "Black Man in the 'White City,'" 354–55; Wanda A. Hendricks, *Gender, Race, and Politics in the Midwest: Black Club Women in Illinois* (Bloomington: Indiana University Press, 1998), 2–3; Anne Massa, "Black Women in the White City," *Journal of American Studies* 8, no. 3 (Dec. 1974): 319–37.

13. Elizabeth G. Linch to Bertha Palmer, Oct. 7, 1891, WCE, Board of Lady Managers, box Feb.–Dec. 1891, Incoming correspondence, CHM; Bertha Palmer to Mary Logan, Oct. 12, 1891, WCE, Board of Lady Managers, box 3, vol. 10, 703–6, CHM.

14. Mrs. J. C. Roberts to Bertha Palmer, Dec. 16, 1891, WCE, Board of Lady Managers, folder Nov. 13–Dec. 16, 1891, Incoming correspondence, CHM; Women's Columbian Association, Aim and Plan of Action, Constitution and Bylaws, carbon typescript (Chicago, Feb. 1891), 2–3, Albion Tourgée Papers, Chautauqua County Historical Society, NY.

15. *Christian Recorder* (Philadelphia), Apr. 13, 1893.

16. Statement dated Mar. 30, 1892, 6152, Albion Tourgée Papers, Chautauqua County Historical Society, NY.

17. *Indianapolis Freeman*, Oct. 3, 1891; Naomi Anderson to Bertha Palmer, Dec. 16, 1891, WCE, Board of Lady Managers, folder Nov. 13–17, 1891, Incoming correspondence, CHM.

18. *Indianapolis Freeman*, Dec. 26, 1891; Massa, "Black Women in the White City," 322–24; Mia Bay, *To Tell the Truth Freely: The Life of Ida B. Wells*, (New York: Hill and Wang, 2009), 156–57.

19. "New York State Afro-American Women's Exhibit," in *World's Columbian Exposition 1893 Official Catalogue*, part 14, Women's Building (Chicago: W. B. Conkey, 1893), 66–67; *Chicago Tribune*, July 22, 1893; Reed, *All the World is Here!*, 27–28.

20. Giddings, *A Sword among Lions*, 248, 256–57; Mark Elliott, *Color-Blind Justice: Albion Tourgée and the Quest for Racial Equality from the Civil War to Plessy v. Ferguson* (New York: Oxford University Press, 2006), 239.

21. *Indianapolis Freeman*, Mar. 25, 1893; *New York Age*, Feb. 18, 1893; Giddings, *A Sword among Lions*, 257–58.

22. *Indianapolis Freeman*, Aug. 19, 26, 1893; Reed, *All the World Is Here!*, 132–33.

23. *Indianapolis Freeman*, July 8, 1893.

24. *Chicago Tribune*, Apr. 30, 1893.

25. *Chicago Tribune*, Aug. 26, 1893.

26. Ibid.

27. *Chicago Tribune*, Sept. 12, 1893; Richard Hughes Seager, *The World's Parliament of Religions: The East/West Encounter, Chicago 1893* (Bloomington: Indiana University Press, 1995). There was, in addition, a Congress on African Ethnology, where Douglass spoke of the history of American slavery. See *Chicago Tribune*, Aug. 18, 1893.

28. Fannie Barrier Williams, "What Can Religion Further Do to Advance the Condition of the American Negro?" in *The Dawn of Religious Pluralism: Voices from the World's*

Parliament of Religions, 1893, ed. Richard Hughes Seager (LaSalle, IL: Open Court, 1993), 142–49; Wilson Moses, *Alexander Crummell: A Study of Civilization and Discontent* (New York: Oxford University Press, 1989), 8.

29. *Chicago Tribune*, Sept. 12, 1893; Williams, "Religious Duty to the Negro," 73–77.

30. Wells to Albion W. Tourgée, July 1, 1893, Ida B. Wells Papers, Special Collections Research Center, University of Chicago Library, and Albion Tourgée Papers, Chautauqua County Historical Society, NY.

31. Ida B. Wells et al., *The Reason Why the Colored American Is Not in the World's Columbian Exposition: The Afro-American's Contribution to Columbian Literature* (Chicago, 1893).

32. On lynching as spectacle, see Hale, *Making Whiteness*, 227–339.

33. Wells, *Crusade for Justice*, 121–24; Giddings, *A Sword among Lions*, 281–82. On Stead see Joseph O. Baylen, "A Victorian's 'Crusade' in Chicago, 1893–1894," *Journal of American History* 51, no. 3 (Dec. 1964): 418–34.

34. For more on black clubwomen see Dorothy Salem, *To Better Our World: Black Women in Organized Reform, 1890–1920* (Brooklyn: Carlson, 1990); Martha S. Jones, *All Bound Up Together: The Woman Question in American Public Culture, 1830–1900* (Chapel Hill: University of North Carolina Press, 2007); Gerda Lerner, "Early Community Work of Black Club Women," *Journal of Negro History* 59, no. 2 (Apr. 1974): 158–67; Anne Firor Scott, "Most Invisible of All: Black Women's Voluntary Associations," *Journal of Southern History* 56, no. 1 (Feb. 1990): 3–22.

35. Willard B. Gatewood, *Aristocrats of Color: The Black Elite, 1880–1920* (Bloomington: Indiana University Press, 1990), 240–42; Anne Meis Knupfer, *Toward a Tenderer Humanity and a Nobler Womanhood: African American Women's Clubs in Turn-of-the-Century Chicago* (New York: New York University Press, 1996), 34–35.

36. Fannie Barrier Williams, "The Club Movement among the Colored Women," *Voice of the Negro* 1, no. 3 (1904): 99–102, reprinted in Mary Jo Deegan, ed., *The New Woman of Color: The Collected Writings of Fannie Barrier Williams, 1893–1918* (DeKalb: Northern Illinois University Press, 2002), 73–78 (quotations throughout from Deegan); Addie W. Hunton, "The National Association of Colored Women: Its Real Significance," *Colored American Magazine* 14 (July 1908): 418–19.

37. Deborah Gray White, *Too Heavy a Load: Black Women in Defense of Themselves, 1894–1994* (New York: W. W. Norton, 1999), 22–24.

38. Jessie Lawson, incoming correspondence, Lawson Collection, Newberry Library, Chicago; Julius Rosenwald Papers, box 14, file 3, Special Collections, University of Chicago Library.

39. Elizabeth Lindsey Davis, *The Story of the Illinois Federation of Colored Women's Clubs* (1922; reprint, New York: G. K. Hall, 1996), 72. The Woman's Era Club of Boston was established by Josephine St. Pierre Ruffin, while in New York, Victoria Earle Matthews and Dr. Susan McKinney formed the Women's Loyal Union. White, *Too Heavy a Load*; Lerner, "Early Community Work of Black Club Women,"160.

40. Mitchell, *Righteous Propagation*, 164–70; White, *Too Heavy a Load*, 31–35.

41. Maureen Ogle, *All the Modern Conveniences: American Household Plumbing, 1840–1890* (Baltimore: Johns Hopkins University Press, 1996), 102–4, 143; Margaret Garb, *City of American Dreams: A History of Housing Reform and Home Ownership in Chicago, 1871–1919* (Chicago: University of Chicago Press, 2005), 113–15.

42. Mitchell, *Righteous Propagation*, 7–9; "A History of the Club Movement among the Colored of the United States of America" (1902), 47, Ida B. Wells Papers, box 5,

folder 13, Special Collections Research Center, University of Chicago Library; Susan L. Smith, *Sick and Tired of Being Sick and Tired: Black Women's Health Activism in America, 1890–1950* (Philadelphia: University of Pennsylvania Press, 1995), 17–19.

43. Knupfer, *Toward a Tenderer Humanity*, 24.
44. *Broad Ax*, Nov. 4, 1899; Gatewood, *Aristocrats of Color*, 211–12; Knupfer, *Toward a Tenderer Humanity*, 35–37.
45. On the statewide work of black women in Illinois, see Hendricks, *Gender, Race, and Politics*.
46. Davis, *Illinois Federation of Colored Women's Clubs*, 119.
47. Ibid., 27–28; Wells, *Crusade for Justice*, 240; Bay, *To Tell the Truth Freely*, 214, 227.
48. Williams, "The Club Movement among the Colored Women," 49.
49. Davis, *Illinois Federation of Colored Women's Clubs*, 28, 31, 118; *Colored People's Blue-Book and Business Directory of Chicago, Ill., 1905* (Chicago: Celerity, 1905), 90–92.
50. Baker, "The Domestication of Politics"; Sklar, *Florence Kelley and the Nation's Work*.
51. Daphne Spain, *How Women Saved the City* (Minneapolis: University of Minnesota Press, 2001); Maureen Flanagan, *Seeing with Their Hearts: Chicago Women and the Vision of the Good City, 1871–1933* (Princeton, NJ: Princeton University Press, 2002).
52. On gambling kingpin John "Mushmouth" Johnson's contributions to the Baptist Church and the "Old Peoples Home," see *Broad Ax*, Nov. 7, 1903; *New York World*, July 25, 1907; Harold Foote Gosnell, *Negro Politicians: The Rise of Negro Politics in Chicago* (1935; reprint, Chicago: University of Chicago Press, 1969), 126–27.
53. Williams, "The Club Movement among the Colored Women," 28.
54. Michelle Mitchell suggests that black women's focus on home ownership implied a rejection of electoral politics as "elusive and fleeting." That may have been the case in southern towns, but northern women used the home to justify participation in urban politics. Mitchell, *Righteous Propagation*, 144.
55. W. E. B. DuBois, "The Work of Negro Women in Society," in *Writings by W. E. B. DuBois in Periodicals Edited by Others* (Millwood, NY: Kraus-Thomas Organization, 1982), 139–44; White, *Too Heavy a Load*, 68.
56. Davis, *Illinois Federation of Colored Women's Clubs*, 25–26, 6, 10, 8, 15.
57. *Chicago Defender*, Jan. 1, 1910.
58. Williams, "The Club Movement among the Colored Women," 49.
59. Ibid., 44.
60. Ibid., 49.
61. There are many histories of the settlement-house movement and biographies of Jane Addams. See, for example, Allen F. Davis, *American Heroine: The Life and Legend of Jane Addams* (New York: Oxford University Press, 1973); Louise W. Knight, *Citizen: Jane Addams and the Struggle for Democracy* (Chicago: University of Chicago Press, 2005); Louise Carroll Wade, *Graham Taylor: Pioneer for Social Justice, 1851–1938* (Chicago: University of Chicago Press, 1964); Graham Taylor, *Chicago Commons through Forty Years* (Chicago: Chicago Commons Association, 1936).
62. Jane Addams, *Twenty Years at Hull-House* (New York: Penguin, 1961), 80–83; Louise de Koven Bowen, *Growing Up with a City* (New York: Macmillan, 1926), 66–67.
63. *Hull-House Maps and Papers, a Presentation of Nationalities and Wages in a Congested District of Chicago, Together with Comments and Essays on Problems Growing Out of the Social Conditions* (New York: T. Y. Crowell, 1895); Kathryn Kish Sklar, "Hull House Maps and Papers: Social Science as Women's Work in the 1890s," in *Gender and American Social Science: The Formative Years*, ed. Helene Silverberg (Princeton, NJ: Princeton University Press, 1998), 127–55.

64. Jane Addams, "The Subjective Necessity for Settlements," in *Twenty Years at Hull-House*, 90–100.

65. Graham Taylor, "The Neighborhood and the Municipality," Taylor Collection, box 29, folder 1681, Newberry Library, Chicago.

66. There is some debate about why white settlement leaders segregated the settlements. Some, like Thomas Lee Philpott, conclude that Addams and Taylor, at best, simply neglected African Americans who were not living nearby and thereby participated in the growing racial segregation of the city. Thomas Lee Philpott, *The Slum and the Ghetto: Immigrants, Blacks and Reformers in Chicago, 1880–1930* (Belmont, CA: Wadsworth, 1991), 79–81. Others call Addams a "cultural pluralist" and highlight the later work of Addams and McDowell in fighting for racial equality. Steven J. Diner, "Chicago Social Workers and Blacks in the Progressive Era," *Social Service Review* 44 (Dec. 1970): 393–410; Rivkah Shpak-Lisack, *Pluralism and Progressives: Hull House and the New Immigrants, 1890–1919* (Chicago: University of Chicago Press, 1990); Elizabeth Lasch-Quinn, *Black Neighbors: Race and the Limits of Reform in the American Settlement House Movement: 1890–1945* (Chapel Hill: University of North Carolina Press, 1993).

67. Jane Addams, "Public Activities and Investigations," in *Twenty Years at Hull-House*, 218; Howard Eugene Wilson, "Mary E. McDowell and Her Work as Head Resident of the University of Chicago Settlement" (master's thesis, University of Chicago, 1927), 33–34; Mary McDowell, "Life and Labor," unpublished manuscript (1914), McDowell Collection, box 3, folder 13, University of Chicago Library.

68. *Chicago Record-Herald*, Feb. 7, 1911; Fannie Barrier Williams, letter to the editor, *Chicago Record-Herald*, Sept. 15, 1906, quoted in Philpott, *The Slum and the Ghetto*, 155–56; Garb, *City of American Dreams*, 194–95.

69. Williams, "The Club Movement among the Colored Women," 114.

70. St. Clair Drake and Horace R. Cayton, *Black Metropolis: A Study of Negro Life in a Northern City* (New York: Harcourt, Brace, 1945), 57; Monroe Nathan Work, "Negro Real Estate Holders of Chicago" (master's thesis, University of Chicago, 1903), 29–31; Philpott, *The Slum and the Ghetto*, 150–52.

71. Alzada P. Comstock, "Chicago Housing Conditions IV: The Problems of the Negro," *American Journal of Sociology* 18, no. 2 (September 1912): 255–56. See also: Louise DeKoven Bowen, *The Colored People of Chicago* (Chicago: Juvenile Protective Association, 1913); Charles S. Duke, *The Housing Situation and the Colored People of Chicago* (Chicago, 1919).

72. *Broad Ax*, Nov. 4, 1899; Wells, *Crusade for Justice*, 249; Knupfer, *Toward a Tenderer Humanity*, 36.

73. Davis, *Illinois Federation of Colored Women's Clubs*, 16–17. Davis remained president of the Phillis Wheatley Club for twenty-eight years, while also serving as president of the state organization. Hendricks, *Gender, Race, and Politics*, 52–53.

74. Davis, *Illinois Federation of Colored Women's Clubs*, 10–11.

75. Williams, "The Frederick Douglass Centre: A Question of Social Betterment and Not of Social Equality," *Voice of the Negro* 1, no. 12 (1904): 601–4, reprinted in Deegan, *The New Woman of Color*, 115; Schechter, *Ida B. Wells-Barnett and American Reform*, 184–86.

76. *Broad Ax*, Jan. 20, 1906; Giddings, *A Sword among Lions*, 446–47, 455; Bay, *To Tell the Truth Freely*, 262.

77. *Broad Ax*, June 23, 30, July 7, 1906; Giddings, *A Sword among Lions*, 459; Knupfer, *Toward a Tenderer Humanity*, 98–99.

78. W. E. B. DuBois, "A Litany at Atlanta," in *Darkwater: Voices from within the Veil* (1920; reprint, New York: Washington Square, 2004), 17–20; Rebecca Burns, *Rage in the City: The Story of the Atlanta 1906 Riot* (Athens: University of Georgia Press, 2009).

79. Wells, *Crusade for Justice*, 284–86; Bay, *To Tell the Truth Freely*, 264–65.

80. Jacqueline Anne Rouse, *Lugenia Burns Hope, Black Southern Reformer* (Athens: University of Georgia Press, 1989), 17, 139n13, 65–72; White, *Too Heavy a Load*, 66–67.

81. Lisa G. Materson, *For the Freedom of Her Race: Black Women and Electoral Politics in Illinois, 1877–1932* (Chapel Hill: University of North Carolina Press, 2009), 21.

82. Materson, *For the Freedom of Her Race*, 25–26.

83. *Chicago Tribune*, Sept. 25, 21, Oct. 9, 1894; Materson, *For the Freedom of Her Race*, 25–28.

84. *Chicago Tribune*, Sept. 11, Nov. 7, 1894.

85. Fannie Barrier Williams, "Women in Politics," *Women's Era* 1, no. 8 (Nov. 1894): 12–13; *Inter Ocean*, Oct. 12, 1894; *Chicago Tribune*, Sept. 21, Oct. 16, 1894.

86. *Chicago Tribune*, Aug. 12, 1894; Materson, *For the Freedom of Her Race*, 28.

87. Katherine E. Williams, "The Alpha-Suffrage Club," *Half-Century Magazine*, Sept. 1916, 12; Wells-Barnett quoted in Giddings, *A Sword among Lions*, 514; Bay, *To Tell the Truth Freely*, 289. See also Ida Wells-Barnett, "How Enfranchisement Stops Lynching," *Original Rights Magazine*, June 1910, 270–72.

88. Lucy G. Barber, *Marching on Washington: The Forging of an American Political Tradition* (Berkeley: University of California Press, 2002), 44–76.

89. Giddings, *A Sword among Lions*, 518, 514–16; *Chicago Tribune*, Mar. 4, 1913.

90. *Chicago Defender*, Aug. 23, 1913.

CHAPTER FOUR

1. *Chicago Tribune*, Dec. 8, 1889; *Indianapolis Freeman*, Jan. 11, 1890; US Manuscript Census, 1900, Chicago Ward 3, Cook, Illinois, reel T623 247, p. 13A, Enumeration District 68; Chicago Lakeside Directory, 1890, reel 9. Lewis and Bryan likely met at a literary society whose meetings were held at Estella's. See *Western Appeal*, June 15, 1889.

2. For a good historiography of race and labor, see Eric Arnesen, "Up from Exclusion: Black and White Workers, Race, and the State of Labor History," *Reviews in American History* 26 (1998): 146–74.

3. Ray Stannard Baker, *Following the Color Line: An Account of Negro Citizenship in the American Democracy* (New York: Doubleday, Page, 1908), 134.

4. Frederick Engels made this point when he argued that the spatial arrangements of industrial capitalism render the inequality and exploitation at the heart of capitalism invisible. Engels, *Condition of the Working Class in England in 1844* (London: George Alwin Unwin, 1950), esp. 45–54.

5. *New York Freeman*, May 1, 1886; Sidney H. Kessler, "The Organization of Negroes in the Knights of Labor," *Journal of Negro History* 37, no. 3 (July 1952): 273.

6. *Inter Ocean*, Dec. 22, 1886, quoted in Kessler, "The Organization of Negroes," 267.

7. Proceedings, National Convention of Colored Men at Louisville, Kentucky, September 24, 1883, reprinted in *The Black Worker: A Documentary History from Colonial Times to the Present*, vol. 3, *The Black Worker during the Era of the Knights of Labor*, ed. Philip S. Foner and Ronald L. Lewis, (Philadelphia: Temple University Press, 1978), 35.

8. *John Swinton's Paper*, Feb. 13, 1887. 1.

9. *Journal of United Labor*, Aug. 15, 1880; Sidney H. Kessler, "The Organization of Ne-

groes in the Knights of Labor," *Journal of Negro History* 37, no. 3 (July 1952): 249; Leon Fink, *Workingmen's Democracy: The Knights of Labor and American Politics* (Urbana: University of Illinois Press, 1983), 169.

10. *Journal of the Knights of Labor*, Mar. 5, 1891.

11. Fink, *Workingmen's Democracy*, 169; *New York Freeman*, Oct. 30, 1886; Kessler, "The Organization of Negroes," 255. On interracial unionism in the Knights of Labor, see, for example, Daniel Letwin, *The Challenge of Interracial Unionism: Alabama Coal Miners, 1878–1921* (Chapel Hill: University of North Carolina Press, 1998), 55–88.

12. *New York Sun*, June 26, 1887, quoted in Kessler, "The Organization of Negroes," 272; *Guide to the Local Assemblies of the Knights of Labor*, compiled by Jonathan Garlock (Westport, CT: Greenwood, 1982), appendix H, 674–80.

13. Richard T. Ely, *The Labor Movement in America* (New York: Cromwell, 1885), 83; Erie West Hardy, "The Relation of the Negro to Trade Unionism" (master's thesis, University of Chicago, 1911), 4–5.

14. *Chicago Times*, Aug. 22, 1888, quoted in Perry Duis, *Challenging Chicago: Coping with Everyday Life, 1837–1920* (Urbana: University of Illinois Press, 1998), 266–67.

15. *John Swinton's Paper*, Oct. 28, 1883. See also Rebecca M. McLennan, *The Crisis of Imprisonment: Protest, Politics, and the Making of the American Penal State* (Cambridge: Cambridge University Press, 2008), esp. 150–51, 181–82.

16. Eugene Staley, *History of the Illinois State Federation of Labor* (Chicago: University of Chicago Press, 1930), 7–8; Richard Schneirov, *Labor and Urban Politics: Class Conflict and the Origins of Modern Liberalism in Chicago, 1864–97* (Urbana: University of Illinois Press, 1998), 213. In 1890, the Trades and Labor Association in Chicago launched its own investigation of convict labor. *Chicago Tribune*, May 21, 1890.

17. *Chicago Tribune*, Jan. 1, 1889.

18. Eleventh US Census, 1890; Isaac Counselor Harris, *The Colored Men's Professional and Business Directory and Valuable Information on the Race in General* (Chicago, 1886), Vivian Harsh Collection, Woodson Library, Chicago; Christopher Robert Reed, *Black Chicago's First Century*, vol. 1, *1833–1900* (Columbia: University of Missouri Press, 2005), 241; *Colored People's Blue-Book and Business Directory of Chicago, Ill., 1905*, compiled by D. A. Bethea (Celerity, 1905), 114.

19. Monroe Nathan Work, "Crime among the Negroes in Chicago: A Social Study," *American Journal of Sociology* 6, no. 2 (Sept. 1900): 208; "Suggestions for Recommendations: Industry," typed report to the Commission on Race Relations, Julius Rosenwald Papers, box 4, folder 5, Special Collections Research Center, University of Chicago Library.

20. *Chicago Tribune*, July 21–25, 1877; *Inter Ocean*, July 20–24, 1877; Pierce, *A History of Chicago*, vol. 3, *The Rise of a Modern City, 1871–1893* (New York: Alfred A. Knopf, 1957), 240–54; James Ford Rhodes, "The Railroad Riots of 1877," *Scribners Magazine*, July 1911, 87.

21. Paul Avrich, *The Haymarket Tragedy* (Princeton, NJ: Princeton University Press, 1984); Carl S. Smith, *Urban Disorder and the Shape of Belief: The Great Fire, the Haymarket Bomb, and the Model Town of Pullman* (Chicago: University of Chicago Press, 1995); James R. Green, *Death in the Haymarket: A Story of Chicago, the First Labor Movement, and the Bombing That Divided Gilded Age America* (New York: Pantheon Books, 2006); Timothy Messer-Kruse, *The Trial of the Haymarket Anarchists: Terrorism and Justice in the Gilded Age* (New York: Palgrave Macmillan, 2011).

22. Fink, *Workingmen's Democracy*, 26; Schneirov, *Labor and Urban Politics*, 216–17.

23. Schneirov, *Labor and Urban Politics*, 216–17, 220; *Chicago Tribune*, Feb. 28, 1887.

24. Schneirov, *Labor and Urban Politics*, 216–17, 220.

25. *Chicago Tribune*, May 10, 1890; *Chicago Daily News*, May 6, 1890.

26. *Chicago Tribune*, May 10, 1890.

27. *Indianapolis Freeman*, May 31, June 7, 1890; *Western Appeal*, May 24, 1890; *Abendpost*, Jan. 22, 1891, reprinted in the *Chicago Foreign Press Survey*, German vol. 2, digitized microform.

28. *Indianapolis Freeman*, June 7, 1890.

29 Ibid.; *Western Appeal*, May 24, 1890; *Chicago Tribune*, May 22, 1890; William C. Pomeroy, *Lords of Misrule: A Tale of Gods and Men* (Chicago: Laird and Lee, 1894), 43; Schneirov, *Labor and Urban Politics*, 320. For a perhaps apocryphal description of Pomeroy's initiation in organized labor, see W. E. McEwen, "Reminiscences," *Labor World* (Duluth, MN), cited in *Mixer and Server*, Apr. 15, 1904.

30. Lady Duffus Hardy, *Through Cities and Prairie Lands: Sketches of an American Tour* (1881; reprint, New York: Arno, 1974), 75–79; Donald L. Miller, *City of the Century: The Epic of Chicago and the Making of America* (New York: Simon and Schuster, 1996), 275.

31. Daniel Bluestone, *Constructing Chicago* (New Haven, CT: Yale University Press, 1991), 114–15. On the movement of factories out of downtown, see Robert Lewis, *Chicago Made: Factory Networks in the Industrial Metropolis* (Chicago: University of Chicago Press, 2008), 31–36.

32. Miller, *City of the Century*, 265–70.

33. Bluestone, *Constructing Chicago*, 143–45; Homer Hoyt, *One Hundred Years of Land Values in Chicago: The Relationship of the Growth of Chicago to the Rise in Its Land Values, 1830–1933* (Chicago: University of Chicago Press, 1933), 149–53. Richard Sennett makes a similar argument about the rationalization of property values in late nineteenth-century Paris. Sennett, *The Fall of the Public Man: The Social Psychology of Capitalism* (New York: Vintage, 1978), 145–48.

34. On the emergence of Loop restaurants and saloons see Duis, *Challenging Chicago*, 152–69; Pierce, *A History of Chicago* 3:469–71.

35. For the distinction between mass strikes and organized labor-sponsored strikes see David Montgomery, "Strikes in Nineteenth-Century America," *Social Science History* 4 (Feb. 1980): 81–104; Schneirov, *Labor and Urban Politics*, 100–103.

36. *Chicago Tribune*, May 10, 1892; *Chicago Daily News*, May 6, 1890.

37. Sullivan quoted in Matthew Josephson, *Union House, Union Bar: The History of the Hotel and Restaurant Employees and Bartenders International Union, AFL-CIO* (New York: Random House, 1956), 10–11. Frances Donovan, describing the work of the waitress in the 1910s, says that most did a lot of "side work," or cleaning. Donovan, *The Woman Who Waits* (Boston: Gorham, 1920), 120–24.

38. Richard R. Wright Jr., "The Industrial Condition of Negroes in Chicago," (bachelor of divinity thesis, University of Chicago, 1901), 22–23; Duis, *Challenging Chicago*, 265; Reed, *Black Chicago's First Century*, 1:249–51; *Inter Ocean*, Jan. 18, 1896.

39. St. Clair Drake and Horace R. Cayton, *Black Metropolis: A Study of Negro Life in a Northern City* (New York: Harcourt, Brace, 1945), 74; Reed, *Black Chicago's First Century*, 1:250, 272.

40. "Our Exchanges," *Christian Recorder* (Philadelphia), Sept. 17, 1885; *Chicago Tribune*, Mar. 28, 1886.

41. *Inter Ocean*, May 1, 1887, May 19, 1890.

42. *Chicago Tribune*, May 10, 1890; Paula J. Giddings, *Ida: A Sword among Lions: Ida B. Wells and the Campaign against Lynching* (New York: HarperCollins, 2008), 344–45.

43. *Chicago Tribune*, May 10, 1890; Apr. 27, 1891. On Kinsleys, see *The Standard Guide to Chicago* (Chicago: Standard Guide, 1893), 39.

44. *Chicago Tribune*, May 22, 1890; *Western Appeal*, May 24, 1890.

45. *Chicago Tribune*, May 10, 1890.

46. *John Swinton's Paper*, May 17, 1885.

47. *Chicago Evening Journal*, July 9, 13, 1886; *(East Saint Louis) Weekly Signal*, July 22, 1886; *(Springfield) Illinois State Journal*, July 14, 1886; *Chicago Evening Journal*, Nov. 20, 1886. Armour quoted in John H. Keiser, "Black Strikebreakers and Racism in Illinois, 1865–1900," *Journal of the Illinois State Historical Society* 65, no. 3 (Autumn 1973): 319.

48. *John Swinton's Paper*, Mar. 20, 1887; John Keiser, "Black Strikebreakers and Racism in Illinois," 317–19; Alma Herbst, *The Negro in the Slaughtering and Meat-Packing Industry* (1932; reprint, New York: Arno, 1971), 18. Eric Arnesen argues that for black workers, strikebreaking was "a form of working-class activism designed to advance the interests of black workers and their families." Eric Arnesen, "The Quicksands of Economic Insecurity: African Americans, Strikebreaking, and Labor Activism in the Industrial Era," in *The Black Worker: Race, Labor, and Civil Rights since Emancipation*, ed. Arnesen (Urbana: University of Illinois Press, 2007), 44.

49. *Inter Ocean*, May 22, 1890; *Western Appeal*, May 24, 1890.

50. *Inter Ocean*, May 18, 1890.

51. *Chicago Tribune*, May 22, 1890; *Western Appeal*, May 24, 1890; *Chicago Daily News*, May 6, 1890. The *Daily News* commented that the waiters were more concerned with increasing pay than with limiting work hours.

52. *Inter Ocean*, Nov. 11, 1890; *Abendpost*, Jan. 22, 1891, reprinted in the Chicago Foreign Press Survey, German vol. 2, digitized microform..

53. Josephson, *Union House, Union Bar*, 14–15, 17.

54. *Chicago Tribune*, Apr. 27, Mar. 8, 1891; Schneirov, *Labor and Urban Politics*, 320. In 1896, Pomeroy had become an ally of Republican Party chairman Mark Hanna and was accused of distributing "immense sums of money" to steer laboring men away from William Jennings Bryan. See Josephson, *Union House, Union Bar*, 22–23; Sklar, *Florence Kelley and the Nation's Work*, 214–15.

55. *Chicago Tribune*, May 17, Apr. 28, 1893; *Inter Ocean*, May 1, 1890. The *Inter Ocean* reported that a "Clark Street restaurant" that employed "colored waiters" promised its waiters a raise from $12 to $18 per week during the fair. The move apparently spurred the new effort to demand $20 per day from all downtown restaurants and oyster houses.

56. *Chicago Tribune*, May 3, 1893; *New York Times*, Apr. 10, 11, 1893.

57. *Chicago Tribune*, May 2, 1893; *Inter Ocean*, May 4, 1893.

58. *Chicago Tribune*, May 4, 1893; *Indianapolis Freeman*, May 4, 1893; *Inter Ocean*, May 15, 16, 1893.

59. Herbst, *The Negro in the Slaughtering and Meat-Packing Industry*, 18.

60. *Chicago Tribune*, July 13, 1893; Herbst, *The Negro in the Slaughtering and Meat-Packing Industry*, 18; Keiser, "Black Strikebreakers and Racism," 319.

61. *Inter Ocean*, July 4, 1896.

62. *Chicago Tribune*, June 5, 1903.

63. *Chicago Tribune*, June 5, 16, 1903; *Chicago Daily News*, Aug. 25, 26, 1903.

64. *Chicago Tribune*, June 6, 1903. The laundresses would again fight for union protections in 1919. *Chicago Whip*, Sept. 20, 1919. On laundresses' work and labor struggles in Atlanta, see Tera W. Hunter, *To 'joy My Freedom: Southern Black Women's Lives and Labor after the Civil War* (Cambridge, MA: Harvard University Press, 1997).

65. Stephen H. Norwood argues that strikebreaking provided black men with a new sense of "masculinity," "allowing black men to challenge white society's image of them as obsequious, cowardly." See Norwood, *Strikebreaking & Intimidation: Mercenaries and Masculinity in Twentieth-Century America* (Chapel Hill: University of North Carolina Press, 2002), 80–81.

66. Ray Stannard Baker, "Capital and Labor Hunt Together: Chicago, the Victim of the New Industrial Conspiracy," *McClure's Magazine* 21, no. 5 (Sept. 1903); *Chicago Daily News*, Aug. 25, 1903. On the shift from black male waiters to white women in other cities, see Dorothy Sue Cobble, *Dishing It Out: Waitresses and Their Unions in the Twentieth Century* (Urbana: University of Illinois Press, 1991), 18–24; Kenneth Kusmer, *A Ghetto Takes Shape: Black Cleveland, 1870–1930* (Urbana: University of Illinois Press, 1976); Mary White Ovington, "The Negro in the Trade Unions in New York," *Annals of the American Academy of Political Science* (June 1906).

67. *Chicago Tribune*, June 16, 17, 1903.

68. *Chicago Tribune*, June 17, 1903; *Chicago Daily News*, Aug. 25, 1903.

69. *Chicago Tribune*, June 16, 1903.

70. *Inter Ocean*, Aug. 25, 1903.

71. *Chicago Daily News*, Aug. 26, 1903; *Inter Ocean*, Aug. 25, 1903, Apr. 30, 1877; Duis, *Challenging Chicago*, 263.

72. *Chicago Tribune*, Aug. 27, 1903; *Chicago Daily News*, Aug. 27, 31, 1903.

73. *Chicago Tribune*, Aug. 27, 1903; *Chicago Daily News*, Aug. 27, 1903.

74. Richard R. Wright Jr., "The Negro in Chicago," *Southern Workman* 35 (Oct. 1906): 560; Lorenzo J. Greene and Carter G. Woodson, *The Negro Wage Earner* (Washington, DC: Association for the Study of Negro Life, 1930), 93–95; Cobble, *Dishing It Out*, 18–21; Donovan, *The Woman Who Waits*, 8–11; Duis, *Challenging Chicago*, 270.

75. Women's Trade Union League of Chicago, *Statement of Facts Concerning Henrici's on Randolph Street* (Chicago: n.p., 1914).

76. Donovan, *The Woman Who Waits*, 59–60; Cobble, *Dishing It Out*, 18–19; Mark Pittenger, *Class Unknown: Undercover Investigations of American Work and Poverty from the Progressive Era to the Present* (New York: New York University Press, 2012).

77. Cobble, *Dishing It Out*, 18–21; Norwood, *Strikebreaking & Intimidation*, 105–6.

78. *Chicago Tribune*, Aug. 27, 29, 1903; Fannie Barrier Williams, "Social Bonds in the Black Belt in Chicago," *Charities* 15, no. 1 (Oct. 7, 1905): 43. On the hardening of racial boundaries of residential neighborhoods see Allan H. Spear, *Black Chicago: The Making of a Negro Ghetto* (Chicago: University of Chicago Press, 1967); Philpott, *The Slum and the Ghetto* (Belmont, CA: Wadsworth, 1991).

79. "Chicago Commission on Race Relations Conference on Trade Unions and the Negro Worker," unpublished outline dated Aug. 16, 1920, Folder "Negro and Civil Rights Items," box 25, Chicago Federation of Labor, John Fitzpatrick Collection, CHM. On labor leaders' concerns about black workers' suspicions of labor organizing see Forrester R. Washington to John Fitzpatrick, Jan. 25, 1919, Fitzpatrick Collection, box 25, CHM; *Chicago Whip*, July 17, 1920.

80. "Negroes Are Out for Busse," box 30, folder 5, IWP; Harold F. Gosnell, *Negro Politicians: The Rise of Negro Politics in Chicago* (1935; reprint, Chicago: University of Chicago Press, 1967), 22; Reed, *Black Chicago's First Century*, 1:251.

CHAPTER FIVE

1. Harold F. Gosnell, *Negro Politicians: The Rise of Negro Politics in Chicago* (1935; reprint Chicago: University of Chicago Press, 1967), 65–66.

2. Charles Russell Branham, "The Transformation of Black Political Leadership in Chicago, 1864–1942" (PhD diss., University of Chicago, 1981), 17–35; Ira Katznelson, *Black Men, White Cities: Race, Politics, and Migration in the United States, 1900–30, and Britain, 1948–68* (New York: Oxford University Press, 1973), 197; Beth Tompkins Bates, *Pullman Porters and the Rise of Protest Politics in Black America, 1925–1945* (Chapel Hill: University of North Carolina Press, 2001), 55–58. Bates contrasts "patronage politics" of the 1910s to "protest politics" of the 1920s and 1930s. Yet, as she notes, black politicians who worked with the machine after 1900 were able to bring jobs and some services to the Black Belt. My point is that successful black politicians were no longer dependent simply on personal relationships with whites but brought needed black votes and precinct workers to the Republican machine and, ultimately, won local office through stressing racial solidarity and using the only political leverage available, the machine. Their effective use of the machine, though it no doubt limited demands for social change, moved them beyond white patron-client politics. As Bates notes, "political possibilities" for migrants in the 1910s in Chicago "were greater than in most urban areas." Bates, *Pullman Porters,* 55.

3. Katznelson, *Black Men, White Cities,* 104; Branham, "Transformation of Black Political Leadership," 455–56.

4. On differences between northern and southern politics in Chicago and other cities, see Howard N. Rabinowitz, "A Comparative Perspective on Race Relations in Southern and Northern Cities, 1860–1900," in *Race, Ethnicity, and Urbanization: Selected Essays* (Columbia: University of Missouri Press, 1994), 219. Other studies of African Americans in northern cities in this period include Gilbert Osofsky, *The Making of a Ghetto: Negro New York, 1890–1930* (New York: Harper and Row, 1966); Marcy S. Sacks, *Before Harlem: The Black Experience in New York before World War I* (Philadelphia: University of Pennsylvania Press, 2006); Leslie Schwalm, *Emancipation's Diaspora: Race and Reconstruction in the Upper Midwest* (Chapel Hill: University of North Carolina Press, 2009); Kimberly L. Philips, *AlabamaNorth: African-American Migrants, Community, and Working-Class Activism in Cleveland, 1915–45* (Urbana: University of Illinois Press, 1999); James R. Grossman, *Land of Hope: Chicago, Black Southerners, and the Great Migration* (Chicago: University of Chicago Press, 1989).

5. Paula J. Giddings, *Ida: A Sword among Lions: Ida B. Wells and the Campaign against Lynching* (New York: HarperCollins, 2008), 484–87.

6. Miller quoted in Gunter Myrdal, *An American Dilemma: The Negro in America* (New York: Harper and Row, 1948), 740.

7. Jones to Washington, Jan. 28, 1904, in *The Booker T. Washington Papers,* 14 vols., ed. Louis R. Harlan (Chicago: University of Chicago Press, 1972–89), 7:417–18.

8. *Chicago Record-Herald,* Mar. 8, 1907.

9. Langston Hughes, *The Big Sea: An Autobiography* (New York: Knopf, 1945), 33.

10. *Colored People's Blue-Book and Business Directory of Chicago, Ill., 1905* (Chicago: Celerity, 1905), 18; Thomas Lee Philpott, *The Slum and the Ghetto: Immigrants, Blacks, and Reformers in Chicago, 1890–1930* (Belmont, CA: Wadsworth, 1991), 147; Allan H. Spear, *Black Chicago: The Making of a Negro Ghetto, 1890–1920* (Chicago: University of Chicago Press, 1967), 14–17; Chicago Commission on Race Relations, *The Negro in Chicago: A Study of Race Relations and a Race Riot* (Chicago: University of Chicago Press, 1922), 17.

11. Richard R. Wright Jr., "The Negro in Chicago," *Southern Workman* 35 (Oct. 1906): 557.

12. Spear, *Black Chicago,* 11, 16; *Chicago Defender,* Sept. 20, 1913.

13. W. E. B. DuBois, *The Philadelphia Negro: A Social Study* (1899; reprint, Philadelphia: University of Pennsylvania Press, 1996), 311; Spear, *Black Chicago*, 20–25.

14. Alzada P. Comstock, "Chicago Housing Conditions, VI: The Problem of the Negro," *American Journal of Sociology* 18, no. 2 (Sept. 1912): 244–45; Fannie Barrier Williams, "Social Bonds in the Black Belt of Chicago," *Charities* 15, no. 1 (Oct. 7, 1905): 40–41; Spear, *Black Chicago*, 20–25.

15. *Chicago Defender*, May 21, 1910. See also Lloyd Wendt and Herman Kogan, *Lords of the Levee: The Story of Bathhouse John and Hinky Dink* (New York: Bobbs-Merrill, 1943).

16. St. Clair Drake and Horace R. Cayton, *Black Metropolis: A Study of Negro Life in a Northern City* (New York: Harcourt, Brace, 1945), 55–56.

17. *Chicago Defender*, Nov. 8, 1913; William Howland Kenney, *Chicago Jazz: A Cultural History, 1904–1930* (New York: Oxford University Press, 1993), 13–15; Nathan Thomson, *Kings: The True Story of Chicago's Policy Kings and Numbers Racketeers: An Informal History* (Chicago: Bronzeville, 2006), 19–48; Michael Harris, *The Rise of the Gospel Blues: The Music of Thomas Andrew Dorsey in the Urban Church* (New York: Oxford University Press, 1992), 51–63.

18. Harry Haywood, *Black Bolshevik: Autobiography of an Afro-American Communist* (Chicago: Liberator, 1978), 37–38.

19. Cynthia M. Blair, *I've Got to Make My Livin': Black Women's Sex Work in Turn-of-the-Century Chicago* (Chicago: University of Chicago Press, 2010), 155; Albert Lee Kreiling, "The Rise of the Black Press in Chicago," *Journalism History* 4, no. 4 (Winter 1977): 134; Davarian L. Baldwin, *Chicago's New Negroes: Modernity, the Great Migration, and Black Urban Life* (Chapel Hill: University of North Carolina Press, 2007), 44–48. Pannell owned stores at Twenty-Seventh and Dearborn, Thirty-Sixth and Armour, and Fifty-First and Dearborn. *Chicago Defender*, July 31, 1909 (see also advertisements).; Writing about the emergence of "civic culture," Robin F. Bachin highlights the "cultural proximity of spaces of respectability and areas of 'vice.'" Bachin, *Building the South Side: Urban Space and Civic Culture in Chicago, 1890–1919* (Chicago: University of Chicago Press, 2004), 247–85.

20. Blair, *I've Got to Make My Livin'*, 140; Blair writes that after 1900, white vice syndicates forced black saloonkeepers out of the Levee. But black entrepreneurs continued to run gambling houses, cabarets, and saloons in the Black Belt. Robert M. Lombardo, "The Black Mafia: African-American Organized Crime in Chicago, 1890–1960," *Crime, Law and Social Change* 38 (2002): 33–65.

21. *Broad Ax*, Sept. 21, 1907; Dempsey J. Travis, *An Autobiography of Black Jazz* (Chicago: Urban Research Institute, 1983), 26. *Colored People's Blue-Book, 1905*, 183, lists the city's only "Old Folk's Home" for black Chicagoans at 610 Garfield Boulevard.

22. *New York World*, July 25, 1907, quoted in Gosnell, *Negro Politicians*, 126; *Broad Ax*, Nov. 7, 1903, Sept. 21, 1907; Junius B. Wood, *The Negro in Chicago* (Chicago: Chicago Daily News, 1916); Spear, *Black Chicago*, 75–76; Baldwin, *Chicago's New Negroes*, 47; Reed, *Black Chicago's First Century*, vol. 1, *1833–1900* (Columbia: University of Missouri Press, 2005), 24, 421–22.

23. *New York World*, July 24, 1907;; Carl R. Osthaus, "The Rise and Fall of Jesse Binga, Black Financier," *Journal of Negro History* 58, no. 1 (Jan. 1973): 39–60; Arnett G. Lindsay, "The Negro in Banking," *Journal of Negro History* 14, no. 2 (Apr. 1929): 192–93. See also J. H. Harmon Jr., "The Negro as a Local Business Man," *Journal of Negro History* 14, no. 2 (Apr. 1929): 116–55. The *Defender* covered Binga's career through the 1930s. See, for example, *Chicago Defender*, Jan. 1, 1910.

24. *Colored People's Blue-Book, 1905*, 138; Kenney, *Chicago Jazz*, 5–7; Henry T. Sampson, *Blacks in Blackface: A Source Book of Early Black Musical Shows* (Metuchen, NJ: Scarecrow, 1980), 119.

25. Taylor to Edward T. Devine, Mar. 4, 1908, box 7, folder 155, Graham Taylor Papers, Midwest Manuscript Collection, Newberry Library, Chicago; Harold F. Gosnell, *Machine Politics: Chicago Model* (1937; reprint, Chicago: University of Chicago Press, 1969), 42–43.

26. *Chicago Defender*, Feb. 4, 1933; Gosnell, *Negro Politicians*, 127–28. A series of *Chicago Tribune* articles describe "tribute money." See, for example, *Chicago Tribune*, Mar. 24, 1901.

27. Katznelson, *Black Men, White Cities*, 197; Branham, "Transformation of Black Political Leadership," 17–18.

28. That year, Morris moved from the First to the Third district. *Chicago Daily News*, Sept. 14, 1907; *Broad Ax*, Dec. 28, 1907, May 16, 1908; Branham, "Transformation of Black Political Leadership," 22–24; *New York Times*, Mar. 3, 1901; Gosnell, *Negro Politicians*, 128; "Illinois General Assembly Research Response," prepared by Amanda Huston, Legislative Research Unit, file 11-092,. http://www.ilga.gov/commission/lru/BlackLegislators.pdf.

29. Helen Buckler, *Doctor Dan, Pioneer in American Surgery* (Boston: Little, Brown, 1954), 70–71; George Arthur, "The Young Men's Christian Association Movement," *Opportunity* 1, no. 3 (Mar. 1923): 17; Bates, *Pullman Porters*, 43–44; Drake and Cayton, *Black Metropolis*, 57.

30. *Chicago Defender*, Mar. 26, Apr. 23, 1910; Kenney, *Chicago Jazz*, 7–9; Mary Carbine, "'The Finest Outside the Loop': Motion Picture Exhibition in Chicago's Black Metropolis, 1905–1928," *Camera Obscura* 23 (May 1990): 9.

31. *Chicago Defender*, Feb. 24, 1912, Jan. 31, 1916, Jan. 16, 1915. See also Leslie Brown, *Upbuilding Black Durham: Gender, Class, and Black Community Development in the Jim Crow South* (Chapel Hill: University of North Carolina Press, 2008).

32. *Chicago Defender*, Feb. 12, 1910, May 8, 1916; Kenney, *Chicago Jazz*, 15; Chad Heap, *Slumming: Sexual and Racial Encounters in American Nightlife, 1885–1940* (Chicago: University of Chicago Press, 2009), 73–80.

33. Vice Commission of Chicago, *The Social Evil in Chicago: A Study of Existing Conditions with Recommendations* (Chicago: Gunthrop-Warren, 1911), CHM; Charles Edward Merriam, *Chicago: A More Intimate View of Urban Politics* (New York: Macmillan, 1929), 25–29; Gosnell, *Negro Politicians*, 115–35; Thompson, *Kings*, 24–25.

34. My analysis of the ways illicit activities shaped licit politics is influenced by James C. Scott's study of anarchist groups in Southeast Asia. See Scott, *The Art of Not Being Governed: An Anarchist History of Upland Southeast Asia* (New Haven, CT: Yale University Press, 2009). 179.

35. As Wallace Best suggests, though discussions and conflicts over the role of the church began before the Great Migration, debates over how the church would respond to the migration were amplified after 1915. Best, *Passionately Human, No Less Divine: Religion and Culture in Black Chicago, 1915–1952* (Princeton, NJ: Princeton University Press, 2005), 13–30.

36. There is much debate about the role of black ministers in guiding local politics, especially before World War II. Some scholars see the church serving as a place to escape the burdens of racism, whether by creating insular communities or focusing on the afterlife. See Benjamin E. Mays and Joseph William Nicholson, *The Negro's Church* (New York: Institute of Social and Religious Research, 1933); E. Franklin

Frazier, *The Negro Church in America* ((New York: Schocken Books, 1974); Carter G. Woodson, *The History of the Negro Church* (Washington, DC: Associated Publishers, 1922); W. E. B. DuBois, ed., *The Negro Church: Report of a Social Study Made under the Direction of Atlanta University; Together with the Proceedings of the Eighth Conference for the Study of the Negro Problems, Held at Atlanta University, May 26th, 1903* (Atlanta: Atlanta University Press, 1903). Some more recent scholars see the early twentieth-century black church as laying the groundwork for activist politics in the postwar years. See Best, *Passionately Human*; Barbara Dianne Savage, *Your Spirits Walk beside Us: The Politics of Black Religion* (Cambridge, MA: Harvard University Press, 2008); James Melvin Washington, *Frustrated Fellowship: The Black Quest for Social Power* (Macon, GA: Mercer University Press, 1986); Milton C. Sennett, *Bound for the Promised Land: African American Religion and the Great Migration* (Durham, NC: Duke University Press, 1997); Clarence E. Walker, *A Rock in a Weary Land: The African Methodist Episcopal Church during the Civil War and Reconstruction* (Baton Rouge: Louisiana State University Press, 1982); C. Eric Lincoln and Lawrence H. Mamiya, *The Black Church in the African American Experience* (Durham, NC: Duke University Press, 1990); William E. Montgomery, *Under Their Own Vine and Fig Tree: The African-American Church in the South, 1865–1900* (Baton Rouge: Louisiana University Press, 1993).

37. W. E. B. DuBois and Monroe N. Work, "The Middle West, Illinois," in DuBois, *The Negro Church*, 83–92; Richard Bardolph, *The Negro Vanguard* (New York: Rinehart, 1959), 105. Fannie Barrier Williams lists twenty-five black churches in Chicago in 1905. Williams, "Social Bonds of the Black Belt in Chicago: Negro Organizations and the New Spirit Pervading Them," in *The New Woman of Color: The Collected Writings of Fannie Barrier Williams, 1893–1918*, ed. Mary Jo Deegan (DeKalb: Northern Illinois University Press, 2002), 118. Robert Lee Sutherland, quotes a letter from Cardinal Mundelein requesting that Saint Monica's Church, later called Saint Elizabeth's, "be reserved entirely for the colored Catholics of Chicago." Robert Lee Sutherland, "An Analysis of Negro Churches in Chicago" (PhD diss., University of Chicago, 1930), 35.

38. *Colored People's Blue-Book, 1905*; Junius B. Wood, *The Negro in Chicago* (Chicago: Chicago Daily News, 1916), 19.

39. Proceedings of the Twenty-Second Quadrennial Conference of the African Methodist Episcopal Church, Chicago, May 2, 1904, 23, AME Archives, Nashville, TN.

40. Daniel Bluestone, *Constructing Chicago* (New Haven, CT: Yale University Press, 1991): 82–85.

41. *Colored People's Blue-Book, 1905*, 16, 25, 36–37; Robin Fleming, "Picturesque History and the Medieval in Nineteenth-Century America," *American Historical Review* 100, no. 4 (Oct. 1995): 1061–94; Bluestone, *Constructing Chicago*, 70–71.

42. DuBois and Work, "The Middle West, Illinois," 83–92.

43. Ibid., 83–92.

44. *New York Times*, Sept. 9, 1916; Sennett, *Bound for the Promised Land*, 124–25.

45. W. E. B. DuBois and Monroe N. Work, "The Middle West, Illinois," and "The Negro Church," in *Atlanta University Publications* (nos. 7–10), ed. W. E. B. DuBois, vol. 2 (1903; reprint New York: Octagon Books, 1968), 61–62. On DuBois's views of the black church, see Curtis Evans, "W. E. B. DuBois: Interpreting Religion and the Problem of the Negro Church," *Journal of the American Academy of Religion* 75, no. 2 (June 2007): 268–97; Barbara Dianne Savage, "W. E. B. DuBois and 'the Negro

Church,'" *Annals of the American Academy of Political and Social Science* 568 (Mar. 2000): 235–49.

46. Martin Summers, *Manliness and Its Discontents: The Black Middle Class and the Trans-formation of Masculinity, 1900–1930* (Chapel Hill: University of North Carolina Press, 2004), 84; Phillips, *AlabamaNorth*, 168–69. Wallace Best writes that by the 1920s, many Chicago ministers took up a "mixed type" preaching style in order to attract southern migrants. Best, *Passionately Human*, 96–99. On white critiques of emotional preaching see Frederick Morgan Davenport, *Primitive Traits in Religious Revivals: A Study in Mental and Social Evolution* (New York: Macmillan, 1906); James Bissett Pratt, *The Psychology of Religious Belief* (New York: Macmillan, 1907), 173–95, 280–304; Ann Taves, *Fits, Trances & Visions: Experiencing Religion and Explaining Experience from Wesley to James* (Princeton, NJ: Princeton University Press, 1999), 308–47.

47. Washington Gladden, "Remarks of Dr. Washington Gladden," in *Atlanta University Publications* (nos. 7–11), ed. W. E. B. DuBois, vol. 11 (New York: Octagon Books, 1968), 206.

48. Journal of Proceedings of the Fifty-Third Annual Session of the Kentucky Confer-ence of the African Methodist Episcopal Church held at Saint Peter's AME Church, Harrodsburg, Kentucky, October 6–10, 1920. 5, AME Archives, Nashville, TN.

49. For example, Vattel Elbert Daniel, "Ritual and Stratification in Chicago Negro Churches," *American Sociological Review* 7, no. 3 (June 1942): 352–61; Rothe Hilger, "The Religious Expression of the Negro" (master's thesis, Vanderbilt University, 1931); Mays and Nicholson, *The Negro's Church.*

50. *Body and Soul*, directed by Oscar Micheaux, 1925. On Micheaux see Patrick McGil-ligan, *Oscar Micheaux, the Great and Only: The Life of America's First Great Black Film-maker* (New York: HarperCollins, 2007); J. Ronald Green, *With a Crooked Stick: The Films of Oscar Micheaux* (Bloomington: Indiana University Press, 2004).

51. DuBois and Work, "The Middle West, Illinois," 85. For excellent discussions of the debates over the role of black churches in the early twentieth century, see Savage, *The Politics of Black Religion*; Best, *Passionately Human.*

52. Richard R. Wright Jr., "The Industrial Condition of Negroes in Chicago," (bachelor of divinity thesis, University of Chicago, 1901), 23–25; Spear, *Black Chicago*, 29.

53. Best, *Passionately Human*, 95.

54. "Suggestions for Recommendations, The Negro Community," typed report for the Chicago Commission on Race Relations, 2, Julius Rosenwald Papers, box 6, folder 5, Special Collections Research Center, University of Chicago Library; Spear, *Black Chi-cago*, 102–3; Grossman, *Land of Hope*, 156–60.

55. Sutherland, "An Analysis of Negro Churches in Chicago," 38.

56. Joseph A. Logsdon, "The Rev. Archibald J. Carey and the Negro in Chicago Politics" (PhD diss., University of Chicago, 1961), 5–6; *Broad Ax*, Sept. 12, 1903. On the establishment of the "political church," see Eric L. McDaniel, *Politics in the Pews: The Political Mobilization of Black Churches* (Ann Arbor: University of Michigan Press, 2008), 5–16.

57. For a full study of Carey's life and that of his son, Archibald J. Carey Jr., see Den-nis C. Dickerson, *African American Preachers and Politics: The Careys of Chicago* (Jack-son: University Press of Mississippi, 2010).

58. Dennis C. Dickerson, *African Methodism and Its Wesleyan Heritage: Reflections on AME Church History* (Nashville: AMEC Sunday School Union, 2009); Lawrence S. Little,

Disciples of Liberty: The African Methodist Episcopal Church in the Age of Imperialism, 1884–1916 (Knoxville: University of Tennessee Press, 2000); Walker, *A Rock in a Weary Land*; Daniel A. Payne, *History of the African Methodist Church* (1891; reprint, New York: Johnson Reprint, 1968); Carol V. R. George, *Segregated Sabbaths: Richard Allen and the Emergence of Independent Black Churches, 1760–1840* (New York: Oxford University Press, 1973). Milton C. Sennett notes that several other prominent black ministers, including Olivet Baptist's E. J. Fisher and Lacey Kirk Williams (who replaced Fisher in 1915) seemed much less interested in Chicago politics, perhaps because Carey so quickly dominated the field. Sennett, *Bound for the Promised Land*, 168.

59. "Quinn Chapel African Methodist Episcopal Church 120th Anniversary Record, 1847–1967," Quinn Chapel Archives, Vivian G. Harsh Research Collection, Woodson Library, Chicago; Roudell Kirkwood, "The African Methodist Episcopal (A.M.E.) Church and the Education of Afrikana Adults: An Historical Study of Quinn Chapel, Chicago, Illinois, 1947–1997," (PhD diss., Northern Illinois University, 2001), 58–59. See also Commission on Chicago Historical and Architectural Landmarks, "Quinn Chapel: 2401 South Wabash, Chicago, Illinois" Ryerson and Burnham Libraries, Art Institute of Chicago. The *Tribune* in 1903 listed the 1898 debt at $40,000. *Chicago Tribune*, July 27, 1903.

60. Logsdon, "The Rev. Archibald J. Carey and the Negro in Chicago Politics," 8; "Dr. Archibald J. Carey," *Half-Century Magazine*, Sept. 1919, 9.

61. Ransom later wrote that McKinley had been scheduled to speak at his church, Bethel, but Carey complained so strongly that the president's visit was moved to Quinn Chapel. Reverdy Ransom, *The Pilgrimage of Harriet Ransom's Son* (Nashville: AME Sunday School Union, 1949), 115.

62. Carey had met McKinley in Florida in 1896 when he stumped for the Republican ticket. Dickerson, *African American Preachers and Politics*, 25, 40; Giddings, *A Sword among Lions*, 378; Calvin S. Morris, *Reverdy C. Ransom: Black Advocate of the Social Gospel* (New York: University Press of America, 1990), 145. Ransom later claimed that AME bishop B. W. Arnett and Alexander Walters, representing the Afro-American League, met with the Republican Party platform committee in the summer of 1896 to insert an antilynching plank. Ransom, *Pilgrimage*, 77.

63. Rayford W. Logan, *The Betrayal of the Negro, from Rutherford B. Hayes to Woodrow Wilson* (1965; reprint, New York: Da Capo, 1997), 87–88. The war likely carried complex and distinctive meanings for black Chicagoans. Sutton E. Griggs, in his novel *Imperium in Imperio: A Study of the Negro Problem* (1899), had laid out alternative possibilities for US imperialism, suggesting that war for empire helped black and white Americans avoid another civil war. See also Amy Kaplan, *The Anarchy of Empire in the Making of US Culture* (Cambridge, MA: Harvard University Press, 2002), 123–24.

64. *Chicago Tribune*, Oct. 9, 1899; Kirkwood, "The African Methodist Episcopal Church," 60.

65. Unsigned letter, Nov. 1, 1901, Archibald J. Carey Sr. Collection, CHM; Logsdon, "The Rev. Archibald J. Carey and the Negro in Chicago Politics," 15–16.

66. Giddings, *A Sword among Lions*, 384.

67. Morris, *Reverdy C. Ransom*, 10–12.

68. Proceedings of the Twenty-First Quadrennial Session of the General Conference of the African M.E. Church held in the auditorium, Columbus, Ohio, May 7– May 25, 1900, 190, AME Archives, Nashville, TN.

69. *Inter Ocean*, July 29, 1900; Annetta L. Gomez-Jefferson, *The Sage of Tawawa: Reverdy Cassius Ransom, 1861–1959* (Kent, OH: Kent State University Press, 2002), 64–65; Ralph E. Luker, "Missions, Institutional Churches, and Settlement Houses: The Black Experience, 1885–1910," *Journal of Negro History* 69, no. 3–4 (Summer–Autumn 1984): 104. Luker makes the persuasive argument that the settlement-house movement was rooted in part in the American missionary movement and was not simply an offspring of the English social settlement. This is an important point because it suggests that African Americans had been involved with and were crucial progenitors of the settlement-house movement.

70. Ransom, *Pilgrimage*, 104–5; Graham Taylor, *The Standard*, Feb. 7, 1903, box 31, Graham Taylor Papers, Midwest Manuscript Collection, Newberry Library, Chicago. See also Taylor, "The Social Function of the Church," *American Journal of Sociology* 5, no. 3 (Nov. 1899), 305–21.

71. Wells, *Crusade for Justice: The Autobiography of Ida B. Wells*, ed. Alfreda M. Duster (Chicago: University of Chicago Press, 1991), 249; Giddings, *A Sword among Lions*, 383–84. On the establishment of kindergartens for black children, see Annie E. Tucker, "Formation of Child Character," *Colored American Magazine*, Feb. 1901, 258–61.

72. *Inter Ocean*, July 29, 1900; *Christian Recorder* (Philadelphia), Jan. 25, 1900.

73. *Inter Ocean*, July 29, 1900; *Christian Recorder* (Philadelphia), Jan. 25, 1900.

74. Morris, *Reverdy C. Ransom*, 135–37; Giddings, *A Sword among Lions*, 421. Richard R. Wright Jr. claimed that the Niagara Movement was initiated at Institutional Church after the men's group invited DuBois to Chicago to discuss his recently published *Souls of Black Folk*. See Wright, *Eighty-Seven Years behind the Black Curtain: An Autobiography* (Philadelphia: Rare Book, 1965), 97, cited in Morris, *Reverdy C. Ransom*, 140.

75. Gomez-Jefferson, *The Sage of Tawawa*, 66–67; Ransom, *Pilgrimage*, 90–91; Katherine Leckie, "A South Side Institution," *Chicago American*, Mar. 1, 1901, cited in Ransom, *Pilgrimage*, 104–5. Though Ransom thought men and women needed different kinds of education, he was among the earliest AME leaders to urge that women be given full voting rights in the church's main governing body, the General Conference. *AME Church Review* 43, no. 169 (July 1926): 25; Lisa Matteson, *For the Freedom of Her Race: Black Women and Electoral Politics in Illinois, 1877–1932* (Chapel Hill: University of North Carolina Press, 2009), 139–40.

76. Ransom to Claude A. Barnett, May 14, 1945, Claude A. Barnett Papers, CHM; Morris, *Reverdy C. Ransom*, 110–11.

77. Ransom, *Pilgrimage*, 143–48; Best, *Passionately Human*, 129–30.

78. DuBois, *The Negro Church*, 85.

79. Journal of the Twenty-third Quadrennial Session, of the General Conference, AME Church, St. John AME Church, Norfolk VA, May 4–21, 1908, 77.

80. See for example Journal of the Twenty-First Quadrennial Session of the General Conference of the African M.E. Church Held in the Auditorium, Columbus, Ohio, May 7–May 25, 1900, 266–67.

81. Wells, *Crusade for Justice*, 292, 295; David W. Wills, "Archibald J. Cary, Sr., and Ida B. Wells-Barnett: Religion and Politics in Black Chicago, 1900–1931," *AME Church Review* 120, no. 395 (July–Sept. 2004), 95; Giddings, *A Sword among Lions*, 458.

82. Journal of Proceedings of the Fifty-Fourth Annual Session of the Kentucky Conference of the African Methodist Episcopal Church Held at Saint James AME Church, Ashland, Kentucky, Oct 25–30, 1921, 56.

83. The ministers were not the sole forces "mapping" the city. The black press, in particular the *Chicago Defender*, issued regular articles describing and defining urban spaces for new arrivals.

84. Archibald J. Carey, "Bishop A. J. Carey Thrills the West Tennessee Conference," in *Christian Recorder* (Philadelphia), Dec. 22, 1922. Clipping in Archibald J. Carey Sr. Collection, Folder 1, CHM.

85. *Chicago Defender*, Mar. 7, 14, 1914, Apr. 28, 1931 (obituary); Logsdon, "The Rev. Archibald J. Carey and the Negro in Chicago Politics," 16–18; Spear, *Black Chicago*, 64–65.

86. A. J. Carey, "The Other Side of the Question," in *Abraham Lincoln: The Tribute of a Century, 1809–1909* (Chicago: A. C. McClurg, 1910), 111; Spear, *Black Chicago*, 64; *Chicago Defender*, Apr. 5, 1913.

87. Dickerson, *African American Preachers and Politics*, 28–30.

88. IWP interview with Annabelle Carey; Sennett, *Bound for the Promised Land*, 149; Best, *Passionately Human*, 131.

89. *Inter Ocean*, May 10, 1905; Carey quoted in Grossman, *Land of Hope*, 230. For a full discussion of the shift in attitudes toward organized labor by black ministers, see Bates, *Pullman Porters*, 74–86.

90. Journal of the Twenty-Sixty Quadrennial Session of the General Conference of the African Methodist Episcopal Church, Held in St. Louis, Missouri, May 3rd to 18th, 1920, 205; Sennett, *Bound for the Promised Land*, 149–50; Bates, *Pullman Porters*, 54.

91. Logsdon, "The Rev. Archibald J. Carey and the Negro in Chicago Politics," 16–17; Quinn Chapel AME Church, *102nd Anniversary Record, 1847–1967* (Chicago, 1967), 25.

92. Lloyd Wendt and Herman Kogan, *Big Bill of Chicago* (New York: Bobbs-Merrill, 1953), 32–33; Douglas Bukowski, *Big Bill Thompson, Chicago, and the Politics of Image* (Urbana: University of Illinois Press, 1998), 13–14; interview with Archibald Carey Jr., quoted in Logsdon, "The Rev. Archibald J. Carey and the Negro in Chicago Politics," 37.

93. Bukowski, *Big Bill Thompson*, 14; Logsdon, "The Rev. Archibald J. Carey and the Negro in Chicago Politics," 36.

94. Logsdon, "The Rev. Archibald J. Carey and the Negro in Chicago Politics," 38; Gosnell, *Negro Politicians*, 50; Dominic Pacyga, *Chicago: A Biography* (Chicago: University of Chicago Press, 2009), 179–80.

95. Gosnell, *Negro Politicians*, 38–39; Pacyga, *Chicago*, 180.

96. Gosnell, *Negro Politicians*, 37–39; Logsdon, "The Rev. Archibald J. Carey and the Negro in Chicago Politics," 39–40; Giddings, *A Sword among Lions*, 385–86; Charles E. Merriam, *Chicago: A More Intimate View of Urban Politics* (New York: Macmillan, 1929), 95; *Outlook*, May 11, 1912, 52.

97. *Chicago Tribune*, Feb. 26, 1901.

98. Logsdon, "The Rev. Archibald J. Carey and the Negro in Chicago Politics," 39; Branham, "Black Chicago: Accommodationist Politics before the Great Migration," in *Ethnic Chicago*, ed. Melvin G. Holli and Peter d'A. Jones (Grand Rapids, MI: William B. Eerdmans, 1984), 33–63.

99. Branham, "Black Chicago," 357–58; Logsdon, "The Rev. Archibald J. Carey and the Negro in Chicago Politics," 24–26; Harrison quoted in Drake and Cayton, *Black Metropolis*, 345.

100. *Chicago Defender*, Sept. 7, 1912.

101. *Broad Ax*, Nov. 2, 1907; Nov. 18, 1911; Gosnell, *Negro Politicians*, 83. Logsdon, "The Rev. Archibald J. Carey and the Negro in Chicago Politics," 40–41.

102. *Chicago Defender*, Mar. 30, 1912; typed letter dated Feb. 23, 1911, from Theodore E. Remi on Charles E. Merriam for Mayor stationery, which lists the "Merriam Committee," Merriam Collection, University of Chicago Library.

103. Typed, undated letter on Young Colored Men's Merriam for Mayor Club stationery, typed call for a "Monster Rally Meeting" on Young Colored Men's stationery, typed note "To the Colored Voter of Chicago" signed "Second Ward Merriam for Mayor Club," typed, undated letter from the Second Ward Merriam for Mayor Club, signed Wm. Floyd Jenkins and A. L. Williams, all in Merriam Collection, University of Chicago Library; "Ida B. Wells," typed MS, Ida B. Wells Papers, box 8, folder 10, p. 4, Special Collections Research Center, University of Chicago Library.

104. Typed, undated letter on Young Colored Men's Merriam for Mayor Club stationery; typed call for a "Monster Rally Meeting" on Young Colored Men's stationery; typed note "To the Colored Voter of Chicago" signed "Second Ward Merriam for Mayor Club; typed, undated letter from the Second Ward Merriam for Mayor Club, signed Wm. Floyd Jenkins, and A. L. Williams, all in Merriam Collection. University of Chicago Library; Colored Blue Book *Colored People's Blue-Book, 1905*, 78; Mia Bay, *To Tell the Truth Freely: The Life of Ida B. Wells* (New York: Hill and Wang, 2009), 282–89.

105. *Chicago Defender*, Aug. 27, Sept. 24, 1910.

106. *Chicago Defender*, Nov. 18, 1911.

107. *Chicago Defender*, Sept. 20, 1913.

108. *Inter Ocean*, Nov. 27, 1906; "Dr. Archibald J. Carey," *Half-Century Magazine*, Sep. 1919, 9.

109. *Chicago Defender*, Oct. 10, 1914.

110. Gosnell, *Negro Politicians*, 38–39. For the investigation of Lorimer see *Chicago Tribune*, Feb. 14, Mar. 8, 29, 31, July 15, 1912. Carey and Lorimer maintained their peculiar friendship until Carey's death in 1931.

111. *Chicago Defender*, July 22, 1911; *Chicago Tribune*, July 11, 1911. Motts's sister, Lucy Lindsay, took over the Pekin. She married Dan Jackson, the undertaker who buried her brother and was later a prominent South Side politician. In 1916, the Pekin's proprietors replaced the theater seats with a dance floor. The cabaret became known as a gangland hangout after two policemen were shot there in 1920. It was later torn down and replaced by a South Side police station. Kenney, *Chicago Jazz*, 7.

112. Kenney, *Chicago Jazz*, 9–10; *Indianapolis Freeman*, Jan. 2, 1915; Gosnell, *Negro Politicians*, 128–30.

CHAPTER SIX

1. *Broad Ax*, May 1, 1915. On DePriest's campaign see Wanda A. Hendricks, "Vote for the Advantage of Ourselves and Our Race: The Election of the First Black Alderman in Chicago," *Illinois Historical Journal* 87, no. 3 (Autumn 1994): 171–84.

2. *Broad Ax*, May 1, 1915.

3. On social identity, particularly ethnic and racial identities, shaping voting patterns, see Hanna Fenichel Pitkin, *The Concept of Representation* (Berkeley: University of California Press, 1967), 81; Melissa Williams, *Voice, Trust, and Memory: Marginalized Groups and the Failings of Liberal Representation* (Princeton, NJ: Princeton University Press, 1998). Much of the scholarship on African American urban politics in the twentieth century has taken for granted that race (sometimes class too) was the

primary factor in voters' decisions. Rufus P. Browning, Dale Rogers Marshall, and David Tabb, *Protest Is Not Enough: The Struggle of Blacks and Hispanics for Equality in City Politics* (Berkeley: University of California Press, 1984); Paul Kleppner, *Chicago Divided: The Making of a Black Mayor* (DeKalb: Northern Illinois University Press, 1985); Manning Marable, *Black American Politics: From the Washington Marches to Jesse Jackson* (New York: Verso, 1985); Raphael J. Sonenshein, *Politics in Black and White: Race and Power in Los Angeles* (Princeton, NJ: Princeton University Press, 1993).

4. Frederick Harris, criticizing Barack Obama's lack of support for African Americans, recently characterized Obama's presidency as a "triumph of symbolism over substance." That view of contemporary politics is open to debate, but the phrase certainly captures DePriest's victory and brief career on the city council. It is worth noting, however, that symbols, at particular moments, can be nearly as important as substance. See Harris, *The Price of the Ticket: Barak Obama and the Rise and Decline of Black Politics* (New York: Oxford University Press, 2012).

5. Allan H. Spear, *Black Chicago: The Making of a Negro Ghetto, 1890–1920* (Chicago: University of Chicago Press, 1967), 78; *Chicago Whip*, Aug. 25, 1923. On DePriest's participation, or lack of action, in city governance, see City Council Proceedings, box Oct.–Nov. 1915, Illinois Regional Archives Depository, Northeastern Illinois University, Chicago. Several scholars argue that black activists effectively became pawns for urban white machines. See, for example, Ira Katznelson, *Black Men, White Cities: Race, Politics, and Migration in the United States, 1900–30, and Britain, 1948–68* (New York: Oxford University Press, 1973); Joe William Trotter, *Black Milwaukee: The Making of an Industrial Proletariat, 1915–1945* (Urbana: University of Illinois Press, 2007), 210–13. Trotter, like Martin Kilson, argues that Chicago was the "exception," where black northerners were able to become incorporated "as an integral part of political machines." See also Kilson, "Political Change in the Negro Ghetto, 1900–1940s," in *Key Issues in the Afro-American Experience*, ed. Nathan I. Huggins, Martin Kilson, and Daniel M. Fox (New York: Harcourt, Brace, Jovanovich, 1971), 167–92.

6. Kilson, "Political Change in the Negro Ghetto"; Charles Russell Branham, "Black Chicago: Accommodationist Politics before the Great Migration," in *Ethnic Chicago*, ed. Melvin D. Holli and Peter d'A. Jones (Grand Rapids, MI: William B. Eerdmans, 1984), 33–63; John D. Buenker, "Dynamics of Chicago Ethnic Politics, 1900–1930," *Journal of the Illinois State Historical Society* 67, no. 2 (June 1974): 260.

7. Charles Russell Branham, "The Transformation of Black Political Leadership in Chicago, 1864–1942" (PhD diss., University of Chicago, 1981), 147–49; John M. Allswang, *Bosses, Machines, and Urban Voters* (Baltimore: Johns Hopkins University Press, 1986); Humbert S. Nelli, "John Powers and the Italians: Politics in a Chicago Ward, 1896–1921," *Journal of American History* 57, no. 1 (June 1970): 67–84. On benefits of urban machines see Stephen P. Erie, *Rainbow's End: Irish-Americans and the Dilemmas of Urban Machine Politics, 1840–1985* (Berkeley: University of California Press, 1988); Robert A. Dahl, *Who Governs? Democracy and Power in an American City* (New Haven, CT: Yale University Press, 1961), 32–62.

8. Charles Edward Merriam, *Chicago: A More Intimate View of Urban Politics* (New York: Macmillan, 1929), 255. The number of wards was increased to fifty in 1923. Since 1935, aldermen have been elected to four-year terms.

9. Merriam, *Chicago*, 231, 261. For examples of aldermanic requests for services see

City Council Proceedings, box Oct.–Nov. 1915, Illinois Regional Archives Depository, Northeastern Illinois University, Chicago.

10. Grace Abbott, *The Immigrant and the Community* (New York: Century, 1917), 256–57; Katznelson, *Black Men, White Cities*, 88.

11. Katznelson, *Black Men, White Cities*, 87–89. See, for example, Schmidt's description of the 1910 aldermanic campaign in the Seventeenth Ward between native-born Republican William E. Dever and Stanley Walkowiak, a Democrat and candidate of the Polish ward boss, Stanley Kunz. John R. Schmidt, *"The Mayor Who Cleaned Up Chicago": A Political Biography of William E. Dever* (DeKalb: Northern Illinois University Press, 1989), 37–38.

12. *Chicago Tribune*, July 12, 13, 14, 1910; Schmidt, *The Mayor Who Cleaned Up Chicago*, 42–43.

13. Harold F. Gosnell, *Negro Politicians: The Rise of Negro Politics in Chicago* (1935; reprint Chicago: University of Chicago Press, 1967), 19; Martin Kilson, "Political Change in the Negro Ghetto," 167–92.

14. Merriam, *Chicago*, 253–54; Douglas Bukowski, *Big Bill Thompson, Chicago, and the Politics of Image* (Urbana: University of Illinois Press, 1998), 20–21.

15. Harold F. Gosnell, *Machine Politics: The Chicago Model* (Chicago: University of Chicago Press, 1937), 183; Maureen A. Flanagan, *Charter Reform in Chicago* (Carbondale: Southern Illinois University Press, 1987).

16. Merriam, *Chicago*, 24.

17. Ibid., 225.

18. Gosnell, "The Political Party versus the Political Machine," *Annals of the American Academy of Political and Social Science* 169 (Sept. 1933): 21; Ray Stannard Baker, "Hull House and the Ward Boss," *Outlook*, Mar. 28, 1898, 769–71; Jane Addams, "Why the Ward Boss Rules," *Outlook*, Apr. 2, 1898, 879–82.

19. Gosnell, *Machine Politics*, 182–85.

20. Gosnell, *Negro Politicians*, 138–39. Precinct captains in the 1910s and 1920s were listed as "porters, tailors, chauffeurs, and common laborers," though ambitious young lawyers often found precinct work a stepping-stone to a city job.

21. Gosnell, *Machine Politics*, 51; Gosnell, *Negro Politicians*, 138–39.

22. Merriam, *Chicago*, 25–28; Nathan Thompson, *Kings: The True Story of Chicago's Policy Kings and Numbers Racketeers: An Informal History* (Chicago: Bronzeville, 2006), 24–25.

23. Merriam, *Chicago*, 53, 225.

24. "Citizens' Association Rooms," Dec. 20, 1884, Citizens Association of Chicago Collection, box 5, folder 1875–1887, CHM.

25. William T. Stead, *If Christ Came to Chicago! A Plea for the Union of All Who Love in the Service of All Who Suffer . . .* (Chicago: Laird and Lee, 1894), 159–69.

26. Allen F. Davis, *Spearheads of Reform: The Social Settlements and the Progressive Movement, 1890–1914* (New York: Oxford University Press, 1971), 188–89; John R. Schmidt, *The Mayor who Cleaned Up Chicago*, 20–21.

27. Merriam, *Chicago*, 102–8.

28 Ibid., 103–4. On the traction wars see Georg Leidenberger, *Chicago's Progressive Alliance: Labor and the Bid for Public Streetcars* (DeKalb: Northern Illinois University Press, 2006).

29. Ida B. Wells, *Crusade for Justice: The Autobiography of Ida B. Wells*, ed. Alfreda M. Duster (Chicago: University of Chicago Press, 1970), 365; Paula J. Giddings, *Ida:*

A Sword among Lions: Ida B. Wells and the Campaign against Lynching (New York: HarperCollins, 2008), 514–15, 543–44.

30. *Chicago Defender*, Mar. 21, 1914, Jan. 16, 9, 1915. The school board apparently did not address the issue. Board of Education Collection, box 39, I Illinois Regional Archives Depository, Northeastern Illinois University, Chicago.

31. "Platform of the Municipal Voters' League, 1907," Citizens Association of Chicago Collection, box 6, folder 1906–1914; Edwin Burritt Smith, "Council Reform in Chicago: What the Municipal Voter's League Has Accomplished," *Municipal Affairs*, June 1900, 351.

32. "Twenty-Second Annual Preliminary Report of the Municipal Voters' League," Apr. 2, 1917, 15, CHM; "Twenty-Fourth Annual Report of the Municipal Voters' League," Jan. 1919, 12, CHM; Gosnell, *Machine Politics*, 67.

33. Gosnell, *Negro Politicians*, 67.

34. Gosnell, *Machine Politics*, 69.

35. Many contemporary commentators noted black Chicagoans' unique position in municipal politics. See, for example, George W. Ellis, "Chicago Democracy and the Negro," typed manuscript, Irene McCoy Gaines Collection, box 1, folder 2, CHM.

36. James R. Grossman, *Land of Hope: Black Southerners and the Great Migration* (Chicago: University of Chicago Press, 1989); Timuel D. Black Jr., *Bridges of Memory: Chicago's First Wave of Black Migration* (Evanston, IL: Northwestern University Press, 2003); Isabel Wilkerson, *The Warmth of Other Suns: The Epic Story of America's Great Migration* (New York: Random House, 2010).

37. *Colored People's Blue-Book and Business Directory of Chicago, Ill.* (Chicago: Celery Printing, 1906), 86.

38. *Chicago Defender*, Dec. 26, 1914; Katherine E. Williams, "The Alpha Suffrage Club," *Half-Century Magazine*, Sept. 1916, 12; "Alpha Suffrage Record," Mar. 18, 1914, Ida B. Wells Papers, Special Collections Research Center, University of Chicago Library.

39. *Chicago Defender*, Jan. 13, 1912.

40. *Chicago Defender*, Apr. 13, 27, May 4, 1912.

41. *Chicago Defender*, July 13, 1912, Mar. 28, Apr. 25, 1914.

42. On the ways the Republican Party took black voters for granted, see Paul Frymer, *Uneasy Alliances: Race and Party Competition in America* (Princeton, NJ: Princeton University Press, 1999), 49–86.

43. Leidenberger, *Chicago's Progressive Alliance*, 97.

44. *Chicago Tribune*, Aug. 9, Oct. 13, Nov. 5, 7 10, Dec. 19, 1906; Giddings, *A Sword among Lions*, 462–65. On Dunne see John D. Buenker, "Edward F. Dunne: The Limits of Municipal Reform," in *The Mayors: The Chicago Political Tradition*, rev. ed., ed. Paul M. Green and Melvin G. Holli (Carbondale: Southern Illinois University Press, 1995), 33–49. Ida Wells-Barnett also blamed her husband's defeat on Rev. Carey and his disapproval of her fund-raiser at the Pekin Theatre. She claimed that the city's ministers did not get out the vote for Barnett. Wells, *Crusade for Justice*, 294.

45. Giddings, *A Sword among Lions*, 462–65.

46. *Chicago Tribune*, Nov. 23 30, 1906.

47. *Chicago Defender*, Nov. 12, 1910; Giddings, *A Sword among Lions*, 466.

48. S. Laing Williams to Booker T. Washington, Nov. 16, 1906, Special Correspondence File, Booker T. Washington Papers, Library of Congress, quoted in Giddings, *A Sword among Lions*, 644.

49. Interview with Mrs. Lucy McNiell Miller by Eloyse Cannon, Jan. 19, 1937, box 10, folder 39, IWP.

50. Gosnell, *Negro Politicians*, 139.

51. Giddings, *A Sword among Lions*, 526–27; *Chicago Defender*, Feb. 22, 1913, May 30, 1914; Philip F. Rubio, *There's Always Work at the Post Office: African American Postal Workers and the Fight for Jobs, Justice, and Equality* (Chapel Hill: University of North Carolina Press, 2010), 35–40.

52. Henry W. McGee, "The Negro in the Chicago Post Office," (PhD diss., University of Chicago, 1961), 2–3.

53. Wells-Barnett, however, later wrote that the president paid close attention to their appeal. Wells, *Crusade for Justice*, 375–76.

54. *Chicago Defender*, Mar. 4, 12, Apr. 2, 1910; Spear, *Black Chicago*, 78.

55. Spear, *Black Chicago*, 78; *Chicago Daily News*, Feb. 18, 1912; Charles Russell Branham, "Transformation of Black Political Leadership," 84.

56. *Chicago Defender*, Apr. 26, 5, 19, July 5, 19, 12, 1913. On full-crew bills see Eric Arnesen, *Brotherhoods of Color: Black Railroad Workers and the Struggle for Equality* (Cambridge, MA: Harvard University Press, 2001), 39.

57. Williams, "The Alpha Suffrage Club," 12; Wells, *Crusade for Justice*, 346; Giddings, *A Sword among Lions*, 535–36.

58. *Chicago Defender*, Feb. 21, 28, 1914; Branham, "Transformation of Black Political Leadership," 83–85; Gosnell, *Negro Politicians*, 74.

59. Second Ward Precinct Map, July 1914, reprinted in Branham, "Transformation of Black Political Leadership, 1864–1942," 87; *Chicago Defender*, Feb. 3, 1912.

60. *Chicago Defender*, Apr. 11, 1914.

61. *Chicago Defender*, Nov. 18, 1911; Rubio, *There's Always Work at the Post Office*, 33–35; "Alpha Suffrage Record," Mar. 18, 1914.

62. *Chicago Defender*, Apr. 4, 11, 1914; *Broad Ax*, Apr. 11, 1914; Wells, *Crusade for Justice*, 346–47; Giddings, *A Sword among Lions*, 537.

63. *Chicago Defender*, Feb. 24, 1914, Jan. 16, 1915; *Broad Ax*, Apr. 11, 18, 1914; Giddings, *A Sword among Lions*, 717–18n47.

64. *Chicago Tribune*, Nov. 28, 1914; Giddings, *A Sword among Lions*, 542.

65. *Chicago Tribune*, Nov. 28, 1914, Jan. 11, 1915.

66. Edward R. Kantowicz, "Carter H. Harrison II: The Politics of Balance," in *The Mayors: The Chicago Political Tradition*, rev. ed., ed. Paul M. Green and Malvin G. Holli (Carbondale: Southern Illinois University Press, 1995), 16–32.

67. *Chicago Defender*, Jan. 2, 1915, Apr. 14, 1914.

68. *Chicago Defender*, Jan. 2, 1915; Nelli, "John Powers and the Italians," 70.

69. *Chicago Defender*, Jan. 30, 1915.

70. *Chicago Defender*, Jan. 16, 23, 1915.

71. *Chicago Defender*, Jan. 2, 1915. Anderson and DePriest stated publically that they had sent telegrams to Madden and other members of the Illinois delegation when an amendment to the Immigration Bill was under debate in the House of Representatives. Both opposed the measure, known as the Reed Bill, which would have barred "alien members of the Negro race" from entering the United States. The amendment was defeated. *Chicago Defender*, Jan. 9, 1915.

72. *Chicago Defender*, Jan. 16, 23, Feb. 13, 1915.

73. *Chicago Defender*, Jan. 23, 1915; Gosnell, *Negro Politicians*, 75.

74. *Chicago Defender*, Jan. 30, Feb. 20, 1915.

75. See, for example, *Chicago Defender*, Jan. 9, 16, 1915.

76. *Chicago Defender*, Jan. 23, 1915.

77. *Chicago Defender*, Feb. 27, 1915.

78. Ibid. Kevin K. Gaines makes this point about the symbolism of African American achievements. Gaines, *Uplifting the Race: Black Leadership, Politics, and Culture in the Twentieth Century* (Chapel Hill: University of North Carolina Press, 1996).

79. *Broad Ax*, Mar. 20, Apr. 3, 1915.

80. *Broad Ax*, Jan. 30, Apr. 10, 1915; Branham, "Transformation of Black Political Leadership," 93–94.

81. *Broad Ax*, Apr. 17, 1915.

82. Gosnell, *Negro Politicians*, 39, 49–50.

83. Lloyd Wendt and Herman Kogan, *Big Bill of Chicago* (Indianapolis: Bobbs-Merrill, 1953), 94–96, 103–14; Spear, *Black Chicago*, 187–89; *Chicago Daily News*, Aug. 13, 1915; Gosnell, *Negro Politicians*, 38–62.

84. *Chicago Defender*, May 1, 1915.

85 Ibid.; Gosnell, *Negro Politicians*, 157, 199.

86. Gosnell, *Negro Politicians*, 55–56; Wendt and Kogan, *Big Bill of Chicago*, 167–68.

87. *Chicago Tribune*, June 14, 1916; City Council Proceedings, May 21, 1917, Illinois Regional Archives Depository, Northeastern Illinois University, Chicago; Branham, "Transformation of Black Political Leadership," 98. On DePriest's support for machine issues see "Twenty-Second Annual Preliminary Report of the Municipal Voters' League," Apr. 2, 1917, 15, CHM.

88. "Young Colored Men's Merriam For Mayor Club," undated letter, Ida B. Wells Papers, box 8, folder 1, Special Collections Research Center, University of Chicago Library; "'Black Devils' of the old Eighth regiment whooped it up," undated typed MS, University of Chicago Library.

89. Gosnell, *Negro Politicians*, 57–58; undated letter from H. K. Barnett on the stationery of the "Young Colored Men's Merriam For Mayor Club," Ida B. Wells Papers, box 8, folder 10, University of Chicago Library; Junius B. Wood, *The Negro in Chicago* (Chicago: Chicago Daily News, 1916), 5.

90. *The People of the State of Illinois vs. Stephen N. Hawley et al. Indictment for Conspiracy, etc.*, filed Jan. 18, 1917, Office of the Clerk of the Circuit Court of Cook County. For copies of the indictments see case CR-10410 through 10419. Unfortunately, the records of the trial are not extant. See also *Chicago Defender*, July 30, Aug. 26, 1916, Jan. 19, 1917; *Chicago Tribune*, Jan. 19, June 5, 12, 1917; Gosnell, *Negro Politicians*, 172–73; Andrew E. Kersten, *Clarence Darrow: American Iconoclast* (New York: Hill and Wang, 2011), 212.

91. *Chicago Tribune*, Jan. 20, 1917.

92. *Chicago Tribune*, June 6, 7, 8, 9, 1917.

93. Gosnell, *Negro Politicians*. 175.

94. *Colored People's Blue Book, 1913–1914*, 534, CHM; Gosnell, *Negro Politicians*, 68.

95. Gosnell, *Negro Politicians*, 76–77.

EPILOGUE

1. *Chicago Defender*, Mar. 20, 1915.

2. *Chicago Defender*, Apr. 3, May 1, 1915; *Chicago Tribune*, Apr. 26, May 15, 1915; Melvyn Stokes, *D. W. Griffith's "The Birth of a Nation": A History of the Most Controversial Motion Picture of All Time* (New York: Oxford University Press, 2008), 150–53.

3. *Chicago Defender*, May 19, 1915, May 26, 1917, Sept. 25, 1915; *Chicago Tribune*, Apr. 18, 1915; Stokes, *D. W. Griffith's "The Birth of a Nation,"* 141–50, 153–60.

4. *Chicago Defender*, Nov. 19, 1910; Perry R. Duis, *Challenging Chicago: Coping with Everyday Life, 1837–1920* (Urbana: University of Illinois Press, 1998), 230–31; Lizabeth Cohen, *Making a New Deal: Industrial Workers in Chicago, 1919–1939* (New York: Cambridge University Press, 1990).

5. Louise de Koven Bowen, *Speeches, Addresses, and Letters of Louise de Koven Bowen Reflecting Social Movements in Chicago* (Ann Arbor, MI: Edwards Brothers, 1937), 198; Kathleen D. McCarthy, "Nickel Vice and Virtue: Movie Censorship in Chicago, 1907–1915," *Journal of Popular Film* 5, no. 1 (1976): 45–46; Lee Grieveson, *Policing Cinema: Movies and Censorship in Early-Twentieth-Century America* (Berkeley: University of California Press, 2004), 73–78.

6. Duis, *Challenging Chicago*, 231; McCarthy, "Nickel Vice and Virtue," 45–46.

7. McCarthy, "Nickel Vice and Virtue," 50–51.

8. *Chicago Defender*, Feb. 2, 1912; Charles Russell Branham, "The Transformation of Black Political Leadership in Chicago, 1864–1942," (PhD diss., University of Chicago, 1981), 85.

9. *Chicago Defender*, Feb. 21, Mar. 21, 1914, May 8, 1915.

10. *Chicago Tribune*, June 5, 6, 1915; *Chicago Defender*, Oct. 9, 23, 1915.

11. *Chicago Tribune*, June 8, 1915.

12. *Chicago Defender*, June 12, 1915; *Chicago Tribune*, June 7, 1915.

13. *Chicago Defender*, June 5, Oct. 30, 1915.

14. *Chicago Defender*, June 12, Nov. 6, 1915.

15. For the best account of the riot, see William M. Tuttle Jr., *Race Riot: Chicago in the Red Summer of 1919* (New York: Atheneum, 1970).

16. *Chicago Defender*, Jan. 10, Feb. 21, 1920. See also Jane Gaines, "*Within Our Gates*: From Race Melodrama to Opportunity Narrative," in *Oscar Micheaux and His Circle: African-American Filmmaking and Race Cinema of the Silent Era*, ed. Pearl Bowser, Jane Gaines, and Charles Musser (Bloomington: Indiana University Press, 2001), 67–80; Patrick McGilligan, *Oscar Micheaux, the Great and Only: The Life of America's First Black Filmmaker* (New York: HarperCollins, 2007); Pearl Bowser and Louise Spence, *Writing Himself into History: Oscar Micheaux, His Silent Films, and His Audiences* (New Brunswick, NJ: Rutgers University Press, 2000).

17. Davarian L. Baldwin, *Chicago's New Negroes: Modernity, the Great Migration, and Black Urban Life* (Chapel Hill: University of North Carolina Press, 2007), 123.

18. Spear, *Black Chicago: The Making of a Negro Ghetto, 1890–1920* (Chicago: University of Chicago Press, 1967), 195–96.

19. *Chicago Defender*, Mar. 23, 1918.

20. Harold Foote Gosnell, *Negro Politicians: The Rise of Negro Politics in Chicago* (1935; reprint, Chicago: University of Chicago Press, 1967), 174–75; Branham, "Transformation of Black Political Leadership," 115–19.

21. *Chicago Defender*, Mar. 23, 1918; Branham, "Transformation of Black Political Leadership," 125–26.

22. *Chicago Whip*, June 24, Oct. 4, 1919, Mar. 13, June 26, 1920, Sept. 10, 1921; Spear, *Black Chicago*, 197.

23. *Chicago Defender*, Feb. 2, 16, 1918; *Abendpost*, Dec. 28, 1929, Chicago Foreign Press Survey, German vol. 2, digitized microform; Branham, "Transformation of Black Political Leadership," 153–54. As Branham notes, despite the People's Movement,

white politicians maintained control of the Second Ward, determining who could run for office and controlling street-level campaign workers through jobs and donations.

24. Gosnell, *Negro Politicians*, 181–84; "Negro Congressmen," box 43, folder 21 IWP. Gosnell also notes that DePriest worried that the House leaders would not seat him because of his indictment. Some "skillful maneuvering" by Mrs. McCormick, representative at large for Illinois and widow of the late Senator McCormick, ensured DePriest was sworn it without complaint.

25. *Washington Tribune*, cited in *Chicago Whip*, July 6, 1929. DePriest, however, was attacked by the black press in the 1930s when he refused to support the fight to overturn the convictions of the Scottsboro Boys, nine black men wrongly convicted of rape in Alabama. See "Negro Congressmen," box 43, folder 21, IWP. For a full discussion of the complex maneuvering among DePriest, other black politicians, and the Republican machine in the 1920s, see Christopher Manning, *William L. Dawson and the Limits of Black Electoral Leadership* (DeKalb: Northern Illinois University Press, 2009), 53–65.